ACTION RESEARCH IN PRACTICE

Partnerships for Social Justice in Education

D1323828

Edited by Bill Atweh, Stephen Kemmis and Patricia Weeks

London and New York

First published 1998
by Routledge
11 New Fetter Lane, London EC4P 4EE

Simultaneously published in the USA and Canada
by Routledge
29 West 35th Street, New York, NY 10001

Typeset in Garamond by Routledge
Printed and bound in Great Britain by TJ International Ltd,
Padstow, Cornwall

British Library Cataloguing in Publication Data
A catalogue record for this book is available from the British Library

Library of Congress Cataloging in Publication Data
Action research in practice: partnership for social justice/edited by
Bill Atweh, Stephen Kemmis and Patricia Weeks.
Includes bibliographical references.
1. Action research in education. I. Atweh, Bill. II. Kemmis, Stephen.
III. Weeks, Patricia.
LB1028.24.A285 1998
97–25558
371.2'07–dc21
CIP

ISBN 0–415–17151–2 (hbk)
ISBN 0–415–17152–0 (pbk)

ACTION RESEARCH IN PRACTICE

This book presents a collection of stories from action research projects in schools and a university. The collection is more than simply an illustration of the scope of action research in education – it shows how projects that differ on a variety of dimensions can raise similar themes, problems and issues. The book begins with theme chapters discussing action research, social justice and partnerships.

The case study chapters cover topics such as: how to make a school a healthier place; collaboration between a university and a state education department; how to involve parents in decision-making; students as action researchers; how to promote gender equity in schools; improving assessment in social sciences; staff development planning; doing a PhD through action research; writing up action research projects.

Bill Atweh is at the Queensland University of Technology, **Stephen Kemmis** is at the University of Ballarat, and **Patricia Weeks** is at Queensland University of Technology.

CONTENTS

CONTRIBUTORS

Charles Arcodia has experience as an educator at both secondary and tertiary levels. He has broad research interests which include individual and corporate ethics, effective leadership and workplace training and development. He is presently teaching within the Department of Business Studies at the University of Queensland.

Tania Aspland is a PhD student within the Graduate School of Education at the University of Queensland. She also teaches curriculum theory and pedagogical studies at the Queensland University of Technology. Her teaching and research interests focus on generating better practices in the areas of culturally responsive teaching, supervision and learning within the emerging culture of the 'new' university context. She has recent publications in the field of curriculum leadership, advocacy-oriented action research, postgraduate teaching and thesis supervision.

Bill Atweh is a lecturer in mathematics education at the Queensland University of Technology. His main research interest is in the areas of social context and social justice in mathematics education. He assumed several administrative roles in course co-ordination mainly at the postgraduate level. He is the past Vice President for Publication for the Mathematics Education Research Group of Australasia. He is the director of the Student Action Research for University Access (SARVA). His publications include journal articles, chapters in books and edited books on research in mathematics education.

Joyce Blanche is a 'solo' mother of two teenage children who were students at the school involved in this particular chapter. She has been self-employed for most of her adult life, and has travelled extensively. A lateral thinker, she hopes to retain her connection with the school and in a collaborative manner have an impact on the welfare and learning process of secondary school students.

Jillian Brannock is currently a senior lecturer in the Faculty of Education at the Queensland University of Technology. She has participated in several national research projects, including the Gender and Professional Practices Project, and the Young People's Attitudes to and Perceptions of Sexual Violence Project. In 1995 she was co-director of the National Youth Affairs Project: Homelessness Among Young People in Australia: Early Intervention and Prevention. Her teaching interests include classroom practice, gender and sexuality issues for teachers, and women's social history. She is deputy Director of the Centre for Research in Policy and Leadership Studies.

Ross Brooker is a lecturer in physical education and curriculum studies in the School of Human Movement Studies at the Queensland University of Technology. He has participated in two recent projects, the Gender and Professional Practices (GAPP) Project, and the Young People's Attitudes to and Perceptions of Sexual Violence Project. He is currently working in a nationally supported collaborative research project (university and school system) focusing on developing a model of curriculum leadership in schools through an action research methodology. His other research interests are curriculum policy and change in physical education.

Clare Christensen is an experienced science teacher who is currently working as a research assistant in the Centre for Mathematics and Science Education at the Queensland University of Technology. She has also worked recently as a part-time tutor in science education and completed her Masters degree in science education. She has been involved in two action research projects as both research assistant and researcher, through an interest in research which is more collaborative and emancipatory then traditional approaches.

Alison Cobb is currently employed by Education Queensland as a project officer for Aboriginal and Torres Strait Islander Boys Participation and Retention. This position is the result of the activities described in this book and focuses on finding alternatives in education for one of the groups of students in our schools who are most 'at risk'.

Susan Monro Cooke was born in Scotland, and grew up in Brisbane. She currently works for the Queensland Health Department, and her background includes nursing and education. A spell out of the full-time workforce when her children were young allowed time for reflection on the state of the world's environment and the futures which will be faced by our children. She is interested in promoting ecologically sustainable public health, and action for change at the local level.

Tom Cooper is Associate Professor and Head of School of the School of Mathematics, Science and Technology Education at Queensland University of Technology. He has been a teacher in mathematics in South Australia and a lecturer in mathematics education in Western Australia, New South Wales and Queensland. His research interests include acquisition and application of mathematics concepts and principles, mathematical problem solving, professional development and teacher change in mathematics, and adult and workplace learning of mathematics.

Julie Davis is a parent with children in primary school. She has been a primary school teacher and now lectures in the School of Early Childhood at the Queensland University of Technology. Her interests include 'whole-centre' approaches to planning for educational change aimed at creating healthy, just and sustainable environments, collaborative processes that enable all members to participate in the change processes lie at the heart of these approaches.

Leonie Daws is the Director of the Centre for Policy and Leadership Studies, Queensland University of Technology. Her research interests centre on gender issues in social and educational policy. The major focus of this work has been educational policies affecting the education of girls. However, Leonie is also involved in researching policies issues arising from rural women's use of interactive communication technologies and issues relating to women and leadership. Much of this research has been carried out using action research. She is co-author of monographs on networking and women in management and young people's attitudes to sexual violence.

Louise Dornan works part-time in the complementary positions of high school teacher and research assistant at the Queensland University of Technology. She has completed her Master's degree in education (Language and Literacy). Her special areas of interest include critical literacy, co-operative learning and action research.

Pamela Dougall 'manages' her family of three young adult children by juggling the many demands placed on her. Between work, study, golf, and the unplanned, she is involved in activities for enhancing her daughter's school.

Lisa Ehrich is an Associate Lecturer in the School of Professional Studies within the Faculty of Education at Queensland University of Technology. She is currently completing a PhD investigating professional development as experienced by primary school principals. The study uses phenomenological methodology. Other research areas include: adult and community education, educational administration, and women in management.

Bob Elliott is an Associate Professor and Director of the Research Concentration in Curriculum Decision-Making in the School of Professional Studies at Queensland University of Technology.

Sonya Gorman is a high school teacher of History and English. She started teaching in 1989 and worked for 4 years in a Queensland country school. She has been at a Brisbane inner city school since 1993.

Janet Granzien was born and raised in Mount Isa (North West Queensland). She married and brought up three daughters and a son. She travelled with her family to England, living there for 2 years, then spent a year in Singapore. She has recently completed a Bachelor of Education (Adult and Workplace Education) and is presently working as a unit supervisor in the QCSC. Her involvement with schools has extended from primary school level up to tertiary level, focusing on the secondary school stream due to her children's involvement at this stage.

Barbara Greer-Richardson worked in advertising as a Media-Buyer in London, Hong Kong and Australia before leaving the full-time workforce to have children. She has seen many changes in the education system in the 14 years her children have been at school and university. She has always been involved as a volunteer in the schools her children have attended, in the classroom, canteen, on the Parent and Citizen Committees and with fundraising. Given a chance, she would do it all over again.

Shirley Grundy is an Associate Professor in the School of Education at Murdoch University, Western Australia. Her research interests include curriculum theory, policy analysis, school-based research and development, school leadership and management and school/university partnerships for teachers' professional development. She has published and taught in the area of qualitative research methodology, particularly action research. For the period 1994–96 she was the joint national coordinator of a large Australian national action research based professional development project in Australia called Innovative Links between Universities and Schools for Teachers Professional Development.

Mary Hanrahan is a fourth-generation Irish Australian and was born in a potato farming district in Victoria. After travelling and living overseas (France and Colombia, South America), she now lives in Queensland, and works as a tutor in technology education while completing her PhD in science education at the Queensland University of Technology. A mother of two sons, her life experiences also include being a secondary English and French teacher, doing a science degree (psychology honours) and teaching in adult literacy. Her research interests include psychosocial learning environments and language of science education.

Stephen Kemmis was until his retirement from Deakin University in June 1994, a Professor of Education (Curriculum Studies), Head of the Graduate School of Education and Co-Director of the Deakin Centre for Education and Change. At the time of his involvement with the PARAPET project, he was an Adjunct Professor at the Faculty of Education at Queensland University of Technology. In 1996–7 he was a Pro-Vice Chancellor (Research) then Deputy Vice Chancellor (Operations) at the University of Ballarat. He has written a variety of journal articles, chapters and monographs on educational evaluation, education reform and theory and practice of action research. He has been a consultant to a variety of projects, programs and agencies in the USA, Britain, Canada, Singapore, Malaysia, Hong Kong, Spain and Iceland. He is now in private practice as a consultant in action research and the development of educational research.

Christine Ling is currently working as Acting Principle at Coorparoo State School. She previously worked at the Valley School Support Centre in the role of Assistant Coordinator, Social Justice, taught in rural areas of Queensland, including Palm Island, and worked in the area of Aboriginal and Torres Strait Islander Education. Her research interests have been in the area of the development of community in schools with a focus on the integration of community development methodology with practice in education. The links between a school climate with a sense of community and the improvements in learning environment for students and their families are important both academically and in practice.

Charmaine McKibbin was a part-time Research Assistant in the Queensland University of Technology's Education Faculty, and a parent of two students at the high school which formed a collaborative research partnership with that university. Her keen interest in the educational importance of a strong relationship between school and family stemmed mainly from her research for her Honours degree into gender equity initiatives in Australian schools. Steeped in the 'politics of education' as a research assistant on the project, she decided to undertake a doctoral thesis on the topic of increased parent participation initiatives in Queensland's government schools. She is currently enrolled in the Faculty of Humanities, Griffith University, Brisbane.

Ian Macpherson is a senior lecturer in the School of Professional Studies at Queensland University of Technology. His areas of academic interest are curriculum studies and teacher education. His current research interest is theorising curriculum leadership for effective learning and teaching and he uses action research approaches which are both critical and collaborative in a range of research and consultancy projects. He takes a praxis view of professional work and works with professional practitioners rather than doing research on them.

Roger Marshall is a teacher with almost thirty years' experience in secondary schools in the United Kingdom and Queensland. At the time of writing this chapter, he was working as an Educational Adviser in Inclusive Curriculum at the Valley School Support Centre in Brisbane. He is now Head of Department, Social Justice at Glenala State High School, in Brisbane's western suburbs.

Christine Proudford is a lecturer in curriculum studies in the School of Professional Studies at the Queensland University of Technology. She has been involved in a collaborative research project between the Queensland Education Department and the School of Professional Studies on theorising curriculum leadership. She is also researching current education policy development in Queensland and its implications for teacher professionalism. Her areas of interest include the sociology of curriculum, the management of educational change and the use of action research in school improvement.

Fazal Rizvi is a Professor of Education at Monash University, having previously worked at the University of Queensland and Deakin University. He has written extensively on issues of social justice and the politics of difference, cultural and educational policy; and racism and multiculturalism as an educational policy. Professor Rizvi co-edits the journal, *Discourse: Studies in the Cultural Politics of Education*, and is a Director of the Australia Foundation for Culture and the Humanities.

Yoni Ryan has worked in educational institutions at primary, secondary, TAFE and university level in Australia and the Pacific. She initially taught English language and literature, but has worked more recently in instructional design, external studies and staff development. She is currently senior lecturer in adult education at the Queensland University of Technology.

Denise Scott coordinates the Teaching, Reflection and Collaboration (TRAC) network for the Academic Staff Development Unit at the Queensland University of Technology. She is a lecturer in Teaching and Learning (Higher Education) and has a particular interest in the role of collaboration and interaction in the teaching/learning process.

Leonie Shaw is a senior education officer in the Effective Learning and Teaching Unit, who has worked for the Queensland Department of Education in the primary field for many years and in particular in effective learning and teaching for the past 5 years. She has been involved in the development of the 'Principles of Effective Learning and Teaching' and the review that has evolved from the principles. A major focus of work in recent times has involved the sharing of effective practice by providing professional development opportunities for teachers and whole schools. Leonie has been involved in activities with the Queensland University of Technology since 1994. She also has a strong interest in the area of middle schooling.

Jill Shepherd is educated and trained in the Queensland education system. She worked for 5 years in country schools; reared a family for 16 years and did contract and supply teaching for several years in a range of schools; and returned to full time teaching in a Brisbane inner city school for 11 years.

Georgia Smeal is the Research Coordinator in the Academic Staff Development Unit at Queensland University of Technology and has formerly co-ordinated two national research projects – the Gender and Professional Practices Project and the Young People's Perceptions of and Attitudes to Sexual Violence Project. She holds a Master of Education degree; her thesis focused on the experiences and practices of feminist physical education teachers in Queensland schools.

Greg Thurlow works in the Queensland Department of Education central office. He has a background in research, policy development and curriculum development at the system level. Recently he has worked in the areas of effective learning and teaching, teacher development, systems curriculum development and learning communities. Curriculum leadership and teacher development issues are the current focuses of his research commitments.

Ros Trost completed her Bachelor of Arts degree and Diploma of Education at the University of Queensland and is currently studying for her Masters degree in Adult and Workplace Education. She is an experienced secondary English and social sciences teacher and has a special interest in vocational education. She is concerned about the stigma attached to vocational education and supports a convergence model of general and vocational education. She is interested in ensuring that students of all ages are extended and challenged to think and learn for themselves.

Jim Watters is a senior lecturer in science education at the Queensland University of Technology. He teaches preservice and inservice teachers as well as conducting research on scientific reasoning and learning in children. His research interests include professional development of teachers and scientific reasoning in young children. He has worked in universities in both a part-time and full-time capacity for most of his career.

Patricia Weeks is a senior lecturer in the Academic Staff Development Unit and coordinator of the Undergraduate Teaching, Learning and Assessment Portfolio at the Queensland University of Technology. Patricia received her Teacher's Certificate (1968) from the School of Education, University of Cardiff, her Bachelor of Education (1984) from the Brisbane College of Advanced Education, Brisbane, her Master of Education (1989) from Deakin University, Victoria and her Doctor of Philosophy (1995) from the School of Curriculum and Professional Studies, Queensland University of Technology, Brisbane. In her research Patricia has investigated the theoretical and practical aspects of facilitating teacher development in higher education. Patricia consults in the areas of teaching and learning in higher education, action research and narrative inquiry.

Mervyn Wilkinson currently lectures in adult learning, programming and workplace education, and change. He lectures at the School of Professional Studies, Faculty of Education, Queensland University of Technology. His PhD studies aspects of organisational change and process consultancy. He is involved in consultancy and research work with schools, school support centres, and in other adult learning institutions, workplaces and organisations as a change management process consultant and facilitator of organisational development and problem solving workshops. He has embraced the action research approach in his consulting work over the last 15 years and sees action research as a significant empowering process for managers and other people in public and private institutions.

PREFACE

The Story of The Book

Bill Atweh, Stephen Kemmis and Patricia Weeks

This book is a collection of stories about action research projects written by people who are involved with the Participatory Action Research for the Advancement of Practice in Education and Teaching (PARAPET) Project at the Queensland University of Technology (QUT). PARAPET is a network of action research projects and researchers, including university staff, teacher support personnel, teachers and parents. Details of the aims and history of the project are given in Part I of this book.

In the second year of its operation, the PARAPET members discussed ways of disseminating the stories of the various projects and sharing the resulting learnings with a wider audience. It is customary for action research projects, especially ones that involve university people, to be published at conferences and in professional journals in the various disciplines. Specialised action research journals, some of which have wide international membership, contain many illuminating stories of projects around the world. However, the group of authors felt that writing a book to tell their stories would illustrate issues of commonality and differences between various researchers and projects not possible in isolated publications.

The projects involved in this collection differed in the educational setting of the practice (classrooms, schools, school community, School Support Centres,[1] universities and so on). They differed in the size and roles of project teams (some were initiated by a sole researchers, some were collaborative). They also differed in their understanding of action research (some aligned themselves more than others to participatory action research concepts as discussed by Kemmis and colleagues). Planning the book allowed the participants an opportunity to look at the big picture view of the individual projects and ask serious questions about their professed aims, their processes, as well as their outcomes. As the group discussed the major issues arising from each project, significant similarities between the projects came to light.

First, by the nature of the group, each project aimed at changing some specific practice using action research. Second, there was a common commitment in all the projects to practices that promote social justice. The group felt the need to learn more about the meaning of the term and critically apply it to understanding what were the real effects of our actions in the projects. Third, many of the individual projects, and PARAPET members as a whole, were involved in developing communities of researchers. The need arose to study how these communities operated, how can they be developed, what were some of the arising problems and how the various groups dealt with them.

Hence, three themes were identified for discussing the different projects in the book: *participatory action research, social justice* and *partnerships in research*. These were not regarded by the authors as isolated themes. In fact, we feel that each chapter in the book addressed in one way or another the following questions:

1   How can social justice in and through education be brought about through the processes of partnership embedded in participatory action research (PAR)?
2   What achievements have we demonstrated, and what difficulties and challenges have we encountered, in working towards this aspiration in our projects?

The process

Traditional researchers follow structured and linear process in the development and implementation of their projects. This involves identifying the need and rationale, developing a plan and implementing it, and finally, reflecting on its successes or failures and publishing the findings. Those involved in action research projects usually follow alternative processes that are more cyclic and iterative. There were several PARAPET meetings where decisions about themes, content and structure of the book were considered along with plans for the development of chapters, editing and rewriting. These details will be omitted here as they often are in reporting action research projects, because of their tediousness. A project story consisting of minutes of the various meetings may not be of interest to the reader. Suffice to say that the group went through several meetings to decide on the process of writing the book and in identifying themes tying the various chapters together. The overall process which we believe is unique for this book will be described briefly here.

After the initial themes were identified as common issues behind many of the projects represented in PARAPET, all participants were invited to submit a short proposal for a chapter. A similar call for expressions of interest was distributed widely to other researchers within the university who may have been interested in contributing to the book and joining PARAPET. A few other proposed chapters were volunteered, two of which found their way into the book, while the others were either judged as not relevant to the aims of the book or were withdrawn by the authors because of time limitations.

At that stage, three people were selected by the group to act as editors and to vet the proposals. The editors were able to comment on the proposals by giving constructive feedback to the authors about writing the first drafts of their chapters. Authors were reminded of the identified themes of the book and were encouraged to address the themes in their chapters. Comments given to authors were of two types – some were specific to the project and others were of general interest to all chapters. In the general comments, the authors were encouraged to give specific details about the practice that their projects aimed to change and the relationships that had developed within the research team and with the participants. Authors were guided by these comments in developing their first drafts.

Based on the group's commitment that the process of editing the book should be a group learning experience, hence, collaborative and democratic, a large part of the editing process and decision making was handled by the authors themselves. To accomplish this, a working conference was conducted in September 1995 to edit the first drafts of the chapters. At this stage, the themes of the book began to crystallise. To address these, the expertise of outside friends of the group, who have written about these themes extensively, were invited to address the working conference. Stephen Kemmis was asked to address the role of action research in changing practice, Shirley Grundy was invited to address issues in creating communities of researchers and Fazal Rizvi was requested to discuss issues related to social justice. These keynote addresses formed the basis for the three chapters in Part 2 of the book.

Each of the other chapters was distributed to at least three other authors from the group for critical comments three weeks before the conference. Each session at the working conference was arranged so that the author(s) could summarise the main points about their chapter, then each discussant would identify the main strengths of the chapter and suggest changes that may enhance it. These short presentations were then followed by general discussion. Each session was chaired by a PARAPET member who summarised the main points raised.

All participants were unanimous in their enthusiasm about the success of the deliberations at the conference. A second similar day was conducted in December where the group discussed the second draft of the chapters. A few weeks later, the editors had one more chance to comment on the third draft. The writing was finalised during the first half of 1996.

The book

Each chapter was written independently and is able to stand alone. Hence, there was no obvious order in which the chapters should appear in the book. Different readers may find certain chapters more appropriate to their practice and needs than others. Nevertheless, as editors, we have sought to provide a structure and an order where some recurrent themes and development of ideas is discernible. The stories are grouped according to the site of practice involved in the project. However, a reader may start and finish anywhere, following whatever order seems most appropriate to them.

Part 1 of the book contains a single chapter relating the story of the PARAPET project. The story was written by Bill Atweh and Stephen Kemmis. To allow for the story to represent the views of all participants of PARAPET, the drafts were distributed to all project participants for comments and suggestions.

As the theme chapters in Part 2 of this book attest, action research, social justice and partnership have all played a major role in educational change over the past decade. The theme chapters were written by the guest speakers at the first working conference, sometimes in collaboration with a PARAPET member. The first chapter, written by Stephen Kemmis and Mervyn Wilkinson discusses the main features of participatory action research and its role in the study of practice. The second chapter by Shirley Grundy problematises the concept of partnerships in research. Finally, Fazal Rizvi discusses recent theories on social justice. All three chapters are used by the various authors in the book in conceptualising and/or reflecting on their projects.

Each chapter in Parts 3, 4 and 5 of this book tells the story of a project. The stories are grouped according to the major site of the practice involved. Part 2 relates three stories of action research projects within the school environment and community. In the first chapter, Julie Davis and Sue Cooke reflect on the issue of 'Parents as partners for educational change: the Ashgrove healthy school environment project'. Both authors are parents of children who attend the primary school. By connecting their individual interests in environmental education and health promotion and utilising the 'Healthy Schools Environment' approach, they have helped to make positive changes to the school environment, not only for the children, but also for the parents and teachers who became involved in this community action research project. They emphasise the value of developing one's own personal theories and conclude their story by quoting the Commission for the Future, 'The future is not some place we are going to, but one we are creating'.

The chapter by Charmaine McKibbin, Tom Cooper, Joyce Blanche, Pamela Dougall, Janet Granzien, and Barbara Greer-Richardson, 'Bridges and broken fingernails', relates the actions of a group of parents who, in collaboration with a university and the Queensland Department of

Education personnel, aimed to increase parent participation in a local high school. The story is a story of determination, and of the gains and losses, of struggles and problems which may arise when different players have different understandings of school change.

An equity project aiming to increase the participation in university study of students from a low socio-economic area forms the context for the chapter by Bill Atweh, Clare Christensen and Louise Dornan, 'Students as action researchers: partnerships for social justice'. Students are not often seen as partners in research. This chapter illustrates how the principles of PAR can be extended to include school students with great benefit to them. The project targets students from low socio-economic schools and their lack of access and participation in higher education.

Part 4 of the book relates stories of collaborative projects which involve partnerships aimed at supporting school teachers and personnel.

Collaborative work with the Queensland State Department of Education provides the background for Chapter 8, 'A journey into a learning partnership: a university and a state system working together for curriculum change', written by Ian Macpherson, Tanya Aspland, Bob Elliott, Christine Proudford, Leonie Shaw and Greg Thurlow. The story illustrates the use of critical, collaborative action research as a vehicle to journey into the development of a learning partnership. The authors discuss the difficulties involved in undertaking collaborative research and, in timely admission, suggest that writing about it is, in fact, much easier than doing it! Through their involvement they are seeking to understand curriculum leadership with curriculum studies as a field of inquiry. The authors demonstrate how, as they continue to learn, they are also developing their own personal practical knowledge into a living educational theory.

Chapter 9, written by Alison Cobb, Chris Ling and Roger Marshall, is entitled 'Change in schools: practice and vision'. All three authors are involved in leadership roles within a School Support Centre at the Brisbane Metropolitan East region of the Education Department. They decided to form a study and sharing group to support each other's work and growth. The structure of the group they have established mirrors that of PARAPET.

In Chapter 10 entitled 'Action research for professional development on gender issues', Ross Brooker, Georgia Smeal, Leonie Daws, Lisa Ehrich and Jillian Brannock report on a federally funded commissioned project. This project provided an opportunity for participants, who included teachers, regional staff and university academics, to clarify their values and reflect on their teaching practice as they relate to gender issues in the school. The chapter argues for professionals to reflect critically on their own, often taken-for-granted practices as a powerful tool with the potential for effecting long-term change.

Chapter 11 entitled 'Collaborative action research: learnings from a social sciences project in a secondary school' is an account of a three-year project undertaken by Ian Macpherson, Charles Arcodia, Sonya Gorman, Jill Shepherd and Ros Trost. University lecturers joined with teachers in a secondary school to find ways of implementing changes in their school in line with recommendations from recent Queensland policy documents on issues such as key competencies, links with industry and student autonomy. The project aimed at the facilitation of changes in teaching and learning practices resulting from recent changes in the prescribed curriculum in the state. This chapter tells the stories of the five people most directly involved in the project. The first part captures some of the issues associated with establishing relationships and reflecting on processes. It continues with reflection and several questions which were raised and remain unanswered. Many useful lessons were learnt in this project about the characteristics of effective teaching and learning.

Part 5 of the book deals with projects involving partnerships within the university context. The section starts with Chapter 12 by Denise Scott and Patricia Weeks, 'Action research as reflective collaboration'. It explores the evolution of the 'Teaching, Reflection and Collaboration' (TRAC) approach to academic staff development at the Queensland University of Technology. The chapter argues that a network of interdisciplinary collaboration and reflection can be more motivating, enriching and productive than individual attempts to undertake action research.

The theme of action research for professional development is also central to Chapter 13 entitled 'Occasional visits to the kingdom: part-time university teaching' by James Watters, Clare Christensen, Charles Arcodia, Yoni Ryan and Patricia Weeks. The authors describe the first stage of a collaborative action research project involving three full-time and two part-time academics who came together to explore the conditions surrounding the employment of part-time lecturers at the Queensland University of Technology. The chapter, which includes numerous comments made by part-timers, details the background to the study, each researcher's story and some personal reflections.

Chapter 14, written by Tania Aspland and Ross Brooker and entitled 'A pathway for postgraduate teaching', discusses the development of a curriculum studies subject in a postgraduate course at a Brisbane university. This chapter portrays and analyses the pathway they have taken in reconstructing and theorising their teaching through action research over a period of four university semesters with two different cohorts of students.

Finally, Chapter 15 by Mary Hanrahan, 'Academic growth through action research: a doctoral student's narrative', demonstrates the power of enacting action research principles to transform both understanding and practice in doctoral research. In an account which suggests much personal and academic growth, Mary shows how individual action research can also be collaborative, as she explores ways of doing research in science classrooms to improve scientific literacy.

The postscript of the book contains a single chapter on collaborative writing (Chapter 16). In the process of writing the above stories, the authors had several opportunities to reflect, not only on their own projects but also on the process of writing about them. Writing action research stories is not often problematised in the literature. Several authors in this book felt that this part of the process that we followed required specific reflection and documentation; learning developed from compiling the book in addition to learning from writing the individual chapters. Chapter 16 is written by Clare Christensen and Bill Atweh and is based on formal and informal interviews with many authors in the book and on the deliberations at working conferences. Once again all contributors to the book were given a chance to comment on the content of the chapter.

NOTE

1   School Support Centres are established by the Queensland Department of Education to provide resources and expertise in support of curriculum change and development in schools in their local areas.

Part 1

THE PROJECT

1

PARAPET

From meta-project to network

Bill Atweh and Stephen Kemmis

The Participatory Action Research for the Advancement of Practice in Education and Teaching (PARAPET) Project is a meta-project connecting people working in a loose collaborative network facilitating exchange of experience across a range of participatory action research (PAR) projects in schools and universities. It arose out of a programme of activities aimed at developing an action research culture at The Queensland University of Technology (QUT). This chapter presents the story and accomplishments of the project in its first year of life, discusses some of the issues and difficulties the project faced and the changes it underwent to deal with them. First, we discuss the context in which it arose.

QUT was established in 1991 by the amalgamation of the Queensland Institute of Technology and the Brisbane College of Advanced Education. While individual academics from both institutions were already involved in research activities prior to the amalgamation, a major task of the new university was to develop a research culture within the whole of the staff and to establish the supporting infrastructure. Supported by policies from the federal government, QUT adopted procedures for concentrating available research funds into a handful of university or faculty research centres and other research concentrations within the various schools. After an initial period of base funding, university and faculty grants to these centres and research concentration areas was on a competitive basis, implying that some problems could arise in collaborative projects across the various disciplines and in developing new research areas.

Along with the changes in research culture at the university, there were changes for staff, too, for example, in finding opportunities for staff development to assist with the application of new research methods and in handling new types of data prompted by changes in social and educational research paradigms. There was also an interest in developing kinds of research that would cross the so-called pure/applied divide in university research, linking university researchers with people in the professions. Funds were available both within the university and from the federal government to develop new expertise and establish new directions in research.

A group of researchers from the Centre for Mathematics and Science Education received a grant from the Mentor Programme of the (Queensland) Consortium for Staff Development Units to bring Stephen Kemmis to the faculty as a Visiting Scholar. The main aim of his visit was to build upon and strengthen the interest and expertise in critical action research that already existed in the faculty.

Stephen Kemmis came to QUT in June 1994 and offered a one-week short course that laid the theoretical foundations of action research as well as the practice of planning and conduct of PAR projects. At the end of the short course, a number of participants indicated that they would like to continue working together and exchanging ideas about action research. The groups consisted of people who have interpreted action research in different ways, yet they shared a commitment for the agenda of social justice, inclusive collaboration and mutual self-development. The PARAPET project grew from this set of associations.

Four months later, in October 1994, the group of people committed to working together as a continuing project group had begun to develop a clearer notion of what a shared project might look like. It could establish links between several PAR projects already under way and others in various stages of development, and initiate a collaborative programme of PAR by the group with an explicit intention of exploring and developing PAR projects, practices and processes.

Members agreed that they would seek opportunities to extend their own PAR practice in their own projects, but that they would work together in a meta-project conducted by the group. Group members formally adopted the name PARAPET as the title for the project, and formally endorsed four purposes for its meta-project:

1   To create a forum in which members could act as critical friends for one another in the process of exploring participatory action research in and through practice.
2   To act as an information exchange, and as a resource for group members: (a) to exchange information about how the different participatory action research projects being conducted by members of the group contribute to the improvement of education and teaching at different levels of education (from school to university) and (b) to share the group's resources of expertise.
3   To act as a study group, developing a programme of study into the improvement of education and teaching through participatory action research, and sharing reading resources among the various projects with which group members are associated.

4   To promote the development of expertise in and a culture of participatory action research beyond the group, and to raise consciousness about the role it can play in educational, cultural and community development.

At another meeting, also in October 1994, the group endorsed an organisational structure for the project based on the approach followed in a project co-ordinated by César Cascante Fernández in Asturias, Spain. According to Stephen Kemmis, the Asturias Project has two meetings per month: one in which participants exchange practical PAR experience arising from project work, and a second, held as a study group meeting, in which participants discuss common readings about PAR, educational research, and critical analyses of developments in education in Spain, especially in Asturias (the province in which project participants are located – mostly in and around the cities of Oviedo and Gíjon). The Asturias group holds its convenors' meetings approximately monthly. Finally, the project has two conferences each year: one for project participants, to discuss practical developments through the PAR projects, and a second more general conference addressing topical issues in the development of education in Asturias and Spain, in which the Asturias project group is joined by other invited speakers and fee-paying participants. The latter conference is held as a contribution to broader professional and educational development, and has sometimes been supported by such educationally progressive professional groups as the Movement for the Renovation of Pedagogy. It was anticipated that this kind of project organisation would permit maximum participation in discussion and sharing of experience, and generate a shared sense of direction and commitment in the conduct of the group's work. The adopted PARAPET organisation was intended to provide for:

1   Some meetings of the whole PARAPET meta-group (about five or six times a year) to discuss participants' PAR projects and reflections on shared readings, as well as attend to organisational matters.
2   More frequent meetings of PAR project groups – that is, of those people working collaboratively on shared projects (perhaps once a month, or more frequently, as required for progress in each project).
3   Regular meetings of project group convenors to co-ordinate and share experience between project groups, and to share ideas about useful readings for study across groups (about once every two months, in the month between whole group meetings).
4   The possibility of conferences and workshops, probably of two kinds, perhaps within the framework of other existing conferences:

   (a)   working conferences of the PARAPET group itself, held with the purposes of sharing experience across the group as a whole, providing a shared time horizon for reporting project work, and creating a basis of project documentation which could lead to the production of joint publications;

(b) more open conferences (like a teachers' conference) at which PARAPET group members (and perhaps others working in similar ways) could share their experience and celebrate their achievements in the presence of an audience beyond the PARAPET group.

With some modifications, this structure turned out to be roughly the way PARAPET worked in 1994–5. The meetings of the whole group tended to concentrate more on working as a study group than on exchanging detailed reports on individual projects. The distinction between a convenors' meeting and whole-group meetings was blurred when it was decided that anyone interested should be able to come to the convenors' meeting. Some planned projects did not proceed (some despite considerable effort and negotiation with potential collaborators), and some projects began to operate semi-autonomously as they pushed ahead to meet their own deadlines and objectives. Towards the end of the first year (by late 1995), other PARAPET and project meetings came to be a little overshadowed by preparations for a planned working conference (devoted to sharing project experiences and reviewing draft reports of projects as a basis for a PARAPET book) and a teachers' conference (reporting project experience and achievements to a wider audience of teachers as a contribution to developing teacher research and inquiry). During 1995, PARAPET established an electronic mail list (PARAPET-L) where participants could receive announcements to meetings and notes of held meetings and participate in discussion about common concerns and issues.

The following two sections outline the major achievements and learnings of the project and discuss some of the issues it faced in its first year of operation. In telling this story we are conscious of the problematics of voice representation. This chapter is written by two authors who were in a leading role in establishing the group and maintaining its progress. Bill Atweh has had a major role in the organisation of Stephen Kemmis's visit and in calling for meetings and summarising the discussion at the meetings. Stephen Kemmis has acted as a participating critical friend and a mentor to many of the PAR projects represented and to the structures and operation of the group. Yet, in writing this chapter, we are aware that we are mainly representing our own view of the events and problems. At least seven PARAPET people have had a chance to read and comment critically on previous drafts of this chapter. While every care has been taken to accommodate their views, arguably, a different story might have resulted if other people had written it.

PARAPET's achievements in its first year

Probably the best way to reflect back at the activities and successes of PARAPET in its first year of operation is to revisit the aims of the meta-project and to reflect on the extent of their achievement.

Objective 1:   *To create a forum in which members could act as critical friends for one another in the process of exploring participatory action research in and through practice.*

PARAPET has planned three types of activities towards the achievement of this goal. First, the regular whole-group meetings were envisaged to allow for members to consider the various issues faced by the different projects and share possible solutions adopted by the different projects. This was only a limited success. The meetings were not regular enough or long enough to allow the relatively large number of projects to have sufficient 'air time' to discuss their difficulties and receive sufficient critical assistance from other participants. Second, one of the aims of the electronic list was to allow for some discussion of specific or general issues and views. One member of the group posted a request for volunteers to become critical friends for a project that she was undertaking. Two other people have agreed to become critical friends to her specific project. Yet in general, the success of this use of the email was limited. Not all members had access to electronic email and many others had not developed sufficient expertise and habits required for such use. Third, the most successful forum for critical friends was the working conference organised at the end of September 1995. During the two days of the conference, writers of reports on each project were able to have a 50-minute session where respondents to their chapter gave constructive comments and criticism of their chapter. The majority of comments were taken in the spirit in which they were given. Attenders were unanimous in their desire to repeat the exercise in December 1995. Perhaps the challenge to the group for the future is to investigate how this aspect of the aims could be further developed and become a regular occurrence.

Objective 2:   *To act as an information exchange, and as a resource for group members: (a) to exchange information about how the different participatory action research projects being conducted by members of the group contribute to the improvement of education and teaching at different levels of education (from school to university) and (b) to share the group's resources of expertise.*

For the same reasons discussed above, the use of the general PARAPET meetings and the email list proved to be of limited success towards the achievement of exchange of information about the successes of the various projects in changing practice in education. However, the publication of this book is to be considered as a significant accomplishment of the group towards the achievement of this aim. PARAPET can be proud of the accomplishment of providing a forum where expertise within the group can be shared. Several of the projects that evolved after the initial group was established, may not have been possible without the sharing of expertise of people from different organisational units from the university and without the critical advice provided by Stephen Kemmis to the proposing team. At least four major proposals for internal and external funds would not have been developed without the networking that occurred through PARAPET.

> *Objective 3:* *To act as a study group, developing a programme of study into the improvement of education and teaching through participatory action research, and sharing reading resources among the various projects with which group members are associated.*

The whole-group meetings were planned for two hours. The first hour was usually spent on project information sharing and general business and the second hour was to be devoted to discussion of a shared reading. Readings on issues related to the principles and conduct of PAR, problematics of the concept of empowerment and on narratives were planned for this year. The discussion below identifies some of the issues faced by PARAPET as a learning organisation. Perhaps one of the challenges that the group faces in the future is to develop mechanisms for the different projects to become more persistent in their attempts to become study groups.

> *Objective 4:* *To promote the development of expertise in and a culture of participatory action research beyond the group, and to raise consciousness about the role it can play in educational, cultural and community development.*

Arguably, PARAPET was most successful in achieving this aim. Four major activities of PARAPET have assisted in promoting the culture of action research within the educational community in the university, in associated schools and in South East Queensland generally. First, a series of six public seminars were conducted at the university on issues relevant to critical theory and action research. Two of these seminars were presented by overseas people visiting the university. Second, the appointment of Stephen Kemmis as an Adjunct Professor to the Faculty of Education enabled him to discuss action research matters with several researchers and postgraduate students embarking on various research studies. This appointment was the first collaborative appointment supported by three schools within the faculty. Third, a teachers' conference was conducted in co-operation with PARAPET, the Queensland Board of Teacher Registration and the Valley School Support

Centre.[1] At least sixty teachers from Queensland schools attended the conference helping to build networks among teachers, School Support Centre staff, board members and university staff with common research and development interests. Fourth, an advanced seminar subject on critical social practice was conducted within the Master of Education degree at QUT taught by Bill Atweh, Stephen Kemmis, Colin Lankshear and Merv Wilkinson. The seminar considered an extensive reading list of classical and modern writing on critical theory and action research and addressed concrete concerns arising in the action research projects of participants.

Some issues faced by PARAPET

We raise these issues here not because they are peculiar to PARAPET: such issues frequently arise in PAR work and PAR groups. On the other hand, by raising them for discussion, we may contribute to the critical and self-critical dialogue of participants as they consider the practice of PAR in their projects and the PARAPET network.

Issues concerning PARAPET as a network

Time

At the planning stage of the project many members may not have been consciously aware that joining a meta-project of the kind PARAPET aspired to be would require a significant time commitment. For example, participating in a PAR project might require something like half a day a week for much of a year; attending PARAPET-wide and project group meetings might require the equivalent of another half-day per month and preparing for and participating in conferences and workshops might require ten (or so) more days of writing, conference planning, attendance and editing of project publications in the course of a year. Taken together, this would be a substantial workload, though for most group members it would overlap with other existing aspirations and responsibilities. At times it was rather difficult to find a time slot where all interested members were able to attend the group meetings. However, we believe that it is unlikely that the time commitments for PARAPET excluded many potential participants, but it did add a new set of demands to most participants' already busy lives and it prevented some from full participation in all meetings.

Being 'central' versus 'peripheral' to PARAPET

Naturally, it takes some effort, energy and resources to keep a project like PARAPET going (for example, calling meetings, distribution of notes from meetings and administering the overall project resources). As is the case for most projects, the task of sustaining the organisation fell more on some members than on others. Partly for this reason, there were differences in the degree to which people associated with PARAPET felt responsibility for maintaining it, and differences in the degree to which it was central to their research interests. While at one level PARAPET encouraged people to affiliate to whatever extent they liked, at another level there was some expectation that people would share a commitment to PARAPET aims – including, for example, participation in meetings and work towards the production of a PARAPET book. Openness about participation was an espoused value of the group, but differences in frequency and types of participation meant that some felt more central to the operations of the collaboration than others.

To describe the structure and functioning of the project, we often used the spatial metaphor of a wheel, with individual projects lying on the perimeter and the PARAPET project on the axis. Maybe this metaphor helps to make such prophecies self-fulfilling; like many organisations – especially ephemeral and voluntary ones – PARAPET may have fallen prey to it.

Further, it was always rather unclear about what projects were 'PARAPET projects' and how and when a project could become one. Likewise, there was some confusion about who was a 'PARAPET member' and how and when one could become one or who was the co-ordinator of a group and who was not. The group managed a mailing list that stood as an unofficial membership list and a list of projects that stood as an unofficial list of PARAPET projects. Membership of both lists was based on expressed interest from the participants themselves. Some attenders were involved in projects that were not listed on the PARAPET list of projects, and conversely some members of the list did not in the end affiliate. Meetings were open and all attenders had equal right to voice opinions and to participate in the decision making process. As discussed below, however, not all attenders felt free to do that.

Difference versus unity

We have argued above that PARAPET was formed by a group of people who shared interests in action research, collaboration and social justice. Yet, as the group progressed in its activities, it had to deal with questions of differences in views between its members. Some members felt marginalised because their views of action research did not match what they perceived as the orthodoxy of the group. Critical discussion of alternative views may have been interpreted by some members to mean that if they subscribe to these views being criticised, they could not be part of the 'inside group'. As evidenced from the various stories told in this book, multiple interpretations rather than a single view of what action research is arose in the group. At times, some attenders at meetings may have been hesitant to express their views or may have felt that their views were not as valued as those of group leaders or those who were perceived as 'experts'. Likewise, questions arose as to the effect of academic status (for example, university lecturers versus postgraduate students) and gender on participation in the decision-making process. At times these differences were experienced as tension between participants – and for some participants more than others. PARAPET sometimes struggled between values of openness and tolerance on the one side, and developing and defending distinctive and different points of view on the other. Of course, it is also true to say that most participants felt that PARAPET did create opportunities to learn more about PAR, to participate in discussions and debates about it, to develop a sense of confidence about using the various discourses of PAR and to consider whether and how they should participate in shaping its future. Arguably, the differences of positioning and affiliation these differences imply were productive for PARAPET – causing participants to problematise difference and to recognise that PAR may (on the one hand) serve different people and groups in different ways, and (on the other, like all processes which begin to attain the status of social technologies) serve the self-interests of some groups at the expense of others.

Territories and boundary-crossing

In institutional contexts, people are generally sophisticated about institutional territoriality, and they can make shrewd judgements about how different activities are likely to unsettle established interests and self-interests. With an organisation like PARAPET, which aspired to be boundary-crossing, rather than to operate entirely within existing organisational structures (for example, solely within the university, or solely within one school or research centre of the university), the decision to operate across established boundaries may be perceived as a decision to be 'outlaw' in terms of existing structures. Certainly, such a decision have meant that PARAPET was perceived as peripheral to the 'core business' of existing structures. This have been destabilising for PARAPET from the point of view of some participants and observers of the project. On the other hand, this location of PARAPET across the university organisational units and, indeed, across the traditional boundaries between the university and school system, was highly rewarding. Members from different disciplines complemented each other's expertise and were able to draw upon the resources of more than one organisational unit within, and beyond the university. Further, the location of PARAPET outside the established university centres implied that it can enter in mutually beneficial arrangements with more than one centre and thus increase its autonomy and effectiveness.

11

A *learning organisation?*

One of PARAPET's aims was to operate as a study group for its members. Some of this happened – perhaps not as much as participants would have liked, and perhaps not through the mechanism initially envisaged (project groups working as study groups and exchanging ideas for readings, rather than whole-PARAPET meetings being partly devoted to discussing shared readings). Part of the reason for this change of structure was the difficulty that some smaller project groups had in sustaining shared readings and discussion. It seemed more efficient to meet as a whole group, even at the expense of 'air time' in discussion for each participant and the need for a little more formality in discussions in a larger group. It may be, however, that disconnecting the study group function from the project groups, and connecting it instead to the whole group meetings, may have created an unintended separation of function between 'theory'- and 'practice'-type forums.

Some participants felt that the discussions of PAR in the group were rather abstract – a year into the project some said that they 'still don't know' or 'are unsure about' what PAR is. Processes intended to *problematise* PAR may have served to *confuse* it, especially in the context of broader debates about different schools of thought in the AR and PAR literature.

A positive outcome of PARAPET has been that a group of university staff agreed to co-teach an advanced seminar on 'Action Research and Critical Social Practice' for MEd (and PhD) students. This allowed for the development of a more structured reading list which could be used with other groups and members of PARAPET.

Working in (and to change?) established institutional cultures

As was suggested earlier, one of the adopted aims of PARAPET was to help develop a culture of collaborative work at QUT and in schools affiliated with its project work. There was a more or less explicit intention to change what was seen as a somewhat individualistic, somewhat specialised, perhaps competitive, style of research operation towards a more collaborative style that could bring teachers and researchers together within and between the university and schools. As comments in the last section indicate, PARAPET was partly successful in achieving this aim, but for some people more than for others – and probably more for people already interested in developing such a culture in collaborative school-focused and school-based work they were doing in other projects. The continuing challenge for PARAPET is to demonstrate some of the strengths and weaknesses of this kind of educational research.

In its first year of operation, PARAPET experienced the tension between the culture of collaboration it aspired to develop and some features of the dominant political economy of universities. For example, promotion policies and funding seem to value individual productivity and competition for scarce rewards more than collaborative work and multiple outcomes for different participants in projects. If institutional practices value individual work above collaborative work and 'products' in the form of publications above impact on professional practice, then there is a bias against the kind of research productivity that PAR research creates. It is also clear that PAR activity may stretch the capacity of staff to meet established work demands. To the extent that PARAPET allows the participants to re-frame their work and modes of operation, it may contribute to a change in organisational culture. To the extent that it is regarded by participants and observers as peripheral or additional to 'mainstream' modes of operation in teaching and research, it may inadvertently contribute to the reproduction of that 'mainstream'.

In school and school support centre settings, PARAPET may also have demonstrated (once again) that the collaborative research culture is still regarded as somewhat peripheral to the main tasks of schools and schooling – as an 'add-on' rather than integral to school operation and development. There are signs that the culture may be changing, but the values may be more rhetorical than real for large parts of the education profession.

PARAPET also demonstrated some of the difficulties inherent in working across the divide between university and school cultures – though it also demonstrates that there are large, and sometimes unexplored territories of mutual interest and reciprocal reward which bring benefits to people in both sets of institutions. PARAPET blurs the boundary between university-based research and school-based research – but it is interesting to note that each proceeds rather autonomously, in ways shaped by its own institutional culture and modes of operation. The cluster of school-focused and school-based projects associated with the Valley School Support Centre turned out to be like a separate PARAPET project of its own; PARAPET recognised and valued these differences, but there were large areas in each group of projects (higher education and school projects) which remained opaque to all participants, even though the organisation aimed for transparency of project work across PARAPET as a whole.

In such ways, PARAPET may have produced some transformations in school and university cultures, and in the relationship between them, but, by being seen as (to some extent) new and innovatory in each culture, it may also have contributed to the general reproduction of the different cultures, leaving many core values and modes of operation unchanged for many people in schools and universities who were not so interested in confronting the issues and challenges of institutional change through PAR.

Project issues

One of the images used to describe PARAPET was that of the 'umbrella' project: a project (or meta-project) which in some sense included the work of other projects. This image suggests that PARAPET was an overarching structure subsuming other projects within its intellectual or organisational ambit. As already suggested, the image may have aggravated some territorial sensitivities. In general, however, participants in PARAPET attempted to see the relationship between the meta-project and the PAR projects of members as mutually nurturing rather than as parasitism or as a territory marked out by conflicts of interest.

Some projects which affiliated with PARAPET actually pre-dated it, for example, the Student Action Researchers Project (see Chapter 7, this volume) and others could just as easily have been initiated without it (for example, the PETPAR project (see Chapter 13, this volume). Such projects stand alone; they do not need to cluster under a common umbrella for protection, but bring their concerns to the PARAPET forum in a search for critical friendship. The extent to which each participating project would be *different* if PARAPET did not exist is a matter for speculation; on the other hand, because PARAPET did (and does) exist, the network of associations it engendered changed the membership of many, perhaps most project teams, and helped to emphasise aspects of each project in line with the overall emphasis of PARAPET on social justice collaboration and change of practice.

Another issue about the character of projects in PARAPET concerns their importance as commodities – especially in the university setting, but also in school support centres. A project has a plan, a programme of work, a set of working relationships and the prospect of products to justify involvement in it. From an institutional point of view, it may be a commodity, offering the prospect of showing achievement and accountability, and the achievement of certain kinds of rewards (like publications which can be redeemed in promotion and tenure decisions or further funding). It also confers certain kinds of rewards on the institutions involved – rewards not limited to such goods as securing additional funds, fulfilling institutional missions, generating publicity, and demonstrating practical engagement in the world of affairs (all of which are increasingly important for universities and service agencies like school support centres). As the philosopher Alasdair MacIntyre (1981: 175) points out, however, there is a difficult and sometimes tension-ridden relationship between the goods external to the practice of projects (the pursuit of money, power and status, for example) and the goods internal to project work (for example, developing the excellences and virtues intrinsic to the practice of education). One explicit reason for creating PARAPET was that it could foster research productivity through collaborative effort; some could read the success of PARAPET solely in terms of the degree to which those involved have produced research findings and publications as a result of their participation. To receive funding from the university, PARAPET had to demonstrate its success in terms of the monies it was able to attract in competitive grants and in terms of the number of publications it was able to produce. It is not only outsiders to PARAPET who use this yardstick as a measure of its success; indeed, it is one of the yardsticks by which participants themselves judge the success of their project work. It might be cynical to see projects primarily as 'commodities', but it would be naive to ignore their character as commodities – especially their capacity to create a structure and rhythm for research and development work (including the sense of a beginning and an end, and the sense of closure that comes with public disclosure of findings as a contribution to debates in the wider field). As with all commodities, however, there can be problems in attributing and gaining ownership of projects, and maintaining a balance between the goods external and the goods internal to PAR work.

The necessity of goods external to a project in relation to goods internal to them is easily demonstrated: some projects simply did not happen without funds to conduct them – with some understandable disappointment in the PARAPET group. At the same time, institutional recognition of the status of funded projects cannot but have a some impact on the internal life of a collaborative group like PARAPET – despite the commitment to collaboration. In a group like PARAPET, the disappointment of missing out on funding may also be made more pointed if 'having a project' is seen as the entry ticket to full participation in the group – not that this was any part of the group's explicit values. Still, PARAPET members, individually and collectively, could not shield themselves from the vagaries of the competitive ethos of the institution; it is worth considering the extent to which the commodity value of projects (from the point of view of the institutions) produced effects in the dynamics and membership of the PARAPET group.

PARAPET has also demonstrated that a range of sources of funding is available for projects, within and outside members' own institutions. Members have sought, and often were successful in attracting funds from such sources as the Australian Research Council (ARC) Collaborative Grants Programme and the National Professional Development Programme (NPDP), but have also learned to be more proactive in seeking the funding and in-kind support from their own and other agencies.

The future for PARAPET

The first change in PARAPET planned for 1996 was a change in the metaphor used to describe its structure and functioning. The concept of a meta-project created some confusion about tasks, memberships and affiliation. The new metaphor adopted by the group is that of a *network* of affiliated PAR projects and people interested in working on PAR projects. Much of the success of a co-operative like PARAPET rests with the activities within the individual projects, and with the interactions that develop across projects. As a network, PARAPET does not have membership and does not own projects. However, we will maintain a lists of affiliated projects and affiliated people for reference and communication.

Towards the end of 1995 participants agreed to a new statement outlining the structure's membership of PARAPET. This statement is seen as a continued and evolving description of the participants' current thinking about the group. The statement acknowledges that PARAPET is a network of 'affiliated projects' that share common characteristics. A PARAPET affiliated project is a PAR project which:

1   aims at the improvement of some practice related to education and training;
2   involves people from within the practice working collaboratively with outside consultants and/or critical friends;
3   agrees to act as a study group exploring shared readings and learnings;
4   agrees to establish mutually educative connections with other affiliated PAR projects.

Each affiliated project has its own aims, functions, processes membership, and manage its own resources. In addition to that, PARAPET is interested in affiliation with projects that are committed to interaction with other projects in the study of PAR and other related issues (point 3 above) and to sharing their learnings to help develop the network (point 4 above).

Further the statement acknowledges the formation of one specific affiliated project: 'Partnerships and Networking for PARAPET (PAN-PARAPET)'. This project consists of people who are interested and willing to put effort into maintaining and directing the future of the network. As an affiliated group, PAN-PARAPET meets the four requirements of PARAPET projects listed above.

1   It has the main focus of developing partnerships and networks to support PAR projects. It has the following mission and objectives:

Mission: through participatory action research, to empower people to transform their social and educational practices in ways that are critically-informed, inclusive and ongoing.

Objective 1   To create forums for people associated with PAR projects to share ideas and to continue theorising participatory action research, and to share information about PAR principles and practices.

Objective 2   To facilitate PAR groups in becoming study groups by action as a resource for publications and other materials.

Objective 3   Facilitate the linking of PAR projects affiliated with PARAPET, and to critically reflect upon itself as a basis for ongoing review and reconstruction of PARAPET.

2   The PAN-PARAPET project consists of people who support the aims of PARAPET and are committed to the development and evaluation of networks and partnerships for action research projects. Anyone affiliated with PARAPET is welcomed to participate in the PAN-PARAPET project.

3   The PAN-PARAPET project acts as a resource identifying readings and other educative materials for study in other PARAPET affiliated projects and it aims to facilitate the study group function in affiliated projects.

4   The PAN-PARAPET project maintains a register of people and their interests, and a list of PARAPET affiliated projects. It aims to provide leadership support for new PAR groups, and attempt to develop networks between affiliated projects and other AR and PAR projects around the world.

NOTE

1   School Support Centres are established by the Queensland Department of Education to provide resources and expertise in support of curriculum change and development in schools in their local areas.

REFERENCE

MacIntyre, A. (1981) *After Virtue: A Study in Moral Theory*, London: Duckworth.

Part 2

COMMON THEMES

2

PARTICIPATORY ACTION RESEARCH AND THE STUDY OF PRACTICE

Stephen Kemmis and Mervyn Wilkinson

Though the process of action research is inadequately described in terms of a mechanical sequence of steps, it is generally thought to involve a spiral of self-reflective cycles of:

- planning a change
- acting and observing the process and consequences of the change
- reflecting on these processes and consequences, and then
- re-planning, and so forth (see Figure 2.1).

In reality the process may not be as neat as this spiral of self-contained cycles of planning, acting and observing, and reflecting suggests. The stages overlap, and initial plans quickly become obsolete in the light of learning from experience. In reality the process is likely to be more fluid, open and responsive. The criterion of success is not whether participants have followed the steps faithfully, but whether they have a strong and authentic sense of development and evolution in their practices, their understandings of their practices, and the situations in which they practice.

In this chapter, we outline of our views about participatory action research (PAR) and its role in the study of practice. We conclude the chapter by a set of questions that are suggested as means for action researchers to reflect on the processes and outcomes of their projects.

Participatory action research

As we see it, participatory action research aims to help people to investigate reality in order to change it (Fals Borda 1979). At the same time, we might say, it also aims to help people to change reality in order to investigate it. In particular, PAR attempts to help people investigate and change their social and educational realities by changing some of the practices which constitute

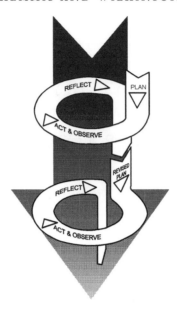

Figure 2.1 The self-reflective spiral in action research

their lived realities. In education, PAR can be used as means for professional development, improving curricula or problem solving in a variety of work situations.

We argue that each of the steps outlined in the spiral of self-reflection is best undertaken collaboratively by co-participants in the action research process. Not all theorists of action research place this emphasis on action research as a collaborative process; some argue that action research is frequently a solitary process of systematic self-reflection. We concede that it is often so, but nevertheless hold that action research is best conceptualised in collaborative terms. One reason is that action research is itself a social – and educational – process. A second and more compelling reason is that action research is directed towards studying, reframing, and reconstructing practices which are, by their very nature, social. If practices are constituted in social interaction between people, then changing practices is a social process. To be sure, one person may change so that others are obliged to react or respond differently to that individual's changed behaviour, but the willing and committed involvement of those whose interactions constitute the practice is necessary, in the end, to secure the change. PAR offers an opportunity to create forums in which people can join one another as co-participants in the struggle to remake the practices in which they interact – forums in which rationality and democracy can be pursued together, without an artificial separation ultimately hostile to both. At its best, it is a collaborative social process of learning, realised by groups of people who join together in changing the practices through which they interact in a shared social world – a world in which, for better or for worse, we live with the consequences of one another's actions.

Central features of participatory action research

We mentioned above that, for many people the image of the spiral of cycles of self-reflection (planning, acting and observing, reflecting, re-planning and so on) has become the dominant feature of action research as an approach. In our view action research has six other key features, at least as important as the self-reflective spiral. They are:

1 *PAR is a social process*: it deliberately explores the relationship between the realms of the individual and the social. It recognises that 'no individuation is possible without socialization, and no socialization is possible without individuation' (Habermas 1992: 26), and that the processes of individuation and socialisation continue to shape individuals and social relationships in all the settings in which we find ourselves. Action research is a process followed in research in settings like those of education and community development, when people – individually and collectively – try to understand how they are formed and re-formed as individuals, and in relation to one another, in a variety of settings – for example, when teachers work together, or with students, to improve processes of teaching and learning in the classroom.

2 *It is participatory*: it engages people in examining their knowledge (understandings, skills and values) and interpretive categories (the ways they interpret themselves and their action in the social and material world). It is a process in which each individual in a group tries to get a handle on the ways their knowledge shapes their sense of identity and agency, and to reflect critically on how their present knowledge frames and constrains their action. It is also participatory in the sense that people can only do action research 'on' themselves – individually or collectively. It is *not* research done 'on' others.

3 *It is practical and collaborative*: it engages people in examining the acts which link them with others in social interaction. It is a process in which people explore their acts of communication, production and social organisation, and try to explore how to improve their interactions by changing the acts that constitute them – to reduce the extent to which participants experience these interactions (and their longer-term consequences) as irrational, unproductive (or inefficient), unjust, and/or unsatisfying (alienating). Action researchers aim to work together in reconstructing their social interactions by reconstructing the acts that constitute them. It is a research done 'with' others.

4 *It is emancipatory*: it aims to help people recover, and unshackle themselves from, the constraints of irrational, unproductive, unjust and unsatisfying social *structures* which limit their self-development and self-determination. It is a process in which people explore the ways in which their practices are shaped and constrained by wider social (cultural, economic and political) structures, and consider whether they can intervene to release themselves from these constraints – or, if they can't release themselves from these constraints, how best to work within and around them to minimise the extent to which they contribute to irrationality, unproductivity (inefficiency), injustice and dissatisfactions (alienation) as people whose work and lives contribute to the structuring of a shared social life.

5 *It is critical*: it aims to help people recover, and release themselves from, the constraints embedded in the social media through which they interact: their language (discourses), their modes of work, and the social relationships of power (in which they experience affiliation and difference, inclusion and exclusion – relationships in which, grammatically speaking, they interact with others in the third, second or first person). It is a process in which people deliberately set out to contest and to reconstitute irrational, unproductive (or inefficient), unjust, and/or unsatisfying (alienating) ways of interpreting and describing their world (language/discourses), ways of working (work), and ways of relating to others (power).

6 *It is recursive (reflexive, dialectical)*: it aims to help people to investigate reality in order to change it (Fals Borda 1979), and to change reality in order to investigate it – in particular, by changing their practices through a spiral of cycles of critical and self-critical action and reflection, as a deliberate social process designed to help them learn more about (and theorise) their practices, their knowledge of their practices, the social structures which constrain their practices, and the social media in which their practices are expressed and realised (see Figure 2.2). It is a process of learning by doing – and learning with others by changing the ways they interact in a shared social world.

The study of practice

Action research and the study of practice

It should also be stressed that action research concerns actual, not abstract, practices. It involves learning about the real, material, concrete, particular practices of particular people in particular places. While of course it is not possible to suspend the inevitable abstraction which occurs whenever we use language to name, describe, interpret and evaluate things, action research differs from other forms of research in being more obstinate about changing particular practitioners' particular practices, rather than focusing on practices in general or in the abstract. In our view, action researchers need make no apology for seeing their work as mundane and mired in history; there are philosophical and practical dangers in the idealism which suggests that a more abstract view of practice might make it possible to transcend or rise above history, and delusions in the view that it is possible to find a safe haven in abstract propositions which construe but do not themselves constitute practice. Action research is a learning process whose fruits are the real and material changes in:

- what people do
- how they interact with the world and with others
- what they mean and what they value
- the discourses in which they understand and interpret their world.

Through action research people can come to understand their social and educational practices more richly by locating their practices, as concretely and precisely as possible, in the particular material, social and historical circumstances within which their practices were produced, developed and evolved – so that their real practices become accessible to reflection, discussion and reconstruction as products of past circumstances which are capable of being modified in and for present and future circumstances. While recognising that every practice is transient and evanescent, and that it can only be conceptualised in the inevitably abstract (though comfortingly imprecise) terms that language provides, action researchers aim to understand their own particular practices as they emerge in their own particular circumstances, without reducing them to the ghostly status of the general, the abstract or the ideal – or, perhaps one should say, the unreal.

If action research is understood in such terms, then, through their investigations, action researchers may want to become especially sensitive to the ways in which their particular practices involve

(a) *acts* of material, symbolic and social
- production
- communication
- social organisation;
(b) which shape and are shaped by *social structures* in
- the cultural
- the economic
- the political realms;
(c) which shape and are shaped by the *social media* of
- language/discourses
- work
- power;

(d) which largely shape, but can also be shaped by, participants' own *knowledge*, expressed in participants'
- understandings
- skills
- values; which, in turn, shape and are shaped by their
(a) acts of material, symbolic and social production, communication and social organisation . . . , and so on.

PAR researchers might consider, for example, how their acts of communication, production and social organisation are intertwined and interrelated in the real and particular practices which connect them to others in the real situations in which they find themselves (situations like communities, neighbourhoods, families, schools, and other workplaces). They consider how, by collaboratively changing the ways they participate with others in these practices, they can change the practices, their understandings of these practices and the situations in which they live and work.

The theoretical scheme depicted in Figure 2.2 takes a view of what theorising a practice might be like: locating a practice within frameworks of participants' knowledge, in relation to social structures and in terms of social media. By adopting a more encompassing view of practice, we may be able to understand and theorise it more richly, and in more complex ways, so that powerful social dynamics can be construed and reconstituted through a critical social practice like action research.

Methodologies and perspectives in the study of practice

Despite its ubiquity and familiarity, what the term 'practice' means is by no means self-explanatory. In theory and research, it turns out to mean very different things to different people. Perhaps one reason for this is that researchers into practice from different intellectual traditions tend to focus on different aspects of practice when they investigate it. The result is confusion. On the basis of their different views about how practice should be understood, different people have different views on how it can and should be improved. To make a start in clearing up some of these confusions, it may help if we distinguish five different aspects of practice emphasised in different investigations of practice:

1 The *individual performances*, events and effects which constitute practice as it is viewed from the 'objective', external perspective of an outsider (the way the practitioner's individual behaviour appears to an outside observer).

2 The wider *social and material conditions and interactions* which constitute practice as it is viewed from the 'objective', external perspective of an

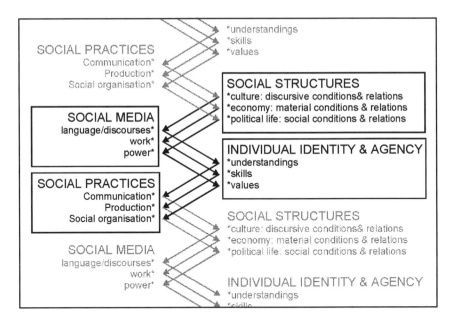

Figure 2.2 Recursive relationships of social mediation which action research aims to transform

outsider (the way the patterns of social interaction among those involved in the practice appear to an outside observer).

3   The *intentions, meanings and values* which constitute practice as it is viewed from the 'subjective', internal perspective of practitioners themselves (the way individual practitioners' intentional actions appear to the individual practitioners themselves).

4   The *language, discourses and traditions* which constitute practice as it is viewed from the 'subjective', internal social perspective of members of the participants' own discourse community who must represent (describe, interpret, evaluate) practices in order to talk about and develop them, as happens, for example, in the discourse communities of professions (the way the language of practice appears to communities of practitioners as they represent their practices to themselves and others).

5   The *change and evolution of practice* – taking into account all four of the aspects of practice just mentioned – which comes into view when it is understood as reflexively restructured and transformed over time – in its historical dimension.

Though different schools of thought in theorising and research about practice in different fields are very diverse in terms of the problems and phenomena they study, and the methods they employ, it is possible to bring some of their presuppositions about problems, phenomena and methods to the fore by making some distinctions around which these differences can be arrayed. For the moment, we want to focus on just two dichotomies which have divided approaches to the human and social sciences: first, the division between those approaches which see human and social life largely in 'individualistic' terms and those which see human and social life largely in terms of the 'social realm', and, second, the division between those approaches which conceive of their problems, phenomena and methods largely in 'objective' terms (from an 'external' perspective, as it were) and those which conceive their problems, phenomena and methods largely in 'subjective' terms (from an 'internal' perspective, as it were). In each case, we want to suggest that these are false dichotomies, and that we can escape from the partiality of each by seeing the two sides of the dichotomies not as opposites, only one of which can be true, but as dialectically related – that is, as mutually constitutive aspects of one another, both of which are necessary to achieve a more comprehensive perspective on practice.

The move from thinking in terms of dichotomies to thinking in dialectical terms might be characterised as a move from 'either or' thinking to 'both and' (or from 'not only . . . ' to 'but also . . . ', or from 'while on the one hand' . . . , to 'also, on the other hand . . . ') thinking. For the time being, however, it suffices to say that it is possible that each of these two dichotomies – individual–social and objective–subjective – can be transcended by seeing them in dialectical terms. Whether or not this is well-founded in logic and epistemology is a matter of philosophical dispute, but we will nevertheless use these distinctions to classify a number of approaches to the study of practice. Figure 2.3 is an attempt to 'map' the interrelating five traditions in the study of practice.

In the light of these considerations, then, we can conceive of five broad traditions in the study of practice. A brief description of each tradition follows.

1   *Practice as individual behaviour, to be studied objectively.* The first perspective on practice sees it primarily 'from the outside', as *individual* behaviour. Those adopting this perspective frequently understand the science of behaviour as *objective*, and apply this view to understanding practice. A variety of traditions in psychology, including the behaviourist and the cognitivist, adopt this view of practice. Research on practice from this perspective adopts correlational or quasi-experimental methods, is likely to use descriptive and inferential statistics and adopts an instrumental view of the relationship between the researcher and the researched, in which the field being studied is understood in the 'third person' (as objects whose behaviour is to be changed). This approach to the study of practice is likely to be adopted when the research question is one asked by people administering organisations,

Focus: Perspective:	The individual	The social	Both: Reflexive-dialectical view of individual-social relations and connections
Objective	**(1)** Practice as individual behaviour, seen in terms of performances, events and effects: behaviourist and most cognitivist approaches in psychology	**(2)** Practice as social interaction – e.g., ritual, system-structured: structure-functionalist and social systems approaches	
Subjective	**(3)** Practice as intentional action, shaped by meaning and values: psychological *verstehen* (empathetic understanding) and most constructivist approaches	**(4)** Practice as socially-structured, shaped by discourses, tradition: interpretive, æsthetic-historical *verstehen* and post-structuralist approaches	
Both: Reflexive-dialectical view of subjective-objective relations and connections			**(5)** Practice as socially- and historically-constituted, and as reconstituted by human agency and social action: critical theory, critical social science

Figure 2.3 Relationships between different traditions in the study of practice

who want to provoke change by changing the inputs, processes and outputs of the organisation as a system (in which people are seen as elements of the system).

2   *Practice as group behaviour or ritual, to be studied objectively.* The second perspective also views practice 'from the outside', but sees it in terms of *the social group*. Those adopting this perspective also understand the study of group behaviour as *objective*. A variety of social psychological perspectives, and structure–functionalist perspectives in sociology, adopt this view of practice. Research on practice from this perspective is also likely to adopt correlational or quasi-experimental methods, is also likely to use descriptive and inferential statistics and is also likely to adopt an instrumental view of the relationship between the researcher and the researched, in which the field being studied is understood in the 'third person' (as objects whose behaviour is to be changed). And, like the first perspective, this perspective would also be likely to be adopted when the research question is one asked by people administering systems, who want to change them by changing system inputs, processes and outputs.

3   *Practice as individual action, to be studied from the perspective of the subjective.* On this view, human action (including practice) cannot be understood as 'mere' behaviour – it must be seen as shaped by the values, intentions and judgements of the practitioner. A variety of approaches in psychology take this view of practice (among them some clinical, some

29

'humanistic', and some 'Gestalt' approaches, to give just a few examples). Research on practice from this perspective generally adopts qualitative methods (including autobiographical, idiographic and phenomenological methods), and is likely to make only limited use of statistics. The field being studied is understood in the 'second person' (that is, as knowing, responsible and autonomous subjects – persons who, like the researcher her/himself, must make their own decisions about how to act in the situations in which they find themselves). This perspective is likely to be adopted when the research question is one asked by people who understand themselves to be autonomous and responsible persons acting in a lifeworld of human relationships and interactions, who believe that changing these lifeworlds requires engaging, and perhaps re-forming, selves and relationships in shared lifeworld settings.

4   *Practice as social action or tradition, to be understood from the perspective of the subjective.* A fourth perspective on practice also attempts to view it 'from the inside', but understands it not from the perspective of the individual acting alone, but as part of a *social* structure that contributes to forming the way in which action (practice) is understood by people in the situation. It also takes a *subjective* view, but it takes into account that people and the way they act are also formed historically – that they always come to situations which have been pre-formed, and in which only certain kinds of action are now appropriate or possible. Moreover, this view is also conscious that it must take into account that people's own perspectives, and their very words, have all been formed historically and in the interactions of social life – they are historically, socially and discursively constituted. Research on practice from this perspective is similar to the third perspective in its likely research methods (though it may also adopt clinical or critical ethnography as a research method, or particular kinds of methods which are very explicit about the role of the researcher in the research – as in advocacies for some feminist approaches to research), its view about practical reasoning and its view of the standpoint of the researcher in relation to others in the situation being studied. In this case, however, the researcher would understand her/himself not only as another actor in a social situation, but also as a human agent who, with others, must act at any particular moment in a situation which is already socially, historically and discursively formed, and in which one is also, to some extent, a representative of a tradition which contests the ground with other traditions (since different and competing traditions about different things are simultaneously and typically at play in any particular situation). In this sense, research in this tradition is likely to understand itself as in some sense 'political' – just as the situations it studies are 'political'.

5   *Practice as reflexive, to be studied dialectically.* The fifth view of practice understands it as 'political' in an even more self-conscious sense – it understands that to study practice is to change it, that the process of studying it is also 'political', and that its own standpoint is liable to change through the process of action – that it is a process of enlightenment about the standpoint from which one studies practice and about the practice itself.

This view of practice challenges the dichotomies or dualisms which separate the first four views from one another: the dualism of the individual versus the social, and the objective versus the subjective. It attempts to see each of these dimensions not in terms of polar opposites, but in terms of the mutuality and relationship between these different aspects of things. Thus, it sees the individual and the social, and the objective and the subjective, as related aspects of human life and practice, to be understood *dialectically* – that is, as mutually opposed (and often contradictory) but mutually necessary aspects of human, social, historical reality, in which aspect helps to constitute the other.

On this view, it is necessary to understand practice as enacted by *individuals* who act in the context of history and in ways constituted by a vast, historical web of *social* interactions between people. Similarly, on this view, it is necessary to understand practice as having both *objective* (externally given) and *subjective* (internally understood and interpreted) aspects, both of which are necessary to understand how any practice is really practised, and how it is constituted historically and socially, and how it can be transformed if people critically transform what they do to enact the practice, transform the way it is understood and transform the situations in which they practice. This view of the relationship between the objective and the subjective is sometimes also described as 'reflexive', since changing the objective conditions changes the way in which a situation is interpretively understood, which in turn changes how people act on the 'external', 'objective' world, which means that what they do is understood and interpreted differently, and that others also act differently, and so on, in a dynamic process of reflection and self-reflection which gives it human action in history its dynamic, fluid and reflexive character. This view of practice thus sees itself explicitly as engaged in making action and making history, and in learning from action and history as something within the research process, not as something outside it (as an outcome or effect which follows from the research).

The reflexive–dialectical perspective on practice thus attempts to find a place for the four previous perspectives in a broader framework of historical, social and discursive construction and reconstruction, and does its best to recognise that people and their actions are not only caused by their intentions and circumstances, but also that people cause intentions and circumstances – that is, that people are made by action in the world, and that they also make action and history. And it aims to see how these processes occur *within the ambit of the research process itself*.

Research on practice from this perspective is likely to adopt research methods which are reflexive – methods like those of critical social science (Carr and Kemmis 1986; Fay 1987), or collaborative action research (Kemmis and McTaggart 1988; Wilkinson 1996), or 'memory work' (Haug 1987). They are reflexive in the sense that they engage participants in a collaborative process of social transformation in which they learn from, and change the way they engage in, the process of transformation. Research conducted from this perspective adopts an 'emancipatory' view of the point and purpose of the research, in which co-participants attempt to remake and improve their own practice to overcome distortions, incoherence, contradictions and injustices. It adopts a 'first-person' perspective in which people construct the research process as a way of collaborating in the process of transforming their practices, their understanding of their practices and the situations in which they practice. Like the fourth perspective on practice, it understands that research is 'political', but it aims to make the research process into a politics which will in some definite ways supersede and reconstruct the pre-existing politics of the settings in which it is conducted – indeed, it aims to be a process in which various aspects of social life in the setting (cultural, economic and political) can be transformed through collaborative action. Recognising that the internal social processes of the setting and the research are connected to, and sometimes conflicting with, wider social and historical processes which the co-researchers cannot suspend or change simply by changing themselves, action researchers need to work in relation to these wider forces rather than simply 'for' or 'against' them.

Though the other four traditions are necessary in their own ways, and for particular kinds of purposes, this fifth tradition is of special interest to those who want to change practices through their own efforts, and especially in participatory, collaborative research. It is a tradition in the study of practice which aims to make explicit connections across the dimensions of 'objective' and 'subjective', the focus on the individual and the focus on the social, the aspects of structure and agency, and the connections between the past and future. The significance of the word 'connections' here deserves special notice. It seems to me that we need to recognise that the study of a practice as complex as the practice of education, or nursing, or public administration (to give just a few examples) is a study of connections – of many different kinds of communicative, productive and organisational relationships between people in socially, historically and discursively constituted media of language (discourse), work and power – all of which must be understood dynamically and relationally. And we should recognise that there are research approaches which aim to explore these connections and relationships by participating in them and, through changing the forms in which people participate in them, aim to change the practice, the way it is understood and the situations in which the practice is conducted. At its best, it seems to me, such a research tradition aims to help people understand themselves both as 'objective' forces impinging on others and as subjects who have intentions and commitments they share with others, and both as people who act in ways framed by discourses formed beyond any one of us individually, and as people who make meaning for ourselves in communication with others with whom we stand.

In terms of the five aspects of practice and the five traditions in the study of practice outlined earlier, a methodologically driven view of action research finds itself mired in the assumptions about practice to which one or another of the different traditions of research on practice is committed. Once accepting one or another of these sets of presuppositions, it may find itself unable to approach (the study of) practice in a sufficiently rich and multi-faceted way – that is, in terms which recognise different aspects of practice, and do justice to its social, historical and discursive construction.

If action research is to explore practice in terms of each of the five aspects outlined earlier, it will need to consider how different traditions in the study of practice, and different research methods and techniques, can provide *multiple* resources for the task. It must also avoid accepting the assumptions and limitations of particular methods and techniques. For example, the action researcher may legitimately eschew the narrow empiricism of those approaches which attempt to construe practice *entirely* 'objectively', as if it were possible to exclude consideration of participants' intentions, meanings, values and interpretive categories from an understanding of practice, or as if it were possible to exclude consideration of the frameworks of language, discourse and tradition by which people in different groups construe their practices. It does not follow from this that quantitative approaches are never relevant in action research; on the contrary, they may be – but without the constraints many quantitative researchers put on these methods and techniques. Indeed, when quantitative researchers use questionnaires to convert participants' views into numerical data, they tacitly concede that practice cannot be understood without taking participants' views into account. Action researchers will differ from one-sidedly quantitative researchers in the ways they collect and use such data, because the action researcher will regard them as crude approximations to the ways participants understand themselves, not (as quantitative researchers may assert) as more rigorous (valid, reliable) because they are scaled.

On the other hand, the action researcher will differ from the one-sidedly qualitative approach which asserts that action can only be understood from a qualitative perspective – for example, through close clinical or phenomeno-logical analysis of an individual's views, or close analysis of the discourses and traditions which shape the way a particular practice is understood by participants. The action researcher will also want to explore how changing 'objective' circumstances (performances, events, effects; interaction patterns, rules, roles and system functioning) shape and are shaped by the 'subjective' participants' perspectives.

In our view, questions of research methods should not be regarded as unimportant, but, by contrast with the methodologically driven view, we would want to assert that what makes action research 'research' is not the machinery of research techniques but an abiding concern with the relation-ships between social and educational *theory and practice*. Before questions about what kinds of research methods are appropriate can be decided, it is necessary to decide what kinds of things 'practice' and 'theory' are – for only then can we decide what kinds of data or evidence might be relevant in describing practice, and what kinds of analyses are relevant in interpreting and evaluating people's real practices in the real situations in which they work. On this view of action research, a central question is how practices are to be understood 'in the field', as it were, so they become available for more systematic theorising. Once having arrived at a general view of what it means to understand (theorise) practice in the field, it becomes possible to work out what kinds of evidence, and hence what kinds of research methods and techniques, might be appropriate for advancing our understanding of practice at any particular time.

Reflection on projects and on PAR

In the discussion above we have presented one, arguably personal, view of what PAR is and its role in the study of practice. Needless to say, this view of what constitutes PAR is not static. It is continuously open to reflection, critique and further development based on new theoretical developments and on empirical experience of action researchers.

We will conclude this chapter by proposing a set of questions for use by PAR researchers in reflecting on their projects' processes and outcomes. These questions are based on issues raised in this chapter. It is important to point out that these questions are not intended as a rigid criterion to judge whether a project is or is not PAR, nor to evaluate projects on how closely they follow the above description. Rather, they are a tool for a more compre-hensive critical reflection on PAR projects.

Naturally, reflection on action research projects is multifaceted. A collab-orative team of PAR researchers often develop significant learning about PAR processes and principles. A parallel set of questions could be developed to allow participants reflection on PAR principles and characteristics them-selves. The construction of such questions is left for the reader.

1 How does the project design follow the Lewinian spiral of cycles of self-reflection (at least in broad terms)?

2 How does the project aim at improvement in

(a) practices?
(b) practitioners' understandings of their practices?
(c) the situations in which the practices are carried out?

3 How does the project aim at involvement of:

(a) those whose action constitutes the practice?
(b) those affected by the practice?

4 How can the project be described as a social process? How does it deliberately explore the relationship between the realms of the individual and the social?

5 How can the project be described as participatory? How does it engage people in examining their knowledge (understandings, skills and values) and interpretative categories (the ways they interpret themselves and their action in the social and material world)?

6 How can the project be described as practical and collaborative? How does it engage people in examining the acts which link them with others in social interaction?

7 How can the project be described as emancipatory? How does it aim to help people recover, and release themselves from, the constraints of irrational, unproductive, unjust and unsatisfying social structures which limit their self-development and self-determination?

8 How can the project be described as critical? How does it aim to help people recover and release themselves from the constraints embedded in the social media through which they interact: their language (discourses), their modes of work and the social relationships of power (in which they experience affiliation and difference, inclusion and exclusion, etc.)?

9 How can the project be described as recursive (reflexive, dialectical)? How does it aim to help people to investigate reality in order to change it, and to change reality in order to investigate it – in particular by changing their practices in a deliberate social process designed to help them learn more about (and theorise)

their practices, their knowledge of their practices, the social structures which constrain their practices and the social media in which their practices are expressed and realised?

10   Which aspects of the project consider practice from a

(a) subjective or

(b) objective or

(c) reflexive–dialectical perspective involving both?

11   What aspects of the project consider practice from

(a) an individual or

(b) social or

(c) reflexive–dialectical perspective involving both?

REFERENCES

Carr, W. and Kemmis, S. (1986) *Becoming Critical: Education, Knowledge and Action Research*, London: Falmer.

Fals Borda, O. (1979) 'Investigating reality in order to transform it: the Colombian experience', *Dialectical Anthrolopogy*, 4: (March) 33–55.

Fay, B. (1987) *Critical Social Science: Liberation and its Limits*, Cambridge: Polity Press.

Habermas, J. (1992) *Postmetaphysical Thinking: Philosophical Essays* (William Mark Hohengarten, trans.), Cambridge: Massachusetts: MIT Press.

Haug, F. (1987) *Female Sexualization: A Collective Work of Memory*, London: Verso.

Kemmis, S. and McTaggart, R. (eds) (1988) *The Action Research Planner*, 3rd edn, Geelong, Victoria: Deakin University Press.

Wilkinson, M. B. (1996) *Action Research for People and Organisational Change*, Brisbane, Australia: Queensland University of Technology.

3

RESEARCH PARTNERSHIPS

Principles and possibilities[1]

Shirley Grundy

The concept of 'professional partnership' has been an influential one in recent educational reform discourses. In the period 1988–96, for instance, we witnessed the Australian States, Territories and the Commonwealth working in partnership on a national agenda, originally articulated through the Dawkins policy statement: *Strengthening Australia's Schools* (Dawkins 1988; see also Grundy and Bonser, forthcoming). During this period employers and unions also found or made spaces to engage in partnership, particularly around issues related to teacher professionalism. This commitment to partnership was articulated in the Teaching Accord (Free *et al.* 1994), being most clearly expressed in two of the objectives and two of the principles underpinning the agreement:

Objectives

- to develop, pursue and monitor educational change on a sound and continuing basis by using a collaborative approach
- to provide for understanding and participation by the profession in implementing educational change

Principles

- Successful implementation of public policy in the education industry depends on the informed participation of the teaching profession.
- There should be collaborative action between the Federal Government, state and territory government and non-government schools systems, and teacher unions, in consultation with all industry stakeholders, to manage educational change and development effectively.

(Free *et al.* 1994: 7, 8)

In an address to the Innovative Links Project National Forum in 1995

Lynne Rolley (Federal Secretary of the Independent Education Union and a joint architect of the Accord) emphasised the importance of the principle of 'partnership' to the agreement:

> Central to the philosophy underpinning the Accord is the notion of partnership – an understanding that there are many stakeholders in the industry of education and that, in the context of it being a mass industry having to operate within the tensions of Commonwealth/State relations, cohesion and integrity can only be maintained by linking arms, so to speak, working collaboratively, and negotiating with each other to advance our respective interests within this complex context.
>
> (Rolley 1995: 10)

In a review of literature around issues relating to the reform of teacher education undertaken by Jennifer Gore for the Innovative Links Project it is claimed: 'Not surprisingly, . . . collaborative and partnership programs are frequently touted as the single most efficient, effective, and important way of reforming both teacher education and schools concurrently' (Gore, 1995: 14).

In this chapter I explore some of the issues relating to this concept of professional partnerships, not so much in relation to teacher education, but in relation to 'research partnerships'.

There are currently two principal manifestations of the professional research partnership. One of these could be called 'researching *for* the profession'. This is a form of partnership which is increasingly being developed because of the restructuring of educational bureaucracies and the consequent tendering out of many research functions that were previously undertaken by research branches located within most State Departments of Education. This is a form of commercial researching partnership where university-based researchers are 'employed' to undertake research on behalf of the profession (or at least the system in which the profession is practised). It is not, however, with this partnership that I am principally concerned in this chapter.

One of the other forms of professional partnership is through the development of professional collaborative research enterprises between groups of educators, for instance, school-based teachers and university-based researchers, parents, school support personnel, students, etc. These forms of professional researching partnership could be characterised as 'researching *with* the profession'.

These are two very different forms of research partnerships; the former a commercial partnership, the latter a collaborative partnership. Each, has possibilities and problems associated with it and each needs to be grounded in sound ethical and operational principles if it is to function successfully. It is, however, upon the latter relationship 'researching with the profession' that I want to concentrate here. Moreover, within that form of professional partnership I focus principally upon the development of partnerships between people whose work is primarily located within the sites of the 'university' and the 'school'. The issues and principles associated with such partnerships have application to varying degrees to other forms of professional researching partnerships (such as between parents and teachers, students and teachers, etc.) and research partnerships involving sites and organisations other than schools, but in this chapter I leave such extrapolations largely to the reader.

Although I am directing my reflections specifically to the professional partnership between 'academic' (or university-based) researchers and 'practitioners' (or school-based teachers), such partnerships can also be instructive as a metaphor for 'within-site' relationships – that is, the relationships within our own professional lives between those aspects of our work principally directed towards the generation of knowledge and understanding (within the site of the university this is principally the portion of the academic's work characterised as 'research') and those aspects of our work principally directed towards practising our profession (within the site of the university this is principally the portion of the academic's work characterised as 'teaching'). In both university and school sites these aspects of professional work are given different weightings of regard. Within university sites 'research' is often privileged (and rewarded) above 'teaching' and within school sites the reverse is often the case. So there is a very real sense in which some of the principles and possibilities relating to across-site partnerships apply also to the development of 'partnership' between the various aspects of our professional work.

Researching with the profession

There is a very real sense in which it is timely to be investigating the implications of professional partnerships. As was indicated by the quotation from Lynne Rolley cited at the beginning of this chapter, 'partnerships' have been regarded as an important political strategy for negotiating the increasingly complex relationships which provide the context for educational work (Rolley 1995). Lasley et al. claim that the tightening economic constraints within which educational institutions are forced to operate make collaborative partnerships 'necessary for institutional growth' (Lasley et al. 1992: 260).

While not wanting to diminish either the pragmatics or the politics of the impetus towards forming professional partnerships, my purpose here is to investigate and advocate professional research partnerships on epistemological and ideological grounds. That is, on the basis of arguments about what knowledge and knowledge production processes are most worthwhile for advancing educational theory and practice, and on the basis of commitments around ideas about how power is and should be distributed and contested in relation to such knowledge production.

Professional research partnerships: a tradition in educational research

The educational knowledge which I have largely been interested in exploring in my work is 'professional' knowledge, that is, knowledge that is intrinsically connected with practice. This is not knowledge that 'informs' practice, or that has practical intent, but knowledge which is embedded in 'praxis' – reflective knowledge in and through action. I have argued for such knowledge both epistemologically and politically in other places (e.g., Grundy 1987), so I will not rehearse such arguments here. What I want to do here is to recognise as problematical that which I and others have advocated in other places at other times, that is, to call into question some of the glib advocacy of professional research partnerships. I call such advocacy into question, not to denigrate or discourage professional researching partnerships, but rather to strengthen such possibilities by subjecting them to an unflinching critical gaze.

There is now a long history of advocacy of the right of educational practitioners to control the production of their professional knowledge. Most clearly this tradition has been associated with 'action research', a form of research which brings action for change (improvement) together with the improvement of understanding and knowledge (research). 'Action' and 'research' are brought together not only into the one process but also into the one person – the inquiring practitioner (see Grundy 1987; Carr and Kemmis 1986).

The valuing of professional knowledge production through the advocacy of action research in Australia has strong links back to a British tradition of 'teacher as researcher', most notably associated with the work of Lawrence Stenhouse. I used as the closing quote in my book *Curriculum: Product or Praxis?* this extract from Stenhouse: 'Curriculum research and development ought to belong to the teacher and . . . there are prospects of making this good in practice. It is not enough that teachers' work should be studied: they need to study it themselves' (Stenhouse 1976: 142, 143).

But Stenhouse was not handing over responsibility for educational research to individual teachers. Indeed the community of the school is advocated as the 'body' where professional action and responsibility should be expressed:

> I value highly the tradition of professional autonomy as the basis of
> educational quality but it seems that this must now be negotiated
> at the school level. . . . [T]he school staff can no longer be seen as a

federal association of teachers and departments: it must be a professional community. And it is with this community that professional
autonomy must lie.

(ibid. 183)

So 'practice' is to be a crucial site and subject of educational research and
'practitioners', understood collectively (in professional communities known
as schools), are to be the researchers.

Even Stenhouse was not, however, advocating the wholesale abandonment
of school and classroom-oriented research to practitioners. He concluded his
1976 book on curriculum research and development with the following
observation:

> Research in curriculum and teaching, which involves the close
> study of schools and classrooms, is the basis of sound development,
> and the growth of a research tradition in the schools is its founda-
> tion. Full-time research workers and teachers need to collaborate
> towards this end. Communication is less effective than community
> in the utilization of knowledge.

(ibid. 223)

Stenhouse's privileging of 'community' over 'communication' suggests a
transformation of the idea that research is conducted by one set of people
and communicated to another set. Rather, professional researching communities are being advocated as communities of inquiry which are characterised
by the sort of two-way processes of communication which partnerships
require.

Research partnerships: the challenge

This idea of a collaborative professional research community would sit
comfortably with the idea of partnership which, we noted earlier, has been
enunciated and supported alike in the Teaching Accord and in the teacher
education literature. Yet in his keynote address at the 1994 Annual
Conference of the Australian Association for Research in Education (AARE),
Ken Zeichner made the claim:

> Many academics in colleges and universities dismiss teacher research
> as trivial, atheoretical, and as inconsequential to their work. Most
> academics who are involved in the teacher research movement
> around the world have marginalized the process of school-based
> inquiry by teachers as a form of teacher development but do not
> consider it as a form of knowledge production.

(Zeichner 1994: 1)

The challenge that needs to be addressed in relation to professional partnerships is implicit in Zeichner's criticism and it is this: Is it possible to construct a legitimate and authentic professional research partnership which would see, for instance, university-based researchers and school-based teachers genuinely participating in a community of inquiry such as Stenhouse envisaged?

In Gore's paper, to which I referred above, she notes from the teacher education literature a number of principles that need to be taken into account for genuine partnerships:

- Democracy is required in partnerships and hierarchical relationships, where expertise is seen to belong more clearly to one set of participants than another, are to be avoided.
- In the planning of the partnership, the distinctive interests of all parties need to be taken into account.
- Trust, communication and understanding of each partner's perspectives should be developed.
- Problems associated with a lack of, or limits on, rewards and recognition of individuals in universities and schools for collaborative activities need to be acknowledged and addressed.
- All involved in the partnership should be jointly responsible for and involved in the planning of the partnership from the very beginning.

(Gore 1995: 19)

These form a very attractive set of principles of partnership. Moreover, they would come as not great surprise to those committed to ideas and practices of professional collaboration. However, if this is the set of principles for effective partnership that can be extracted from the literature, then the possibilities of forming genuine researching partnerships with professional practitioners seem remote. There are both cultural and structural impediments to such genuine partnerships which are not overcome merely by glossing the different positioning of the professional partners.

The first of Gore's principles could be interpreted as implying that one of the bases for the formation of productive partnerships is the elimination of notions of expertise, that is, the elimination of the ascribing of expertise to one set of participants rather than another. Attempts to represent research as 'reflective practice' and 'what teachers do anyway', belittles both research and reflective practice as does the portrayal of university researchers as 'teachers' in a different guise. To gloss over the differential expertise of the researching partners is to call into question the very nature of and rationale for the partnership. The crucial elements of this principle (elements that I would not want to dispute) are 'democracy' and 'hierarchy', but we do not demonstrate a commitment to democratic principles or challenge hierarchy by eliminating the value of the differing expertise that the partners in a professional community of inquiry bring to the research task. However, because of the deeply embedded histories of those in both the school and the academy, the non-hierarchical recognition of differing sources and forms of expertise is problematical. But the problem is not solved by the elimination of the idea of expertise.

The second and fifth principles relating to planning and the acknowledgement of differing interests also represent principles that are easier to assert than to live. Here the structural impediments arising out of what Connelly and Clandinin refer to as 'the rhythms that develop around the cyclic organization of time in our institutions' (Connelly and Clandinin 1994: 92) militate against living these principles. Of course, as Teitel (1994) notes, many partnerships exist on the margins of both school and university life and, hence, are constructed around mutual interest, informal associations and mutual agreements. However, if such partnerships are to be mainstreamed, especially as research partnerships, they will become subjected to structured timelines and formal procedures, particularly with respect to applications for and the administration of funding. Developing funding applications in genuinely collaborative ways so that the 'distinctive interests of all parties are taken into account' is extremely difficult. For instance, where is the time to come from for teachers to engage in the planning and writing of research proposals funded through university-based grants schemes? The partnerships for most collaborative research projects are formed after the funds have been obtained, but this has implications for whose questions and interests the research is really addressing.

The fourth point relating to the limits on rewards from both sides of the partnership is an equally complex one. It isn't just that there are few rewards for teachers who involve themselves in research, although that may well be the case. Within the academy there are disincentives for engaging in collaborative research. Take as one example the 'research quantum' (a reward system for universities based increasingly upon research productivity measured by publications). A university researcher who published with another who is not either a staff member or postgraduate student of the university is credited with only a portion of the weighting that the publication would attract in the index. Similarly, promotion and tenure committees ask for the proportion of collaborative publications to be ascribed to the applicant to be specified. The obvious implication is that collaboration reduces the amount and value of individual contributions. Connelly and Clandinin further note that 'ethical guidelines are set up to require university faculty to protect school personnel as subjects rather than to support them as collaborators' (*ibid.*: 94). The AARE Ethics Statement, for instance, has a useful section on collaborative research and joint authorship, but the collaborators and joint authors are imagined to be postgraduate students or other university-based personnel.

Given these difficulties with what at face value is a very attractive set of principles, the prospects for genuine professional research partnerships are not bright.

Research partnerships: some possibilities

Read as a set of principles of possibility, however, these principles do open up prospects for the development of communities of professional inquiry – professional researching partnerships. In what follows, I explore some principles of possibility for professional research partnerships.

The issue of 'parity of esteem' of the knowledge and expertise of school- and university-based practitioners needs to be seriously worked through. The elimination of hierarchy does not mean the elimination of different forms or sources of knowledge. However, the differences need to be delineated, indeed, they need to become the subject of research themselves. Of course 'parity of esteem' for expertise will be strongly dependent upon the other principles of partnership – trust, comparable rewards, recognition of distinctive interests. It should not be assumed, however, that these will lead to 'parity of esteem' for the expertise of the various partners. The question of expertise needs to be addressed explicitly.

Recognition of the 'distinctive interests of the partners' should add breadth and depth to the research programme where those 'distinctive interests' are represented in the research questions which shape the research. The issue of 'For whom is this a question?', if addressed, will result in far richer research programmes. One tendency here is to switch the emphasis towards the research questions of school-based educators. The research principles of the Innovative Links Project privileged school- and teacher-generated questions. The principles of operation explicitly state: 'Affiliated academic associates are committed to working with schools on a school's research and reform agenda . . . [and] give precedence to the research questions generated within the school setting, rather than within the academic environment' (The Innovative Links Project 1994).

While this is appropriate as a short-term strategy designed to counterbalance the traditional control of the educational research agenda exercised by university-based academics, as a principle of long-term partnership it is problematical. Eventually the principle of 'parity of esteem' should provide a basis for research questions to be generated out of educational work in a multitude of sites by practitioners of all kinds engaged in work in those sites, rather than the privileging of one source of research questions over another.

For this to be possible, however, professional partnership research needs to be understood and practised in terms of *research programmes* and *researching communities*, rather than one-off projects. In this way parity of esteem and trust will build over time. It will also facilitate participation in all phases of the research planning by all participants. The establishment and operation of such research communities will have work organisation implications both for university-based and school-based partners.

The work organisation implications referred to above may imply that members of the academic community need to understand the industrial contexts within which school-based researchers work. University researchers, working in genuine partnership with school-based researchers may be able to play important advocacy and support roles in the struggle for professional recognition of research as a legitimate and essential work practice for teachers. Similarly, school-based researchers will need to understand and take a similar supportive, even advocacy, role in relation to the work practices of their academic colleagues.

If such professional partnerships are to flourish, we need to develop outlets for joint writing between university- and school-based researchers. This will entail exploring in greater depth issues related to collaborative writing.

Conclusion

In this chapter, the concern has been with professional partnerships between different persons. The issue of partnership, however, can also be interpreted as a personal matter. For me this entails the possibility of the integration of all aspects of my professional/academic life and history.

The link for me is between my positioning as a university-based researcher and as a member of the profession. If I see myself as a integral member of the education profession, then that participation needs to include my work as researcher as well as my work as teacher. Moreover, I am interested in my profession being a research-oriented profession, that is, not just a profession which grounds policy and practice in sound research (though that is vitally important) but one that is itself a community of researchers. Not, however, token researchers – real researchers. That means that those of us who devote a large proportion of our work to the practice of research need to form researching partnerships with those who traditionally have not regarded research as a work practice.

NOTE

1 This chapter is a paper, originally presented as a keynote address at a PARAPET conference in 1995, and later integrated into my Presidential Address to the Australian Association for Research in Education (AARE) in November 1995. That address appeared in the 1996 issue of *The Australian Educational Researcher*, 23 (1): 1–15.

REFERENCES

Carr, W. and Kemmis, S. (1986) *Becoming Critical: Knowing through Action Research*, Geelong, Victoria: Deakin University Press.

Connelly, M. and Clandinin, J. (1994) 'The promise of collaborative research in the political context', in Hollingsworth, S. and Sockett, H. (eds) *Teacher Research and Educational Reform: Ninety-third Yearbook of the National Society for the Study of Education*, Chicago: University of Chicago Press, pp. 86–102.

Dawkins, J. (1988) *Strengthening Australia's Schools: A Consideration of the Focus and Content of Schooling*, Canberra: Australian Government Printing Service.

Free, R., Burrow, S. and Rolley, L. (1994) *Agreement between the Commonwealth Government and the Teaching Profession through their Teacher Unions Providing for an Accord to Advance the Quality of Teaching and Learning*, Canberra: Office of the Minister for Schools, Vocational Education and Training.

Gore, J. (1995) 'Emerging issues in teacher education', mimeo, The Innovative Links Project, Perth, Western Australia: Murdoch University.

Grundy, S. (1987) *Curriculum: Product or Praxis?* London: Falmer Press.

Grundy, S. and Bonser, S. (forthcoming) National Initiatives and Primary Schooling, in Sachs, J. and Logan, L. (eds) *Meeting the Challenges of Primary Schooling*, London: Routledge.

Lasley, T., Matczynski, T. and Williams, J. (1992) 'Collaborative and non-collaborative partnership structures in teacher education', *Journal of Teacher Education*, 43 (4): 257–61.

Rolley, L. (1995) 'The role of unions in the Innovative Links Project', *The Big Link*, no. 3: 10.

Stenhouse, L. (1976) *Introduction to Curriculum Research and Development*, London: Heinemann.

Teitel, L. (1994) 'Can school–university partnerships lead to the simultaneous renewal of schools and teacher education?' *Journal of Teacher Education* 45 (4): 245–52.

The Innovative Links Project (1994) *Information Pamphlet*, Perth, Western Australia: Murdoch University.

Zeichner, K. (1994) 'Beyond the divide of teacher research and academic research', paper presented as a keynote address at the Annual Conference of the Australian Association for Research in Education, Newcastle, Australia, November.

4

SOME THOUGHTS ON CONTEMPORARY THEORIES OF SOCIAL JUSTICE

Fazal Rizvi

The immediate difficulty one confronts when examining the idea of social justice is the fact that it does not have a single essential meaning – it is embedded within discourses that are historically constituted and that are sites of conflicting and divergent political endeavours. Thus, social justice does not refer to a single set of primary or basic goods, conceivable across all moral and material domains. Its social meaning, as Michael Walzer (1983) has pointed out, is historical in character. It needs to be acknowledged, however, that injustice does have a material reality that is readily recognised by those who are subjected to it. Those who are hungry or poor or homeless or physically impaired do not need abstract definitions in order to be able to recognise their plight or indeed the inequities they might confront. If this is so, then the idea of social justice has practical significance. It needs therefore to be articulated in terms of particular values, which, while not fixed across time and space, nevertheless have to be given specific content in particular struggles for reform.

It remains a fact however that the idea of social justice is a highly contested one. It does not represent a timeless or static category. It has been interpreted in a variety of ways to reflect changing social and economic conditions. Indeed, even the Australian Labor Party (ALP)[1] does not have, and never has had, a uniform understanding of the idea of social justice. It is, for example, possible to identify a number of traditions which can be found within the ALP with respect to the meaning and significance they ascribe to the idea of social justice. Throughout its one hundred years of history, these traditions have struggled for supremacy. Indeed, it may be argued plausibly that it is these differing understandings of the notion of social justice that are the basis of the formation of the various factions within the ALP (MacIntyre 1985). The current policy priorities simply represent the triumph of one particular understanding over others, for it is only within the framework of the currently dominant understanding of the concept that it is possible to reconcile the government's competing discourses of social justice and economic rationalism.

The three main traditions of thinking about social justice found within the ALP, and the Australian society more generally, can be identified as: 'liberal-individualism', 'market-individualism' and 'social democratic'. The liberal–individualist view conceptualises social justice in terms of fairness. In recent philosophical literature, perhaps the most outstanding contemporary advocate of the view of social justice that emphasises justice as fairness is John Rawls (1972). To derive his principles of justice, Rawls constructed a hypothetical state of ignorance in which people did not know of the social position they might occupy in the future – with regards, for instance, to their income, status and power, and also to their natural abilities, intelligence, strength, etc. In such a state, Rawls argued that most people, if they were acting in their own self-interest, would select those principles of conduct that were likely to do them the least amount of harm and maximise their chances of happiness. From this 'veil of ignorance', as Rawls called it, people would want to protect themselves from the various possibilities of misfortunes.

This philosophical projection led Rawls to suggest two principles fundamental to any morally sustainable view of justice. First, each person is entitled to the most extensive basic liberty compatible with similar liberty for others. And second, there should be the most equal distribution of primary social goods, unless unequal distribution was to the advantage of the least favoured. The first principle implied individual freedom, while the second principle suggested that the state had a special responsibility to create policy initiatives and programs directed towards 'removing barriers, arising from unequal power relations and preventing equity, access and participation'.

Rawls's theory of social justice has been enormously influential in most western countries. During the 1960s and '70s, it led to the social democratic settlement, which included programmes of affirmative action, as well as some, though not as many as some imagine, redistributive policies. In the 1990s, Rawls's views are still promoted by a section of the ALP, most notably by Andrew Theophanous (1993), a leading parliamentarian in Australia, whose book, *Understanding Social Justice* uses Rawls to provide a blueprint to steer the federal government's social justice strategy towards a liberal definition. What Theophanous's analysis does not make clear, however, is how his government's economic rationalism can be reconciled with the Rawlsian redistributive philosophy he promotes.

In opposition to Rawls's view, Nozick (1976) has advocated a view of social justice based on a market-individualism that emphasises desert. Writing in the tradition of Locke and Sidgwick, Nozick argued that Rawls's theory focused on the issues of distribution and ignored the issue of people's entitlements to what they produced. Most theories of social justice, he pointed out, focus only on the end distribution of holdings; they pay little attention to the processes by which holdings were acquired. Nozick suggested that it was the justice of the competition – that is, the way competition was carried out and not its outcome – that counts. Nozick argued for a minimal state, limited to the functions of protection against force, theft, fraud, entitlement of contracts and so on – that is, the protection of individuals to exercise their liberty. He thus rejected redistributive notions of social and economic justice. His entitlement theory suggested that it was unjust for the state to transfer property that belonged to individuals. Any transfer of holdings was to be left to the markets.

Now while the differences between Rawls and Nozick are considerable, they both assume that people always act in their own self-interest. They both consider individualistic liberty as a value prior to any consideration of distribution of goods. And they both assume community to simply be the sum of the individuals who reside in it.

The other tradition of thinking about social justice within the ALP – the social-democratic tradition – is based on a very different set of assumptions. It is derived from Marx and stresses the idea of needs. As Beilharz has pointed out:

> it is qualitatively different from the preceding understandings, in that need is viewed as a primary rather than a residual category, and it is this which sets this view off from the charity-based arguments about the 'needy' which are compatible with either the 'desert' or the 'fairness' principles. This 'needs' tradition highlights a more collectivist and co-operative image of society.
>
> (Beilharz 1989: 94)

It is important to note that the two traditions of individualism (represented by Rawls and Nozick) and the social-democratic tradition rest on very different understandings about the nature of the relationship between social justice and the market. Nozick in particular regards the market as the most basic provider of social justice, of employment, services and welfare. The state is seen simply as a vehicle for promoting the activities of the market, and it is assumed that the market, if left to operate freely, will be able to deliver distributive fairness on its accord. According to the social-democratic view, on the other hand, as Agnes Heller (1987) has pointed out, while the idea of social justice may not necessarily be incompatible with markets, it is unlikely to be achieved unless the market is controlled in sufficiently rigorous ways. State activity is thus seen as 'market replacing' (Heller 1987), correcting its excesses, and minimising the costs of its arbitrary exercise.

In Australia, as in other western countries, market-individualism, and the view of social justice as desert, has become increasingly dominant over the past decade or so. As Beilharz argued, the social justice strategies of governments appears to be based on the hope:

> that the economy itself can be steered in the direction of 'social justice' – a non-sequitur outside the logic of markets, necessarily introducing residual welfare mechanisms in order to buoy up the human flotsam which cannot negotiate justice for itself through the market. To argue in this way is necessarily to introduce the logic of charity, and the language of the 'needy', for there are citizens, and there are those outside the city gates, who are deserving compassion.
>
> (Beilharz 1989: 92–3)

These assumptions necessarily introduce deficit considerations, with women, migrants, people with disabilities and the poor, and especially the unemployed, becoming the disadvantaged to whom the market, through its agency, the state, may choose to have a compensatory responsibility. Beilharz suggests further that social justice understood in this way thus becomes not so much a universal ethical principle as an administrative principle, the practical symbol of which is targeting of funds to ameliorate the most harmful consequences of market activity.

Certainly, in Australia, the federal Labor government's social justice strategy seems to incorporate some of these assumptions. It suggests that freedom, prosperity and equity can only be delivered by the expansion of markets. With such a reliance on the market, the government's major responsibility becomes that of 'good management' of the social and cultural conditions necessary for capital accumulation. Labor's restructuring programme may be seen in this light. Among the assumptions that lie behind the restructuring is the belief that the less the state is involved in market operations the better. Thus, tariffs have been cut, controls on the conduct of the market have been reduced, controls over banking and finance have been removed, tax breaks have been given to speculators to borrow abroad, new concentrations of wealth and media have been permitted and a programme of the sale of public enterprises has been commenced. And all this has often been justified on the grounds that free association of buyers and sellers in an open market will in the end bring a fair and equitable exchange. Moreover, it is assumed that with an expanding economy, it will be possible to do more for the disadvantaged.

What is clear, then, is that a conception of social justice has now been found by Labor which is consistent with the requirements of capital accumulation that give markets a freer reign. Social and educational policies and programmes are now subjected to this piece of ideology. The view of social justice now emerging in the form of a consensus is a contradictory amalgam of Rawlsian redistributive principles and Nozickian entitlement theory. In

Australia, it seems that while the Nozickian ideological framework has not yet been totally accepted, at least to the extent it has been in Britain, New Zealand and the United States, it has nevertheless gained considerable policy ascendancy.

Regarding the United States, Michael Apple (1988) has argued that there is now a recurrent conflict between property rights and person rights. A property right, he suggests, vests in individuals the power to enter into social relationships on the basis and extent of their property, while person rights are based on simple membership in their social collectivity. Person rights involve equal treatment of citizens, freedom and expression of movement, equal access to participation in decision making in social institutions, and reciprocity in relations of power and authority. According to Apple, these rights, which were won in the 1960s, have been under sustained attack in the past two decades. In the process, the meaning of what it is to have the social goal of equity has re-articulated. He argues:

> The citizen as 'free' consumer has replaced the previously emerging citizen as situated in structurally generated relations of domination. Thus the common good is now to be regulated exclusively by the laws of the market, free competition, private ownership and profitability. In a sense the definitions of freedom and equality are no longer democratic but commercial.
>
> (Apple 1988: 11)

While it would indeed be an overstatement to suggest the absolute triumph of property rights over person rights in Australia, a great deal has already happened to raise the issue of what is wrong with the Nozickian view of social justice, why it should concern educators and how its logic might be confronted.

Nozick's view of social justice is located in the processes of acquisition and production, rather than redistribution. Its moral consequences should be disturbing to all educators because as Barry (1973) has noted, a market view of social justice eliminates all transfer payments through the state, leaving 'the sick, the old, the disabled, the mothers with young children and no breadwinner and so on, to the tender mercies of private charity, given at the whim and pleasure of the donors and on any terms they choose to impose'. The freedom a market concept guarantees individuals benefits the privileged in a disproportionate way.

Market-individualism refuses to supply social goals for economic allocation, substituting for them procedural criteria for the proper acquisition of income and wealth. But such a view individualises the processes of production and acquisition. The activity of production in modern industrial societies is more social in character than Nozick appears to assume. All economic activity depends upon a network of co-operative relations between individuals. It is the social dimension of acquisition which makes distribution problematic in ways Nozick does not acknowledge.

Furthermore, what seems also to be assumed by Nozick is that equality in respect of acquisition of material wealth is somehow unrelated to equality in respect of power. But as Norman has pointed out:

> trapped as he is within his individualistic assumptions, he [Nozick] still seems to think in terms of individuals being forced to put their individual property into a social pot. He ignores the possibility that what goes into the pot may be, from the start, socially produced and socially owned.
>
> (Norman 1987: 152–3)

What these arguments show is that market criteria are insufficient for determining social and educational policy, and that solely procedural criteria for the fairness of competition are insufficient for achieving social justice. To consider them so is to privilege the economic – and view it as somehow unconnected to the cultural and the social. It is the 'social' in the notion of social justice that we need to stress. The moral idea of social suggests above all the need to develop a sense of co-operative community in which rewards are not determined simply on the basis of productive contribution, but also on the broader considerations of need and the human rights which everyone has to participate in social life to the best of her or his ability. A community that is not genuinely co-operative cannot be just.

In co-operative communities everyone benefits from participating in activities and in social institutions that are collectively productive. One can have a more productive life if one shares one's energies with others, in relations of open trust which enable one to see others as allies rather than competitors. Co-operation broadens one's interests and enlarges people's practical outlook by sharing the concerns of others. Beyond the benefits to individuals, co-operation also contributes to the general welfare of society, leading to general happiness. Market-individualism, on the other hand, favours only those who are already advantaged.

This reference to co-operation highlights the need to consider the historical and cultural particularities of our moral lives. As Warnke has noted, if we are to move beyond thinking about justice in abstract and universalistic ways then 'The theory of justice becomes an attempt to understand what a society's actions, practices and norms mean, to elucidate for a culture what its shared understandings are so that it can agree on the principles of justice that make sense to and for it' (Warnke 1994: 5). But this also requires taking note of the diversity of views and traditions that exist in most modern societies. Increasingly in recent years this recognition has led to a focus on difference, raising a range of theoretical and practical dilemmas which cannot be ignored.

In his book, *Spheres of Justice*, Walzer (1983) has posed one such dilemma which is critical to our educational work: how should educational policy and practice best respond to a society that is both heterogeneous and, it is to be hoped, committed to social justice and democracy. In a complex society, asserts Walzer, the idea of 'simple equality', as access so that everyone gets the same thing in the same form is neither achievable nor desirable. It is not achievable because people do not have the same means and capacities, and it is not desirable because people do not have the same needs. This has been historically demonstrated in Australia and elsewhere in that centralised uniformity of educational provision has proved over and over again to be insufficient for achieving social justice. For example, a system that encourages integration of all 'special needs' students into regular schools works on the assumptions of uniformity and cannot be just for all students with disabilities. Relevant differences in relative power, capacities and aspirations of students and parents must be acknowledged without risk to the notion of social justice.

Taking into account such heterogeneity, Walzer argues for a 'complex equality', which involves the distribution of different social goods according to different criteria. But this involves the old Aristotelian problem of how to determine what counts as 'relevant difference' that might require different treatment for a just situation to ensue. Clearly, criteria of justice are required that reflect the specificity of goods, their social significance and the variety in interests and capacities of the recipients. So rather than invoking the normative principles that would apply in all cases, from either the rights of individuals or the promise of universal emancipation, what is required is an organisational structure that enables the widest possible participation in order to develop context-specific meanings and criteria appropriate to particular spheres. This means that systems should generate general principles of social justice which are broad enough to allow for specific adaptation in different contexts, including schools and classrooms.

Walzer's is a significant step forward in its recognition of the contemporary politics of difference – in the diversity of inflections that can found within the category 'people with disabilities', as well as the diversity of interests they represent. In this, Walzer takes the political claims of the contemporary social movements seriously. However, he does not recognise the extent to which social movements have changed both the conception and the politics of social justice. As Nancy Fraser points out:

> the struggle for recognition is fast becoming the paradigmatic form of political conflict in the late twentieth century. Heterogeneity and pluralism are now regarded as the norms against which demands for justice are now articulated. Demands for 'recognition of difference' fuel struggles of groups mobilised under the banners of nationality, ethnicity, race, gender and sexuality. Group identity has supplanted

class conflict as the chief medium of political mobilisation. Cultural domination has supplanted economic exploitation as the fundamental injustice. And cultural recognition has displaced social-economic redistribution as the remedy for injustice and the goal of political struggle.

(Fraser 1995: 68)

Of course, material inequality has not disappeared but is now seen as articulated with demands for recognition of difference. What is also clear is that the distributive paradigm, as Iris Marion Young (1990) calls it, within which the major traditions of thinking about social justice are expressed, is no longer (if it ever was) sufficient to capture the complexities of injustice. This observation is consistent with analysis presented above of the limitations of the policies of access and equity, be it in the form of integration or any other form.

The distributive paradigm is concerned with the morally proper distribution of benefits and burdens among society's numbers. Paramount among these are wealth, income and other material resources. This definition however is often also stretched to include non-material goods such as rights, opportunity, power and self-respect. These are treated as if they were material entities subject to the similar logic to zero-sum game. So what marks the distributive paradigm is a tendency to conceive social justice and distribution as coextensive concepts. Young has identified two major problems with this way of thinking about social justice. First, she has argued that it tends to ignore, at the same time as it often presupposes, the institutional context that determines material distribution. Its focus is on consumption rather than on mode of production. As a consequence, it cannot account for those injustices that occur in the processes of social exchange and cultural formation. Second, in treating non-material goods like power, values and respect as if these were commodities, the distributive paradigm tends to misrepresent them. It obscures issues of decision-making power and procedures as well as of divisions of power and culture which can often lead to the perpetuation of gross injustices.

With the work of feminist scholars like Nancy Fraser and Iris Marion Young, a new mode of thinking about social justice is clearly emerging. While the distribution paradigm was associated with concepts like interest, exploitation and redistribution, this new paradigm is concerned to focus attention also on issues of identity, difference, culture domination and recognition. The distribution paradigm saw injustice as being rooted in the political–economic structure of society which results in economic marginalisation and exploitation and denial of access and equity, and often adequate material standard of living. The remedy was assumed to require political–economic restructuring; but at least greater access and equity. The recognition paradigm does not dismiss these concerns as irrelevant but suggest that they do not exhaust the range of injustices that occur in human societies. Chief among these is the injustice resulting from cultural disrespect. Fraser (1995) argues that injustice can also be rooted in social patterns of representation, interpretation and communication, which result in cultural domination, non-recognition and disrespect

The semiotic issues of representation, interpretation and communication are highly relevant to the concerns for justice in the education of students with disabilities because it is in education that students learn to develop their sense of self-worth and acceptable modes of social communication. As we have already pointed out, the practices of integration, have only promoted access for students with disabilities; they have done very little in changing the culture of schooling so that those with disabilities feel recognised and valued. Pedagogic and curriculum practices have remained largely unchanged with respect to the need to cater for a wide range of differences which are now acknowledged to exist in schools. Schools are still based on the assumptions of homogeneity and uniformity. They still require conformity and obedience to rules that are based on the requirements of administrative convenience rather than moral principles.

For there to be genuine social justice, cultural and symbolic changes to the ways schools are structured are clearly needed. According to Fraser (1995), the politics of recognition requires social transformation in ways that would change everybody's sense of self. But the most significant insight that has emerged from this discussion is that reform for educational justice is complex, and requires attention to not only the issues of political economy of schooling – of concerns of access and equity – but also of issues of the culture of schooling; that is, the way things are named and represented, the manner in which difference is treated and the ways in which the values, significations and norms which govern life in schools are negotiated and established.

NOTE

1 At the time of writing this chapter, the Australian Labor Party was in goverment. Hence this chapter discusses theories of social justice within the then government policies.

REFERENCES

Apple, M. (1988) 'How equity has been defined in the conservative restoration', in Secada, W. (ed.) *Equity in Education*, London: Falmer Press, pp. 7–25.

Barry, B. (1973) *The Liberal Theory of Justice*, Oxford: Clarendon Press.

Beilharz, P. (1989) 'Social democracy and social justice', *The Australian and New Zealand Journal of Sociology*, 25 (1): 85–99.

Fraser, N. (1995) 'From redistribution to recognition: dilemmas of justice in a "post-socialist" society', *New Left Review*, July–August, 68–93.

Heller, A. (1987) *A Theory of Needs*, Cambridge: Polity Press.

MacIntyre, S. (1985) *Winners and Losers*, Sydney: Allen & Unwin.

Norman, R. (1987) *Free and Equal*, New York: Oxford University Press.

Nozick, R. (1976) *Anarchy, State and Utopia*, Oxford: Blackwell.

Rawls, J. (1972) *A Theory of Justice*, Oxford: Clarendon Press.

Theophanous, A. (1993) *Understanding Social Justice*, Melbourne, Australia: Elikia Press.

Walzer, M. (1983) *Spheres of Justice*, Oxford: Blackwell.

Warnke, G. (1994) *Justice and Interpretation*, Cambridge: Polity Press.

Young, I. M. (1990) *Justice and the Politics of Difference*, Princeton, NJ: Princeton University Press.

Part 3

PARTNERS IN CHANGE
School-based projects and collaborations

5

PARENTS AS PARTNERS FOR EDUCATIONAL CHANGE

The Ashgrove Healthy School Environment Project

Julie Davis and Sue Cooke

Unless we change we'll get where we're going.
(Anon, Quoted in Birch 1993: 107)

Parents are under-recognised agents for change in schools. This chapter is about a school community project in the primary school which our children attend. The two authors were key actors in the initiation and development of the project; however, the full project team consisted of around fifteen enthusiastic parents, teachers and the principal, with a much larger group of students, teachers and parents also involved at various times in different activities. The experiences and insights of this learning community created by the project are presented here.

The project seeds were germinated in late 1991 to early 1992, during brief conversations in the welcoming environment of a local community kindergarten. As parents of young children who had recently started school, and with younger ones still at pre-school, we discovered that we shared similar feelings, concerns and interests in relation to our children's transition to school. Chatting briefly in the pre-school playground we reflected on the contrasts between the two settings and the nature of our children's experiences in them. The nurturing, personalised and responsive social interactions between teachers, children and parents in a small child-appropriate pre-school setting, contrasted markedly with the much larger, more impersonal and harsher physical and social world of the school. Through conversations with other parents, colleagues and friends, we realised that the concerns we were feeling in relation to our own children were shared by many other parents, some teachers and in many schools.

While we wanted our children's intellectual, physical and social development to be nurtured by their schooling, we were equally motivated by the desire that they be empowered by their education, not only to cope in the world in which they will grow up, but also to contribute positively to it. Our talks led us to realise that we had similar perspectives on issues of environment, health, education and long-term sustainable futures. We also agreed on the need for integrated, holistic, collaborative, participatory actions for change. Connecting Julie's interest in environmental education and Sue's in health promotion, we recognised the potential to address concerns about the school using the 'healthy schools' approach (British Columbia Ministry of Health 1991). Such an approach, we felt, would make positive changes for our children, address teachers' concerns and involve parents. It would also make the most of Education Department initiatives for devolving power and responsibility to the local level, *and* model processes for creating sustainable healthy futures for all.

Global issues, local perspectives

Our initial motivation for commencing this project related to our own children's growth and development. On both a deeper and broader level though, our actions were motivated by concerns about environmental and social issues as diverse as global atmospheric warming, uncontrolled urbanisation, deforestation and personal and family fragmentation.

Undeniably, the final years of the twentieth century are a period of increasing uncertainty, instability and rapid change. Today's children are already living in a world where environmental damage, social injustice and appalling ill-health are major features of the global landscape and where future options for healthy, just and sustainable living are being foreclosed through current actions and lifestyles. We believe that children, with the biggest stake in the future, will bear the consequences of decisions and actions that are currently being made or avoided (Davis 1994). It is increasingly being recognised that global environmental change is eroding the very life-support systems of the Earth, and that this is a threat of major consequence to the world's living species, including humankind (Brown *et al*. 1992; McMichael 1993).

The first global conference on health promotion, at Sundsvall in Sweden in 1991, *Supportive Environments for Health*, clearly linked developments in the health arena with public concern over threats to the global environment, stating:

> Humankind forms an integral part of the earth's ecosystem. People's health is fundamentally interlinked with the total environment. All available information indicates that it will not be possible to sustain the quality of life, for human beings and all living species, without drastic changes in attitudes and behaviours at all levels with regard

to the . . . environment. Concerted action to achieve a sustainable, supportive environment for health is the challenge of our times.
(United Nations Environment Programme 1991: 5)

It is our belief that one of the greatest tasks for society, then, is to equip children with the skills, attitudes and knowledge necessary to change current patterns of action and to secure healthy, just and sustainable futures. Reflection on our children's beginning experiences of schooling, though, gave us little evidence that this challenge was going to be met. Indeed, it seemed clear that schooling, like most of society's institutions, was struggling even to recognise the challenge, let alone understand and develop processes and strategies necessary to meet it. It seemed equally clear to us that a participatory action research (PAR) approach to implementing the health-promoting school concept was taking a big step towards meeting the challenge.

Health-promoting schools and PAR

The principles of health promotion are predicated on the notion of community and personal action for creating healthful change in just and sustainable ways. This approach also recognises that health is created in the settings of everyday life and that education is fundamental to these processes of change. Schools therefore have been recognised as potentially key settings for the creation of health (Lavin *et al.* 1992; Nutbeam *et al.* 1993; Young and Williams 1989).

A health-promoting school strives to put into practice the action directives of the World Health Organization's (WHO) Ottawa Charter for Health Promotion (World Health Organization 1986). These directives are to:

- *build healthy policy* – making healthy choices the easy choices
- *create supportive environments* – a socio-ecological approach to health
- *strengthen community action* – empowerment for effective community action to achieve better health
- *develop personal skills* – education and life skills, increasing options available to individuals
- *reorient services* – going beyond clinical curative services, and re-focusing on the total needs of the whole person, with all sectors having a role to play in creating health.

The health-promoting school concept involves the deliberate orientation for health of three main elements of a school. The first element is the place of health education in the 'formal' curriculum and the manner in which teaching and learning take place. This includes actively participative methods focusing on the real concerns of students. The second element is the 'hidden' curriculum or ethos of the school which is created by its physical and social environment. This could include school policies, facilities and the relationships between students and teachers, and between students themselves. The third element is the relationship between the school and its community – i.e., between school, home, the wider community, and environment (Cooke 1994; Young and Williams 1989). The health-promoting school process is an approach that has, at its heart, the empowerment of all the members of a school community – children, parents, teachers and the wider community – in collaboratively making changes in the school environment, inclusive of all its social, political, physical and personal dimensions. It is overtly a democratic, non-hierarchical decision-making process.

The student-centred socio-environmental skills and learning-focused approach embodied in the health-promoting school concept contrasts in significant ways with traditional health education which has confined itself largely to teacher-centred content-oriented classroom teaching of the formal health education curriculum. In this latter view, students are more often seen as passive recipients of information, divorced from the real world context beyond the classroom walls. However, there are significant differences between health-promoting school programmes around the world, in relation to the fundamental educational and social changes called for by the rhetoric of health promotion. Analysis of the literature indicates that there are wide differences in the ways the concept is interpreted and enacted in practice, with existing programmes spanning a continuum between the two approaches (Cooke 1994).

The Ashgrove Project has deliberately attempted to position itself at the health-promoting school end of the continuum. The PAR project at Ashgrove was initiated by the school community, for the school community. Essentially community self-development, it has promoted action learning for health through a process which is progressive, cyclical (or spiral), iterative and accountable to the community (Cooke 1994). Progress or action is based on reflective critical assessment of the current situation by those affected by it, and outcomes of actions are in turn observed and subjected to critical reflection, leading to further planning and action (Cooke 1994; Kemmis and McTaggart, 1988; Wadsworth 1993). Change is not simply a benefit of the action research process – it is fundamental to it and happens throughout. Our experience of the Ashgrove Healthy School Environment Project suggests that using a PAR approach is entirely congruent with the health-promotion philosophy. The participatory action research approach reinforces the health-promoting school's practical capacity to empower individuals and communities to take action for healthier lives and healthier environments.

The project

About the school

Ashgrove State Primary School, catering for around 500 students (from Pre-school to Year 7) is a middle-sized inner-Brisbane primary school in a well-established suburb. The school has always had an excellent reputation, is recognised as a leader academically and in sport and music. There are twenty-six teaching staff including part-time, full-time and visiting specialist teachers, and nine non-teaching staff. In 1992 the physical facilities included the rather imposing main school building – a traditional two-storey red-brick structure typical of public buildings constructed in the first half of this century – a smaller wooden building with four classrooms and a small creative skills centre (converted from an old toilet block). The grounds encompassed a sports oval and several smaller play areas, a pool, two bitumen tennis courts and a large bitumen assembly and games area between the main buildings. The first impression a visitor might have gained was of stately buildings in green and leafy grounds. Closer examination, however, would have revealed that, typical of schools built in this 1930s style, a number of significant constraints impacted on the effective delivery of quality education, both inside and outside the classroom.

By 1992 increasing awareness of some of these constraints led to general school community dissatisfaction with aspects of the school environment. In particular, the Year 1 playground was degraded, dusty, uninteresting and contained play equipment which was deemed to be dangerous and was ultimately condemned. It was this generalised discontent with the existing environment, seen to offer little comfort, stimulation or shade, which provided the opportunity to implement a healthy school environment project. The project aimed at improving the physical and social environment of the school through empowering children and adults alike, to actively create the type of school environment they wanted.

The Story of the Project

As already noted, health-promoting school initiatives may differ widely from each other, based not only on differences between contextual factors impacting on the settings, but also on differences in the orientation of key participants towards health promotion, educational and social change. The Ashgrove Healthy School Environment Project has been shaped by its own unique combination of personal and contextual influences. Some of these are:

- It was initiated by parents rather than teachers as in most other projects.
- It has a strong community development orientation.

- It is holistic, dealing not only with human interactions but also with the relationships between people and environments.
- It has developed a different way for parents to relate to the school and for teachers and parents to relate to each other.
- It overtly links social justice, health promotion and environmental education.
- It has widened and strengthened links for the school with community groups, and local and state government.
- It is both responding to and being part of recent initiatives at local, state and federal government levels for greater pro-active community input and participation.

At its broadest level, the project at Ashgrove aims to educate children and adults to be active democratic citizens who, collectively and individually, can take action for healthier lives and healthier environments (Ashgrove State School 1993; Jensen 1992). More specifically, it seeks to enable children and adults to create and sustain healthy environments, starting with practices, policy and relationships in the school grounds. Adopting the Canadian Healthy Schools process (British Columbia Ministry of Health 1991: 7) as a guide, our particular project used the following inclusive and actively democratic five-step process:

Step 1   Create a shared vision of a healthy school.
Step 2   Select the priority issues.
Step 3   Develop an action plan.
Step 4   Put the plan into action.
Step 5   Evaluate progress and plan for the future.

Following are details of each of the steps taken as we proceeded to build a healthy school at Ashgrove through PAR. The remainder of this section briefly describes the process and major activities of the first two to three years of the project and reflects in particular the perceptions of the chapter authors, as initiators and key actors in the early stages. This overview provides a context for the next sections which report reflections on the project by a wider participant group of parents, teachers and principal who together make up the active learning community for this project.

Step 1 Creating a shared vision of a healthy school environment

As neither of us had been previously involved in Ashgrove school activities or decision making, introducing the health-promoting school concept to the school community, let alone getting a project up and running, presented us with our first challenge. Early in 1992, Sue, as a member of the Healthy Cities Queensland: Healthy Schools Working Party, approached the principal to talk about the healthy school concept as a possibility for overcoming issues specific to Ashgrove School as well as for dealing with other educational challenges including the increasing devolution of decision making and management to school communities. The principal agreed with the concept in general but suggested that the Parents and Citizens (P&C) Association was the appropriate forum to raise and further discuss the healthy schools idea. However, an initial letter describing healthy schools and the potential benefits for the school of working towards such an ideal, elicited no response. It was not until the connection was made between the healthy school process and the pressing need for redevelopment of the Year 1 playground (see Figure 5.1) that the concept was seen as having any practical relevance. After the P&C meeting, Sue was invited to convene the then defunct Grounds Committee of the P&C.

Although taking on the convenorship of the P&C's Grounds Committee seemed at first tangential to our intention for implementing a healthy school process, on reflection we realised that it did indeed present a real opportunity to use an integrated holistic process for social, environmental, health and educational change. We realised that it was not enough to raise concerns and suggest solutions without also taking an active part in creating changes. With some trepidation, having no 'grounds' or project management experience, or even P&C experience, we agreed to co-facilitate the process. We suspected it could prove time consuming and personally challenging! Little did we realise that our involvement in the project would

Figure 5.1 The Year 1 playground in 1992: stimulus for action

provide the foundation for our respective Masters' dissertations. This story, in fact, draws on our reflective journals, focus group and individual interview transcripts gathered during the initial three years of the project.

The next three months or so were a period of learning and awareness raising for us and also for the school community. As we began systematically to investigate the situation, informally consulting with teachers, groundsmen, parents, children, authorities and people with knowledge and expertise about schools, school grounds, landcare and 'learnscaping', we communicated key points regularly through the school newsletter. Taking a broad view of health as *well-being* with physical, social, emotional and spiritual dimensions, we broadened the playgrounds agenda by raising issues such as the importance of play for children's development, and the impacts of aesthetic, physical and emotional environments on play and learning. We particularly stressed the benefits, for both children and adults in the school community, of deciding our own needs and priorities for a healthy school environment, and of working together to plan and achieve these as important 'lessons for life'. In these ways we were raising general interest and awareness in the school community about the project. We were also linking the concept of 'healthy schools' to children's broad growth and development, both inside and outside the classroom, with links also to the benefits of supportive physical and social environments for education generally.

We then began to provide opportunities for everyone in the school community to take part in the planning process, and actively to mobilise support. An initial 'visioning' workshop was held with a small group of interested parents. This involved a guided imagery process where participants were asked to imagine their ideal healthy school environment, and share these imaginings with other group members to elicit the common themes. A visioning workshop held with the teachers produced remarkably similar 'visions'. At this meeting, one of the teachers volunteered to be the teacher representative and liaise between the embryonic Grounds Committee and the school staff. Further consultation and collaboration to ensure the widest possible school community input included surveying opinions of families and teachers using written questionnaires, and feeding the collated results back to the school community.

Our desire to make sure that every child in every classroom was actively involved in the process was seen by some teachers and parents as not only unnecessary, but quite impractical. Demonstrating commendable initiative, however, the Student Council with the encouragement of their liaison teacher, carried out verbal polling of the student population, visiting all classrooms and talking to students in the playground. They collated their results, and presented them to us at a lunchtime Student Council meeting. The students themselves had demonstrated, in an active and assertive way, their desire to be part of shaping the school environment in which they, after all, are the major stakeholders.

The resultant mountain of information collected from parents, students and teachers validated our original concerns about the physical and social school environment, and indicated that many in the school community shared these. The school community also had considerable enthusiasm and many good ideas about how to make improvements. We set about collating, analysing and summarising the information and reporting it back to the school community via the school newsletter. The resultant 'shared vision' was of greener, friendlier and more diverse school grounds. On a basic level this translated into a general desire for shade and shady seating, more interesting play spaces for children, extra opportunities for outdoor learning and a more supportive social climate, particularly for the younger students.

Step 2 Selecting the priority issues

Analysing the information gathered in the visioning stage of the process in these early months in 1992, the following emerged from the data as priority health and environment issues for the school community:

- sun safety
- the urgent need to redevelop the degraded junior playground
- children's happiness in the playgrounds (creating a supportive school environment, both physically and socially)
- the 'greening' of the school grounds (local action for ecological sustainability)

In August 1992, five months after raising the idea of 'healthy schools' with the school community, we called the first public meeting and officially reconvened the Grounds Committee. This first meeting involved small group work and plenary sessions in a short workshop format, to model a democratic organisational management style and create a supportive environment for individual and community participation and development. The sixteen people who attended this first meeting, included the principal, teacher, and fourteen parents, who then became the core of the Ashgrove Healthy School Environment Project Team.

Considering the breadth of information which had been gathered both from within the school community and our research beyond the school, it became apparent to the new Grounds Committee members at this meeting that there was little point in continuing to make *ad hoc* changes to the grounds outside the context of a 'whole grounds' plan. Problems of drainage, erosion, location of buildings, sheds, pathways, playgrounds, gardens and entrances – land degradation and land use factors – all needed to be considered together as they each impacted upon the others and influenced the functionality and aesthetics of the whole school environment. The group agreed at this meeting that the school needed to develop a master plan for the redevelopment of the whole school grounds, with the Year 1 playground a priority for action. It also agreed to continue using a collaborative and consultative, participative planning process.

A key task in this stage was mediating between interest groups and keeping the focus on children's broad health needs. Having constructed a shared vision of the ideal school environment broadly agreed to by all sectors of the school community, meant that individual differences in viewpoints were able to be transcended and a sense of community, of working together for common goals, became apparent. The following comment illustrates this:

> It's made part of the community . . . a more cohesive group. By community I mean teachers, students and parents, because we're working together for the one thing.
>
> (School principal)

A date was set for the first major planning workshop to be held two weeks later. Its optimistic goal was to complete a site analysis and develop concept plans on which to base the flexible master plan, for development of the school grounds over perhaps the next fifteen to twenty years, in a single Saturday afternoon workshop!

Step 3 Developing action plans

Over the months of October and November, in a series of well-attended participative workshops (parents, teachers and a student representative), and with extensive community consultation and feedback between workshops, two major action plans were developed – a Sun Safety Policy, and a Whole School Grounds Concept Plan. The first-draft concept plan was modified and areas or projects prioritised as short, medium or long-term priorities, after broad school community comment and suggestions. School community consultation involved a range of strategies: displaying the draft plans on noticeboards at school entrances and in the central foyer, with paper, pencils and comments boxes attached, weekly newsletter items and feedback surveys, personal telephone calls and regular invitations to telephone committee members with concerns or suggestions or to get involved. A most valuable strategy was also the informal face-to-face 'chats' with other parents as children were being collected from or dropped off at school, or while waiting for swimming lessons or sporting activities to finish. This participative and iterative process aimed to involve the whole school community in decision making which balanced both short-term, immediate needs with long-term strategic planning.

Learning how to organise, co-ordinate and facilitate the planning process was concurrent with intense learning about the technical aspects of whole-school planning for key participants (Cooke 1994). Where the team did not have the necessary expertise, or it was not available in the school community, we consulted outside experts on the understanding that we chose to work with experts 'on tap' not 'on top' (Baum 1990). The project team also hoped that these outside consultants would be able to complete detailed planning more quickly and efficiently, and to ensure the plans met safety, legal and bureaucratic requirements.

For the authors, as facilitators, the feeling was often that we were 'flying by the seat of our pants', literally one step ahead of the complex process we had set in train only a few months earlier! This was an extremely creative and exciting time, however, and high levels of energy and expectation flowed in sections of the school community, including teachers, parents and students. Some key participants were putting enormous amounts of time and effort into the process. It was also at this time that some parents, teachers and ancillary staff began voicing criticism that nothing had been done in the playgrounds; that the project was 'all talk and no action', and that therefore both the project and its advocates warranted condemnation. This negativism added to the stresses already being experienced by some of the most active participants in the process, who were indeed voluntarily expending huge amounts of energy on the process and combining this with family, paid work, study and other community commitments.

Step 4 Putting the plans into action

Although the Whole School Grounds Redevelopment Project is really only one aspect of a broader agenda for change in the school, it is the most visible aspect of the Healthy School Environment Project. Equally important is that the process models inclusive collaborative decision making and action, and is empowering both students and adults for active participation in life, both individually and collectively.

Action on the Year 1 playground, which became stage one of the new Junior Playground in the Whole Grounds Plan, began in earnest in May 1993. The focus in this stage was on school community action – actually *doing* it. By putting energy and time into including all stakeholders and into co-ordination, and by maintaining clear, open-communication channels over the planning and implementation periods, creative and productive partnerships have been developed between students, parents and teachers, and with the broader community. It is these dynamic partnerships which have enabled an impressive range of results to be achieved by the school. These include:

• *Sun safety*: The comprehensive Sun Safety Policy has been implemented, resulting in a broad range of health-promoting changes including uniform and timetable changes, providing shade structures, modelling and promotion of effective sun-safe behaviours such as wearing hats and using a sun screen.

- *Grounds redevelopment*: Stage one of the long-term Whole School Grounds Plan has been implemented, beginning the transformation of the grounds into comfortable, shady, stimulating 'outdoor classrooms' and play areas. The P&C agreed to pay for a qualified landscape architect to draw up detailed working drawings based on the school's very detailed brief, and in consultation with a play environment consultant. P&C funds were also used to pay a contractor to undertake complex earthworks, drainage and construction of a large, free-form sandpit and proposed water-play area which lie at the centre of the new junior playground.

The enthusiastic support of both our local city councillor and our state MP, who were kept informed from the earliest conception of the plans, has been invaluable both at the local 'on the ground' level, and also in terms of expediting our progress through the various bureaucratic labyrinths surrounding our social institutions such as schools. Under a state government scheme to employ long-term unemployed people and refurbish Queensland schools, our school was one of many in Queensland to benefit from the provision of skilled labour and materials, allowing us to complete a large part of the hard landscaping including construction of paths, paved areas, garden beds, seating, retaining walls and other features. Native plant seedlings were provided by Greening Australia community nurseries and a local branch of 'The Men of the Trees'. Local businesses and school community contacts have also contributed as did the Education Department through existing subsidy schemes on many of the materials required, including the shade structure over the sandpit.

Many parents and children 'bought' turf by the square metre (once again organised by the Student Council and an actively involved teacher), and laid it in pouring rain on a Sunday morning 'working bee'. Working bees have also seen parents, children and teachers paving, mulching, planting and maintaining the thriving native gardens. Children are now playing in the new junior playground, which has a number of discrete but connected 'spaces'. These include several connected play platforms, a large and deep free-form sandpit adjoined by large sandstone boulders, landscaped gardens bordered by informal seating and a small performance space or amphitheatre. It is often the site for class group activities such as reading, science, art and music, across all grades, and is a popular meeting place for parents and children after school and on weekends.

We were able to thank the many people and organisations who had contributed to the project when the school community celebrated the official opening of the new junior playground in April 1994 (see Figure 5.2). The playground provided a delightful environment for the congratulatory speeches from state and local government representatives and Education Department dignitaries, and we shared a (healthy!) breakfast in the dappled morning sunlight.

Figure 5.2 The new junior playground 1994. A greener, shadier, more interesting and friendlier place for playing and learning

Step 5 Evaluating and planning for the future

In action research, evaluation and further planning are in-built and continuous. Meetings, workshops and to a lesser extent working bees, have provided a forum for joint critical reflection, where participants review the effectiveness of recent actions and plan further steps. While the new junior playground is evidence of visible success, reflection on our progress towards achieving the overarching aim of children's active participation in creating a healthy environment initially left us somewhat disappointed in the overall level of their involvement. Recognising that teacher participation is critical to children's participation has, in more recent times, redirected the project's focus towards more teacher/curriculum aspects as a way of ensuring greater decision making and action by the children. While grounds development is still a major agenda item for the Healthy Schools Project, this reorientation has led to some new directions outlined below.

Development of a Supportive School Environment Policy is in progress, using inclusive participatory strategies as modelled by the Healthy School Environment Project. Co-ordinated by a teacher active in the project, this policy-development has deliberately encouraged active student participation. As students canvassed student opinion, ensuring that all children in the school were given a say, the resulting policy more clearly reflects children's viewpoints on behaviour management strategies.

Another development that will strengthen curriculum links and increase teachers' and children's participation is a joint project between the Ashgrove school community and a school in the Danish Health Promoting School Network, part of the World Health Organization's European Health Promoting School Project. This initiative has involved a teacher from the Danish school liaising at Ashgrove with children and teachers to develop a twin project for school and community action for health and environmental goals based on children's own concerns and investigations. Children in the two schools have exchanged introductory letters and messages by facsimile and email. In 1996 one Ashgrove teacher visited Denmark for in-service activities and networking with teachers from health-promoting schools in various European countries.

A further action plan has involved university environmental education students working with the Student Council, students and teachers, towards the establishment of a school-wide paper recycling programme. Together, these later developments have provided greater opportunities for teachers' involvement, and in doing so, for increasing children's participation in creating their own healthy school environment.

As we continue with this PAR project, we continue to reflect and evaluate. We do this individually, together, with other participants, our families, through our participation, reading and research. The camaraderie developed through these often extremely productive exchanges is important for sustaining the individuals involved as well as the processes for change. The next section of this chapter outlines some of the insights gained as a result these of reflective engagements.

Reflection on the project

> Any group which is attempting to do something new and different . . . poses a threat.
>
> (A parent)

After nearly four years of using PAR in the Healthy Schools Environment Project, a considerable amount has been achieved. The inclusive, holistic approach modelled has resulted in obvious 'on-the-ground' changes, but more fundamentally, changes in the way the school community approaches and carries out change. However, there has been, and continues to be, a dynamic tension between the usual *ad-hoc* ways of doing things and the desire to plan, reconceptualise and act in deliberately holistic and participatory ways.

Our view is that the flat, collaborative power-sharing nature of PAR and the healthy schools approach is fundamentally different from the hierarchical top-down model pervasive in our society. Essentially PAR and health promotion/healthy schools represent a paradigm change, from a hierarchical and anthropocentric world view to an egalitarian, inclusive and ecological one (Cooke 1994). The comments from project participants (parents and teachers) in the following pages, illustrate their awareness of the dichotomy between entrenched patterns of perceptions and actions, and those being modelled by the project, and go a long way to explain the nature of the challenge of implementing this type of project.

Social justice, democracy and inclusivity

In a climate of increasing social change, schools, too, are undergoing change. Teachers are under pressure from all sides of the political spectrum for change in many aspects of their work, including school organisation and management, the relationships between teachers and parents, and what and how they teach. Uncomfortable as it is, this climate of uncertainty also presents real opportunities for change. While there is major institutional, political and some public pressure being exerted for 'back to basics', reductionist and economically efficient approaches to education, our project, however, has sought to put holistic, inclusive thinking for health and the environment on the educational agenda during this period of change.

Both the health-promoting school concept and emancipatory environmental education are built on the notion of social justice as reciprocity in relations of power and authority. This means that we are about developing a sense of co-operative community where participation contributes to a collective sharing of energies, and the development of relations of open trust where people see each other as allies rather than as competitors (see Chapter 4 by Rizvi, in this volume).

Further, the view of social justice seen through the lens of health promotion and environmental education redefines social justice to take into account intergenerational equity, the ability of future generations to meet their needs uncompromised by the actions of the present generations. This focuses attention on issues related to the natural environment and the need to be serious about children's involvement in democratic processes for change.

In fact, the health-promoting schools approach appears to have a clear place in the moves for greater community participation in school management, or devolution, fostered in recent times. The Ashgrove Project has demonstrated that such approaches can, indeed, be highly effective in economic terms, by harnessing and co-ordinating school and community resources and skills to achieve common goals. The project is a grassroots community initiative, which has deliberately adopted long term, change strategies over short-term ones. In contrast, many current pressures impacting politically and socially on schools appear to be bureaucratic, top-down and short-term in nature.

Our experience at Ashgrove suggests that the Healthy Schools project, with its PAR processes, is realigning relationships, with parents, children and school staff working together, solving common problems and sharing in the solutions. It is changing practices, social relations and values and represents an action-oriented democratisation of social practices and decision making within the school (Davis 1994). The effectiveness of such an approach can be surprising as illustrated in the following comment from one of the teachers in the school:

> What interests me . . . is when you do get people together, by and large they're willing to find common ground. . . . What I've liked about it is that everyone involved has really been together as a community and worked on the project in a properly positive way, for the common good.
>
> (A teacher)

A comment from the principal indicates his recognition that the process has modelled non-hierarchical decision making.

> I would be just another person to consult and not necessarily a person who is conceived of as being the apex . . . .I'm on the same level as everyone else on the staff of the school here, and the parents.
>
> (The principal)

Parents were aware that the project modelled a co-operative and more equitable alternative to the more familiar adversarial ways of doing things.

> You come to the vocal minorities, the motivated minorities who control what goes on. So we are not vocal, and we are not yackity!
>
> (A parent)

> That's right. That goes against our way of doing things which is co-operation, . . . problem solving, active communication and participation.
>
> (A parent)

The importance of modelling these processes was not lost on parents or teachers.

> I think that's a really important thing, to model the behaviour of a democracy. So in that way it's empowering kids because . . . when they grow up they're more likely to attend meetings and do their bit, or have their say, and not let the world walk over them. They know how to go about things so to me that's the empowering bit.
>
> (A teacher)

Parents have also been empowered by participating in the process.

> For me, being involved in this has personally shown me that all sorts of things can be done, once you start talking to other people. . . . Whereas once upon a time I would have said, 'Well nothing's ever going to change', from working on the committee, although I feel as though my personal contribution is very small compared to others, it's shown me that all sorts of things can really happen.
>
> (A parent)

> Yes, anything's possible!
>
> (A parent)

While there has been acknowledgement of the positive contribution that participatory approaches have made within the school, sustaining these inclusive processes for change has not always been easy. As in the community generally, even committed participants in the project were more familiar with hierarchical, 'expert', adversarial and specialist management approaches. Social institutions, including schools, replicate existing inequitable power relations between people (Apple and Weis 1983; Giroux 1989; Huckle 1991), and reinforce the non-recognition of the natural environment.

Hierarchical decision making tends to exclude views held by those outside the powerful elite of the dominant social paradigm. As the project progressed an underlying concern was that we would not be seen as just another 'interest group' pushing yet another 'single issue' at the expense of others' views. We were careful to make the decision-making process as transparent as possible by explaining the participatory processes being used, continually seeking inputs and providing detailed feedback at every stage. Another part of this essential transparency has been focusing attention on the natural environment where the same processes of exclusion have acted to marginalise it, ensuring that it continues to be ignored, degraded and over-exploited.

Including children

While there is increasing acceptance of the principles of greater democratisation in decision making and action by adults in the school, our goal for the project has always been the active participation of children in creating positive change. For many parents, their motivation in regard to the project was the active involvement of children in the transformation of the school grounds. They saw children's participation as a way of equipping them with the skills, attitudes and knowledge necessary for healthy, just and sustainable futures. We were initially disappointed at the level of children's involvement, indeed even in the recognition by many teachers and parents of the importance of children's active involvement. This was a major frustration for many of the parents involved.

> One more difficulty is getting kids, the students, involved in the project.
>
> (A parent)

Generally speaking, in the early stages of the project at least, teachers and some parents saw children simply as users of the improved physical environment rather than as decision makers or actors in creating the changes.

> The idea of children's involvement is one of limited involvement. If you think there's maybe 20 people in the parent body actively involved, now you don't expect 200 parents to be actively involved, you know that's unrealistic. So I think we should keep those same goals for kids. There's no way you can involve 200 kids.
>
> (A teacher)

This is perhaps not possible immediately; but the essence of the project is exactly that: that *every* child has the same opportunity to be involved, and to participate actively, in real lessons for life. This early adult wariness about extending democracy to include children is demonstrated in this reflection.

> I think that until . . . adults feel totally comfortable with the process themselves, it's very difficult then to introduce children into the situation. Possibly you know, if you used this process with children, they might operate it much better than adults do!
>
> (The principal)

Finding more effective ways to ensure children have opportunities to participate actively has emerged as an important priority for the project team and has led in more recent times to a shift in project focus. The grounds redevelopment orientation of the project has given way to greater emphasis on more teacher/curriculum aspects.

Seeing things differently

Not only has the project been concerned with inclusive practices in the school, but it has also been concerned with changing perceptions. For example, different ways of seeing the school grounds were based on new understandings of 'the environment'.

We talk about the environment now in a way we didn't when I was growing up. I think we are aware now about how important the environment is in many different ways.

(A parent)

Yes, in a broader sense too, rather than in a narrow sense. Just a comment on the project, I guess it was a bit of an eye opener for me in a way, because I work in an environmental area, but I think in a fairly narrow way. You know, like water quality, air quality, noise and all those sorts of things. But really it is a much bigger issue and of course that's where I've found it really interesting. The quality of life is really what we are talking about, isn't it?

(A parent)

The grounds project was concerned with *whole grounds* planning rather than *ad hoc* solutions which offered quick and simplistic results. Specifically this has meant a reorientation from short-term 'quick fix' actions to integrative, strategically planned processes for ongoing and longer-term change.

What I thought we desperately needed as a school was a better playground – better grounds all over – the whole picture rather than just working on isolated little projects that someone thinks is great, and then in 10 years' time you see that this doesn't fit the big picture. Then you say, let's get rid of that and start over. What a wasted effort!

(A teacher)

It's not about putting an extra fort in the playground, this is a plan for the next 20 years. . . . It's a complete revision of the way in which we have looked at everything to do with playgrounds.

(A parent)

We found we were also reconceptualising the relationships between play, learning and the outdoor environment. Now, the playground is increasingly perceived as an outdoor classroom, utilised informally by children during school breaks and for teacher-initiated activities during class time.

[T]he fact that playgrounds haven't been looked at as being an essential part of school life and things seem to be very geared to inside buildings and what's happening inside a classroom. Whereas in the playground, that's where a lot of skills to relate to people are learned. Or not learned!

(A parent)

Doing things differently

We have also been doing things in a different way, as illustrated in the following reflections and participant comments.

Using a partnership model for decision making when most of us have been conditioned to work hierarchically is challenging and has to be nurtured.

> [The usual approaches] seem to be confronting and critical but 'Healthy Schools' is less direct, trying to get people to see there is a problem without having to be told. . . . It's a process, not one-offs. It is non-combative and non-confrontational.
>
> (A parent)

We are all novices, learning about the process as we were doing it ('building the bicycle while riding it!')

> It's the fact that we have modelled the process, that we have kept going and have always demonstrated to people that we are not experts but we are managing . . . we have the same sort of adequacies and inadequacies as anyone else but we can still keep doing this together.
>
> (A parent)

It takes a long time, both in terms of the changes 'on the ground' and in changing the way things are done.

> [There was] criticism around the school that everything was taking so long. But I think if you're going to do it properly, you've got to put that time and effort into the thing.
>
> (A parent)

For a group of volunteers, who have family, study, work and other personal commitments, this has been a real challenge.

> It is difficult finding time because a lot of people don't like coming back on the weekend and a lot of parents work full time and the only time they can come is nights and weekends, so it's a bit tough to get together.
>
> (A teacher)

> It's the competing pressures. Our life is not getting any easier and it's not going to get any easier in the future either.
>
> (A parent)

Participants in the project have sometimes been surprised by the resistance to change from both parents and teachers. Negative feedback is the loudest and is debilitating for participants.

> I'm feeling really bogged down because there is not a lot of positive feedback, in fact the reverse. I don't think the majority of people feel negative about it, it's just that the ones who do are very loud about it!
>
> (A parent)

The project has used resources which would otherwise have been utilised in other areas of the school, causing some dissatisfaction.

> People's perceptions of how much things cost can cause trouble.
>
> (A parent)

> And several people were very vocal about amounts of money spent.
>
> (A parent)

At times, there have been uncertainties as to the boundaries of decision making between parents and teachers.

> We can sort of recommend. We are not decision makers *per se*. We don't have the power to make decisions do we?
>
> (A parent)

These innovations represent a paradigm shift in thinking, in ways of organising and responding to the issues and problems in the setting. The new processes modelled by the project have been recasting relationships between people, and between people and their environments. They are non-hierarchical, participatory and inclusive, enabling changes to be initiated and implemented jointly. As Kuhn points out, paradigm transition is likely to be contested, characterised by upheaval and argument and may take a generation to occur (Kuhn 1970).

> I think that's what has taken some time for some people to come to terms with. It's been such a radical change to what they have been used to.
>
> (A teacher)

> Different, yes. This is radical! . . . I'm not surprised that there's been problems in the school community. As a matter of fact, I'm surprised we've got this far!
>
> (A parent)

Not unexpectedly, then, the transition to new ways of seeing things and doing things at Ashgrove has led to a fair amount of negativism and loss of momentum. Recognising that these difficulties, tensions and dilemmas stem from challenging the status quo with new paradigm solutions has enabled us to deal more philosophically with the frustrations. This has allowed us to focus on the more positive aspects and potentials of the process. For many the benefits are clear. In the words of one of the first teachers to embrace the project:

> A healthy school environment should not only be seen as a new playground for Ashgrove. It should be seen as a group of like-minded people endeavouring to reach out to each other for each other. In a sense it gives true meaning to the term 'community'. Teachers, parents, principal, P&C members, committee organisers – after two years of ups and downs, those titles are no longer barriers but rather roles we play in assisting our school to move forward to become a better place for us all.
>
> (A teacher)

Principles, practices and observations

Although the participatory process used has been systematic and basically simple, the reality can be very untidy, at times chaotic! However, it is *vital* and *creative* and has led to the development of supportive and open relationships, and some great improvements in the school environment. Clearly it has not always been easy, but there is general consensus that it has been worthwhile. Many participants believe, like us, that such participatory projects represent an essential shift towards empowering people for creating healthy, sustainable futures. In our experience a number of principles and practices helped to sustain the momentum of the project and may be important characteristics for successful engagement in other PAR projects. These principles are:

1 Effective communication is fundamental. Communicating and educating on behalf of and about the project – its purposes, strategies, plans, achievements and difficulties – is a key element to its success. Taking every opportunity to restate the values and principles underlying the processes being used is important.

2 Creating a 'shared vision' is an essential component to participation. This gave participants an aim, derived from their own concerns and viewpoints, but which had the validation of the whole school community. As a result, activities were able to be conducted within a framework that reflected general community support. This broad canvassing of opinion also engaged/enlisted people with a wide range of

80

skills and interest. This diversity enabled creative, innovative and integrated solutions to our problems.

3 Change can come from any part of an organisation. Parents, and indeed children, can be effective initiators of change and are a largely untapped resource in schools as key contributors to the change processes, not simply as recipients or endorsers. However, support from the principal and some teachers at least, is very important.

4 Adults need 'empowering' too, so they can effectively become models for children. The social structures and hierarchical decision-making processes into which we have been socialised, have marginalised us all to some extent. Adults need to become aware, committed and empowered to challenge the 'dominant paradigm'. Only then can we effectively model for children the principles of democratic participation for long-term sustainable change. Children, however, may more readily demonstrate such processes and may therefore be very effective models and teachers for adults, both parents and teachers.

5 Criticism and conflict are to be expected and can be seen as an indicator that paradigm shift is under way, as new ideas and new ways of operating confront the usual ways of doing things. Both within the school and with the wider community, it takes a while for the participatory approach to be accepted and utilised, instead of the usual entrenched adversarial styles. Suggesting people see things and do things in fundamentally different ways is often personally threatening. For some, the transition is too big a leap altogether. Active project participants also had to learn not to be too sensitive to criticism, and not to take it too personally.

6 Changes do not come quickly. The participants experienced the frustration of balancing the pressure to 'do something concrete quickly' against the desire for thoughtful, strategic planning for long-term change. Gaining widespread acceptance for taking the longer view is an incremental process at best. We found also that recognition for the project and its achievements, beyond the immediate school environment, appeared to assist in legitimising the project within the school, adding to its local support.

7 With the increasing range of educational initiatives making demands of teachers, curriculum change and children's involvement may take longer to evolve for a parent-initiated project. However, community development aspects are likely to be stronger where parents are driving the process.

8 The project doesn't happen by itself. The commitment of key facilitators has been essential. Consider co-facilitation of such projects. Our experience was that having a 'critical friend' was invaluable, and possibly sanity saving. It requires sustained, organised commitment to ensure opportunities are created for the participation of all stakeholders. The

successes achieved by the project were due to the many hundreds of hours of voluntary effort from parents, teachers, principal, children and consultants and other stakeholders in the wider community. The appointment and resourcing of school project managers (including time) to promote, maintain and co-ordinate school community participation would be very helpful.

9 There is a danger of volunteer burnout. The project team is made up of volunteers from within the school community – parents, teachers and the principal – who have a range of personal, family, career, community and study commitments. At times these other demands impact on the project, slowing it down, and sapping energy. Of course, working through the 'system' of writing proposals, seeking approvals for funding and capital works can also be time-consuming, frustrating and exhausting.

10 Measuring outcomes for projects which make long-term investments in building futures which are healthy, just and sustainable can be difficult. Outcomes such as the development of a sense of community or individual and community empowerment, or indeed, reductions in skin cancer incidence, are not easily observable or measurable. Consequently, short time frames or narrow criteria for reporting progress will be inappropriate. Monitoring and evaluation needs to be flexible. In the Ashgrove project, the PAR process has proved useful for monitoring, recording and evaluating change.

Conclusions

What we have discussed in this chapter is one school community's efforts to improve its working environment – not only the physical features of the landscape but, as importantly, the processes by which decisions are made and changes are enacted. As illustrated in this chapter, the project has had considerable success and some difficulties, in responding to the particular needs of the Ashgrove school community. Success is clearly evident in the outdoor environment of the school, particularly in relation to playground and sun-safety issues, resulting in more interesting, stimulating, safe and supportive environments for children's play and learning.

As important as these outcomes are, there have also been significant changes in the social relationships within the school. While changes in power relations have been at times uncomfortable, the synergy resulting from people working together has unleashed creative energy, forged new friendships and working partnerships and led to innovative solutions to long-standing problems. The project is creating an inclusive learning community, exemplifying concepts of personal and community empowerment which are fundamental to PAR health promotion, environmental education and broader educational reform.

Particularly heartening is increasing recognition for children's inputs into decision making and action. In changing from its initial parent-driven grounds orientation to a stronger teacher/curriculum focus, the project more readily allows for children's active engagement with health-promoting principles, actions and values. Clearly, the project will have its greatest effect when action in the three spheres identified in the literature – ethos and environment, curriculum and school/community relationships – is mutually reinforcing and indeed integrated.

The Ashgrove Healthy School Environment Project is still in the initial stages of a long-term plan for the development of a healthier school environment. The project will result in a better environment for nurturing the social, intellectual, physical and emotional aspects of the children and adults who pass through the school. More important, though, is the sense of agency and optimism developed in those who take part in creating the changes. As we have highlighted throughout this chapter, the project's successes have hinged on using participatory processes. Ironically these same inclusive processes have generated many of the tensions and dilemmas faced by participants. The transition from adversarial, fragmentationalist, short-term processes to inclusive, holistic, futurist approaches is not easy, but we have demonstrated that these alternative strategies can and do make a difference.

Many schools are facing the challenges, difficulties and dilemmas of responding to current calls for social, economic and educational reform. While the Ashgrove experience is certainly not a blue-print for change for other schools to follow, it does, however, show that when individual interests and concerns are harnessed for collective action, significant change pertinent to the needs of that community, can be made.

Perhaps projects such as this, linking parents, teachers and children in partnership, also offer a way to lift thinking collectively beyond short-term problems and solutions and to direct energies towards the adoption of long-term actions. Such projects may then provide the initial tentative steps towards creating a citizenry that builds futures that are healthy, just and sustainable (Davis 1994). These are the *real* lessons for life!

> The future is not some place we are going to,
> but one we are creating.
> The paths to it are not found
> but made,
> and the activity of making them
> changes both the maker
> and the destination.
> (Commission for the Future, Australia, 1989, quoted in Davis
> 1994: 118)

REFERENCES

Apple, M. and Weis, L. (1983) *Ideology and Curriculum*, London: Routledge & Kegan Paul.

Ashgrove State School (1993) *Healthy School Environment Project*, (pamphlet), Brisbane, Australia: Ashgrove State School.

British Columbia Ministry of Health (1991) *Healthy Schools: A Resource Guide for Teachers*, Victoria, Canada: British Columbia Ministry of Health, Office for Health Promotion.

Baum, F. (1990) 'The new public health: force for change or reaction?' *Health Promotion International* 5 (2): 145–50.

Birch, C. (1993) *Regaining Compassion for Humanity and Nature*, Sydney: New South Wales University Press.

Brown, L. R., Flavin, C. and Kane, H. (1992) *Vital Signs: The Trends That Are Shaping Our Future 1992 and 1993*, London: Worldwatch Institute.

Cooke, S. (1994) 'Creating health promoting schools: participants' experience of the Ashgrove Healthy School Environment project', unpublished Master of Public Health thesis, Brisbane, Australia: Griffith University.

Davis, J. (1994) 'Empowering the school community for change: an evaluation of participation in the Ashgrove Healthy School Environment Project', unpublished Master of Environmental Education thesis, Brisbane: Australia: Griffith University.

Giroux, H. A. (1989) *Schooling for Democracy: Critical Pedagogy in the Modern Age*, London: Routledge.

Huckle, J. (1991) 'Education for sustainability: assessing pathways to the future', *Australian Journal of Environmental Education*, 7: 43–62.

Jensen, B. B. (1992) 'Environmental health education – introduction and basic concepts' mimeograph, Copenhagen: Research Centre of Environmental and Health Education.

Kemmis, S. and McTaggart, R. (eds) (1988) *The Action Research Planner*, Geelong, Australia: Deakin University Press.

Kuhn, T. S. (1970) *The Structure of Scientific Revolutions*, Chicago: Chicago University Press.

Lavin, A. T., Shapiro, G. R. and Weill, K. S. (1992) 'Creating an agenda for school-based health promotion: a review of twenty five selected reports', *Journal of School Health*, 62 (6): 212–26.

McMichael, A. J. (1993) *Planetary Overload: Global Environmental Change and the Health of the Human Species*, Cambridge: Cambridge University Press.

Nutbeam, D., Wisem, M., Bauman, A., Harris, E. and Leeder, S. (1993) *Goals and Targets for Australia's Health in the Year 2000 and Beyond*, Canberra: Australian Government Printing Service.

United Nations Environment Programme, World Health Organization and Nordic Council of Ministers (1991) *Sundsvall Statement on Supportive Environments for Health – Action for Public Health*, Third International Conference on Health Promotion – Sundsvall Conference: Sundsvall, Sweden, June.

Wadsworth, Y. (1993) *What Is Participatory Action Research?* Melbourne, Australia: Action Research Issues Association.

World Health Organization (1986) *Ottawa Charter for Health Promotion*, Copenhagen: World Health Organization, Health and Welfare Canada, and Canadian Public Health Association.

Young, I. and Williams, T. (eds) (1989) *The Healthy School: A Scottish Health Education Group*, Edinburgh: Scottish Health Education Group.

6

BRIDGES AND BROKEN FINGERNAILS

*Charmaine McKibbin, Tom J. Cooper, Joyce Blanche,
Pamela Dougall, Janet Granzien and Barbara Greer-
Richardson*

This chapter tells the story of a group of parents who tried, in collaboration
with a project co-ordinator, school personnel, university researchers and
Queensland's Department of Education personnel, to increase their participation, in different ways and to differing degrees, in an urban inner city
state high school. This project was part of a federally funded Queensland-
based research project to improve teaching and learning in the senior years
of a secondary school.

In Chapter 2, this volume, Kemmis and Wilkinson argue that: 'action
research aims to help people to investigate reality in order to change it,
and, . . . at the same time, it also aims to help people to change reality in
order to investigate it'. This chapter represents some 'ordinary people' who,
over time, became a group of parents committed to seeking ways of
changing themselves in order to improve school effectiveness in recognising
parents as valued partners in the educational journey of their children. Their
project was based upon participatory action research (PAR).

This account follows a chronological progression from initiatives to stumbling blocks to resolution, with parents being the main characters. It is
characterised by perceived 'conflict' and 'disorder', by formal ('official') and
informal activity, by attempts to keep some protagonists 'in their place', and
by changes in the status of some protagonists. It begins with parents feeling
alienated from the affairs of the school. One parent expressed her feelings in
the following way:

> Somewhere between primary school and high school, I had either
> lost my confidence or had it taken away from me in matters relating
> to my child's education. My opinion had never been sought in the
> high school system, and I was later to learn that the high school
> culture, in fact, placed little value on my opinions when I tried to

express them. It was even said by people at the school that high school was the time to let go of your children.

(Barbara, parent)[1]

With university researchers, parents, administrators and teachers sharing the stage, this story could be told from a multiplicity of perspectives. However, in this account, parents describe their expectations, motivations, experiences and disappointments. They discuss how they faced new horizons and goals, overcame the challenges and obstacles to participation, and prevailed in their attempts for more recognition (see Chapter 4, by Rizvi, this volume) as legitimate partners in the schooling of their children.

This chapter has been compiled by parents and researchers. Due to the abundance of material and the number of co-authors, the commentary of the parent story is imparted by the parent/co-ordinator who is the first author. This is counterpoised by placing substantial vignettes of parent testimony throughout the text.

Because of the length (2.5 years) and scope of this project, many issues regarding parent participation arose within its life. In this chapter, however, we limit discussion to only some of the issues, particularly: (a) the demonstrated achievements and options available for levels of parental participation in schooling (or the perceived reality from departmental to local site perspectives); and (b) the benefits or emancipatory effects of PAR as a means to understand and promote social reforms, such as increased parent participation and productive partnerships between home and school.

Policy context/governmental initiatives

In the late 1980s, national and state-wide programmes to renew senior schooling converged with other school reform programmes, such as Queensland's Department of Education initiatives, to increase parent participation. These governmental initiatives drew a response from some parents who wished to be able to play a stronger role in the 'education journey' of their children, if only to convey what their children's education meant to them. Other Australian states have experienced local school-based management, or the 'devolution' process over longer periods of time than Queensland, and 'these processes have resulted in greater demands, in both time and money, on parents and school communities' (Martino 1995: 3).

Queensland initiatives to increase wider school community participation were introduced in two reports: *Focus on Schools* (Department of Education, Queensland 1990a) and *Focus on the Learner* (Department of Education, Queensland 1990b). Of particular importance in *Focus on Schools* is the issue of participation. The publication states:

All members of a democratic society are entitled to participate in the education system. The public education system, therefore, needs to promote the right of school communities to participate, and to provide suitable consultative mechanisms and procedures to facilitate this process.

(Department of Education, Queensland 1990a: 39)

The Queensland Department of Education's policy manual stated that:

1   It is the Department of Education's policy to devolve greater responsibility to schools through the process of school-based decision making.
2   In devolving responsibility to schools, the Department of Education is conscious of the need to ensure that school-based decision-making is as effective, efficient and socially just as possible.
3   Each school is accountable to its own school community and through the government, to the general public. Collaborative School Development Planning and Review is an important component of this process.

(Department of Education, Queensland 1992, Section 1)

In light of this, the then Minister for Education claimed that the Queensland government was 'undertaking the greatest encouragement of parental and community participation in schools ever seen in Queensland' (Comben 1993: 33). The Queensland Department of Education's Corporate Plan for 1994–1998 (Department of Education, Queensland 1993) affirmed this stance and suggested that parents would play an integral part in these reforms. It stated that schools would be empowered to manage their affairs through the delegation of responsibility. The plan widely acknowledged that wide representation of community views in school decision-making processes can have a positive effect on the learning outcomes of children and that it is every principal's responsibility to promote and support genuine parent participation activities in his or her school. The plan concluded by stating that: 'the practical implementation of this participation is a major task for principals in the coming year' (p. 5).

The 1994 budget of the Queensland Department of Education provided money for (a) activities to skill parents for participation in school based management; and (b) employment of Parent Development Officers to work with parents. When writing about 'School Based Management' and reform of the state school system, Queensland's Director-General of Education stated:

One of the main thrusts of the current movement to reform state school systems in Australia is the move towards school-based

88

management. School-based management is about the delegation of power away from a centralised bureaucracy to schools and communities. The push for school-based management is not unique to Queensland nor is it a recent development. Movements towards school-based management can be found in all Australian States and Territories.

(Peach 1994: 9)

In this, the Director General was supported by the then Queensland Premier (Goss 1994), who stated that the education of our children is so important that the whole community needs to be involved in that education for the sake of the whole future of our society.

Focus on the Learner, however, identified the importance of partnerships: 'Senior schooling will be most successful for students when worthwhile partnerships are forged between students, teachers, parents and community' (Department of Education, Queensland 1990b: 4). In this, government initiatives are attesting to the importance of partnerships in education reforms. As a result of a wide review of literature on teacher education, Gore (1995) in Grundy's chapter (Chapter 4, this volume) concludes: 'Not surprisingly, collaborative and partnership programs are frequently touted as the single most efficient, effective, and important way of reforming both teacher education and schools concurrently'.

However, it should be noted that forming productive partnerships, as a means of disseminating new social reform programmes of increased parent participation in schools, does have some prerequisites. Miller and Rose (1990: 1) argue that 'governmentality', which they translate as state intervention into all aspects of life for the social welfare of the population, has come to depend on existing technologies, social activities and authority associated with expertise. They contend, therefore, that positive outcomes for social reform programmes require attention to be given to: 'the complex processes of negotiation and persuasion involved in the assemblage of loose and mobile networks that can bring persons, organisations and objectives into alignment' (*ibid*.). Furthermore, as Grundy in Chapter 4, this volume, highlights, positive outcomes also require attention to be given to the importance of 'parity of esteem', where 'the knowledge and expertise of school and university based practitioners [and, in this case parents] needs to be seriously worked through'.

Levels of parent participation

The development of parent participation has seen a proliferation of types of parent involvement in schooling. Epstein (1987: 14, cited in Mawdsley and Drake 1993) identified five different levels of parent involvement in schools: *Level 1* – involvement that is restricted to being concerned about children's health, safety, supervision, discipline, guidance, and learning at home; *Level 2* – involvement which includes communication between parents and school; *Level 3* – involvement in which parents act as volunteer tutors and as supporters and spectators at school events and student performances; *Level 4* – involvement in which parents assist the school by overseeing learning activities at home; and *Level 5* – involvement in which parents take part in school decision making, governance, and advocacy. Soliman (1991) and Winlock (1994) have identified similar levels of school-community interaction. Kellaghan *et al.* codified parent involvement programmes as proximal, intermediate and distal as follows:

> Activities that focus on teaching and learning may be described as *proximal*; those that do not relate directly to teaching and learning but to supporting these activities may be described as *intermediate*; more remote educational activities may be regarded as *distal*.
>
> (Kellaghan *et al.* 1993: 32)

The parents' project

In early 1992, a high school of approximately 1,100 students and approximately 800 parent sets, decided to develop a senior school curriculum framework to review and renew its teaching in Years 11 and 12 based on government reports and initiatives, particularly the *Focus on the Learner* document (Department of Education, Queensland 1990b). They approached a Brisbane-based university for support, and thus was born a broader collaborative programme, which included several individual projects, one of which centred around parents and the school community. At the commencement of the programme, the school had not yet developed special structures to meet the new Department of Education guidelines with respect to parent participation in school decision making.

The action research context

The method adopted by university workers in their collaboration with the school and the parents was based on the PAR model (Foote-Whyte 1991; Kemmis and McTaggart 1988). In Chapter 2, this volume, Kemmis and Wilkinson state that action research is 'a social – and educational – process'. It is concerned with 'actual practices, not practices in the abstract. It involves learning about the real, material, concrete, particular practices of particular people in particular places'.

Foote-Whyte (1991) identified a form of action research, PAR, which involves people in the community under study participating actively with the professional researcher throughout the research process, from initial design to the final presentation of results and discussion of their action implications. He argued that PAR ' contrasts sharply with the conventional model of pure research, in which members of organisations and communities are treated as passive subjects' (p. 20).

Further, Foote-Whyte contended that PAR begins by discovering a problem which the community believes important and depends for its success on the commitment of the participants. He argued that in PAR, researchers must be willing to 'relinquish the unilateral control' they traditionally maintain over research and 'must rely upon rational discourse and processes of persuasion' (p. 241) to effect planning and implementation of the project. An important component of this project was the collaboration of parents with the project co-ordinator, who was also a parent at the school, as well as other university staff.

The programme context

The wider programme with the school initiated four projects in Science, Social Science, English and with parents. Researchers were employed to work collaboratively with teachers and parents. Grundy, in Chapter 3, this volume, on partnerships, suggests that the type of collaborative research programme which includes 'school-based teachers, university-based researchers, parents, school support personnel, students, etc.', could be characterised as: 'researching with the profession'.

The co-ordinator of the parent project worked with parents attending their meetings, keeping records, working on the other related projects and participating in discussions. It involved social as well as research activity. As part of her role within the programme, the co-ordinator collected copies of meeting minutes and correspondence, kept field notes on activities and undertook surveys and interviews. This material was combined, reorganised and summarised to form the basis of project reports and publications.

The Parents' Survey

The parent involvement began with an initial Parents' Survey. It became the basis of the action research project, as it furnished a common point of reference for all interested members of the school community. It focused on parents' and guardians' perceptions of the school and their participatory role in the school (see McKibbin *et al.* 1994). This survey was divided into three sections. Part A included questions of parents' perceptions of schooling, and whether their expectations were being met. Some questions focused on whether the school provided an education geared to the students' interests, abilities and career futures, and the usefulness of communications and school support services. Part B surveyed parents' understanding of initiatives by the Queensland Department of Education to promote more participation within schools. Part C sought parents' socio-economic background and other demographic details. The Parents' Survey also offered respondents the opportunity to write comments.

The survey was distributed to parents and guardians (also called parents from here on) via students within their Homegroups. Items in regular newsletters were sent home requesting parents to complete them and return them to the school. Student names were ticked when the survey was sent home and crossed ticked when they were returned. A list of parent names of non-returned surveys was compiled by the Homegroup teacher. If a student had not returned a completed survey, another one was issued. Phone calls were made at the end of the year to gather as many surveys as possible. Specific attention was given to the non-English-speaking background parents through their co-ordinator, and to the Aboriginal and Torres Strait Islander parents through their support officer. Parents who were interested in any further discussions of issues relating to the survey were able to register their names and phone numbers on the tear-off section on the back page.

The school had approximately 800 parent sets and 367 surveys were returned, a return of almost 50 per cent. The survey responses were coded and entered on computer for analysis by SPSS. The responses for each question were collated and anecdotal information was recorded and combined into a coherent structure to illuminate the coded findings. When asked in the Parent Survey for areas in which they would like to become involved, the majority of parents chose: (i) school policy; (ii) curriculum development; (iii) parent–student–teacher forums; (iv) fund-raising; (v) classroom support; and (vi) clerical assistance. The Parent Survey indicated that 93 per cent of responding parents 'agreed' that a good home–school partnership was essential for their children's education, and indicated that over 62 per cent wanted more involvement in school activities. Nevertheless, responses also indicated that 79 per cent had no involvement. One parent expressed her sense of alienation,

> Somehow when my child left primary school to enter high school, I had lost touch. I didn't feel that comfortable contact that I had felt at the primary level. The school wasn't just up the road any more, parents didn't pick up and drop off their children any more and therefore didn't get to know other parents. There was no school fete, where we all pulled together to raise funds for something which would improve our children's school and therefore, their education. Apart from the traditional areas of canteen and uniform shop, the school felt closed. It was very different.
>
> (Barbara, parent)

Parents' activities

The parent activity began when forty parents registered their names and phone numbers on the tear-off section of the Parents' Survey, expressing their interest in further discussion of issues emerging from it. After the survey responses had been analysed, invitations were sent out to these parents to attend a meeting at the end of 1993 to discuss the results. University researchers and school administration staff were present. Thirty-two parents replied and twenty parents attended on the night. One of the parents reflected:

> On this particular night I gravitated towards the table with a few familiar faces of other Grade 8 parents, and as we discussed our response to the survey results, I felt a little embarrassed that our issues would seem a bit protective. I was very relieved to hear how widely shared they were amongst this fairly large group of parents, across the age range of students, and felt convinced that we had some common goals to work towards together.
>
> (Narelle, parent)

Beginnings

This initial meeting in November 1993 was planned and organised by the project co-ordinator, with assistance from a member of the administration staff. The co-ordinator facilitated the meeting. During the evening, parents were given an opportunity to discuss survey results, and several key issues were raised by the twenty participants. These were collated by participants at the meeting into four areas.

1 *Discipline*. Parents raised the issues of negative peer pressure, disruptive classes and poor study habits. They believed that the negative peer pressure induced non-achievement. They questioned whether there were enough support staff and resources to support teachers and students.
2 *Communication*. Parents commented that they felt that communication between them and the school could be improved. There were requests for more information to parents on homework tasks and the idea that there be liaison with the various subject teachers re due dates of major assignments. There was particular attention given to improving counselling for students concerning subject selection and their needs. There was a discussion of the role of the 'Homegroup' class.
3 *Extended hours*. Some parents requested that the library hours could be extended.
4 *School Advisory Council*. Some parents wanted further information and discussion on the idea of a School Advisory Council to advise the

principal. The principal at this meeting, however, suggested that a School Council would be more beneficial than an Advisory Council.

During this meeting to disseminate and discuss results, some parents suggested holding a second informal meeting before the new school year to discuss survey issues. The project co-ordinator, however, sent out invitations to the initial forty parents and those staff who had indicated some interest in the project to attend this meeting, to be held in the school's common room in December 1993. The purpose was to discuss some of the issues prioritised at the first meeting, and to give parents an opportunity to participate in setting an agenda for directions the following year. Only two parents were able to attend this December meeting, with no staff present. The co-ordinator arranged to meet with them and to assist in planning the next meeting in February 1994. As a result of this, and subsequent meetings set up to discuss the outcomes of the Parents' Survey, a small group of parents formed a fairly unstructured organising committee interested in more parent/school collaboration. A common concern among participants was the wish and preparedness to be more involved in their child's school.

However, the desire to become more involved was not without apprehension. One parent interprets her experiences of participation over time:

> At the time the Parents' Survey came home, I was becoming more and more conscious that when my daughter had any problems at school or made comments about things that happened at school, I didn't have any answers. It was that foreign country with the culture I didn't understand. The survey gave me an opportunity to make some comments, both positive and negative. When I attended the results evening, I was surprised to hear how much in common my feelings were to those expressed by other parents. I was very interested when asked to join in further discussion and participate in the action research for parents' participation in schools. I could see this was going to be an opportunity for me to learn and perhaps be a more supportive parent to my child than I had been able to be since her transition into high school. It is at this point I feel I bought a ticket for a ride on a roller-coaster.
>
> (Barbara, parent)

Within the first week of school in 1994, the current principal was seconded to the Regional Office of the Department of Education. He was replaced by an acting principal. The relationship with the principal was seen as crucial to parent participation in the school (Beattie 1985; Vertigan 1994), where perceived difficulties can emerge due to a lack of clarity between central control, powers of principals and teachers, and these new roles for parents. This was supported by Dimmock and Hattie (1994) who alluded to much confusion and anxiety associated with roles and responsibilities within devolution. The notion of partnerships as a 'two-way process of communication' (see Grundy's Chapter 3, this volume), was important for parents and the project. However, the secondment of the school's principal appeared to become a major factor which influenced the direction of the parent project.

Meetings and decisions

The decision was to plan the next meeting in February. The co-ordinator sent invitations to the original forty parents, administration staff and to all teachers. Invitations were extended to new and existing parents through newsletter articles. The newly appointed Parent Development Officer (PDO) for the local region of the Queensland Department of Education was also invited to discuss her role with parents who were interested in more participation in schools. A member of the Executive of the Queensland Council of Parents' and Citizens' Association (QCPCA) was invited too. At this stage, students were not involved in the project.

Attendance by parents at the February 1994 meeting was a disappointment. Only six parents attended. However, the regional PDO and the QCPCA Executive Member did attend, as did two administration staff, (one being the new acting principal), one Head of Department (HOD) and five teachers. At this meeting, it was agreed that the best way to deal with the majority of key issues prioritised at the November meeting, and outlined in this meeting's agenda was to increase communication between teachers, students and parents, to enable more awareness of the others' values and expectations. Discussion took place on the following issues: (i) the school community network; (ii) the student council; (iii) parent–teacher nights; (iv) parent–teacher interviews; (v) student reports; (vi) open days; (vii) notice board; (viii) subject handbooks; and (ix) homegroup classes.

As the Parents' Survey (McKibbin et al., 1994) indicated that 93 per cent of responding parents 'agreed' that a good home–school partnership was essential for their children's education, and indicated that over 62 per cent wanted more involvement in school activities, the meeting suggested the following methods for increasing liaison between parents and the school:

1   Monthly community network meetings at which parents, teachers and students can discuss expectations and problems and receive feedback.
2   Evaluating present situation with regard to liaison between home and school.
3   Contact person for each year level, e.g., a helpful key parent.
4   A school newspaper – not to take place of present newsletter, but a community- and student-orientated newspaper, which includes photographs, etc.

A major suggestion was the establishment of a parent meeting place – a place where parents are welcome, for example, to have a cup of coffee, meet other parents, meet teachers and read background material. The meeting decided to take further action on this, to search for a suitable location and to make parents become aware of its existence. This was seen as building a bridge between home and school, particularly for parents who experienced varying degrees of anxiety about facing unfamiliar school surroundings. Problems about identification of visitors to the school were raised in relation to this meeting place. It was decided that all visitors should notify the school's front office.

Suggestions of an I.D. badge or sign-in sign-out book were given. This matter was left to be discussed further at another meeting. The meeting concluded by agreeing to meet again in late March. The date was left in the hands of the small group who continued to maintain interest and a preparedness to be more involved. The co-ordinator reflects upon the February 1994 meeting, which highlighted the diversity of social positions and perspectives within one school community:

> The meeting was very stimulating for all attendants – both parents and teachers were quite vocal. It was, however, an unwieldy meeting and reactions to discussions varied. One member of the administration staff indicated a lack of support through facial expressions and body language. The caretaker principal appeared very interested, and said that he would benefit from parent participation as the Collaborative School Review (CSR) was about to be instigated at the school. He supported involvement of parents and asked to be filled in on proposals. One of the heads of department at the school strongly argued that communication between administration, teachers, parents and students could be addressed and improved. In this, the meeting appeared to act like a mirror of the school with respect to communication and school–community participation, in that it was difficult to define or delineate any 'common unity'.

> (Charmaine, co-ordinator)

Planning began on the fourth meeting in March. Invitations were issued to the forty parents, with consultation held with some administration staff. The organising group decided to hold it at the home of one of the keen participating parents, and to make 'parents' self-reflection' the focus of the meeting. This was arranged to enable parents to take stock and evaluate their commitment to participation, and the means of doing so. One parent expressed some differences between formal and informal meetings:

In stark contrast, it was so easy to speak at an informal meeting of parents at a parent's home – where everyone felt comfortable in talking freely about the issues concerning them in a lively, relaxed way. This day crystallised for me one of the main barriers to parent participation in high schools – how can we preserve the ideas and ideals that arise with the ease of parents simply talking together about their students, when it becomes necessary to communicate these same ideas in more formal settings of Parents' and Citizens' (P&C) committee meetings, school forums, etc.?

(Narelle, parent)

It was agreed at this meeting that the issues which emerged from the Parents' Survey should remain the focus of the parent activities. The enthusiasm and energy of this small group was generated through agenda items such as: (i) a review of levels of parent participation in the school; (ii) skilling for more effective parent participation; (the Department's Regional Office had advertised for applications from groups to offer in-service to parents and teacher/parents on participating in their local schools. We applied for and received a grant to run such a seminar for high schools in the Region); (iii) setting up and advertising the parent meeting place; and (iv) organising a social event, initiated at the November meeting by a parent and an administration staff member.

Ten parents and one of their students attended the March, 1994 meeting. They used the meeting as an opportunity to meet socially, as well as to discuss future directions for parent involvement. The co-ordinator also took the opportunity to discuss PAR methodology, which encourages all participants to become researchers. She stressed that the future directions of parent/school liaison really depended upon what parents wanted to do, as well as their commitment to it. In other words, it was of no use to develop means by which parents could actively participate in their school, if they were not willing to work at it. One parent's commitment became clearer:

I found it very supportive at this stage of my eldest daughter's education, to be given continuing invitations through the project to talk with other parents about their own and their students' experiences of high school – to work out what were important issues, and what could be 'talked over' and 'let go'. And then the project, through Charmaine's questioning, challenged me to *decide where* I could be involved comfortably and to *choose* an area where I would feel happy to ask other parents and students if they would like to be involved, and where I did not expect the barriers to parent participation to be too daunting.

(Narelle, parent)

The group of ten parents and one student wanted to streamline their efforts and showed their determination to participate. They decided to take on the formal name of *'Students and Community Consultative Group'* (SCCG). They decided upon thirteen activities to inform their future. These included: (i) to elect a Chairperson and a Secretary; (ii) to hold regular meetings; (iii) to become affiliated in some way with the P&C, but not responsible to it (only to the principal); (iv) to communicate useful material to the wider school community through a regular article in the school's official weekly newsletter, under the title of 'Parent Speak'; (v) to suggest a Student Council be formed (to include all students); (vi) to provide an opportunity for parents to attend 'Student Forums'; (vii) to look into the matter of parents attending vital policy discussions at the school (but missing out through lack of opportunity caused by their daytime work commitments); (viii) to organise and promote opportunities for parents to become skilled in parent–school participation (through 'certified' workshops jointly arranged by Regional Office Parent Development officers and the university); (ix) to set up the parent meeting place in the school (to be called the 'parent resource area') during the daytime and to look into its utilisation at night time for meetings; (x) to organise a social event, a 'pot luck' meal, where the individual Homegroup teachers, students and parents could get together informally to meet each other early in the school year, then later on whenever appropriate; (xi) to look into responses to newsletter articles requesting parents with problems to come forward and to arrange contact between respondents and teachers; (xii) to hold another meeting in April, hopefully in the new parent resource area with the issues prioritised at the first meeting continuing to lead future discussions; and (xiii) to use 'Parent Speak' initially to advertise what has transpired so far, as a result of the Parents' Survey.

Initial outcomes

Out of the thirteen activities proposed, participants decided to adopt six of them. These were: (i) newsletter articles from the principal to parents; (ii) the 'Parent Speak' newsletter items; (iii) the school–community communication network; (iv) the parent resource area; (v) the social event (although that became more of a school-based initiative); and (vi) setting up sub-committees of the P&C to discuss educational issues. However, these attempts met with mixed success.

The acting principal organised newsletter articles to address educational issues discussed at the February 1994 meeting. In the first of these items, the principal described how he would canvass the range of activities offered at the school. The principal wanted to advertise these to the school community to ensure that they met students' needs. The second newsletter provided assessment schedules for each subject area in each grade. This was done to enable parents to be informed of assignment due dates so that they could ensure that students did not neglect their study. This was welcomed and commended by parents.

Parent Speak newsletter items were successful. Two parents reported on interesting and informative events and articles as a means of reaching other parents. The Parent Speak items became a regular part of the newsletter and offered useful parent information from various other parent networks. The school–community network never really got started. There had always been a great variety of things happening at the school. However, these tended to occur as isolated pockets of activity, inducing what appeared to be a fragmented school community. The project co-ordinator suggested that by contacting these small groups and informing them of what was happening elsewhere, a school community network could become an outcome which may, over time, form the nucleus of a possible School Board or School Advisory Council. The acting principal's immediate response was to request that things proceed slowly. The caretaker principal asked that parents do nothing on this matter until the principal returned. A parent did endeavour to set up a 'telephone tree'. However, finding the time to do this was difficult and nothing substantial emerged at that time.

The parent resource area was set up, but not without some controversy. The planning for this began with a search of the school to find a suitable place. After discussions, parents and administration staff agreed to trial for one term, a parent resource area in a corner of the teachers' common room. However, on the way to this position, the organising group had to overcome an initial hiccough with a newly appointed senior staff member's last-minute objection, as previously that particular area was used for visiting trainee teachers. The SCCG also found a refrigerator and other facilities for the area. Although not utilised extensively by the school's parents, the parent resource area has become accepted to the point that the initial one-semester trial period was extended to the end of that year. Now there is a special room in the school set aside permanently for parents. The social event was successfully run, but with its own controversy. Some administrators and teachers from the school withdrew their support. This is discussed below.

Moves to set up P&C sub-committees on educational issues were not initially successful. These moves arose from parents' needs to find ways to address the matters raised in the Parents' Survey, which resulted in frustration in locating appropriate structures. It was becoming quite obvious that it was not an easy task to find ways for people to become more involved. As one parent stated: 'We kind of got the message that this was a bit of a "closed shop"!' This led to some parents beginning to see themselves and others negatively, as one wrote:

In retrospect, it occurred to me that I was perceived as a trouble-maker: who was I to think I could come up with a solution so quickly and brashly say so? Where did I come from? Whose barrow was I pushing? What's my issue here? In fact, the verbals did not convey their real response to me, the body language revealed this. The non-verbal behaviour was totally incongruent with the verbal response. It confirmed my initial assumption – I was perceived as a threat to this established body of people and was treated accordingly: with absolute deference. My envisaged style of parent participation was momentarily shattered. However, I realised then and there that the 'softly-softly' approach of 'if you can't beat 'em' mentality was the only one to adopt in this case. One has to know the rules of the game to play in the ball park to effect the necessary outcomes, with attitudinal change almost impossible to achieve without stepping onto the playing pitch.

(Jan, parent)

When some SCCG members asked if sub-committees could be set up within the P&C committee to look at educational issues concerning parents, it was questioned whether the P&C's constitutional regulations allowed such changes. The school's administration also questioned whether the more active SCCG parents were representative of the whole school's parents. Some of the parents who had responded to the Parents' Survey and continued to be involved in the project, and others who became involved afterwards, had a preference not to be involved in the school's formal parent body for different reasons. One parent gave her explanation:

As my children were in a new school I knew nothing about, I decided to be active in some way to be a support to them. I attended the P&C's Annual General Meeting. My impression was that the people involved had been involved for some time. A new parent raised a number of issues that seemed relevant. These issues were addressed in a manner that discouraged discussion. . . . At that time I decided that, despite my desire to support my students, I would not attend the P&C committee meetings.

(Pam, parent)

The proposal to set up sub-committees of the P&C was not accepted by the acting principal. It did not go to the P&C meeting. It appeared that no progress was made on the school community network, originally suggested by the project co-ordinator, but taken over after the February meeting. The organising parent group began to feel like 'outsiders' for various reasons. One of the parents recounts:

We realised and were informed after a very short time, that the official voice of parents in a school was the P&C committee, and in fact we did not want to be fighting against the P&C committee, but rather to try to create awareness, so that educational matters and concerns could be raised and discussed through the correct forum.

(Joyce, parent)

Conflict

As the activity of the SCCG continued, some tension arose amongst the SCCG members, school staff, students and P&C executive members, mostly over the planning of the social event. This tension became particularly noticeable when the organising parent was trying to gauge the available resources for the event, namely the use of the hall. A parent recalls:

Most of us did not have a deep enough understanding of the school problems or the political undercurrents in the education system. Looking back, we did not know enough to really contribute or to disagree. This was probably the first block that we came across. At the same time, one of the parents suggested a function to promote the different aspects of the school. This appeared to be well received at the time, but when enthusiasm created a breakdown in control, the brakes were applied in different ways to students, staff and parents. Our baptism by fire occurred when the function was being organised. This was very demoralising, and it became obvious that parent participation was not as easy or as pleasant as it sounded.

(Barbara, parent)

The social event held in July 1994 did not go ahead as initially intended because some heads of departments in the school withdrew their support for various reasons. The parent who accepted the task of co-ordinating the event could not sustain the support of departments within the school. School facilities such as kitchens could not be used by parents without approval. The social event was perceived by some at the school as becoming 'too grand', as well as being 'usurped' by the social's organising parent. A parent reflects:

At the end of the first term I was contacted by another parent, and asked if I would like to be involved in a social event committee. Without any historical reference point, it was difficult to work out why problems were occurring between some of the [school] members and the parents involved in the committee. By the time the event was held, there seemed to be almost a complete breakdown in liaison between the students who were most involved, and the parents organising the event. The reasons for this remain a mystery to me as it was in the school's interest to have cohesion and co-operation between all people involved in the social event.

(Pam, parent)

However, the organising parent, other parents, students and school staff successfully ran the social event, which attracted funds for students in the Senior School. Attendance of parents was very good and those attending appeared to enjoy the feast of food and entertainment. After the resounding success of this event, parents and teachers began to see each other as working towards similar goals. Nevertheless, this situation was not to be repeated the following year, where parents generally were not requested to participate in the event.

The conflict and tension indicated that parent involvement was more problematic than official policy documents indicate. Finding new ways of negotiation became the means of galvanising this small group of parents. The group changed its name to the Collaborative Action Research Group (CARG), to widen its appeal and focus on information gathering and research. One of the parents comments:

By this time we had realised that the existing school/parent body was not aware of the broader changes that were [being initiated] or were occurring, or were possible, and it was a very frustrating time. We seemed to be blocked at every turn. . . . Having our meetings on a fairly regular basis, attending different conferences, even getting to know each other's problems from the past and present, and each other's students, melded our group even further and gave each other moral support to overcome (or work under and around) the barriers.

(Joyce, parent)

Nevertheless, it became difficult for the project to run as a collaborative project between the school and the university. Open divisions appeared between administration, project workers and the parents. The administration did not appear to want the kind of parent activity that the project was supporting. The project parents were called a 'splinter group' by some administration personnel.

A new start

The situations described above made it obvious that if parents were going to participate in schools, they would need to act in a professional manner, be as informed as possible and to find ways to enable them to work within the school's present organisational structures and culture. Hence, parent skilling workshops were organised for high school parents in the local region in May and June, 1994. The project co-ordinator, together with the Parent Development Officer from the local School Support Centre,[2] and a member of the school staff, successfully applied for a Department of Education grant for running a parent skilling workshop for high school parents (and those from surrounding schools). The workshop consisted of one day plus a follow-up week night. The workshops informed and skilled parents in better decision-making processes, and provided the potential for establishing a broader parent network. It also provided an opportunity for parents to gain more confidence:

> In the beginning, outside of our parent group, I was often not sure enough of myself, or the point of view I might want to put to speak out. It was easy for others who felt themselves the absolute authority on these matters to 'shoot me down in flames' or more often than not, just put me down. That doesn't happen anymore. I make sure I am always prepared, as much as possible, for any meeting I go to, so I can not be dismissed or thought of as unprofessional.
>
> (Barbara, parent)

The project now began to look for ways in which parents could 'more acceptably' re-enter school activities. The parent co-ordinator arranged individual and group meetings with Stephen Kemmis, an adjunct professor at the university, offering seminars and consultations on action research at that time. Having expertise in participatory action research methodology as a means of enhancing educational change and social justice, Kemmis suggested more formal or structural ways in which parents could successfully participate. Two opportunities presented themselves: the Collaborative School Review in 1994, and the P&C Committee. Even though some of the parents were not very familiar with, nor comfortable with attending formal meetings for various reasons, they now realised that they had to become more involved and assertive in the usual parent forums. As one parent stated:

> Our flow chart continued on to the Annual General Meeting of the school's P&C meetings, where we as a group of parents, who never ever became involved in the formal structures for parents, decided that if we were to effect change, the only way available was through existing formal school structures. Some of us became elected to executive positions.
>
> (Joyce, parent)

In the beginning of 1995, some of the parents were successful in becoming executive members of the P&C. A 'Welcome Back' social occasion was also organised for teachers and new parents in 1995. It was well received and highlighted a need for such occasions to become part of the school routine. It was perceived that an era of more positive negotiation emerged between these parents and school staff in their new formal executive capacity. One parent recollected:

> When members [were] elected to the Executive of the committee, the P&C committee meetings started to change because we were raising issues which we felt needed to be addressed. We continued to meet and get to know each other and understand each other, and were therefore able to encourage other parents and each other to continue.
>
> (Joyce, parent)

In the meantime, the original principal's seconded position was made permanent, and the acting principal was replaced briefly with another acting principal, before a new permanent principal arrived. The new principal appeared to understand the kind of interest in parent participation that the 'splinter group' was seeking. Personal and structural outcomes realised in 1995, however, must be attributed to the effects of PAR and the continual efforts of the organising parent committee of 1994. A teacher observed:

> Through the project, I was encouraged by the parent participation and supported their involvement. I attended a workshop with the parents wearing my teacher's 'hat', and was impressed by their awareness of the skills they needed to develop. I was embarrassed and hurt, however, when they attempted to become more involved in school decision making, only to be rejected. I was proud when they persevered, and elated when they presented a co-paper at a conference with such confidence – they found strength from one another. I was confident that they would bring about change.
>
> (Sandra, teacher)

In the end, the parents felt that they had made progress. They became official members of the P&C. The 'Welcome Back', a social gathering for teachers and parents was a great success and has been continued by the P&C and the principal in the following year. Parents on the Executive were appointed to various school management committees set up within the school, and one parent became a part-time Parent Liaison Worker for part of a term. A forum on 'Behaviour Management' was organised at the school by parents and some school staff, with a sub-committee of P&C members and teachers setting out to construct a survey to inform future policy directions. A report emerged with recommendations for further action, some of which were accepted by the teachers. There was success with grant applications for various projects at the school. A discussion on the School Advisory Council was organised as part of a P&C meeting by some members of the Executive. The formation of a high school P&C cluster group was also organised by some parents on the Executive Committee. A 'whiteboard' agenda was introduced into P&C meetings, enabling participants to have their concerns raised at the meeting, and addressed where possible. The P&C agenda and reporting format was also re-organised to encourage a more 'user-friendly' atmosphere for parents at meetings.

All six of the project parents attended and participated in a Social Justice Conference, organised by the Valley School Support Centre, where five of them gave their individual testimonies of experiences, an awareness of the need for self-development and the need to be taken seriously as educational partners. One parent sought audience participation to gain a broader understanding of the Education Department's initiatives, asking questions such as: Why? What and whose purpose does it serve? What outcomes are envisaged? and How will they be achieved? They sparked some lively debate. Students from the school also participated in the conference. There has also been increased discussion at meetings regarding school and educational issues as a result of school forums.

Reflection and learning

Looking at the project in retrospect, there appeared to be positive changes in the parents – in terms of their self-efficacy and how they operated with respect to the school. At the beginning of the project, the parents appeared to operate mainly at Epstein (1987) *Level 2* – involvement which includes communication between parents and school; and *Level 3* – involvement in which parents act as volunteer tutors and as supporters and spectators at school events and student performances. The SCCG parents aimed for Epstein (1987) *Level 5* – involvement in which parents take part in school decision making, governance and advocacy. As a result of PAR, the active parents managed a shift from Epstein's (1987) *Levels 2 and 3* to part of the way to *Level 5*. The SCCG tried to move parents from *distal* to *proximal*, in terms of Kellaghan *et al.* (1993).

Issues of parent–school collaboration

There have been many successful outcomes from the parent perspective. However, there are five issues which need to be elaborated upon in relation to parent/school relations. First, there is the issue of the involvement of the uninvolved. Some project parents expressed a sense of loss of influence and alienation in relation to the education of their children when they left primary school to enter high school. This led them to aspire for more recognition, encouragement and support from the school, as valued partners in the schooling of their children.

However, rather than imagining that it is 'the norm' for parent participation to occur, in fact it was quite the reverse. At least half of the 800 parents in the school responded to the Parents' Survey. Of those only about forty parents wanted to make contact with the school and the university staff for further involvement. Of those only about five parents continued their ongoing participation in the project. Some factors which contributed to this low rate of parent participation include: ethnicity; work commitments; school meeting times; disinterest; parents' lack of confidence, knowledge and skills in understanding school routines; and the lack of appropriate structures for their participation, as proposed in various policy documents.

These outcomes also make it clear that it is one thing to 'abstractly' imagine that the school community exists, and that it is 'inherently' able to participate. It is another, nevertheless, to '[learn] about the real, material, concrete, particular practices of particular people in particular places' through PAR, as Kemmis and Wilkinson suggest in Chapter 2. The parent activity, which began when forty parents registered their names and phone numbers as interested in further discussion of issues, whittled down to a handful when the project was really under way.

The turning point for parents to 'take the reins' happened during the March 1994 meeting initially, and later at the Annual General Meeting in 1995. Until those times, the project was directed more by the school and university researchers, overall. As one parent summarised:

> Overall I found contact with university staff to be a very supportive, welcoming recognition of this parent's wish to continue my involvement in my student's schooling, though knowing this would have to be in a new capacity than as a primary school parent. I greatly appreciate the persistence the parent/researcher showed in pursuing positive goals, and the project has helped me to look at ways to focus my energy in the future, rather than the temptation to 'give up' through the frustrations of communication in formal and discomfiting meetings.
>
> (Narelle, parent)

Second, as new structures for parent participation had not yet been created in early 1994, this meant that the P&C was the only arena in which parents could formally participate. However, some of the SCCG parents observed that the P&C did not function as a forum for educational matters. Members of the SCCG, therefore, went outside the usual school environment to gain more information and support. This appeared to create a tension between increased parental knowledge and existing structures, with all their complexities. One parent reflected:

By its very nature as an academic institution, a school has inherent structures which will be in conflict. Like circles within circles these structures reflect their own agendas based on many influences (e.g., personalities, goals and bias). Learning how to negotiate between these, collaborate with, reject or simply ignore the differing agendas, has been and will continue to be my greatest challenge as a parent actively participating in my students' school. . . . As yet, I have not learned to walk through this maze without the sense of walking on eggshells. The easiest path would be to confine my activities to canteen duty. I could then rest on my laurels of having had involvement that has increased profitability in savings on labour costs.

(Pam, parent)

The third issue was the apparent inconsistency between the type of parent involvement espoused by the Education Department and sought by these parents, and the school's readiness to accommodate such initiatives. Participating parents were not convinced that the school was aware of, or prepared for, these broader changes that were being initiated and encouraged by the Department of Education policy documents. This apparent lack of awareness appeared to create an insensitivity towards parents who wanted to be more involved. The participating parents' original focus on educational issues resulting from the Parents' Survey, therefore, shifted over time to those of being 'kept at a distance'. Parents express their perceptions in the following way:

What appeared to be a cultural climate of mistrust, apprehension, fear, at times intimidation, but most apparent of all, sheer ignorance of the potentiality of parent participation was a prime reason for some parental involvement.

(Jan, parent)

Some 18–20 months down the track, these participative parents who became involved initially because of concern for their students, have discovered that they, the parents, are the ones who have probably benefited the most in the learning procedure.

(Barbara and Joyce, parents)

It must be acknowledged that parents also needed to be helped to understand school routines and to be confident enough to understand and participate in meeting procedures. That takes time. It also became important for parents to find their own levels of participation, wherever they felt comfortable. What they wanted was 'parity of esteem' and to work towards common goals, which can cut across barriers. Within the time frame of this study, parents and researchers also had five different people overall, to work with in the role of school principal. Management styles and attitudes appeared to be significant factors. One parent reflected:

> It is difficult to remember, analyse or integrate past issues when I am continually conscious of current issues and events. Yet the formation of the latter have largely been influenced or determined by the management styles of the past.
>
> (Joyce, parent)

In projects such as this, continuity of school personnel would have been advantageous to enable 'the complex processes of negotiations and persuasion involved in [such assemblages] of loose and mobile networks' (Miller and Rose 1990: 1) to occur. The perceived difficulties encountered, and the amount of time and energy expended by parents, led to frustration as evident in the following comment:

> I sometimes feel angry and frustrated that although we have made some in-roads into the system, it always has to be such a struggle. I feel we are being tolerated under great sufferance and any opinions or ideas we wish to discuss are automatically discouraged in a similar fashion to the way a government in power treats proposals by the opposition. There seems to be such a tremendous resistance which I can only assume is a fear of losing complete control. So what do we have? The government on one hand saying its policy is one of encouraging parents to participate, and school administrations finding that participation is difficult to accommodate and perhaps even threatening. . . . I hope most of all that we can all join together and make the education of our children a joint effort, acknowledging each other's skills and talents and realising that we can do it better if we do it together. I hope we can learn to respect each other's jobs and motives, know that there are lines that cannot and should not be crossed on both sides, but complement each other's areas of expertise and accommodate each other's views and opinions.
>
> (Barbara, parent)

The fourth issue relates to the role of the parent. As 'ordinary people', parents were perceived as having no status in relation to the school unless they fitted into their 'appropriate', demarcated zones. It was difficult to locate these zones at times, when parents 'collectively' desired to be taken seriously. The need for acknowledgement of the positional differences between 'the teacher', 'the principal' and 'the parent', as well as the complementarity of such roles suggested in the quote above, parallel similar concerns discussed by Grundy in Chapter 3, this volume. Grundy argues that productive research partnerships are dependent upon: 'trust, comparable rewards, [and] recognition of distinctive interests'.

Parents came to appreciate the distinctiveness of their roles, rights and responsibilities from those of the teacher. Some participating parents came to realise through their involvement, that they needed to have the broader picture in mind of what schools can do. That is, schools deal with members of the population on a broad scale. To accommodate individual needs and desires, therefore, is difficult in such a setting. One parent reveals:

> My own personal evolution over the past twelve months has been interesting and is still very incomplete. Increasingly I found I enjoyed the stimulation of politics and power. We recognised the need to be a part of the broader community in education circles and I have used my attendance at various workshops, conferences and meetings to influence outcomes. I recognise that I enjoy the ability to try to influence outcomes by making suggestions, by analysing the various propositions and prioritising (a skill developed at the workshop) and by communicating. I reviewed my own personal evolution. I didn't like what I saw. My aim in life is to be supportive of my children and to be involved in a positive way in the community. Although I enjoyed the politics and the ability to influence outcomes, I didn't like the way that I was doing it.
>
> (Pam, parent)

Some parents acknowledged that roles and responsibilities needed to be stated up front for them. One of the parents commented:

> If a parent is to become part of the school community, the role of a parent needs to be made clear from the start. The barriers that you cannot move are the worst – you cannot move them because they are more or less invisible – they are part of the establishment. Probably the most deterring barrier, but not the most obvious, is the fact that parents are not 'qualified' from the viewpoint of the majority of persons employed by the Department.
>
> (Joyce, parent)

The final issue regarding parent–school collaboration relates to parents' personal growth. Although some project parents initially expressed a lack of interest in attending formal school meetings, some parents decided to change themselves in order to bring about change. This happened particularly within the P&C meetings, once parents became more 'official' members of it.

This year, in my role as an executive member, I was asked to chair the P&C Committee Meeting. I could have got out of it and passed the Chair to one of the other executive members with more experience to handle it, but I felt this would be a real 'cop out'. So for me this wasn't an option. I spent a lot of time making sure I knew the correct procedure for running a meeting. I bought a book on the subject of running meetings, which I studied front to back. I was given other reading material by a friend on controlling a meeting. I sought advice from others and I made sure on the evening of this event, I went into the meeting with confidence and a degree of excitement at the prospect of achieving something that to others may seem simple, but to me in the early days of my involvement, would have been terrifying and impossible.

(Barbara, parent)

PAR issues

In relation to PAR, there are three points to note. The first is that parents benefited from the support given by the university. The Parent Project initially had a lot of support from the project co-ordinator, who was also a parent at the school for six years. This was a significant factor within the life of the study. She in turn had support from the university in terms of access to other researchers and its infrastructure. This enabled the co-ordinator to communicate constantly with parents and teachers via invitations, phone calls, newsletter articles, teachers' morning notices, numerous meetings and occasional morning teas. This part-time position, however, became a full-time occupation as evening meetings, weekend workshops and conferences were attended, not only by herself, but by other 'volunteer' parents. Numerous networks and contacts were made. This meant that parents who became interested in the project had to have the available time to become involved, particularly when they became 'official' members of the school community.

The PAR model also meant that parents acted as colleagues with university researchers. In this they saw themselves as partners in a wider movement for change, for example the social justice initiatives of the Queensland Department of Education, and were able to see the limitations they experienced in the light of this wider movement. These limitations parallel some 'dilemmas and tensions' expressed by Davis and Cooke in Chapter 5, this volume, on parents as agents of change, where participatory projects appear to be 'at odds with the usual organisational styles/management practices of schools'.

The second point relates to practices of self-reflection. From the outset, participating parents were encouraged by the researcher to be informed, to record events, outcomes and perceptions, both individually or collaboratively. This was intimidating and new for some parents, whilst others maintained that it was useful:

> This task enabled me to become more reflective. It gave me entirely different perspectives at times, and enabled me to see more clearly 'cause and effect'. More frequently now, I decline to come to a quick decision until I have had the opportunity of examining all the considerations. I have learned to 'listen' more positively and quietly to others and have found it is not necessary to put forward an opinion on every subject raised. I have learned to travel more slowly.
>
> (Joyce, parent)

Another parent who perceived that her 'adult' status was threatened when she entered the school's territory, made a conscious choice to change this perception.

> I felt I should take on the demeanour of the 'child' who must be in obeisance of the teachers and especially the principal. When met with an autocratic style of management, I at first found that I dealt with it by being nice and trying to be liked. However, . . . in the best interests of . . . students . . . I made a clear choice that . . . I would take on the role of 'adult'.
>
> (Pam, parent)

Some specific practices that the group tried to refine were: (i) finding ways which included and skilled participants at meetings, such as rotating the chairperson and the recorder of minutes; and (ii) containing meetings where everyone kept on track and dealt only with agenda issues. This was necessary as some meetings became unstructured 'talk sessions' to relieve pressures and a lack of esteem, but this was avoided as much as possible, due to time constraints and a perceived lack of purpose. Parents also recognised over the duration of the project, that to concentrate and work on a few issues at a time, appeared to bring more success than trying to do too much at once.

The third point is to emphasise the importance of a strong community or group of parents who are willing to work together. In spite of a seeming lack of 'common unity' across six individuals at times, the parents always tried to be as unified and inclusive as possible. Maintaining friendship was paramount. At times, it would have been easier for parents 'to quit'. Rather than giving up, they became even more determined to be involved in the school. The personal pain associated with alienation appeared to galvanise the group. The solidarity that emerged from regular informal meetings, also enabled individuals to become stronger at more formal, public meetings.

In seeking 'social justice', 'recognition' and 'respect' for concerns of parents, and the numerous roles that they can play in the educational journey of their children, this story highlights how change occurred, over time, for some parents as well as their roles within the school. First, participating parents changed significantly from the time they filled out the Parents' Survey to when they took up formal positions within the P&C. As noted previously, a lack of interest or a willingness to participate in formal school structures such as P&C meetings, was registered by most of them from the outset. Over time, however, these parents actually set out to help create a base for involvement of more parents, through changing the structure of participation, in addition to changing the forms of their own participation.

Second, it was only when parents recognised their own needs for personal development and skills, that their successful participation became possible. Personal and group development associated with this PAR project, became a necessity to overcome (or work under and around) the perceived barriers of parent participation. However, this only became a reality for them when they went outside the school grounds to form productive partnerships with Education Department personnel, university staff, QCPCA members and other parents, and when they passed on important information gained through their research. The parent co-ordinator also realised over time, that the 'powerful social dynamics' associated with just one school community, necessitated further investigation. It became the subject of her doctoral research.

Hence, this narrative indicates just how difficult it is for 'persons, organisations and objectives' to be brought 'into alignment'. Nevertheless, these participating parents hope that their efforts were not in vain.

> 'Bridges' were and are still being attempted to be built between teachers, administrative staff and parents; simultaneously broken fingernails are a common phenomenon amongst parents of secondary school students and the 'benefits' of parent participation will, I envisage, have a far-reaching effect on the educational, political, economic, and most importantly, the social context of our richest resources: our children.
>
> (Jan, parent)

NOTES

1 All parents and teachers agreed to use their first name except Narelle, which is a pseudonym.
2 School Support Centres are established by the Queensland Department of Education to provide resources and expertise in support of curriculum change and development in schools in their local areas.

REFERENCES

Beattie, N. (1985) *Professional Parents – Parent Participation in Four Western European countries*, London: The Falmer Press.

Comben, P. (1993) 'Increasing community participation in schools', *School Talk*, September, 33–6.

Department of Education, Queensland (1990a) *Focus on Schools*, Brisbane, Australia: Department of Education.

—— (1990b) *Focus on the Learner*, Brisbane, Australia: Department of Education.

—— (1992) *Program Management PM-01 – Collaborative School Development Planning and Review* (Section 1, Policy and Procedures. 21.12.92), Brisbane, Australia: Department of Education.

—— (1993) *Corporate Plan 1994–1998*, Brisbane, Australia: Department of Education.

Dimmock, C. and Hattie, J. (1994) 'Principals' and teachers' reactions to school restructuring', *Australian Journal of Education*, 38 (1): 36–55.

Epstein, J. (1987) 'Paths to partnership: what we can learn from federal, state, district, and school initiatives', *Phi Delta Kappan*, January, 345–49.

Foote-Whyte, W. (ed) (1991) *Participatory Action Research*, London: Sage Publications.

Goss, W. (1994) 'Keynote address', presentation made at Queensland Council of Parents' & Citizens' Association Annual Conference, Caloundra, Queensland, April.

Kellaghan, T., Sloane, K., Alvarez, B. and Bloom, B.S. (1993) *The Home Environment and School Learning*, San Francisco: Jossey-Bass.

Kemmis, S. and McTaggart, R. (eds) (1988) *The Action Research Reader*, 3rd edn, Geelong, Victoria: Deakin University Press.

McKibbin, C., Cooper, T., Arcodia, C. and Doig, S. (1994) *Parents' Perceptions of an Inner City School* (technical report), Brisbane, Australia: Queensland University of Technology, Centre for Mathematics and Science Education.

Martino, J. (1995) *Secular, Compulsory and 'Not-so-free', Education*, ACSSO working paper no. 2, Melbourne: Public Sector Research Centre.

Mawdsley, R. and Drake, D. (1993) 'Involving parents in the public schools: legal and policy issues', *West's Education Law Quarterly*, 2 (1): 1–14.

Miller, P. and Rose, N. (1990) 'Governing economic life', *Economy and Society* 19 (1): 1–31.

Peach, F. (1994) 'School based management', *School Talk*, November, 9–11.

Soliman, I.K. (1991) 'State control and parent participation: analysis of recent reports', *Australian Educational Researcher*, 18 (1): 53–73.

Vertigan, L. (1994) 'School self-management', *Education Alternatives*, September, 3.

Winlock, L. S. (1994) 'Parents as partners', *Thrust for Educational Leadership*, October, 36–9.

7

STUDENTS AS ACTION RESEARCHERS

Partnerships for social justice

Bill Atweh, Clare Christensen and Louise Dornan

The project reported here aims at increasing the participation of students from low socio-economic backgrounds in higher education. It is a Participatory Action Research (PAR) project between a group of high school students, some of their teachers and university staff. Atweh and Burton (1995) have discussed the role of students as researchers and located it within three perspectives.

First, because research is a political activity, this approach is based on the principle that *the providers of information are the owners of that information.* Any use made of such information should directly benefit the providers themselves. Further, involving the groups or individuals who are facing a problem in the process of finding a solution embeds the solution in the context, making it more appropriate and more likely to be implementable than a more abstract solution derived by 'experts'. Several researchers have identified the role of research in empowering the researched community involved (Freire 1970; Giroux 1986, Kemmis and Carr 1986). This stance has been used to argue for collaborative research (Stenhouse 1975), participatory research (Horton and Zacharakis-Jutz 1987) and educative research (Gitlin 1990). In education such research activity often leads to teachers and university researchers working together to solve educational problems. The students as action researchers (SAR) model carries that argument further by asserting that students, as the ultimate beneficiaries of the educational enterprise, should be regarded as partners in the research process.

Second, this approach adopts the practice of *students researching students.* This is consistent with principles of ethnographic research, particularly those adopted by some feminist researchers (see, for example, Herbart 1989), who argue that the view from inside a group should be obtained from the inside by using participant observation. Serious questions can be raised about the meaning and possibility of participation when an adult, with different academic experience and often different social background, attempts to 'participate' in the world of young people. As Denzin notes, 'The researcher who has not yet penetrated the world of the individuals studied is in no firm position to begin developing predictions, explanations and theories about that world' (Denzin 1986: 39). Evidence from research suggests that the same principle applies when students research aspects of their own culture. Perspectives and data that may not have been possible using other techniques become available. For example, Schwartz (1988) has shown how students interviewed by other students were able to confide in them that when they do school writing, even if they are writing to a real audience, they write what they think the teacher wants to hear.

Third, this approach adopts the view that *participating with students as co-researchers is an expression of trust and respect for their ability to find creative solutions to their current life problems as well as an opportunity for them to nurture this ability*. The employment of students in research into significant questions provides students with 'intrinsic motivation for talking, reading and writing, and has the potential for helping them achieve mature language skills' (Goswami and Stillman 1987: 1). Increasingly, education systems are under pressure to be more relevant to students' needs, one of the most important of which is the systematic generation of one's own knowledge for the solution of real problems. Cole (1981) points to a paradoxical situation where students reach psychological maturity earlier than in previous generations, yet spend an increasing amount of time in the school which operates in a culture of dependency. He quotes Coleman (1972) who says:

> The student role of the young person has become enlarged to the point where that role constitutes the major portion of their youth. But the student role is not a role of taking action and experiencing consequences. . . . It is a relatively passive role, always in preparation for action, but never action.
>
> (Cole 1981: 7)

This chapter discusses the use of SAR in an equity project,[1] aimed at increasing the participation of students from low socio-economic backgrounds in higher education. The following two sections review the literature on the involvement of young people in genuine research projects and on the question of access to university as an equity issue in Australian society.

Young people as researchers

Student engagement in research activities such as planning, collecting data and information, analysing and report writing is not uncommon in education. For teachers, the primary aims of these projects are to develop skills and attitudes towards research and to develop the students' own knowledge. Yet only infrequently does this knowledge form the basis for decision making or for solving real problems. In the context of the project reported here, the research undertaken by students is conceived differently. Here the emphasis is on genuine attempts to generate knowledge useful for action. SAR is a partnership between experienced researchers and students to undertake research similar to that conducted by professional researchers. The desired outcome of this approach to research is that the students will increase their knowledge about their world and that this knowledge will lead to action by them.

SAR is a relatively new development in educational research. A review of literature yielded only a handful of funded research projects that employed this technique. Schwartz (1988) reported on a study to investigate the effect of the use of the electronic network on the writing abilities of students. Alder and Sandor (1990) used young unemployed people to conduct a study on homeless youth as victims of crime. Although initially money was a factor that made these young people volunteer for the project, Alder and Sandor reported that the young people also shared a commitment to increasing knowledge about, and possible solutions to, the problems of the homeless. Alder and Sandor argued that the second motivation was strong because the young people persisted with the project even after the funding ceased. The young people were trained in research techniques and then they planned and conducted the interviews and transcribed and analysed the data. Alder and Sandor reported that the students felt confident in planning and conducting interviews and were pleased with themselves for having acquired these skills. The results of the research were presented at public meetings, which was seen as a highlight of the project for some of the participants in that it provided a public acknowledgement that their project was worthwhile. A third study employing young people in paid research work was conducted in Melbourne (Slee 1988). The study aimed to identify the educational needs of 13–14-year-olds, needs that appeared not to be met by the education system, and to review the existing Education Unit at the Good Shepherd Youth and Family Service. A fourth study reported by Knight (1982) described work done in several schools by young people independently investigating different aspects of vandalism. Henry and Edwards (1986) employed young people to investigate the effect of school on students from non-English-speaking backgrounds. More recent studies at the Queensland University of Technology used young people as researchers to study sexual violence and young people (Daws *et al.* 1995) and youth homelessness (Crane *et al.* 1996). None of these studies involved activities that the young people have carried out based on their findings. This constituted a major component of the project reported here. Atweh and Burton (1995) reported on a study involving a whole class of A-level Sociology students in the United Kingdom participating in a research activity not unlike the one reported in this chapter.

Equity and access

The inequity in Australian education systems has been documented by several social researchers and government reports (Connel *et al.* 1982; Henry *et al.* 1988; Western 1983). This inequity has been particularly pertinent with regard to opportunities to obtain university qualifications and the resulting increase in opportunities to gain greater access to the benefits, privileges and power available in our society. In a wide-ranging review of literature on patterns of participation in Australian post-secondary education, Anderson and Vervoorn (1983) presented the following caricature of a university student:

> He's the son of a doctor, lawyer, or someone else with a house in [the upper middle class suburbs of] Saint Ives or Kew. Because his parents wanted to have the best education money could buy they sent him to a private school, to study academic subjects and learn the importance of not getting his hands dirty. He went direct from school to college, avoiding the real world en route except for glimpses through the windscreen of the sports car his parents bought him. After a few years he too becomes a doctor or lawyer, and so begins to accumulate the money necessary to build a house larger than his father's and to send his children to university.
>
> (Anderson and Vervoon 1983: 1)

Although conceding that, like all caricatures, this was simplifying a complex picture and exaggerating some of its features, Anderson and Vervoorn argued that the results of the different studies reviewed presented a picture not far removed from the caricature. Of more concern to them was the observation that such imbalance has been stable for some years. As they concluded, 'graduation from higher education has been and remains a sought after prize. It opens the door to the prestigious professions, social status, economic security and positions of leadership' (*ibid.* 1). The fact that this prize may be inaccessible to a large portion of the population is a major concern that the participants in the current project shared.

Australian Government policy on university access was outlined in its 1990 document, *A Fair Chance For All: Higher Education That's Within Everyone's Reach* (Department of Employment, Education and Training 1990). Six groups were identified as under-represented in Australian universities: people with disabilities, Aboriginal and Torres Strait Islanders, women, people from non-English-speaking or socio-culturally disadvantaged backgrounds and those from isolated or rural areas. Action by institutions so far has prioritised women in non-traditional areas and people with disabilities. Common strategies have been awareness and support programmes, bridging programmes, special entry schemes, school links, curriculum review, child care and professional development.

In 1993, an Evaluation of Equity and Access Report was published by the Department of Employment, Education, Training and Youth Affairs (DEETYA). Data from their Australian Youth Survey in 1991 showed that considerable inequities continued to be experienced by young people from socio-economically disadvantaged backgrounds. These students experienced lower retention rates in Year 12, lower Year 12 completion rates and low rates of transfer to higher education (DEETYA 1993). Research showed that reasons related to intrinsic differences in families from different socio-economic backgrounds. It would appear that families from higher socio-economic groups are more likely to provide greater support and encouragement for continued education, have higher expectations for their children and are more likely to send their children to private schools than those from low socio-economic groups (Ainley and Sheret 1992). There is thus a need for equity programmes and these are now in place in most institutions. However, despite special entry schemes in thirty-one institutions, in 1991 only nine of these institutions had met their own participation targets for students from low socio-economic backgrounds (DEETYA 1993).

Rationale of the current project[2]

The research component of the present project was conceived at two levels. First, the students were involved in a SAR project, which aimed at increasing the participation in higher education of students from low socio-economic background schools, and the university staff were involved in a PAR project, which aimed at investigating the facilitation of SAR. Action research was seen as a valid model for achieving the aims of both levels of this project.

The aims of the Students as Action Researchers project in its first year of operation were developed by the participating students to:

1   survey the attitudes of students from a low socio-economic background towards higher education, career expectations and plans, and self-concept of ability for higher education;
2   investigate the effect of some background factors as they affect the factors in 1, in particular: gender, work and education of parents, ethnic background, age and year level, and area of residence;
3   investigate the effect of other people on students' attitudes, in particular: peers, parents, and teachers;
4   investigate the level of students' knowledge about options at university and the sources of such knowledge;

5 develop some case studies of past students from disadvantaged back-grounds who have attended university;
6 make recommendations for future action to alleviate the gap between the university and students from a low socio-economic background.

In the second and third years the aims of the project were to:

1 bridge the gap between the university and the school cultures by acting on the recommendations from the previous year;
2 increase academic activity and its status within the school community;
3 increase the school's status within the wider community.

Over the same period, the Facilitating Student Action Research Project undertaken by university staff, aimed to:

1 investigate the advantages and constraints of conducting collaborative action research in partnership between high school students, their teachers and university staff;
2 investigate the use of action research in an equity project.

Elsewhere in this volume, Kemmis and Wilkinson (Chapter 2) identify six characteristics of action research: it is a social process, participatory, collaborative, emancipatory, critical, and recursive. Based on these features, Table 7.1 summarises the rationale of using the action research model at both levels of conceptualisation of the project: the collaborative project with SAR researchers, and the Facilitating of SAR by school and university staff.

The Students as Researchers Project resulted in two reports (Borowicz *et al.* 1992; Bajar *et al.* 1993) and a video (Bajar *et al.* 1994) that speaks in the students' voices. This chapter will concentrate on the findings related to the second level of the project, that is the Facilitating SAR Project.

The project

The context

The Inala State High School is located in a very low socio-economic suburb on the western outskirts of Brisbane.[3] The school has a higher Aboriginal and Torres Strait Islander population than many similar schools in the region, and a significant Vietnamese population. A situational analysis of the school (Middleton 1991) indicated that: (a) 72 per cent of adults in the area were educationally disadvantaged; (b) the number of single-parent families was six times the Brisbane average with 75 per cent of the families depen-dent on Social Security benefits; (c) the school had suffered from a 'brain drain' during the past few years, with many of the more academic students

Table 7.1 Summary of rationale underlying the action research model

Action Research Characteristics	Students as Action Researchers	Facilitating Student Action Research
Action research is a social process: It deliberately explores the relationship between the realms of the individual and the social.	The lack of participation in university is a social problem affecting certain groups in society as well as an individual problem for some students. Many of the causes of lack of participation are structural and cultural and not solely personal.	The research process should be responsible to the people it investigates, not only increasing the researcher's knowledge. Researchers should reflect on the processes and outcomes of their research practice in social terms. Dominant educational research discourses define valid and respectable findings; alternative discourse is needed to justify research in terms of its practical impact on social justice in education.
AR is participatory: It engages people in examining their own knowledge (understanding, skills and values) and interpretive categories (the way they interpret themselves and their action in the social and material world).	Students are able to participate in meaningful research activities; they will benefit from the knowledge generated to make personal and collective decisions for action. Views about the problem as experienced by people from the inside are likely to be of practical use, and have direct practical impact on improving university participation; they can also offer a fresh basis for reviewing expert views from the outside.	Researchers should reflect upon the process of generation of knowledge as well as on the outcomes of their research. University research should be reflexive. It should demonstrate the reflectivity that it encourages in others.
AR is collaborative and practical: It engages people in examining the acts which link them with others in social interactions.	Students can work with adults in mutually respectful and pedagogically useful ways to solve real problems. Students benefit from developing teamwork skills. Cooperative situations are conducive to learning. Students develop direct benefit from engaging in real 'real life' activities.	Separation between the researched and researcher can be bridged to increase effectiveness of research. Research need not be seen as a "lonely activity". Researchers can benefit from being critical friends to each other.
AR is emancipatory: It aims to help people recover and release themselves from the constraints of irrational, unproductive, unjust and unsatisfying social structures which limit their self-development and self-determination.	Developing awareness of differences between their lived culture and the culture of the university can help disadvantaged people bridge the gap between the two cultures. To increase participation in higher education, students need to develop skills that are needed in higher education at the same time as they are learning about the university culture. Students need reassurance that they can generate valid knowledge through careful research of their own.	Demystifying the research process makes it more accessible and potentially more accountable to the public. The hegemony of the traditional paradigms of research needs to be challenged; in particular the primacy of the 'objective' voice from outside over the 'subjective' voice from the inside promoted by the so called 'scientific' method. The role of research in emancipation in contrast to 'giving a voice' needs to be examined. (Troyna, 1994)

Table 7.1 (continued)

Action Research Characteristics	Students as Action Researchers	Facilitating Student Action Research
AR is critical: It aims to help people recover and release themselves from the constraints embedded in the social media through which they interact: Their language (discourses), their modes of work and the social relationships of power (in which they experience affiliation and difference, inclusion and exclusion).	Students from disadvantaged backgrounds may use language and adopt forms of work and relations to others characteristic of tertiary institutions. By becoming aware of the differences between their own school culture and that of the university they can make new critical connections between the two cultures. In developing research experience students can become more critical of the findings and results of other research on tertiary access. Increased awareness of the students about their world can lead them to useful solutions of the problems affecting their lives.	University culture may not value social justice action as 'proper research'. Traditional roles of researchers/researched need to be examined. AR can be used effectively to combine the university commitments to research and community work.
AR is recursive (reflexive, dialectical): It aims to help people to investigate reality in order to change it and to change reality in order to understand it – in particular by changing their practices in a deliberate social process designed to help them learn more about (and theorise) their practices, the social structures which constrain their practices and the social media in which their practices are expressed and realised.	Students can be trusted to be creative in finding solutions to their problems and in reflecting upon these solutions. In order to benefit from equity projects, disadvantaged students need an increased understanding of their social conditions and this increase in understanding would allow them to act to change these conditions.	Researchers should reflect on the different paradigms of research and the constraints under which they operate in order to achieve a more socially critical research activity. This approach to research requires all participants to re-examine and change the usual relations between students, teachers and university staff.

choosing to transfer to nearby schools in higher socio-economic areas; (d) about 80 per cent of the students commencing Year 8 had some form of special needs in learning; and (e) half of the student population had suffered a moderate to severe emotional or mental trauma. However, as the school principal was quick to add in describing the student and suburb population: 'Don't get me wrong. Some of the best people I have ever met live in the suburb, and some of the best students in the world are in this school.' Middleton's situational analysis also indicated that 'most teachers had a real sense of love and caring for the students' (Middleton 1991: 8).

The project has been going on for four years, 1992–1995. In 1992, nine students from Years 11 and 12 were selected by the project liaison school teacher who supervised the students' participation in the project. This selection was based on the students' academic achievement, gender, social and racial backgrounds. Of the selected group, six were females, one was a mature-age student (aged 22 years) and three were Vietnamese. In spite of the school's efforts, no student from Aboriginal and Torres Strait Islander background volunteered for this project. Seven of the students were receiving AUSTUDY assistance.[4] Most of these students believed that their parents and teachers were encouraging them to succeed in school and to consider higher education. However, they were less sure about their parents' and teachers' beliefs in their abilities. In the following two years, all Year 12 students who had participated in the project when they were in Year 11, were invited to continue their involvement, and new group of Year 11 students was recruited.

Project plan

At its commencement, the project team consisted of four university researchers who shared a commitment to social justice and equity issues, a representative of the special entry programme at the university, and the participating school teacher. This group met regularly during the year to discuss the progress of the project and the planning and implementation of the student visits to the university. Students had weekly meetings at the school under the supervision of the school teacher to work on the project. University staff visited the school periodically to provide some sessions on specialised needs identified by the students and/or their teachers and to maintain contact with the students during the year. Membership of the research team from the university varied from year to year as some left due to other commitments and new people joined.

During the first year of the project, the nine students were employed by the university as research assistants to: (a) attend training sessions at the university; (b) plan the study, gather from their community the data required to identify the need to increase student participation in higher education; (c) analyse the data and write a report from this investigation with appropriate recommendations. These three tasks corresponded to the three stages into which the first year of the project was organised.

The first stage consisted of four days of training and planning at the university. Physically locating the project at the university was important for achieving the aim of bridging the gap between the students' culture and that of the university. The students received some financial assistance to cover transport to and from the university. This training session was conducted during the mid-year school holidays. During these days, the students (a) considered the social issues of disadvantage and education; (b) heard the experiences of university staff who came from backgrounds similar to the students; and (c) undertook training sessions to gain library, computer and research skills, including the development and use of questionnaires and interviews. After the initial sessions, much of the university staff's involvement in the training and planning days became reactive because of the involvement of the students in decision making. Specific planning for the following stages of the project was most intensive during these days, as the university staff reacted to the proposals of the students.

The first decision made by the students was to identify the aims of their research in brainstorming sessions (later summarised by university staff). To achieve these aims, the students decided to divide into two research groups, one to plan a questionnaire with which to survey current students' attitudes to and problems with education, and the other to prepare a script for interviews with past students, in order to develop case studies about their experiences. The rest of the time during these first training and planning days was devoted to developing the instruments and trialling them on each other. The university staff provided advice when needed.

The second stage of the project involved the collection of data. Students received support from the school to go into classes to conduct the survey. The case study group conducted their interviews outside class time. The students worked on this stage of the project independently from the university team, but under the supervision of the participating school teacher.

The third stage of the programme was conducted at the university over seven days during the September school holidays. During these days, the students analysed their data, reflected on the project as a whole, made recommendations from the findings and wrote the final report (Borowicz *et al.* 1992).

A similar overall structure of activities was followed during the second to fourth years of the project, with the emphasis then to develop activities that aimed at increasing the participation of students from low socio-economic backgrounds in higher education. In these subsequent years, the students commenced their deliberations on needed action by considering the findings and recommendations from the previous year's report. They identified areas of most urgent need and the required action to address them. The students' own interests and constraints were also taken into consideration.

Lengthy negotiations resulted in the formation of groups to conduct four activities in 1993. In the first year, the students identified the lack of a home environment conducive to study and the lack of parental ability to assist in academic matters as major problems to be addressed. Hence, the Homework Centre Group was formed to take up the task of establishing a twice-a-week after-school study group in the school library. Teachers were recruited by the students to participate as tutors. Rewards of various sorts were granted to regular attenders at the homework centre.

A second group of students identified the problem of students' lack of knowledge about the university as their concern and planned the University Shadowing Experience, targeting Years 11 and 12 students who were considering going to university. This group organised students to spend a day at some university faculty. In their visits to the university, the students were able to discuss their plans with university lecturers, attend selected lectures and talk to university students.

The third group identified the need of the whole school community, including students, parents and other community members, to be aware of the option of university and concerns and issues related to studying at university. This need gave rise to the establishment of the Publicity Group which undertook the writing of articles to community newspapers, education department publications and the major Sunday newspaper in Brisbane. They also wrote articles about the project in the school newsletter for the parents and advertised the activities of the other groups widely within the school.

The final group, the Buddy System, identified the lower secondary school as a priority area to commence informing students about the university option. This group organised visits to the university by all Year 8 students who were met by their 'buddies', who were university students. These visits were reciprocated by visits from the university students to the school to conduct some activities there.

At the end of the second year, the students wrote a report (Bajar *et al.* 1993) on their activities. Each group identified their major successes and some of the difficulties encountered. Each group also made recommendations for future work on the project.

The third year was similar to the second, except that instead of writing a report, the students developed resource material designed to assist future students and other schools to conduct similar activities. A group of students produced a 10-minute video about the project, explaining its rationale, aims and methods (Bajar *et al.* 1994). The video targeted other schools catering for students from similar socio-economic backgrounds who might be interested in commencing similar projects.

Findings of the facilitating student action research project

The informal observations of the students working on their projects were combined with the field notes, transcriptions of university staff interviews with the students, and the students' report, to provide a base of information on which the university staff could evaluate the project. The following analysis was conducted by the university authors and negotiated with the teacher from the school. As discussed earlier the Facilitating Student Action Research Project aimed at investigating the use of collaborative action research in partnership with high school students, and the use of action research in an equity project. The major findings about each aim will be discussed in turn.

Conducting action research with students

Team work

One of the main features of the organisation of this project was its basing on team work. Working on the research project gave students the opportunity to reflect on their own abilities and to learn new skills. Because they worked in teams they were able to divide the tasks, making best use of the skills of all. Some typical comments about their roles included the following: 'Well I think team work was a big part. We all relied heavily upon one another I think, lecturers and the students.' Another student reflected on the project in the following words: 'It was simple. Easier than I thought. I thought it needs more working and all that but really it's team work and we finished things earlier than we thought because we work in a team. [If] we do it alone, it would take time, real long time.'

Although the students saw the benefits of team work, they also reflected on the problems that arose. During both sessions at the university, there were a few moments where real conflict arose between individual students or between groups of students. This conflict of ideas between students was highlighted by one student as follows:

> Everybody has different viewpoints in regard to the actual survey. Like when we were sitting around discussing things that I sort of picked up on that not all of us agreed on certain aspects that we were talking about. I knew quite a few of the people who actually took part in the project with me. I thought I knew them pretty well but when we got into the research thing I found out how differently each of us actually were. We weren't as close or related as I thought we were.
>
> (Student researcher)

Another problem arose because of the perceptions of the unequal amount of work that the different students performed. One student commented on differences in work rate as follows:

> The thing that came across to me was that the reason why we had to come back for longer [time] was just because we didn't all pull our weight. I mean some of us pulled more weight than others and that was one thing that I think we should try to avoid if you done [sic] it again.
>
> (Student researcher)

The student was asked how such a situation should be handled: 'I don't know cause it's really hard. because I mean I hate to hurt anyone's feelings.

Which is *me* and I don't know how to handle it.' Asked whose job it was to handle the situation, the student said

> I think it's really our job. We have to really pull them into line. Say, hey, you know, you're not pulling your weight, you know, you've got to do this and you've got to do that and give them a deadline so they finish that by. And they think, 'Oh Wow, I've done it' so they can actually feel proud of themselves. And then we'd feel proud too cause they'd actually done it. (laughs) Instead of us doing it.
>
> (Student researcher)

There was also concern about differences in the preferred working styles of the students. Some preferred breaking into small groups or even working individually to do specific small tasks and then integrate them in the large group. Others preferred to work in groups all the time. Skills required for working in groups was an aspect of the project that was addressed in separate sessions during the second and third years of the project.

Development of research sense

The students involved in this project demonstrated considerable critical appreciation of the research process. This is clearly illustrated in the research reports that they produced. In general, the students found the writing of the final report difficult yet challenging. They required considerable assistance in editing and formatting as well as guidance in generating conclusions from the data. Yet, in the report they revealed substantial maturity in their ability to be reflective and evaluative. The report contained evidence that these students had developed a good 'research sense'. For example, they were able to identify the strengths of questionnaires as a method for research which enabled them to 'question a large anonymous audience, within a minimal amount of time' (Borowicz *et al.* 1992: 2). At the same time, they were able to identify some of the pitfalls in designing and conducting surveys, that is, 'The design of the survey relied heavily upon the brain' (*ibid.*). They also identified that the attitude of the data collector towards the respondents was a major factor in obtaining valid information. They concluded that 'one must commit oneself to the task, taking a professional outlook and reflecting this image toward the respondents' (*ibid.*: 3). Similarly, they were not afraid to go beyond the data and raise hypotheses about its meaning and causes. In noting that 71 per cent of the boys and 29 per cent of the girls have university aspirations in spite of the fact that girls indicated that they enjoy school more than boys, they were able to provide the following explanation: 'Possibly this may be due to a lack of female role models who have completed university other than teachers, as well as early motherhood which is common in [this suburb, rather than women concentrating on careers]' (*ibid.*: 21).

The second year's report (Bajar *et al.*. 1993) contained a chapter from each of the four groups conducting school activities, with introductory and concluding chapters. Due to lack of disciplined diary keeping, the students found it difficult to reconstruct the year's events for the purposes of writing the final report. Perhaps this was too much to expect of the students with limited experience in report writing; perhaps it is an activity that reminded them of schoolwork. In spite of this, the reports highlighted the main achievement of each group in the year, identified the main problems faced and made some recommendations for the next stage of the project. The students were able to show a sense of evaluation of problems faced and to learn from them. For example, the Publicity Group wrote:

Our group had to deal with a number of problems such as a difference in timetabling, finding space in the school newsletter and obtaining a computer to use on a regular basis. All the members of the Publications Group met once a week with the other Year 11 students in the project to discuss our progress throughout that week and what we plan to do next. The Year 12 students in the project also met, but at a different time. Because of these differences in timetabling, we sometimes found it difficult to conduct interviews with the Year 12 students. Despite this, we organised some interviews at lunch times and during group meetings on holidays and at night. To a smaller extent, we had to know what each group was doing at a particular moment, and to gather that information to write articles. This was also difficult because so many things were happening at the one time within the individual groups. We solved this problem again by organising lunch time and group interviews. We also asked for any general information be passed on to us. It was hard to form a close liaison among so many people, working with second hand information in most cases. Therefore it was harder to write accurate articles, but we tried to make them as accurate as possible.

Another problem we faced was getting space for our articles to be published in the school newsletter. We have submitted several articles to the editor, but as yet none have been published. However we are working on it.

We found it difficult at first to find a computer to use on a regular basis to type up and save our reports for future references, but luckily the school library supported us and providing we are booked in, have given us unlimited use of their computers.

> Despite these minor problems, our group worked hard to achieve our goal of raising public awareness of the . . . project.
>
> (Bajar *et al.* 1993: 17–18)

Students were also able to be critical of the whole structure and conduct of the collaborative project. In deciding how much advice to give to students in their task we were guided by two considerations. First, we were careful not to expose the students to decisions which we did not think that they were prepared to make. Many of these students have faced failure many times before, and our responsibility was to avoid their involvement in tasks which were too demanding, possibly leading to further failure. Second, we aimed to ensure that the report produced by the students had some credibility as a research report. Perhaps we regarded this aspect of the project more as an apprenticeship for the students to develop research skills rather than a partnership. Hence, an attempt was made to ensure that the questions on the surveys were clearly worded and piloted and so on and that the report writing was at a reasonable academic level. This led to some concern in the minds of at least two students. For one student, the input from the university staff gave the students a sense of lack of ownership over the project. She felt that 'we were doing it all for them sort of thing'. To her the task was a job that you had to do to please the employer. Another student felt that the students were used as guinea pigs in a experiment to see how the methodology can be utilised. However, not all students felt this alienation from the aims of the project. Perhaps there is a lesson for us, that we needed to trust the students more.

The use of action research for equity projects

Breaking the barriers with the university

One of the aims of the project was to increase the students' familiarity with university life. The interviews showed that being invited to perform research at a local university with other students their own age, to experience a new environment, new challenges and to learn new skills, proved to be very rewarding for these students. The students expressed positive views about the experience. For a number of the students, universities had been perceived, prior to the project, as an alien environment. They didn't know anybody who had gone to a university. As one student put it:

> They don't think uni [sic] is for them.
>
> (Student researcher)

Upon the completion of the project, one student commented with some surprise that:

I didn't think it would be such a big place . . . how sociable people are! . . . Like, at first, I thought it might be like school. . . . They're not trying to go around big noting themselves like school kids are.

(Student researcher)

Another student described her experience of university in the following words:

I used to think university was this monstrous place. I thought it was a really difficult place to get into, that the lecturers were these sort of people high up on a pedestal. Our teachers said that when you go to university, the lecturers are not like teachers, they aren't there twenty-four hours a day. You've sort of got the feeling that you only get to see them for whatever lecture you have and then they are off and you never get to see them again and then you are stuck with all this work and I used to think how dreadful it would be. Like . . . I like the responsibility and freedom the teachers allow me here but I also like the fact that they are there. And I sort of got the feeling that if I go to university they won't be there. But , . . . um, it's not like that at all, you're human too (laughter). I thought that the lecturers got on really well with us. You know they treated us as adults even though we actually aren't . . . I felt comfortable at the university. I didn't feel out of place or anything like that. It didn't scare me like I thought it would. I don't know why most people think that university is for the most intelligent people, people with status or something like that. It's like school except that it's much bigger. There are a lot more people. People seem to be running around a lot more.

(Student researcher)

While students did enjoy coming to the university to perform a part of their project, this was a cause of some concern for a few of them. Some students required three different means of public transport to get to the campus, which clearly was inconvenient. There was an additional consideration that, according to one of the teachers, for some of these students, unaccustomed to great mobility outside their immediate area, going outside their suburb was a somewhat traumatic experience. One participating student, described by her teacher as one of the best students in the school, refused to find work placement outside her own suburb. According to the participating teacher, taking the bus to go to the city is an ordeal for some of these students. Significantly, one of the problems identified by the students in the first-year survey about the causes of lack of participation in university education was the geographical isolation of their suburb. Locating part of the project at the university was thus crucial to building bridges between these students and university life.

Benefits to the students

In the introduction to this chapter we outlined three principles guiding the development of this project. The first principle was that the students participating should benefit directly from the experience. Such benefit could best be illustrated by the following quotes from three students. The first student talked about how the project had benefited her.

> I didn't think that I would actually become so involved in the project. Like, I didn't actually know what it was about. Then I became very interested in it because I wanted to. The project benefited my friends, the up and coming seniors and whatever. I didn't think that I could handle the responsibility that was, no it wasn't forced on me, like there was so much responsibility. . . . Well, I thought it was very huge, even though there were a lot of people in it. It took a lot of time . . . and I didn't think that I could handle something that big. But I think that I came out pretty good and I'm pleased with the result. . . . I didn't think that I would be able to handle the work load . . . but with a lot of time planning, you know, certain things set around certain times? Yah, I did, and I was really pleased with myself. Well looking at the first draft of the final report, I sat there looking at it thinking, we couldn't have done this. It was the biggest thrill to look at it and say, 'That is mine!'. . . . It has boosted my self-esteem a lot. I'm very proud of myself for this and I feel very capable of undertaking a project so large, like, I'd be willing to do it again just to see if it would actually turn out like this again, but I feel very capable.
>
> (Student researcher)

Another student identified confidence as her primary gain.

> I've always been the type of person who sits in class and, if I don't understand I'll wait for the end of the class to, you know, ask the teacher. But ever since then I ask them during class. Cause I always used to worry what people would say. Oh, you're dumb or something, but it just doesn't worry me any more. . . . It [the project] made me realise that not all my doors are closed to uni [sic], that I do still have a chance and I'm going to do everything that I can to get there.

The third student discussed her new determination to go on to university.

I think it's got me to think of university more. Cause like, I, even six months ago I wanted to go to university but I didn't want to put the effort in to get good marks and I was only just sitting on sounds. But now I've picked my grades up to, like, Bs and As I've got and I've surprised myself too. And my marks are getting better and my Dad's a lot happier and everybody is a lot happier. . . . It's making me more confident about getting to the end of Year 12 and getting into university. And I really want to go now more than I thought I did.

(Student researcher)

Another benefit from the project arose from the fact that the nine students came from different ethnic backgrounds. The students appeared to gain understanding of each others' cultures. This is illustrated by the experience of one girl who said:

When I came here I just hang around the, you know, my people, the Vietnamese people, and I didn't really socialise with other people and I thought those people must be bad and all this. But now that I done the survey there's heaps of people that [are] real nice.

(Student researcher)

There were many other less tangible, yet important benefits to the students. In the conduct of the project, the students decided to raise some of the funds needed for the project by themselves. In order to provide prizes and gifts from regular participation in the Homework Centre and to assist students from the senior school to travel to the university in the University Shadowing Programme, the students wrote letters about the project to local community groups and businesses seeking their support. Similarly, when the main newspaper in the state carried less than complimentary reports about the problems in the school, the students involved in this project wrote letters to the editors defending the school, citing this project as an example of the interesting things that were happening at the school. Teachers at the school attributed the great confidence that the students showed in these actions as directly related to their involvement in the project.

The benefits from the project extended beyond the students directly involved in its conduct to others in the school community. In discussing the effect of the project on the culture of the school, Campbell *et al.* reported the following observations.

Until 1992 very few students were entering university. This has now changed with the introduction of affirmative action programs of special entry to the two nearest universities. For instance, among students completing year 12 in 1992, none entered university without special entry provisions, but 12 (15% of year 12 students) obtained university entrance under the affirmative action programs. Similarly, among students completing year 12 in 1993, two students entered university through mainstream access and five through special entry access. Once these students enter university through a special entry channel they achieve as well as students entering through the normal route. Of the above 12 students obtaining special entry in 1993, all have passed all of their subjects in their first academic year, with a grade point average of 4.8 (where 7 represents a high distinction and 4 a pass). Three have achieved so well that they have upgraded to more prestigious courses.

(Campbell *et al.* 1995: 9)

Issues in facilitating student action research

Students in this project were involved in developing action research skills at the same time as they were becoming more aware of the university culture. Unlike other research activities that often are carried out in the school, this project involved 'real' real-world problem that the students worked on. It generated localised knowledge and was followed by action. Thus, at the same time as the students were developing skills in research they were developing knowledge about aspects of their world and were changing aspects of their world.

Arguably the success of these students, often previously considered academically not capable, can be attributed to the connection of their research activity to their lived experience. Lived experience was considered a vital factor in changing the students' beliefs about themselves and their environment (Campbell *et al.* 1995). The students' experiences in this project affected their beliefs about their own potential and their career options, whereas prior exposure to public information (university brochures, television and newspaper advertisements and talks by guidance officers) might have been to no avail.

Some of the issues of facilitating student research as experienced in this project, in particular those related to the themes of this book, will now be considered.

Possibilities and limitations of partnership

In considering the issues of developing communities of professional inquiry or research partnerships (as discussed in Grundy's Chapter 3, this volume), considerable 'parity of esteem' can be said to have existed in this project. The university researchers relied enormously on the work of the teacher in the school and generally deferred to her decisions and judgements about how the research and activities were conducted in the school. Both the university researchers and the teacher respected the suggestions of the students in relation to the design and implementation of the student survey and the later school-based actions. The students' knowledge and understanding of the student population's needs and beliefs and attitudes were crucial to the success of the actions. On the other hand, the students showed a willingness to accept the assistance of their teacher and the university researchers in learning the basic processes of research. Thus, different members of the partnership contributed different forms of knowledge.

In their published reports, students wrote their own account of the project. These reports were intended for, and have been read by an audience including teachers and university researchers beyond the school and the university. Not only the students' actions but also their accounts of them have been accepted and respected by their teachers in the school, university staff and by others in the community.

In spite of the successful collaboration, it is naive to assume that all the players shared identical agendas. In her chapter, Grundy discussed the importance of recognising the 'distinctive interests of the partners'. This project was the result of collaboration between three groups of people, each with their own interests and expectations. The researchers from the university provided the initial idea of the project and its general aims. Their interest was at two levels: first, an equity concern to improve the access of young people from a socio-economically disadvantaged community to higher education, and second, a research concern to investigate the methodology of research using students as researchers. The teacher in the school saw the project as developing student academic skills and confidence and improving access to university. Although her contribution was fundamental to the success of the project, she was less concerned about the theoretical and research aspects of the project. For example, although she was invited to be involved in the writing process of this chapter from the beginning, she hesitated for a long time before accepting to join the writing team. Writing was not part of the role that she has constructed for herself in her job as a teacher. Further, the students were offered an opportunity to explore a genuine issue of possible interest to them, their peers and the school and, in the process, to enhance their research skills. Most of the students were interested in access to university. Although the teacher and the university researchers were not personally affected by the possibility of university access as the students were, they shared a commitment to social justice that included university access. We believe that this shared commitment of all partners to improving university access accounted for the success of the collaboration.

At times, however, there were some clashes between the interests of the three groups of participants. For example, students tended to be less interested in thinking about social issues on a larger scale and to be more task oriented than the university staff and their teacher. Also, during the period leading to the second session with the students at the university, the students expressed concern to their teacher about the planned programme of activities for the three days. They felt that some of the more general skill development sessions such as social action and group work during the first session were not of particular interest or use to them in doing the project. They were very anxious to get on task even before they received what the adults perceived as necessary training.

Further tension arose between the practical constraints of what it was possible to accomplish from the point of view of the university researchers and the students' idealism. For example, in planning the Buddy System between Year 8 and university students, the student group hoped that each of the eighty students in the school would be teamed up with a university student for the duration of the year. The structure of university courses and the distance between the university and the school, would have made this proposal impractical. Trying to renegotiate this with the students to target only some of the more needy students created a temporary loss of trust and goodwill between the students and their teacher and the rest of the research team. What was very heartening about this temporary disruption to project harmony was that we felt that the students had developed their own under-standing about the issues related to equity and equal opportunity and were willing to stand up and fight for them. Perhaps there is a reminder here that in PAR projects negotiations may lead at times to inevitable but not neces-sarily insurmountable tension between the different participants.

Another difficulty encountered in the process of collaboration related to the clash between the culture of the school and that of the university. In their school life, the students are accustomed to being told what to do and how to do it and it took considerable time for them to become used to accepting responsibility and making decisions for themselves in this project. In the early stages of the project, students were very hesitant to express their disagreements with the teachers and the university staff. As the project progressed they felt much freer to voice dissent. For example, at one stage in the project students complained about the communication links they had with the university. They objected to messages or information having to be passed through the deputy principal and requested that their teachers be the school contact for the project, since this made communication more effi-cient. Their freedom to express disappointment and to argue with the university team was a sign of a feeling of ownership of the project that they developed over time.

It was at times difficult to strike a balance between freedom and control, particularly in relation to ensuring that the students did not have a disheart-ening experience of failure. Some students expressed some concern about the issue of control and ownership of the project. University staff decided on the main research problem which was limited to equity issues by the conditions of funding. The students generally felt comfortable with this, probably because the research question was clearly focused on issues directly affecting them and their community. With other aspects of the project, however, some expressed concerns about ownership. For example, university staff and the teacher were concerned to challenge students only to a point where they could experience success and for this reason did influence the direction of the project in certain areas. As discussed above, most students accepted this but some were less comfortable about it.

Possibilities and limitations of action research with students

Students in this project were involved in a research project that involved understanding aspects of their school world and action to change that world for increased access to university study. They were thus involved in action research. In evaluating the use of action research with students, we shall revisit the characteristics of action research identified in Table 7.1, presented earlier.

First, at the commencement of the project, when students were asked to identify some reasons why few students from their school go to university, their first reaction was 'Because they are lazy'. At the conclusion of the first year's research, the reasons identified by the students for lack of participation in higher education reveal significant awareness of the role of the social context and environmental factors that make university consideration uncommon among these students. We believe that as a result of this project students have increased their awareness of the social conditions under which they live. This is in line with the characteristic of action research being *social*.

Second, the students themselves being both researchers and researched implied that the project was *participatory*. This was of great benefit to the students on many fronts. It allowed them to develop their self-esteem and research and writing skills useful for university study. It also allowed the development of their knowledge about the university by direct experience. Finally, the project gave the message to the rest of the school that young people from that school could accomplish success in intellectual and academic activities.

Third, this project has demonstrated that *collaboration* between university researchers, school teachers and students is possible. As argued above, this collaboration has its problems and limitations that need to be addressed.

Fourth, the effect of this project on changing school or university structures may have been limited. Student *emancipation* was in the form of enabling the students to take advantage of the existing provisions and structures that allowed students from their background to gain entry to the university. As discussed above, this emancipation was also demonstrated in the students' lobbying their teachers and community organisations to support aspects of their activities.

Fifth, the students have demonstrated that they have developed some *critical* understanding of aspects of the research process. They were able to reflect on the methods they used to gather information and to make some hypotheses on some of the results they obtained. The activities that the students planned and conducted have shown that they have understood the complex dimensions of the problem of access to university, and that they were determined to attempt to address these factors. Their activities involved reaching out to the students, their teachers, parents and community organisations.

Last, the project was limited in the amount of theorising of the social conditions and practices that these students live under. As we argued above, students in this project were very task orientated and have shown limited interest in theoretical discussion and deliberations. This project was limited in being integrated with other aspects of the students' school work.

The considerable success of the project was due to the support that it received from the school and in particular, the participating teacher. The school support was in the form of allocating time on the student and teacher's timetables for the work on this project. The teacher's support was in the form of day-to-day organisation of the project and her sustained enthusiasm and commitment over a three-year period. Considering the multitude of demands on student and staff time in today's high schools, this is significant support for the project. In spite of this support, however, the project, both in its methods and aims, has remained to a certain extent outside the mainstream activities of the school. Very few teachers were informed about the project. With the exception of tutoring in the Homework Centre and assistance in the production of the video, all the support that the students have received came from the participating teacher involved in the project. Credit for the students' work has not been given in any subject. As far as we know no subject in the school has attempted to discuss the aims and findings of this project with the students, nor has the teaching in any subject been changed to use the skills developed by the researching students.

NOTES

1   The project has been funded since 1992 by grants from the Faculty of Education, the Equity Board, and the Centre for Mathematics and Science Education, at the Queensland University of Technology.
2   Several people have contributed to the design and implementation of this project during the last five years. Special thanks to: Derek Bland, Jennifer Campbell, Kayleen Campbell, Alan Cook, Tom Cooper, Roger Slee, Sandra Taylor and Glenice Watson.
3   As a result of an amalgamation with another school, it now known as Glanala State High School.

4   AUSTUDY is an allowance provided by the federal government for students studying at high school and university based on the annual income of parents. In monetary terms it is equivalent to the unemployment benefit paid by the Department of the Social Security.

REFERENCES

Ainley, J. and Sheret, M. (1992) *Progress Through High School – A Study of Senior Secondary Schooling in NSW*, Australian Council for Educational Research.

Anderson, D. and Vervoorn, A. (1983) *Access to Privilege: Patterns of Participation in Australian Post-secondary Education*, Canberra: Australian National University Press.

Alder, C. and Sandor, D. (1990) 'Youth researching youth', *Youth Studies*, 9 (4): 38–42.

Atweh, W. and Burton, L. (1995) 'Students as researchers: rationale and critique', *British Educational Research Journal*, 21 (5): 561–75.

Bajar, R., Brennan, K., Deen, A., James, S., Nguyen, J., Nguyen, T., Owens, K., Peace, G., Rice, R., Rilatt, C., Strachan, K. and Tran, U. (1993) *Bridging the Gap: A University Access Project*, Brisbane: Centre for Mathematics and Science Education, Queensland University of Technology.

Bajar, R., Brennan, K., Do, M., Nguyen, J., and Tran, U. (directors) (1994) 'Bridging the gap' (video), available from Centre of Mathematics and Science Education, Locked Bag #2, Red Hill, Queensland, 4059, Australia.

Borowicz, B., Davis, N., James, S., Le, T., Nguyen, T., Owens, K., Pham, H., Strachan, K. and Wilkins, C. (1992) *Finding Out*, Brisbane: Centre for Mathematics and Science Education, Queensland University of Technology.

Campbell, J., Cook, A. and Dornan, L. (1995) 'Empowerment through student-initiated action research: exploring tertiary paths in a multiply disadvantaged school', *Education Research and Perspectives*, 22 (1): 80–9.

Cole, P. (1981) *Youth Participation Projects*, Melbourne: Victoria Institute of Secondary Education.

Coleman, J. (1972) *How Do The Young People Become Adults?* Centre for Social Organisation of Schools Report, no. 130, Baltimore: John Hopkins University.

Connel, R., Ashenden, D., Kessler, S. and Dowsett, G. (1982) *Making the Difference: Schools Families, and Social Division*, Sydney, Australia: Allen & Unwin.

Crane, P., Brannock, J., Ray, L., Campbell, J., Smeal, G. and Atweh, B. (1996) *Homelessness Among Young People in Australia: Early Intervention and Prevention*, report to the National Youth Affairs Research Scheme, Hobart: National Clearinghouse for Youth Studies.

Daws, L., Brannock, J. Brooker, R., Patton, W., Smeal, G. and Warren, S. (1995) *Young People's Perceptions and Attitudes to Sexual Violence*, report to the National Youth Affairs Research Scheme: National Clearing House for Youth Studies, Hobart.

Denzin, N. (1986) *The Research Act: A Theoretical Introduction to Sociological Methods*, New York: McGraw-Hill Book Co.

Department of Employment, Education and Training (1990) *A Fair Chance for All: Higher Education that's within Everyone's Reach*, Canberra: Australian Government Printing Service.

—— (1993) *National Report on Australian Higher Education*, Canberra: Australian Government Printing Service.

Freire, P. (1970) *Pedagogy of The Oppressed*, New York: Hodder & Hodder.

Giroux, H.A. (1986) 'Radical pedagogy and the politics of student voice', *Interchange*, 17 (1): 48–69.

Gitlin, A. (1990) 'Educative research, voice and school change', *Harvard Educational Review*, 60 (4): 443–66.

Goswami, D. and Stillman, P. (1987) *Reclaiming the Classroom: Teacher Research as An Agency for Change*, New Hampshire: Boynton Cook.

Henry, C. and Edwards, B. (1986) *Enduring a Lot: The Effect of The School System on Students with Non-English Speaking Backgrounds*, Canberra: Human Rights Commission.

Henry, M., Knight, J., Lingard, R. and Taylor, S. (1988) *Understanding Schooling: An Introductory Sociology of Australian Education*, Sydney, Australia: Routledge.

Herbart, C. (1989) *Talking of Silence*, Lewes, Sussex: Falmer.

Horton, A. and Zacharakis-Junz, J. (1987) *Empowering the Poor: Participatory Research as an Educational Tool*, paper presented at the Annual Meeting of the American Association for Adult and Continuing Education: Washington DC. (ERIC Document # ED287978), October.

Kemmis, S. and Carr, W. (1986) *Becoming Critical: Education, Knowledge and Action Research*, London: Falmer Press.

Knight, T. (1982) *Youth Advocacy Report: A Student Initiated Project*, a report to the Vandalism Task Force, Melbourne: Department of the Premier and Cabinet.

Middleton, M. (1991) Options report: Inala High School, unpublished document, Brisbane: Inala State High School.

Schwartz, J. (1988) 'The drudgery and the discovery: students as research partners', *English Journal*, 77 (2): 37–40.

Slee, R. (1988) *Education Action Research Report*, Melbourne, Australia: Good Shepherd Youth and Family Service.

Stenhouse, L. (1975) *Introduction to Curriculum Research and Development*, London: Heinemann.

Troyna, B. (1994) 'Blind Faith? Empowerment and educational research', *International Studies in Sociology of Education*, 4, 3–24.

Western, J. (1983) *Social Inequality in Australian Society*, Melbourne: Macmillan Company.

Part 4

PARTNERS SUPPORTING
SCHOOLS CHANGE

8

A JOURNEY INTO A LEARNING PARTNERSHIP

A university and a state system working together for curriculum change

Ian Macpherson, Tania Aspland, Bob Elliott, Christine Proudford, Leonie Shaw and Greg Thurlow

This chapter tells the story of a journey into a learning partnership involving a group of university researchers from Queensland University of Technology and a group of systemic personnel from the Effective Learning and Teaching Unit of the Queensland Department of Education.[1] It is a story whose events are part of an ongoing saga, so there is an unfinished quality about it. The story is set within the context of the State Education Department in Queensland, and more particularly within the Department's Effective Learning and Teaching Principles Statement (Queensland Department of Education 1994).

Antecedents of the learning partnership which began in 1994 are to be found in a number of smaller research efforts which focused very heavily on research as a collaborative relationship involving university and school personnel. These smaller efforts might be regarded by some as more valid examples of collaborative research than the learning partnership presented in this chapter. The focus of the story in this chapter involves the establishment and maintenance of a partnership which is a facilitating framework for university and schools personnel to research matters relating to effective learning and teaching at the school level. The partnership *per se* is not so much an example of collaborative research as it is a facilitating framework which supports collaborative efforts at the levels of critical inquiry and transformative action in various parts of a large system.

Such a focus does not lessen the significance of the story. In fact, we believe that such a focus strengthens the contribution which this story can make to the insights and understandings about collaborative work, because we are working at a level which traditionally is much closer to the levels of systemic policy making, and consequently to the sources which shape systemic cultures. Working directly with teachers is undoubtedly essential in talking about collaborative forms of research. However, to focus on these efforts alone is to deny the parallel necessity to collaborate at other levels in order to challenge and reconstruct (via hearing, listening to and taking account of teachers' voices) systemic hegemonies which continue to exhibit hierarchical and linear tendencies. We believe that our work is, in a sense, a conduit which allows teachers' voices to be heard and listened to in the heady corridors of policy making.

In telling the story, we want to be aware of the sorts of issues which Grundy raises in Chapter 3, this volume, about partnerships and change – 'Parity of esteem', 'distinctive interests of the partners', 'researching communities', 'understanding the industrial contexts of school-based researchers' and 'outlets for collaborative writing'. These are issues which we have met in the events leading to our story and we shall talk about them as this chapter draws to a close.

The story, then, is our living educational theory (see McNiff 1993, Whitehead 1989) about working together in developing a view of curriculum leadership for effective learning and teaching, and using this ever-evolving view to inform ongoing curriculum change through transformative action by teachers at the school level.

Context of the learning partnership

The principles of effective learning and teaching

The recently released *Principles of Effective Learning and Teaching* by the Queensland Department of Education (1994) reflect a commitment 'to ensuring that all students attending state schools are provided with the opportunity to obtain a comprehensive, balanced and equitable education' (p. 1). All five principles place a heavy emphasis on learning in the belief that the education alluded to above 'promotes the holistic development of each individual, and ensures that students are provided with opportunities to prepare them for their present and future lives' (*ibid.*).

The principles, developed in 1993, were derived from a review of exemplary practices in years P-12 across the state, and from an extensive literature review. The principles were developed collaboratively with approximately 200 teachers, and drafts were circulated to all state schools for comment during the developmental stage. The five principles are as follows:

- Effective learning and teaching is founded on an understanding of the learner.
- Effective learning and teaching requires active construction of meaning.
- Effective learning and teaching enhances and is enhanced by a supportive and challenging environment.

- Effective learning and teaching is enhanced through worthwhile learning partnerships.
- Effective learning and teaching shapes and responds to social and cultural contexts.

The rationale in developing the principles was to formulate a corporate position on learning and teaching which would draw attention to exemplary practices that would enhance learning and assist individual school communities in this task. They were designed to focus on the fact that effective learning and teaching is not a final state to be achieved but, rather, a way of thinking about learning and teaching so that continual improvement occurs. Similarly, they were designed to highlight the fact that the school is a learning community and learning refers to all members in the community. Thus, the principles were seen as underpinning teacher learning as much as student learning.

In 1994 a statement of the principles was distributed to all state schools together with a set of possible awareness-raising activities. In a letter to school principals, the Director General of Education indicated that every principal should take up these suggestions in order to introduce the principles into the school communities for which they were responsible. Schools reacted to this directive in diverse ways, and it is this diversity that we have tried to capture through our research.

For our story, the fourth principle of effective learning and teaching stated above is particularly relevant. Aspects of this principle include:

- Learners and teachers take time to reflect critically and creatively on their practices.
- School administrators, parents, caregivers, paraprofessionals, specialist support teachers and other members of the community participate in the learning–teaching process.

This chapter develops within the context of this principle and its accompanying aspects. It links with Stenhouse's (1975) well-known idea which asserts that teachers, in the end, will be central in changing curriculum by understanding the contexts within which it operates; it argues for a worthwhile learning partnership based on collaborative inquiry into the effective learning and teaching principles as an example of curriculum policy formulation and practice; and it sharpens the focus for this inquiry to curriculum leadership for effective learning and teaching.

It would appear that the processes associated with developing the *Principles of Effective Learning and Teaching* statement reflect Stenhouse's assertion. Here you have a set of principles which may be applied in a variety of mixes in the diverse range of learning settings across the system; and which emerged from an identification and recognition of already existing exemplary practice in teaching/learning settings.

There is also a claim which Fullan makes. He believes that 'connection with the wider environment is critical'. He says:

> For teachers and schools to be effective two things have to happen. First, individual moral purpose must be linked to a larger social good. Teachers still need to focus on making a difference with individual students, but they must also work on school-wide change to create the working conditions that will be most effective in helping all students learn. Teachers must look for opportunities to join forces with others, and must realise that they are part of a larger movement to develop a learning society through their work with students and parents. It is possible, indeed necessary, for teachers to act locally, while conceptualising their roles on a higher plane.
>
> (Fullan 1993: 38–9)

How effective learning and teaching might be understood by teachers who will change the world of the school through collaborative inquiry, how notions of curriculum leadership might sharpen the focus of such inquiry, and how action research, which is both critical and collaborative, might provide an overall approach for collaborative inquiry are important considerations in this chapter.

Antecedents of the learning partnership

Small-scale collaborative research studies (see Macpherson and Proudford, 1992; Aspland *et al.* 1993; Aspland *et al.* 1996) which focused on curriculum policy formulation, interpretation and implementation within the context of senior school curriculum policy provided one starting point for the establishment of the learning partnership. These studies attempted to celebrate the centrality of teachers in curriculum decision making and their voice on matters relating to curriculum policy formulation, interpretation and implementations was reported to policy makers at the systemic level.

With the arrival of the *Effective Learning and Teaching Principles* statement, personnel from the Effective Learning and Teaching Unit approached the university to explore possible ways of working together in the area of effective learning and teaching. Using our small-scale research studies as a basis, we entered into negotiations with personnel from the unit concerning possible collaborative working arrangements. Both the university and the unit made funds available to support work in 1994. And so it was that the birth of the collaborative research group took place.

While the proposed intentions of such a project were clear, and strong commitment to the project in place, the way forward remained problematic.

It became the source of anxiety and uncertainty in the formative stages of the project as we tried to articulate our interests in the project professionally and juggle the differing agendas that were significant at this stage. We had to be responsive to the emerging relations within the team – each member cautiously putting forward his/her claims while at the same time remaining sensitive to those of the other partners, particularly those who were entering the research field. In many ways such cautiousness prolonged the beginning phases of the study, but in the long term proved to be fruitful in establishing a positive collegial working ethos that continues to this day.

Two small-scale research studies provided a launching-pad for further investigation. *The Effective Learning and Teaching Principles* statement appeared to be eminently suited to provide a policy-type context for such investigation. An investigation which focused on its formulation at the system level, interpretation at the school level and implementation at the classroom level (as experienced and perceived by classroom teachers) would provide further insights about curriculum decision-making practices of systems, schools and teachers. Such insights would continue the attempts by systems, schools and teachers to work together in worthwhile learning partnerships with a view to the enhancement of effective learning and teaching. Such insights, we claimed, come powerfully and perceptively from the world of teachers, and it is teachers who, in the end, will change the world of the school. We believed that it is teachers who best understand the world of the school, and it follows that policy makers in the broader contexts of schools, systems and society should listen to the messages which their understandings bring to our processes of policy formulation, interpretation and implementation. We considered it important to explore how the *Effective Learning and Teaching Principles* statement had listened to teachers' messages and what the spin-offs have been in the daily lived experiences of teachers and learners in classrooms.

Giving birth to the learning partnership

And so we had a focus to begin work. We decided to investigate the processes of dissemination of, and subsequent practices associated with, the *Effective Learning and Teaching Principles* statement. In particular, the research was concerned with the extent to which teachers felt that their existing practices were in harmony with these principles; the extent to which the principles influenced their practice; and particular conditions that were conducive to changing practice to be more in keeping with the principles. In order to investigate these issues, two parallel projects were established.

Project A

This project focused on the levels of awareness and use of principles by teachers, managers and support personnel in a range of schools across the state. To this end, a questionnaire was developed and distributed to teachers in a range of different school types. Four rural high schools, four rural primary schools, ten provincial high schools, ten provincial primary schools, five metropolitan high schools and five metropolitan primary schools were included in the sample. Schools were selected to be representative of the various interests of the state system.

This project highlighted the facts that:

- There are significant variations between regions concerning the introduction and acceptance of the principles.
- While individual teachers reported awareness of the principles, considerable work is still required for them to consider the principles collaboratively.
- There are differences between the way males and females responded to the principles.

In general, the project indicated the need for curriculum leadership structures to be well established in order to infuse the principles into schools' practices.

Project B

This project consisted of in-depth studies in eight schools – including metropolitan, provincial and rural schools. Staff from each school (teachers and administrative staff) were interviewed in face-to-face situations in metropolitan contexts and through teleconferences for others. From the accounts of these interviews conclusions about factors which would promote acceptance of the principles and factors which facilitate educational change were identified.

With reference to the former category, it was concluded that a number of factors were significant. These included a recognition and acceptance of good practice, appropriate professional development programmes, promotion of collaborative efforts, linking of the principles with teachers' needs and curriculum leadership and a supportive community. In the latter category were factors such as a sense of ownership, facilitative styles of leadership, receptiveness to change and professional development.

In general, the study concluded that while the initiative and its documents had been useful in assisting a number of teachers to improve practice, the impact was even across schools and even within schools. In this sense, the fact that both projects highlighted the importance of leadership in schools is significant. The broad conclusions were based around five integrated themes.

1   *The language of the documents.* Concern was expressed that the documentation was couched in language which encouraged teachers to think of the principles in a competency framework, compared to a developmental framework. As a consequence they felt that each principle was to be mastered and, once mastered, could be put aside. Instead, the intention of the initiative was to encourage development of learning and teaching at all levels within the school. A more 'user friendly' document would have been appreciated.

2   *Schools as learning communities.* A general conclusion from both Project A and Project B was that schools did not see themselves as learning communities. In broad terms it may be concluded that strategies are needed which assist schools to adopt a more critical and developmental approach to their work and address the view that learning is applicable to all members of a school community – not just students.

3   *Leadership in schools.* These projects point to the need for leadership to be developed at all levels in the school. There is a need to move away from the view of leadership as management. What is required is a view of curriculum leadership which includes an holistic view of planning, strategies of assessment and reporting in terms of a well-constructed learning and development framework and a pedagogy which is continually being addressed.

4   *Prioritising initiatives.* Many schools reported that they were often inundated with a range of initiatives and found it difficult to integrate such initiatives into a coherent plan. Again this points to the need for leadership skills so that school staff can develop comprehensive and inclusive views of curriculum. At the same time, principals need to know the relative importance of different system initiatives.

5   *Conditions of development.* With all initiatives, time is a crucial factor and this is no exception. From this study it is clear that time is essential if perceptions and values are to be addressed. All studies on curriculum change point to the importance of available time in introducing change. In this sense, change must be conceived of in terms of altering perceptions, values and attitudes and not simply about doing things.

Pausing to reflect on the learning partnership so far

In both the antecedent research studies and in the 1994 study, our research emphasis was working *with* teachers not *on* teachers. Teachers were researching with us on matters of mutual professional interest. All three studies had teachers participating with us in collecting, analysing and reporting data. From the antecedent study in 1993 (Aspland *et al.* 1993: 27) we concluded that:

- The collaborative nature of the approaches used in the study engendered an interest in participation in terms of both the collection and interpretation of data.
- The opportunities provided for group sessions contributed to the analysis and validation of data, to the professional development of participants and to the transmission of significant messages to administrative personnel.
- The use of teachers' voices conveyed significant messages about their curriculum decision making to administrative personnel.
- The use of negotiation with the participants and stakeholders contributed to determining further investigations and action.

It was at this point that we considered it important to inform our emerging living educational theory of working collaboratively with a review of relevant literature (Beck and Black 1991; Campbell 1988; Feldman 1993; Knight *et al.* 1992; Kyle and McCutcheon 1984; Levin 1993; Lieberman 1992; Miller 1992; Oakes *et al.* 1986), which found that there can be limitations as well as benefits in collaborative forms of research. Johnston, M. (1990) argues that all projects are not suited to the collaborative approach, nor is less collaborative research necessarily less adequate.

We also discovered that there are benefits to be achieved from collaborative research that focused on practical problems which are experienced and defined by teachers, for it has the ability to produce prolific results, not only for the improvement of practice, but also more productive development of curriculum theory itself (Kyle and McCutcheon 1984). Collaboration between teachers and researchers promotes engagement in critical thinking and practice, thus constructing knowledge and cultivating the participants' capacity to structure and appropriate their knowledge and understandings (Beck and Black 1991). This, therefore, increases the credibility of the interpretations of the data as all participants contribute to the interpretations (Johnston, M. 1990).

Collaborative inquiry, we found, leads to improved professional performance of university researchers and school teachers. It also has other unanticipated benefits. These include increased awareness of effective instructional practices, sharing ideas among group members, giving teachers a voice to communicate significant ideas and a supportive atmosphere for problem solving regarding instructional challenges (Aspland *et al.* 1993; Oakes *et al.* 1986; Stevens *et al.* 1992). Collaborative procedures can lead to a wide range of questions about educational theory and practice becoming the subject of systematic inquiry (Kyle and McCutcheon 1984). Writing about collaboration is much easier than doing collaborative research (Levin 1993).

From this brief review, we summarised the limitations of collaborative inquiry as follows: ethical concerns; moral and political problems; value conflicts; issues of power and authority; democratic participation; inequalities in the actual circumstances of individual involvement and in the process itself; and contradictions and role dilemmas when teachers come to suspect 'a hidden agenda' behind the researchers' self-proclaimed promise of a teacher-defined and teacher-directed approach to professional development. (These are elaborated below.) Consequently, differences in perspective between the researchers and the teachers could lead to a context which embodies difficulties, dilemmas and misinterpretations, whilst attempting to relate research as a process of inquiry to the needs and concerns of teachers.

We noted in our reading that, in more recent years, university researchers were moving towards viewing teachers as participants in research rather than seeing them as subjects. (Feldman 1993). The teachers' reflections in our 1993 study (see Aspland *et al.* 1996) emphasise their appreciation of this change in the relationship between the university researchers and the teachers and of the researchers' attitude concerning the object and purpose of the research. Research by Day (1991) supports the teachers' reflections, and he points out that research and staff development can be one and the same enterprise, and that it can be practical and emancipatory for all participants if it follows a 'partnership model'.

The teachers in our 1993 study felt that is was significant that they were able to interact with others and to be given the opportunity for valuable reflection. Stevens *et al.* (1992) see this as an unexpected benefit of collaborative inquiry. It was also noted in the reflections that understanding about the need to value ideas of other individuals when developing policy was also reinforced. Feldman (1993) as well as Oakes *et al.* (1986) support this by quoting a definition by Tikunoff *et al.* (1979) who claim that 'collaboration recognises and utilises the insights and skills provided by each participants' (quoted in Oakes *et al.* 1986: 547).

Power and authority, as argued by Miller (1992), are issues which tend to challenge 'the fit' of some research projects with the collaborative inquiry mode. The teachers' reflections showed that the administrative management styles and the politics at play between the different organisations can impact on a collaborative inquiry approach.

Not all written reflections were positive ones regarding the 1993 study. The responses stated that their understandings were already at a very high level because of their involvement in curriculum decision making at their school. It was stated that the other schools in the project were not operating at the same level of curriculum decision making for teachers.

However, the teachers appreciated that they were not tied to the constraints of an established agenda of research hypotheses. Rather, they valued the flexibility achieved through an agenda of questions and concerns, as advocated by Oakes *et al.* (1986), which often changed as different levels of working consensus were reached. This type of feedback was useful in reshaping our work in the following year.

The 1994 study (Projects A and B) proved valuable in developing collaborative links between the Effective Learning and Teaching Unit in the Queensland State Education Department and the Curriculum Decision-Making Research Concentration at Queensland University of Technology. It formed the basis of applications for funded collaborative research projects focusing on curriculum leadership to facilitate effective learning and teaching in schools and the basis for a further study in 1995 which aimed to develop a model of curriculum leadership for effective learning and teaching.

But reviewing literature and documenting reflections were insufficient in themselves to take our living educational theory further. We needed to theorise about what we were focusing on and how we were working together. We pondered for some time as to what was happening within the partnership as well as the project, and why it was happening in particular ways. It was from this theorising that we conceptualised an approach to collaborative research and a view of curriculum leadership for effective learning and teaching.

Conceptualising an approach to collaborative research: critical collaborative action research

From the reflections presented above, we are now at liberty to argue that the collaborative approach to research used in the three studies has the potential to assist personnel at systemic and school levels to better understand and transform the processes associated with curriculum policy formulation, interpretation and implementation. Central to this is our reliance on and faith in the use of teachers' voices to convey powerful messages to system and school-level personnel. The Stenhouse quote with which we began: 'It is teachers who, in the end, will change the world of the school by understanding it' (Stenhouse 1975), perhaps needs to be extended to read: 'It is everyone associated with schools who, in the end, will change the world of the school by understanding it critically, collaboratively and transformatively.'

The collaborative research approach to which we are actively committed has been conceptualised as *critical collaborative action research* because it is research which had an emancipatory intent of empowering its participants, not just to understand their social reality within their school settings, but to change it (Smith 1993) in ways that are personally meaningful at differing levels to all participants. Based on the lessons learnt here, we were proposing that critical collaborative research could be characterised in the following ways:

- *Collaborative*. Practitioners and researchers engaged in collaborative action work together as a group continually defining and redefining the purposes of the research;
- *Critical*. Underlying assumptions and beliefs are acknowledged; curriculum trends, policies and practices are seen to be problematic and contestable; and further action is tied to critical frameworks which focus on social justice and empowerment for all.
- *Action-oriented*. It demands direct involvement and influence from the real world experience of practitioners where the problems of practice are framed, possible solutions are determined, solutions are enacted, and results are reviewed, reflected upon and reconstructed.
- *Honest*. Generating high levels of trust and relationship building amongst all participants is essential.
- *Contributory*. Roles should be negotiated not imposed and responsibilities are clearly defined and self determined.
- *Communicative*. Interaction among group members should occur frequently.
- *Real*. Realistic expectations are set regarding time lines, and what's possible in particular contexts.
- *Equitable*. Power and authority over design, process, and outcomes are shared.
- *Meaningful*. Teachers are valued as persons not as research objects, they are actively involved in the research process, they can tell their story.
- *Representative*. Acknowledgment of the professional, social and emotional needs of teachers takes place.
- *Sustained*. Time for reflection and reconstruction is an integral feature of the process.
- *Transformative*. Empowerment to make change happen, and not just to explain or understand it, is of utmost importance.

(Aspland *et al*. 1996)

As we entered the next phase of the alliance, we called on these characteristics to be guiding principles for continuing the learning partnership which was seeking to understand the complexity of factors which impact on teachers as they try to live out in their classrooms the implications of policies and curriculum statements associated with effective learning and teaching.

If research aims to interpret and reflect upon such lived experiences, as well as upon the beliefs and understandings of teachers, then, the collaborative approach, in the form of critical collaborative action research, can be argued as the way to proceed. It offers to teachers, as researchers, opportunities to tell stories of their experiences in ways that inform and transform future practices in a critical and enlightening manner.

Research partnerships that adopt these principles of procedure have the potential for teachers to feel empowered as curriculum practitioners and leaders in their respective professional work contexts by:

- accessing opportunities to contest current trends, policies and imperatives at national, state and systemic levels which are seemingly centralising control over curriculum decision making;
- making connections with significant others in planning for transformative action at local and broader levels of context;
- engaging in research which allows them, within a collegial community to critique their practice, transform their work and be accountable for their actions.

Within this approach to collaborative inquiry, research methodologies became very much associated with research relationships so that teachers' voices could ultimately be heard in conveying messages. To strengthen this relationship, and as teachers' stories became central to the research community, we decided in 1995 to enhance our action research, by adopting narrative methodologies to elicit teachers' views about curriculum leadership for effective learning and teaching.

A range of authors have successfully incorporated narratives as a central feature in the analysis of teachers' professional knowledge (Clandinin 1985; Clandinin and Connelly 1988, 1990, 1992; Johnston, M. 1990; Johnston, S. 1988, 1990; Miller 1992; Paley 1990). Narratives are the most successful way to access teachers' thinking about their practice (Carter 1993) for teachers are best positioned to know their practice. Teaching episodes, such as the ones under investigation here, are reported as 'narratives in action', expressions of themselves and their thinking in a particular situation (Clandinin and Connelly 1985: 195).

Based on Gough's recent work (1994), we have begun trialling an innovative way of interpreting narrative as 'fiction'. This may prove more useful in research inquiries of this nature, for it offers to the research community greater opportunity to generate links between existing practices or 'present reality' and 'past or future possibilities' that have emerged or are likely to emerge in teachers' work (Gough 1994: 47). These opportunities, it is contended here, are likely to be more enriching than the simple interpretation of narrative which traditionally has been arrived at through processes of reflection and reflexivity, processes that sometimes fall short of the proactive thinking that is central to informative research. Moreover, the specific development of the narrative advocated by Gough (1994) proposes that the use of fiction brings to the research context a 'diffracting lens' — a phenomenon that is useful in the reconstruction of teachers' curriculum thinking.

In 1995, we invited teachers in four schools (two primary and two secondary) to participate in the writing of narratives, engaging in follow-up conversations, collaborating in analysing the narratives and eliciting themes which will contribute to our tentative model of curriculum leadership for effective learning and teaching. Teachers enthusiastically participated in each of these phases and found it a worthwhile experience, both professionally and personally.

While this work was proceeding as a negotiated action emanating from our earlier work in 1994, we were also working together in developing an application for an Australian Research Council (ARC) Collaborative Research Grant to support our ongoing work in 1996 and 1997. Happily, we were successful in receiving this grant, and currently we are feverishly gearing up for the next two years.

As the collaborative inquiry continues in 1996 and 1997, we are further developing our principles guiding critical collaborative action research as one way of engaging in collaborative inquiry which will be further inform by extending the project to include multi-method methodologies (Brewer and Hunter 1992) at a system-wide and at site-specific levels. We aim to elaborate our conceptions of curriculum leadership for effective learning and teaching and to implement actions which are appropriate for the ongoing empowerment of teachers and learners.

Conceptualising curriculum leadership for effective learning and teaching

Our work to date (which, remember, began back in 1992!) has brought us to the point where we want to continue theorising about curriculum leadership. We are keen to develop a view of curriculum leadership which is empowering for teachers and transforming for their curriculum practice. The notion of curriculum leadership is becoming the substantive focus for our work, and it is a focus which has developed as part of our living educational theory. It has not been something which has been imposed upon our work. A background for this view was needed, and so we returned to further reviewing of literature and theorising our ideas. This theorising is outlined in the following paragraphs.

Leadership is well recognised as a key phenomenon in considering how organisational priorities can be realised in a diverse range of settings, including education and curriculum (Sergiovanni 1984). Recent curriculum research has indicated that there is much to be gained by viewing a curriculum leader as anyone interested in improving the current situation, and monitoring, improving, and implementing curriculum changes (Alberta Department of Education 1992; Hannay and Seller 1991). However, real processes of curriculum leadership in schools are complex, subtle, incorporate many different power forces and can be exclusive to the educator who wishes to be a curriculum leader (Cairns 1981; Kee 1993; McIntyre 1984). This is due, in part, to the limited voice teachers have at present (Hannay and Seller 1991). Although the research and theory in the field of curriculum has long had a rich conceptual dialogue (see, for example, Schwab 1969), there remains little evidence that this dialogue has affected school practices (Harris 1986). Teachers seeking to exercise curriculum leadership in the classroom often have an understanding of professional phenomena in limited terms framed by inadequate discourses and inappropriate theories (Elliott and Calderhead 1993; Hannay and Seller 1991). When this occurs, it is likely that participants in the processes have views of curriculum leadership framed by technologies of management, administration and power rather than framed by the human context of their work. This is the way leadership has been defined in school contexts, and this is the view which is supported by the literature which addresses curriculum leadership as an issue for principals and administrators (see, for example, Bailey 1990). Our continuing collaborative inquiry is seeking to identify those social and professional preconditions that are necessary for the development of curriculum leadership that facilitates effective learning and teaching and to identify those processes that assist participants to move towards adopting personal theories which incorporate such ideas.

The articulation of a living educational theory about curriculum leadership (Whitehead 1989) is leading to the development of a model of curriculum leadership that will hopefully facilitate effective learning and teaching in schools. Generating a living educational theory has called on us as participants to produce descriptions and explanations of our own development in their professional work in education (McNiff 1993; McNiff *et al.* 1992; Whitehead 1989). In the present instance, the living educational theory has been the participants' personal theories of curriculum leadership. These personal models, or living educational theories, have been converted into the beginnings of a model of curriculum leadership. Such a model extends curriculum theory and professional knowledge about curriculum leadership. It will, therefore, be of value to both partners – to the university, in terms of curriculum studies as a field of inquiry in higher education programmes; and to the State Department of Education, in terms of improving curriculum practice as it relates to effective learning and teaching. In addition, our work will be of value to teachers and, most importantly, to students. It will provide the basis for the empowerment of teachers as curriculum leaders who see their role in terms of leaders leading learning. This focus on learning is a national priority in terms of improving the effectiveness of Australian schools, which in turn, benefits students by enhancing the quality of education that they presently enjoy.

Our hopes for work in 1996 and 1997 assume that abstracted theories of curriculum, leadership or current curriculum leadership *per se*, will not shape curriculum leadership practice. To date, literature within curriculum as a field of inquiry has centred on curriculum, leadership and curriculum leadership from an organisational perspective (e.g., Brady 1992; Chapman 1990; Glatthorn 1987; Havelock 1973; Huberman 1973; Morrish 1978; Huberman and Miles 1984; Marsh 1988a, b; Owens 1987). It has only been in more recent times that there has been a discernible shift to a focus on their personal – the teacher as an individual in the pursuit of professional practice as a curriculum practitioner (Clandinin and Connelly 1992; Connelly and Clandinin 1988; Elliot, R. G. *et al.* 1993; Fullan 1992a, b; Fullan and Hargreaves 1992; Gitlin 1992; Goodson 1992; Hargreaves and Fullan 1992; Johnston *et al.* 1991; Rudduck 1991; Ross *et al.* 1992; Simon 1992). It is a more person-oriented and inside-out perspective of curriculum and of the teacher as a curriculum practitioner which theoretically informs the developing understanding and living educational theory of curriculum leadership in this inquiry.

Thus, our efforts are seeking to understand curriculum leadership within curriculum studies as a field of inquiry and to guide a system's support of its teachers as curriculum leaders from an inside-out rather than from a top-down perspective of policy shaping, interpretation and implementation. We are taking a critical, yet constructive perspective of policy formulation (see Pinar 1992; Smith 1993).

Recent government reports (for example, the Finn Review Committee 1991), draw attention to the fact that this country's economic and social future is dependent on the quality of schooling. Underlying this quality is the nature of leadership that exists in school settings. National agendas clearly point to changing learning and teaching curriculum initiatives, particularly those highlighting key learning areas and their profiles and performance standards. Our continuing investigations will provide information on ways in which curriculum leadership can be improved to ensure such initiatives are translated into appropriate practice in school sites.

There is a clear desire by most teachers to adopt these national initiatives. What is not clear for them, however, is how to translate policy into practice in current settings so that they can adopt the role of leaders of learning and leaders of learners. To this end, our ongoing work will seek to identify aspects of the school curriculum environments (namely, the social contexts, the organisational structures, school curriculum frameworks) which interact with those factors which may facilitate opportunities for teachers to engage in curriculum leadership practices. It is as we seek to clarify our own understandings about curriculum leadership that we will develop ways of further investigating curriculum leadership for effective learning and teaching and of further enacting (by teachers), supporting and sustaining (by systems and other agencies) curriculum leadership practices.

Identifying what we have become more aware of

It is always useful to reflect on experiences and to elicit growth points from them (for example, see Macpherson *et al.* 1994). Already in this story, we have identified progress points upon which further investigations and actions have been built, keeping very much in mind the overall action research approach within which our work is situated.

In telling our story, we have probably been using the action research cycle more implicitly than explicitly. Nevertheless, we have tried to highlight some aspects which we value strongly and feel committed to. These aspects are summarised in the following statements:

- We are working with people as partners and not on people in our research efforts.
- We are developing substantive and procedural agendas out of our working together and our mutual understanding of work contexts and priorities.
- The focus of our ongoing work is discussed and negotiated rather than imposed from without or from the perspective of one party in the learning partnership – we are making connections with each other.
- Our efforts endeavour to transcend an exclusive emphasis on technical and practical matters and to incorporate critical and emancipatory perspectives through reviewing of literature, theorising our work and building an ever-evolving living education theory about both the substance and the processes of our work.
- We are aware of the need to sustain the learning partnership by paying attention to such details as principles and procedures which will facilitate and strengthen our partnership and hopefully avoid (or at least mitigate the effect of) tensions and dilemmas which are inevitable in any relationship.
- We have a commitment to engage in research as a relationship (a learning partnership) which has benefits for all parties in the partnership (action components, therefore, are most important as part of our ongoing work).
- We are looking for ways of documenting our work, both within the boundaries of the project and in broader professional forums in ways that are ethically sensitive to such issues as the handling of 'tricky' data and intellectual property.

These statements reflect much of what Grundy identifies in Chapter 3, this volume, about partnerships and change in terms of research as relationships.

They are signposts which we cannot ignore as we move ahead. By stopping and reading the signposts, we have continued our journey with few (and hopefully fewer) breakdowns.

On pausing to read these rather broad signposts, we have also engaged in a self-renewing process asking ourselves: 'What have we become more aware of as we have established and sought to maintain the learning partnership?' Here are some of the things we have learned, and are continuing to learn about:

About collaborative inquiry

- Collaboration is not easy. Sustaining collaboration is even more difficult.
- Expectations of the different partners may not always be shared in terms of the substantive and the procedural elements of a collaborative investigation.
- Different institutional constraints and pressures need to be understood through regular discussion, and built into plans for proceeding.
- Levels of collaboration within each set of partners and between both sets of partners need to be clarified and reconstructed to address changing situations.
- Accountability and intellectual property issues need to be considered up-front in order to avoid tensions and debates which could damage partnerships.
- The sorts of characteristics about critical collaborative action research outlined earlier cannot be assumed – they have to be worked on consciously and deliberately, and they must permeate all aspects of coordinating and participating in the project.

About curriculum leadership for effective learning and teaching

- You may expect too much to happen too soon. For example, an emerging model of curriculum leadership might have been expected by the end of 1995, but the difficulties associated with trying to reach workable consensus quickly need to be recognised. A set of ideas that may be the ingredients of a model of curriculum leadership are probably easier to identify than the articulation of a workable model at this stage.
- The overall methodological framework must not be forgotten, and it is easy to be bogged down with the frustrations of the present, and to forget that the present is only part of a bigger picture. Partners must remind themselves that they are in it for the long haul, and that in two years' time, if we are at the same point that we are now, then the project

will have failed. There still may not even be definite and conclusive answers then – rather there may be new questions!

- Everyone who facilitates learning is a curriculum leader. We are quite clear that it is enabled by certain qualities within a school curriculum environment (which has three elements at least), and that there are a number of mediating factors which work on the individual psychologies of teachers which give them a predisposition to engage in curriculum leadership practices (which we see as having two categories). The dynamic and ongoing interplays among these various elements, factors and practices need to be captured in an articulated model of curriculum leadership which can then be used as a tool to provide broad-brush pictures of curriculum leadership as well as detailed and specific pictures of patterns of and possibilities for curriculum leadership at particular school sites. The tool has investigative as well as action-oriented aspects to it. It provides opportunities to be critically reflective of the what is and to be critically informed and empowered to transform the roles and practices associated with curriculum leadership.

About future collaborative inquiry and action

- It takes a long time to establish a collaborative working relationship.
- In ongoing work, all partners must ensure that something worthwhile is being gained from the collaboration – one partner should not be seen to be getting all the benefits. The ongoing dilemmas associated with the balance of theory and practice, the acceptance or the contestation of policies and the complexities of teachers' work provide a necessary context for considering outcomes.
- Ongoing work needs to documented and advocated in appropriate forums, in order to address the dilemmas and complexities alluded to above in meaningful and constructive ways.
- Ongoing work should increasingly be seen as having an impact upon policy and practice, which in a sense advocates and legitimises action research approaches.
- Ongoing work needs to have both investigative and action components, if it is to satisfy all partners, and if it is to have an impact upon the transformation of curriculum practice by teachers who see themselves to be empowered curriculum leaders.
- An emphasis on 'institutionalising' change processes associated with action research approaches is important so that they will be supported after research funding is finished. This could occur, for example, with the partnership having a culture which seeks further collaborative funding.

Concluding for now . . .

On reflection, our experiences upon which this story is based affirm the usefulness of action research approaches as a basis for working together for curriculum change. These approaches, taking account of the things we have been made more aware of should, we believe, be both critical and collaborative and reflect those characteristics which we have identified. Then, teachers have the chance to be curriculum leaders who are empowered to contest existing trends and policies, to collaborate in planning for transformative action and to reconstruct their roles and practices in ways that will impact on continuing curriculum change.

This, then, is our story, and our living educational theory to date. Our account of the events is probably an imperfect one, and certainly one which is incomplete! Our learning partnership is currently involving two parties – university and systemic personnel. As events unfold, the partnership will grow, new challenges will emerge and exciting opportunities will become available in order to expand and refine our living educational theory about collaborative ways of approaching curriculum change and about curriculum leadership for effective learning and teaching.

The journey and the story will continue. You will hear from us again!

NOTE

1   While the print version of the story was largely constructed by Tania Aspland and Ian Macpherson, it was developed in consultation with all partners. It is, then, the story of the six people who formed the partnership.

REFERENCES

Alberta Department of Education (1992) *Curriculum Leadership and The Principalship* (report no. ISBN–0–7732–1114–1), Edmonton: Calgary Board of Education (ERIC Document Reproduction Service No. ED 364 953).

Aspland, T., Macpherson, I. and Proudford, C. (1993) 'Teachers' curriculum decision-making practices at the classroom level: implication for curriculum policy formulation at the system level', paper presented at the Australian Association of Research in Education Annual Conference, Fremantle, West Australia.

Aspland, T., Macpherson, I., Proudford, C. and Whitmore, L. (1996) 'Critical collaborative action research as a means of curriculum inquiry and empowerment', *Educational Action Research* 6 (2): 93–104.

Bailey, G. D. (1990) 'How to improve curriculum leadership – twelve tenets', *Tips for Principals from NASSP*, Reston, Va: National Association of Secondary School Principals.

Beck, D. and Black, K. (1991) 'Redefining research relationships: two heads are better than one', *The Alberta Journal of Educational Research*, 37 (2): 133–40.

Brady, L. (1992) *Curriculum Development*, 4th edn, Sydney: Prentice Hall.

Brewer, J. and Hunter, A. (1992) *Multimethod Research: A Synthesis of Styles*, Newberry Park, California: Sage.

Cairns, G.L. (1981) *The Role of The Principal in School-based Curriculum Development in Tasmanian High Schools*, Armidale, NSW: University of New England.

Campbell, D. (1988) 'Collaboration and contradiction in a research and staff development project', *Teachers' College Record*, 90 (1): 99–121.

Carter, K. (1993) 'The place of story in the study of teaching and teacher education', *Educational Researcher*, 22 (1): 5–12, 18.

Chapman, J. (ed.) (1990) *School-based Decision-making and Management*, London: Falmer Press.

Clandinin, D. J. (1985) 'Personal practical knowledge: a study of teachers' classroom images', *Curriculum Inquiry*, 15 (4): 361–8.

Clandinin, D. J. and Connelly, F. M. (1985) 'Personal practical knowledge and the modes of knowing: relevance for teaching and learning', in Eisner, E. (ed.) *Learning and Teaching Ways of Knowing: Eighty-fourth Yearbook of the National Society for the Study of Education, Part II*, Chicago, Illinois: University of Chicago Press, pp. 174–98.

—— (1988) 'Studying teachers' knowledge of classrooms: collaborative research, ethics, and the negotiation of narrative', *The Journal of Educational Thought*, 22 (2a): 269–82.

—— (1990) 'Narrative experience and the study of curriculum', *Cambridge Journal of Education*, 20 (3): 141–255.

—— (1992) 'Teacher as curriculum maker', in Jackson, P. (ed.) *Handbook of Research on Curriculum*, New York: American Educational Research Association, pp. 363–401.

Connelly, F. M. and Clandinin, J. (1988) *Teachers as Curriculum Planners*, New York: Teachers' College Press.

Day, C. (1991) 'Roles and relationships in qualitative research on teachers' thinking: a reconsideration', *Teaching and Teacher Education*, 7 (5/6): 537–47.

Elliott, R. G. and Calderhead, J. (1993) 'Mentoring for teacher development: possibilities and caveats', in McIntyre, D., Hagger, H. and Wilkin, M. (eds) *Mentoring: Perspectives on School-based Teacher Education*, London: Kogan Page, pp. 166–89.

Elliott, R., Aspland, T., Johnston, S., Macpherson, I., Proudford, C. and Thomas, H. (1993) 'Review of curriculum studies and of teaching curriculum studies in higher education' (unpublished manuscript), Brisbane, Queensland University of Technology, School of Curriculum and Professional Studies.

Feldman, A. (1993) 'Promoting equitable collaboration between university researchers and school teachers', *Qualitative Studies in Education*, 6 (4): 341–57.

Finn Review Committee (1991) *Review of Young People's Participation in Postcompulsory Education and Training*, Melbourne: Australian Education Council.

Fullan, M. (1992a) *Successful School Improvement*, Buckingham: Open University Press.

—— (1992b) *The New Meaning of Educational Change*, 2nd edn, New York: Teachers College Press and OISE Press.

—— (1993) *Change Forces: Probing the Depths of Educational Reform*, London: Falmer Press.

Fullan, M. and Hargreaves, A. (eds) (1992) *Teacher Development and Educational Change*, London: The Falmer Press.

160

Gitlin, A. (1992) *Teachers' Voices for School Change: An Introduction to Educative Research*, London: Routledge.

Glatthorn, A. (1987) *Curriculum Leadership*, Glenview, Illinois: Scott, Foresman and Company.

Goodson, I. (ed.) (1992) *Studying Teachers' Lives*, New York: Teachers' College Press.

Gough, N. (1994) 'Narration, reflection, diffraction: aspects of fiction in educational inquiry', *The Australian Educational Researcher*, 21 (3): 47–76.

Hannay, L. M. and Seller, W. (1991) 'The curriculum leadership role in facilitating curriculum deliberation', *Journal of Curriculum and Supervision*, 6: 340–57.

Hargreaves, A., and Fullan, M. (eds) (1992) *Understanding teacher development*, New York: Teachers' College Press.

Harris, I. B. (1986) 'Communicating the character of deliberation', *Journal of Curriculum Studies*, 18: 115–32.

Havelock, R.G. (1973) *The Change Agent's Guide to Innovation in Education*, Englewood Cliffs: Educational Technology Publications.

Huberman, A. M. (1973) *Understanding Change in Education: An Introduction*, Paris: UNESCO.

Huberman, A. M. and Miles, M.B. (1984) *Innovation Up Close: How School Improvement Works*, New York: Plenum Press.

Johnston, M. (1990) 'Experience and reflections on collaborative research', *Qualitative Studies in Education*, 3 (2): 173–83.

Johnston, S. (1988) 'Focusing on the person in the study of curriculum in teacher education', *Journal of Education for Teaching*, 14 (3): 215–23.

—— (1990) 'Understanding curriculum decision-making through teacher images', *Journal of Curriculum Studies*, 22 (5): 463–71.

Johnston, S., Macpherson, I. and Spooner, A. (1991) 'Towards a research agenda in curriculum decision-making' (unpublished manuscript), Brisbane, Queensland University of Technology, School of Curriculum and Professional Studies.

Kee, K. N. (1993) *Teachers' Response to School-based Curriculum Development*, Clayton, Vic: Monash University.

Knight, S., Wiseman, D. and Smith, C. (1992) 'The reflectivity–activity dilemma in school–university partnerships', *Journal of Teacher Education*, 43 (3): 269–77.

Kyle, D. and McCutcheon, G. (1984) 'Collaborative research: development and issues', *Journal of Curriculum Studies*, 16 (2): 173–9.

Levin, B. (1993) 'Collaborative research in and with organisations', *Qualitative Studies in Education*, 6 (4): 331–40.

Lieberman, A. (1992) 'The meaning of scholarly activity and the building of community', *Educational Researcher*, August/September, 5–12.

Macpherson, I. and Proudford, C. (1992) 'Empowering teachers for changed curriculum practice at the classroom level: an inside-out perspective from downunder', paper presented at the Bergamo Conference: Curriculum Theory and Classroom Practice, Dayton, Ohio, April.

Macpherson, I., Trost, R., Gorman, S., Shepherd, J. and Arcodia, C. (1994) 'Collaborative action research: lessons learned from a Queensland example', paper presented at the Australian Association for Research in Education Annual Conference, Newcastle, Australia, November.

Marsh, C. J. (1988a) *Curriculum: Practices and Issues*, 2nd edn, Sydney: McGraw Hill.

—— (1988b) *Spotlight on School Improvement*, Sydney: Allen & Unwin.

McIntyre, J. S. (1984) *Subject Coordination in Victorian State Secondary Schools: Case Studies of Subject Coordination during Times of Change*, Melbourne: Monash University.

McNiff, J. (1993) *Teaching as Learning*, London: Routledge.

McNiff, J., Whitehead, J. and Laidlaw, M. (1992) *Creating A Good Social Order through Action Research*, Dorset: Hyde Publications.

Miller, J. (1992) 'Exploring power and authority issues in a collaborative research project', *Theory into Practice*, 31 (2): 165–72.

Morrish, I. (1978) *Aspects of Educational Change*, London: George Allen & Unwin.

Oakes, J., Hare, S. and Sirotnik, K. (1986) 'Collaborative inquiry: a congenial paradigm in a cantankerous world', *Teachers' College Record*, 87: 545–61.

Owens, R.G. (1987) *Organizational Behaviour in Education* (3rd ed.), London: Prentice Hall.

Paley, V.G. (1990) *The Boy Who Would Be a Helicopter: The Uses of Storytelling in the Classroom*, Cambridge, MA: Harvard University Press.

Pinar, W. (1992) 'Dreamt into existence by others: curriculum theory and school reform', *Theory into Practice*, 31 (3): 228–35.

Queensland Department of Education (1994) *Principles of effective learning and teaching*, Brisbane, Queensland: Publishing Services for the Studies Directorate.

Ross, E. W., Cornett, J. W. and McCutcheon, G. (1992) *Teacher Personal Theorising: Connecting Curriculum Practice, Theory and Research*, Albany: State University of New York Press.

Rudduck, J. (1991) *Innovation and Change*, Philadelphia: Open University Press.

Schwab, J. J. (1969) 'The practical: a language for curriculum', *School Review*, 78: 1–23.

Sergiovanni, T. J. (1984) 'Leadership excellence in schooling', *Educational Leadership*, 41: 4–13.,

Simon, R. (1992) *Teaching Against the Grain: Texts for a Pedagogy of Possibility*, Toronto: OISE Press.

Smith, R. (1993) 'Potentials for empowerment in critical education research', *Australian Educational Researcher*, 20 (2): 75–93.

Stenhouse, L. (1975) *An Introduction to Curriculum Development*, London: Heinemann.

Stevens, K., Slaton, D. and Bunney, S. (1992) 'A collaborative research effort between public school and university faculty members', *Teacher Education and Special Education*, 15 (1): 1–8.

Whitehead, J. (1989) 'Creating a living educational theory from questions of the kind, "How do I improve my practice?" ' *Cambridge Journal of Education*, 19: 41–52.

9

CHANGE IN SCHOOLS

Practice and vision

Roger Marshall, Alison Cobb and Chris Ling

We, the authors of this chapter, are educators. The things we have in common include: working together on programmes in the social justice field; we see ourselves as active learners; we get excited about working for change for the better in education; we enjoy exploring innovative approaches to our work; we believe that significant change must start with looking at our own practice. Despite all these shared qualities, we are far from being clones of each other. We bring to our work a diverse range of backgrounds both in our personal and professional lives. We think in very different ways. We approach our work from different perspectives. Often we have to work very hard to come to a shared understanding of our perceptions about issues we are working on.

In 1994 and 1995 we have been working together at a School Support Centre[1] in Brisbane. Our work could be broadly described as assisting people in school communities to solve problems and address issues which arise in the local context as they seek to meet the needs of individuals and groups in the school community and of society.

Our work has been greatly influenced by the environment created in the aftermath of the change of government in Queensland in 1989 from years of Conservative governments to Labor.[2] The period since this change has been full of paradoxes for educators with an interest in social justice. On the one hand, policies have been put in place which espouse principles of inclusivity and participation. Strategies designed to institutionalise review and reflection upon practice have been mandated. The social justice advocate has been able to draw upon these policies and strategies to give authority to her or his advocacy. On the other hand, many of us have felt that our advocacy has become more problematic as resistance to top down imposition of social justice initiatives has grown. It seems that the institutionalisation of social justice and reflective practice has, at best, had only partial benefits. While many people have used the emphasis upon these practices to make their advocacy and resource allocation more legitimate, the very fact that they are institutionalised allows the practices to be portrayed as less likely to be authentic and more likely to make demands upon people's time and energy, thus feeding resistance and detracting from the desired outcomes.

We believe that there is and will always be a strong argument for social justice advocacy and critical reflective practice to be seen as an authentic non-institutionalised activity.

The core of the work we describe in this chapter is cultural change rather than institutional change. The mandating of change has created a role for us to build our work around aligning professional practice with the ideals of the state's social justice agenda. We see our task as working to support the ongoing development of a reshaped professional culture in which educators redefine the way they see their roles and their relationships with others in the school community through critical reflection on their practice.

Looking back we realise that we have, in the work we report below, been working through a cycle that we can now call Data – Hunch – Action – Data. Our chapter is framed in this way. Our data are the conclusions that we draw from reflections upon our work; our hunches are our best guesses about what might work, they are often developed collaboratively and our actions are the processes we choose to pursue individually and together.

Our purpose in writing this chapter together is to share with others what we have learned from projects we have worked on, the kinds of dilemmas we have faced individually and together, the processes we have developed and followed and our thoughts on the implications of what we have learned for our future practice. The reader should be aware that what follows is a constructed framework of a sequence of events written in hindsight. The usefulness of this construct requires to be tested by the reader.

Initial data

By the start of 1995 we found that there was a group of us working in school support centres who were working in the role of facilitators of projects in which groups of teachers, administrators, students and parents were coming together to deal with dilemmas they faced in their school communities. The projects were diverse. They included:

- a project to develop reflective practices in a school attempting to develop a more inclusive curriculum and to document the processes the school experiences;
- a regional student forum;
- student action research into the participation and retention of Aboriginal and Torres Strait Islander boys;
- a regional project to support alternate approaches to managing conflict;
- a school principal group investigating alternative models to develop inclusive practices;

- a support group for parent liaison workers;
- the organisation of a conference to celebrate these and other projects.

Though the projects were diverse, the role of facilitation and leadership in them seemed to be a common denominator which linked our work. Our hunch was that there would be benefits for us in treating this commonality as an opportunity to reflect collaboratively upon our own practice.

First-phase hunch: the emancipatory myth/metaphor and social justice through participatory action research

This was not a hunch chosen at random. Neither was it a choice which would have surprised anyone who had worked with us or had been associated with us. Action research and action learning are methodologies which we seemed to be advocating for at every opportunity. We were highly aware of this and we were also highly aware that this was no chance phenomenon. We could explain our choice of action research/action learning as a primary methodology in the fight against injustice by saying that it is grounded in a firm theoretical base. However, that is too superficial an explanation.

A more convincing understanding comes from the concept that our beliefs and actions in the present are shaped by underlying 'metaphors and myths, images and visions' that we form of possible futures (Boulding 1979; Innuytella and Wildeman 1995; Polak 1962). This concept of individuals and societies being drawn towards images of the future was outlined by Fred Polak, a father of the modern field of Futures Studies, in *Image of the Future*.

Polak saw certain images of the future as carrying charges of unusual potency, the explosion of which creates for the society in question a vision of a totally new possibility. The society will then respond to the vision by mobilising its energies in new ways. Thus, new phases of civilisation are generated. One such triple charged time-bomb is the utopia image, which has repeatedly exploded in the history of western civilisation. The last explosion perhaps only fizzled out in the 1930s when it spawned a genre of anti-utopias in the work of Huxley and others, which closed the breach in time. Writing in the early 1950s, Polak called for the generation of new images to revitalise a disillusioned post-war Europe, which had spent its utopian charges.

The metaphors, myths, images and visions of the future which shape our present behaviours and our choice of participative action research (PAR) as a key methodology, can be argued to be part of just the kind of new images Polak was looking for. As early as 1979, Elise Boulding (1979) was able to discern: 'the development of a new image, a new time bomb, which may have many charges in it for future explosions in subsequent civilisations' (p. 6). The new image that Boulding discerned is:

[N]ew because we know the world differently now. This image is founded on the Gaia hypothesis, that the planet itself is an organic entity, and on . . . a concept of the noosphere, the knowledge sphere which encircles that planet. It envisions a localist world order based on very complex understandings of the interrelationship of physical, biological, social and spiritual phenomena. The noosphere becomes translated into a world wide information net which replaces present hierarchical power orderings and which releases individual potential while enhancing world well-being. . . . It is new in our time because it was not possible to think of the planet in this way before the twentieth century. It blends understandings of the cosmos from Buddhist, Hindu, Islamic, and folk tribal traditions with the Judao-Christian cosmology and the cosmology of science.

(*ibid.*)

Danah Zohar and Ian Marshall in a wonderfully evocative opening to their book *The Quantum Society: Mind, Physics and A New Social Vision*, in which they explore in detail the implications of the thinking of quantum physics for the social sciences, describe the choice of myth/metaphor open to us thus:

We can think of society as a milling crowd, millions of individuals each going his or her own way and managing, somehow, to coordinate sometimes. This is the Western way.

We can think of society as a disciplined army, each member a soldier marching in tight, well-ordered step. Individual differences are suppressed for the sake of uniform performance. This is the now discredited collectivist way.

Or, we might think of society as free-form dance company, each member a soloist in his or her own right but moving creatively in harmony with others. This is the new way.

(Zohar and Marshall 1993: 1)

It is this final metaphor of the free-form quantum dance company, with creative harmony between individuals and their environment, contrasted here with the images of the modern age and the failed images of its demise, that underpins the world view of a growing number of us.

The part of this metaphor for the future, which draws our work towards it in the fight against injustice in public education, has been that of a society and social institutions characterised by minimal necessary constraints upon self-realisation and self-determination (Young 1994). This vision was given a more concrete form in the image of the 'socially critical school', so effectively described by Stephen Kemmis, Peter Cole and Dahle Sugget (1983) over a decade ago. This is an image of the school curriculum as an instrument of liberation for the participants in schooling (teachers and parents as well as students) as they work and learn together by actively confronting the social issues facing young people in our society. Key elements in the image are a sense of community and meaningful, effective participation, collaboration, negotiation and self-reflection.

This, as is argued above, is not a metaphor which stands alone. It is part of a 'web of myth' carrying the image of emancipation and liberation through the adoption of an approach to knowledge generally known as critical theory. It is enunciated in its essence by Habermas in the theory of cognitive interests (Habermas 1971; 1972; 1974).

PAR is a special part of this emancipatory vision. It is a practical way of acting out the myth. It can be argued to have the key elements of socially critical schooling, sense of community, collaboration, negotiation and self-reflection embedded into it. Indeed it can be analysed and shown to be authentic critical practice (Grundy 1987). To those drawn by the vision of emancipation and individuals and society in harmony with the universe, it is a means by which the vision may be transposed into reality. Perhaps this is why it has become recommended means of improvement in many fields of human endeavour to be heard and read about wherever the task of improvement to the human condition is discussed.

For a group of people, drawn as we are by the emancipatory metaphor of the future, the choice of the action research/action learning methodology was certainly no surprise.

First-phase action: an action learning circle

At the start of 1995, then, the formation of an action learning circle in which the group could collaboratively reflect upon and investigate and change for the better our practices as facilitators of action research or action learning projects in schools was the course of action upon which we embarked.

In pursuing such a course, more than just a heuristic sense that this is the right sort of direction to take is needed. There is also a need for some mastery of the technology of the process, a way of organising the group so that it has a sense that its time is going to be spent in worthwhile activity. There is a need for structure in the way the group is organised to work together, and most importantly there is a need for someone to take responsibility for ensuring that that structure is in place and is utilised to make the group workable.

In the case of our group at the start of 1995, Roger took responsibility for this technical aspect of our collaboration. At our first meeting it was agreed that we would meet every second week for the first three times, and monthly thereafter. Each meeting would be approximately two hours long and would be in two basic parts: a sharing of reflections upon a common reading and a sharing of reports and reflections upon our projects. In order that our learnings were documented in a systematic kind of way, two strategies were adopted:

1   Before each meeting each member would write up a short report on her or his project using a common format and common headings. This ensured that the group was able to share in the reflections individuals were experiencing. It also served to form a running record of each project as it evolved.
2   At the end of each session a fifteen-minute time slot was put aside for the group to brainstorm together what were the underlying themes or issues that were emerging during our sessions.

Between meetings, Roger took the responsibility for collecting together and distributing to other members copies of the common readings, the running reports people were compiling of their projects and notes of the proceedings of the meetings, including a summary of the themes and issues which were emerging in the final brainstorming sessions.

At this early stage there was a concern in our minds that the whole project might lack cohesion. The projects themselves were very different in nature and the reflections that people were experiencing upon their own work were also very different. To counteract this there was a high level of energy in our discussions together and an agreement that the efforts made to put aside long timeslots in heavy work schedules for this sort of activity was worthwhile. However, there was little indication in the early stages that our joint deliberations might lead us to the kind of substantial collaborative learnings which were to emerge in the second half of the year.

Some indication of the diversity and individuality of the projects and the members of our group can be gained from the three case study stories which we present here.

Three case studies – participants' stories

Alison's story: Aboriginal and Torres Strait Islander boys' participation and behaviour management projects

These projects initially evolved in March 1995 out of several issues, concerns and needs expressed by Indigenous Education Workers (IEWS), Aboriginal Student Support and Parent Awareness (ASSPA) committees, school staff and Aboriginal community and Torres Strait Islander community concern over the increasing trend for Aboriginal and Torres Strait Islander boys to be involved in behaviour incidents, as well as, suspensions/exclusions within the region.

Data collected for the annual review of the Aboriginal and Torres Strait Islander Tertiary Aspirations Programme (AITAP) also indicated that the participation rate in this project of boys was half that of girls. This was surprising given that enrolment statistics indicated that the numbers of Aboriginal and Torres Strait Islander boys and girls enrolled in the region were generally equivalent.

The resulting rise in the stress levels of IEWs in trying to cope with school-based behaviour management issues meant that we needed to develop together some strategies to address these issues. So we set out to develop a frame of work for this 'project'. A regional steering committee was established comprising of Community Education Counsellors and the National Aboriginal and Torres Strait Islander Education Programme Team, with a view to increasing the group once we had identified people from within the community who were interested in working together. Our hunch was that perhaps an effective programme lay in gathering Aboriginal and Torres Strait Islander people from the local community in order to discuss and establish a broader scope or foundation of issues upon which we could build. We felt the need to find out whether Aboriginal and Torres Strait Islander parents, communities and organisations were encountering similar experiences. Our aim was to work collaboratively with school communities to develop responsive strategies via an open forum.

In April, a Regional meeting of Aboriginal and Torres Strait Islander parents, IEWs, community organisations and government departments met to discuss the cultural and gender contexts that affect the participation rates of Aboriginal and Torres Strait Islander boys. Our role was to facilitate a process of partnerships between the National Aboriginal and Torres Strait Islander Education Programme, school communities and community agencies. This meeting was very well attended and provided a wealth of information for us to explore. Key concerns arose in relation to the following:

- the importance of recognising of cultural identity;
- encouraging student self-acceptance via inclusive school practices;

- the need for positive role models;
- stereotyping and self-fulfilling efficacy;
- institutional racism and marginalisation;
- inappropriate and inadequate prevention strategies;
- the need for increased parent participation and consultation;
- student learning difficulties.

Difficulties in achieving positive outcomes for behaviour management processes were attributed to the school approach, educational services provided, a non-inclusive curriculum, lack of communication and cultural support.

Chris Sarra, a guidance officer from Trinity Bay State High School, has also written on similar issues and places the recognition of cultural identity to the forefront of effective learning and teaching for Aboriginal and Torres Strait Islander students:

> Aboriginal to me is growing up in a way of life where things like family and sharing comes before everything else. It's growing up surrounded by lots of brothers, sisters, cousins, uncles and aunts. It's knowing the stories of the past both good and bad. It's taking pride in the knowledge that our people were here from the start. It's giving your brother or sister a loan and not expecting it back; but knowing that they'll come good for you when you are in need. It's a spiritual thing that many of us may not fully understand. It's knowing, practising, and being a part of all these things . . . even before money came out!
>
> (Sarra 1995: 1)

The emerging dilemma subsequent to identifying perceived barriers to Aboriginal and Torres Strait Islander boys' participation and retention, was how to address these concerns? Did the students themselves feel the same way as parents and the community?

My hunch was that a new direction in the future implementation of behaviour management requires consideration with a commitment to a more serious approach to equitable practice representing Aboriginal and Torres Strait Islander voices.

Behaviour management and the paradigm of control

Current behaviour management policy discourse tends to deny outside critique and inquiry. It appears to be constructed via well-developed top-down implementation, sometimes creating a veneer of participatory democracy to generate a sense of ownership at the various levels of the public education organisation (Slee 1995). The development of appropriate behaviour management policies can only occur via the facilitation of responding to the particularity of different sites and varying interpretations. An examination of the construction of identity and normality in the creation of knowledges within mainstream ideology further complicates social and educational outcomes for Aboriginal and Torres Strait Islander students.

> Culture, in this view, is seen as made up of the products of great minds – books, music, plays, pictures and so on. These cultural objects and the appropriate feelings and attitudes about them exist in a publicity-determined hierarchy of value. Education thus becomes the process of making children familiar with the hierarchy of cultural objects and internalising the public standards of evaluation and appreciation of them. This leads to seeing the curriculum largely as a hierarchy of contents, and education as the gradual mastery of these contents. In such a view, authority is important. The authority of culture itself, which the student has to internalise in order to become, as it were, fully human, and the authority of the teacher and other school officers as the representatives or – better – the embodiment of cultural values. Access to the highest cultural objects requires mastery of a considerable body of academic knowledge and skills, and pressure is required to ensure that children and students work hard to attain these. The value of their attainment justifies the pressure or distress in their pursuit.
>
> (Egan 1989: 32

In an education system where Aboriginal and Torres Strait Islander identities may not be recognised and supported, the expression of self is denied. Egan adds:

> Because culture, and the knowledge which is prerequisite to it, has been to the forefront, the educational task has been interpreted as getting the subject matter logically organised and into the child. There has not been much sensitivity to the child's typical ways of making sense of the world, nor to the individual differences among children (except in terms of intelligence, which is interpreted as the regulator of the rate and quantity of knowledge that can be gotten in). Nor has there been much attention to children's typical patterns

of development in this tradition, because it has generally been assumed that the mind gradually grows and conforms with the shape of the knowledge that it takes in. By mastering the set of rational modes of enquiry, largely through learning their various products, the individual will become an educated, rational, cultured human being. The progressivist weakness has perhaps been the excessive sensitivity to the child's experience, development, needs and interests, with too little attention to the degree to which knowledge can drive development, create interests and generate quite new and distinctive needs.

(Egan 1989: 34)

Two projects

Two distinct strategies emerged. One course of action needed to be based in the 'here-and-now' of the issues, working with students who are considered 'at risk' of not completing senior schooling or entering a downward spiral of negative influences. In order to establish an understanding of the depth and breadth of participation, retention and behaviour management issues, a regional scan involving the collection and analysis of case studies from schools was conducted. A complementary project was also initiated jointly by the Regional Quality Assurance and School Review Unit and the Aboriginal and Torres Strait Islander Education Programme. This project aimed at investigating earlier reports indicating racial tensions contributing to a significant proportion of suspension and exclusions of Aboriginal and Torres Strait Islander students.

The steering committee would have the role of co-ordinating this project and of continuing the development of an inter-agency approach. The group was therefore broadened to include indigenous Police Liaison Officers, youth programmes and school community personnel. Its work was co-ordinated by Waverley Stanley, whose commitment to its ongoing development is outstanding.

The second course of action was to develop a pilot programme of preventative strategies in three interested state high schools. A significant component of this programme involved development of PAR projects conducted by teams of four or five senior male students in three high schools within the region. This project was co-ordinated by Bill Atweh of Queensland University of Technology and myself.

The focus of these projects was to investigate cultural and gender components in student construction of self-identity and how this affects the participation of Aboriginal and Torres Strait Islander boys in senior secondary schooling, as well as, in further tertiary studies. Students were trained as research assistants at the university and paid a nominal wage for the time spent working on the projects on weekends. (This was a new set of experiences for many of the boys participating in that they had not previously visited a university campus.) Student teams determined the direction they were to take in gathering data to analyse. The boys surveyed target groups within Aboriginal and Torres Strait Islander communities within the Metropolitan East Region and across rural and urban Queensland, including parents, students at school, students who had left school, etc. They also interviewed successful Aboriginal and Torres Strait Islander men.

This was a similar project to one carried out by Bill Atweh and his colleagues with students from low socio-economic areas which is reported elsewhere in this book (see Chapter 7).

Roger's story – the Yoban High School learning support projects

In 1995, a team of four people were appointed to the teaching staff of Yoban High School, a small school of 300 students and twenty-five teachers as a 'learning support team'. At the same time, eight students were transferred to the school from a senior special school. These were students with mild intellectual impairments, learning difficulties and/or a history of disturbing behaviours in schools. The appointment of the team was perceived in the school community as being linked to the transfer of these students.

In the minds of the school's principal and the committee responsible for allocating the human resources to the project, the mission of the team was to assist the school in the development of a more inclusive curriculum. That is, assisting the school to cater for the transferred ex-special school students and the many others in the school perceived to have similar needs for a more appropriate learning programme.

My role in the project was generally to assist the team to reflect upon their work with a particular focus upon the documenting of any learnings which accrued. (It should be noted that the core team I was working with was the four newly appointed teachers, the guidance officer and the principal.) I conceived of this role as being to shape the

173

project into one of action research/action learning characterised by collaboration, action and reflection in order to change the practices of the team and through them, others in the school.

As I put together reports on this project for other members of the facilitators' action learning group, I was very aware of some big question marks hanging over the whole project and in particular my work in it. There were questions like:

- To what extent is the project seen by members of the group and others in the school, as the implementation of a policy being imposed from outside the school? Am I seen as an agent of the department sent in to impose this policy? What impact might this have on my work?

- To what extent am I seen as an outside 'expert' in inclusive practices? Do I want to be seen in this way? How would this influence my work?

- What should an action research project be like? Is this project really action research? Is action learning a better name for what we are doing? Are there things I should be doing to make this into better action research?

- To what extent are the rest of the team committed to the action research concept? Is this just an idea I am imposing and which they are prepared to humour me on? Do others resent the amount of time I want them to spend on reflection and dialogue? Do they see the writing demands as being pointless and of little relevance?

- Am I seen as a member of the team and/or of the school or am I just seen as an interfering outsider?

Chris's story: participation in leadership

Through my work with the School Support Centre I have had a growing awareness of the role of conflict as an obstacle to school development and improvement and indeed as a great source of unproductive stress. Initially I wanted to explore ways of addressing this issue with schools. However, as the group started to meet, I realised that my real interest was with the issue of learning how to foster participation effectively in action learning and research in my position of leadership within the Support Centre.

As the development of the action learning and research activities emerged, I realised that the real focus for my learning was to do with the process itself. My question was about how, in my role in the Support Centre, I could create the conditions, the culture, that would support the growth of action learning and research as a collaborative activity and a key form of ongoing professional development.

My hunch was to work in two ways. One was through sponsoring school-based projects, making funding available wherever possible for teacher release for reflective action, and providing co-ordination for meetings to focus on learning and reflection. The second was to sponsor the formation of 'learning circles' with people who worked across the six support centres in the region. In general, I wanted to demonstrate leadership to members of the Support Centre that I valued action learning and research and agreed with our attempts to use these approaches to improving the way we work. As the year progressed, two developments influenced the development of reflective practice in the centre. One was the development of the Community Development Course, which is described in this chapter. The other was the decision to reduce the amount of time I was devoting to individual supervision of members of the staff and to initiate group sessions for the discussion of important issues of practice. These sessions brought together participants from different but not unrelated fields and became important sources of professional development and mutual support. I found them to be far richer sources of learning than the individual sessions previously held and they built a real sense of interdependence between the participants. The strength of these reflective practice sessions grew while I was acting in another position and relieved by Roger.

My learnings about both the centre-based and school-based approaches has developed considerably. The effect of geography on people's capacity to meet regularly and develop supportive cultures has become clearer to me. My hunch is that locating these projects in a single work site has many strengths and while it would not be the only way to proceed, it seems to me at this point that even in a metropolitan area, that travel across sites requires high motivation.

I am now more aware of the difficulties posed when a person in an official leadership position promotes such activities. The issues of parity of esteem as highlighted by Shirley Grundy in Chapter 3, this volume, should not be minimised. In fact, a great deal of attention needs to be directed here. Compliance, direct or indirect, is a poor motivation for involvement in reflective practice and a major obstacle to successful learning.

I am also now quite wary of taking a 'project approach'. My observation of both my own and others is that can lead to the artificial construction of projects to legitimise participation and in some cases, funding. It may be better to start with the exploration of smaller concerns and questions and build wider themes over a period of time for some participants.

First-phase data: developing themes, issues and dilemmas

Though our approaches and our projects were very different, cohesion was brought to our group by the common themes and issues which quickly emerged as we reflected together upon our work. There were common dilemma's facing all of us as we sought to play the role of facilitator to our projects. Dilemmas which would lead us to considerable changes in the way our group operated and the content of our learnings during the second half of the year. In broad terms, the issues were:

- Whose agenda are we trying to address in our projects? Is it a top-down agenda imposed by the system, the bureaucracy, or is it the real agenda of the participants?
- To what extent are we using our status as outsiders perceived to have some expertise in order to influence the agenda?
- How can one as an outsider engage with and stay connected with the issues of people without being a full participant in the situation?
- To what extent do participants in our projects withdraw from acceptance of responsibility for shaping their own situation? In what ways is it possible to assist them to accept this responsibility and work together to reshape their situation?
- How does one maintain the energy for change and addressing key issues in the face of resistance and a reluctance to engage in situations where conflict is encountered?
- How does one assist others to maintain energy for working together to address injustices in the face of the difficulties posed by the tyrannies of time and distance?
- How can we make the voice of the participants heard and how can we ensure a parity of esteem for what that voice is saying?

Second-phase hunch – community practice

As we tried to respond to these issues, the links to some material on community development practices became more apparent to members of the group. Of great influence upon us were the ideas of Tony Kelly and Sandra Sewell (personal communication). There was a growing sense that the skilling offered by community development practitioners could offer the type of development that was needed to break out of the top-down/bottom-up nexus. The idea being that training in this area would renew the confidence members needed for a bottom-up approach in a top-down environment. This training offered the opportunity to include a new paradigm in the repertoire available to education practitioners.

The basic method of community practice, as we understood from our communications with Tony Kelly, is one of bonding and banding. The community practitioner is able to 'walk in the shoes' of community members, to see the world through their eyes. She or he is also able to work in a way that enhances the possibility of people coming together to act to change their situation. In a handout at a training semianar, Kelly provided the following quotes illustrating the two principles .

Principle One: Bonding

Walk in my moccasins for a while
Listen, listen and then listen some more
Work with the people not for them
Carry your agenda lightly
Come down, come in, come alongside
See through our eyes

Principle Two: Banding

[M]aybe, just maybe, if we join together we can do what we could not do on our own
Many hands make light work
Not yours, not mine, but ours
The sum of the whole is greater than the sum of the parts
(Kelly 1995)

It seemed to us that if community development practices enabled community workers to 'get alongside' marginalised and disaffected people and bring them together to take action to change their world in some way, then the skills and knowledge of these practices would assist us in our work with people in school communities.

Community development practice in many ways comes from a different view of how to develop society than does school education. Schooling is essentially a social development strategy. It is characterised by a top-down institutionalised approach to societal improvement with centralised bureaucracies determining for people courses of action and learnings which will assist in the development of a better society and fulfilment for individuals. In contrast, a community development strategy would be characterised by a bottom-up non-institutionalised approach in which participants determine their own courses of action.

However, it is also clear that community development practice is firmly grounded in the same emancipatory myth/metaphor as social critical schooling as discussed above – the myth/metaphor that drives the actions of members of our group and many others pursing social justice in education. This is abundantly clear from the following discussion of the principles and aims of community development by Taylor:

> Community development is concerned with change and growth – with giving people more power over changes that are taking place around them, the policies that affect them and the services they use. It seeks to 'enable individuals and communities to grow and change according to their own needs and priorities' (Standing Conference on Community Development (SCCD) 1990) rather than those dictated by circumstances beyond their boundaries. It works through bringing people together to 'share skills, knowledge and experience' (SCCD 1990), in the belief that it is through working together that they will reach their full potential.
>
> It aims to promote participation in the democratic process on the premise that policies and services will be immeasurably improved if people traditionally at the receiving end are able to play a central part in their development. But there are many people who do not have the confidence to engage in public life, to influence the services they use or the environments they live in. Many, for example, have been conditioned by professions, institutions or services which marginalise them and treat them as passive recipients, expecting them to accept without question decisions made on their behalf. It is often through talking to others in a similar situation that they begin to realise that their experience is shared. From this foundation, many people begin to gain the skills and confidence to take an active part in the services they use and the environment they live in.
>
> It is particularly concerned to challenge the individual prejudices and institutional discrimination which isolate, divide and exclude people from their communities and society at large.
>
> (Taylor 1992: 6–7)

Thus, by mid-1995, we were set to embark on a new course of action a new way to develop paradigms and practices consistent with our driving emancipatory myth/metaphor.

Second-phase action: a community practice training course

The decision was taken that in the period between July and early October of 1995, a training course in community development practices would be organised in which members of the group and other support staff working with them would be able to participate. The course was a substantial one. It involved some sixty hours in duration over five full-day and eight half-day sessions.

This marked a substantial change to the nature of our group. On a surface level, it meant that it would be extended in membership and that there would be a heavier time commitment for participants. At a deeper more substantial level, it also meant a very different approach to learning. The fact that this was a training course meant that its objective was to change and shape the practices of the participants in a certain way. That is, there was to be a deliberate attempt to have members learn skills and techniques and to develop the ability to apply them in their practice.

This did not imply that collaborative reflective practice was to be abandoned. On the contrary, an action learning/action research approach was central to the methodology of the course. The half-day sessions in the course were devoted to case studies in which participants reported upon and shared their reflections upon projects they were undertaking.

There was, however, a major difference in the qualities of these shared reflections. The central method of the course was to assist participants to develop a practice framework. A set of perspectives from which to view and analyse situations and use to develop responses. Ultimately each participant would develop their own individual framework, but to start with we agreed to learn the 'head, heart, hand' framework of our trainers (Kelly and Sewell 1988). The advantage of having such a practice framework is that it gives one a language in which to talk about and reflect upon one's practice. Thus, now when we were reflecting upon our projects, we had much better tools for sharing and extending our learning. It soon became evident to us that to attempt to undertake approaches like supervision of each other's practice was not really possible without an understanding of the practice framework we were each operating from.

Second-phase data: ways of thinking about our dilemmas

As we embarked upon the community development training course together an early result for us was the influence of developing flexibility in thinking and making judgements about situations as a part of our practice framework. As we applied this flexibility to the dilemmas and issues we faced in our projects, new perspectives on these issues and dilemmas began to emerge giving us new data upon which to work and with which to shape our practices.

The thinking dimension is one of two which constitute the 'head' part of the 'head, heart, hand' framework that we adopted for our training course. The other dimension is politicking. Discussion of the thinking dimension here, brief though it may be, is intended to illustrate how having a practice framework which enhances one's understanding through giving different perspectives on a situation can be of assistance in making judgements about one's practices.

The language that people use in discussing issues reveals five different commonly used kinds of 'social logic' or thinking:

- *Heuristic logic* – a logic in which the intellectual task is to evoke a common meaning. For example, people can invoke the ideas of peace, or love or liberation to motivate and mobilise each other. Great social movements have been built upon the foundations of heuristic knowledge. Though it must be noted that the vagueness of such ideas can often mask large difference, and, in the mind of an idealogue fix the meanings for all time.
- *Binary logic* – in which the intellectual task is to make a commitment to choice. This is perhaps the most common form of social logic of the modern western culture. Our physical, behavioural and social science are grounded almost exclusively in binary logic. In it two factors are seen as separate, mutually inconsistent or contradictory, and from these factors a choice must be made. The pressure to make a decision and a choice is often of great use to us in ensuring that movement occurs and decisive action is taken. However there are also great drawbacks to binary logic. For example: if there are only winners and losers, people will reward or punish each other accordingly; if 'you have to look after yourself because no one else will' then you will expect others to do the same and there can be no cooperation.
- *Dialectic logic* – in which the intellectual task is to hold the tension between two factors. This is the logic of dialogue between two factors. It can have the disadvantage of endless backing and forthing between the two in a sea of relativities or

it can be a means of opening up the possibilities closed off in order to make a binary choice. It also has the great advantage of having change embedded into the process. In dialogue, new positions and understandings emerge from the bringing together of differing or opposing positions.

- *Synthetic logic* – in which the intellectual task is to move two factors forward by means of their synthesis. To take a social example, loggers and conservationists may be seen as the thesis and antithesis of a particular contradiction. The solution of synthesis in this situation may be to bring the two together to form a project team to conserve resources and generate local employment. Again the creation of synthesis implies the creation of social change, making this a powerful form of social logic.

- *Trialectic logic* – in which the intellectual task is to grasp a sense of wholeness which emerges from the inter-relationship of at least three sets of factors. In contrast to one or two factor logics trialectic logic establishes (at least a third independent factor as a point of focus. This third point is not a point of synthesis as in synthetic logic, but a factor in its own right. The trialectic of the three factors held together gives a wholeness to the whole situation which makes creativity and change possible. Consider, for example, the *space, relationships, tasks* trialectic in terms of community. To live where there are no people cannot be community. To be with people in a common space but with no shared tasks is not community either. To be at war with one another is to have shared space and shared tasks but it is not community because relationships are missing. Whereas to live in a shared space and relate with others in the pursuit of shared tasks is to build community.

(Kelly and Sewell 1988: 12–30)

As we set out to apply this insight into the forms which social logic commonly takes to the kinds of dilemmas we had been facing in our projects, the first point to hit us was the propensity in our thinking towards the application of binary logic to any situation. Our views of the dilemmas was clearly influenced by some entrenched oppositional thinking: oppressed versus oppressor; insiders (people working in schools) versus outsiders (people like ourselves based outside schools); dominating experts (ourselves) versus dominated people (our clients in schools); our voices versus our clients' voices; correct action research procedure versus incorrect action research procedure; etc. It was clear to us that this binary logic was putting constraints upon us which could threaten to impede the progress of our projects.

Further, it was apparent that the application of some trialectic logic could prove productive. For example the 'space, relationship, task' trialectic referred to above is of obvious use to us. Our work in all of our projects is very much involved in forming relationships with people who work and live in a defined space and bringing them together to achieve given tasks. Each factor in this trialectic is equally important and deserving of our attention as are the relationships between the factors, for example, the effects that the nature of the tasks we are undertaking have upon the relationships, the impact of the physical space upon our ability to accomplish the tasks, etc. The problematics of this trialectic are all referred to for example in Chris's story above.

Perhaps of even more significance and relevance to the issues and dilemmas which were concerning us in our projects in the first half of 1995 is the 'experts, leaders, people' trialectic. So many of our concerns and issues seemed to centre upon the relationships between people in the various sectors of this trialectic and in particular upon the issue of 'parity of esteem' for the perspectives and knowledge of these various groups, which is raised by Shirley Grundy in her theme chapter (Chapter 3) of this book. Kelly and Sewell write about this trialectic as follows:

> [W]hile we need leaders to take initiatives and people to support them, we also need experts to provide knowledge. Without leaders we have a lot of information and the person power to something with it, but no direction to follow. Without experts, we still have the person power, and now a direction to follow, but no informed base for action. Without people we have the know-how and the will to do something, but no take-up or on the ground support. We need all three to get something moving, to sustain it and carry it forward as far as possible. Without trialectic logic we can make narrow based judgements: natural leaders are cut down to size for 'big noting themselves'; experts are put down as 'egg-heads'; the people are lumped together as a 'mindless rabble'.
>
> (Kelly and Sewell 1988: 33)

Put in this way it can be seen that parity of esteem makes a great deal of sense and yet one suspects that it is the problematic of this issue which causes most difficulty in achieving the kind of community building which those of us driven by the myth/metaphor of emancipation strive for. The ability to apply such trialectic logic rather than binary logic on a consistent basis might be a prerequisite to addressing the issue of parity of esteem in a meaningful way.

Second-phase action and data – part B: what was happening to the projects

During the period from July to October in which we were together with twelve colleagues, undertaking the Community Practice Training Course, our projects were continuing on. What was happening in these projects and in several other similar projects which constitute our work in the School Support Centre gives us a continuous stream of new and rich data to inform our learnings. As can be seen from these reports of two of the projects previously referred to, the progress made on the projects is rarely predictable and certainly not always as one would desire it to be.

Roger's story continued – losing contact with the Yoban High Project

At the end of semester one in July 1995 there were two highly significant and unexpected turns of events which were to impact significantly upon my work on the Yoban High School Learning Support Project. First, the principal of the school was appointed to a new position in a larger school and took up the position immediately. Her place was taken for the rest of the year in an acting principal capacity by the deputy principal who had little working knowledge of the project, as she had been on leave for much of the first half of the year. Second, I myself unexpectedly had the opportunity to work in an acting capacity in Chris's assistant co-ordinator position at the School Support Centre, while she in turn acted as a coordinator.

An outcome of all of this unexpected change in circumstances was that I found it very difficult to maintain contact with the group at the school left to continue work on the project, and this just at a time when everything was thrown into considerable disarray by the loss of the outgoing principal. In effect, the project lost two significant leadership figures at the same time. Work on the project did, of course, carry on. The people involved had to regroup and I was able to keep some contact with them as they did so. However, in the new order of relationships which formed my role was a considerably different one.

When I was eventually able to devote any real time to working on the project again in term four 1995, I found a situation of considerable doubt about the direction in which the project was currently going and about whether it would be able to continue in 1996. There were persistent, and probably well-justified, rumours that resources would be withdrawn from the learning support team in the shape of transfers to other schools for some people. And, even if this did not occur, there was considerable doubt about the direction the project might be expected to take when a new permanent principal was appointed at the start of the new school year.

In summary, the project as I had known it had fallen apart. It was going through a protracted period of what would prove to be either: at best a transformation into a new project; or, at worst a slow death. In either case my role in it was likely to be either a marginal one or no role at all.

Alison's story continued – Aboriginal and Torres Strait Islander boys' participation and behaviour management projects

The Behaviour Management Project for 'At Risk Boys'

The emerging dilemma for this project was that it was becoming very large and enormously time consuming. It was evident that I could not possibly continue to work on this project as well as maintain the role of co-ordinating the Aboriginal and Islander Tertiary Aspirations Programme (AITAP), which was seen as being my main role.

What we were able to do with this project was make alternative arrangements for the project to go ahead with adequate resourcing to do it full justice. Through the collaborative efforts of Roger and myself, we were able to advocate in the regional behaviour management forums for regional support for a submission for state funding for the project. The outcome of this was that a full-time project officer was employed in 1996 and 1997 to pursue this project in the region. Funds have also been made available to support the work of the project.

This has been a bonus in terms of resources. However, I feel the best achievements from community involvement in behaviour management has been in the development of colleague networks beyond the Queensland Department of Education. The gathering of community skills and a genuine commitment being undertaken by community groups to provide collaborative support to Aboriginal and Torres Strait Islander youth at risk has been very positive.

Students' PAR projects in collaboration with QUT

This project went ahead in 1996 in an expanded form. Bill Atweh and myself were closely involved in leading the project, which included girls' research teams. The results from the boys' project in 1995 are yet to be fully utilised within schools. Once published, I feel it is essential to transform the findings of the students' research from 'report' status to being a practical tool for change within schools. Unless this occurs, the efforts of these students will be lost in the ongoing 'paper shuffle' of the education system.

I feel that this project was highly successful as an 'authentic' activity whereby the agents of change for students, were students, rather than educators. The experiences taken from this project has led most of the men involved into tertiary studies – equipped with a broad understanding of the issues surrounding the need for greater retention and participation of Aboriginal and Torres Strait islander boys in tertiary studies. More importantly it has given these students the knowledge and skills to *complete* these studies successfully.

Current hunches: time to sum up, take stock and decide 'where to from here?' – again

An inescapable characteristic of the cyclical action research approach is that there is never a finishing point. That must be evident to the reader at this stage of our account of our work. The best that one can hope for is that there will be times when one can take time out to reflect upon what are the main lessons one has learned to this point in the ongoing process; and in doing so discern some indications of what might be good actions to take next.

What, then, do we see as the main aspects of our learning from our collaboration in 1995? We will conclude for now by a brief sharing of our current hunches.

First, a key insight for us is that we are driven in much of our choice of ways of viewing situations and in the choice of actions to respond to what we see by the underlying 'myth, metaphor, image or vision' of a society characterised by minimal constraints upon self-determination and self-realisation.

As interpreted by Elise Boulding (1979), the translator of his work into English, Fred Polak classified the images that societies form into four broad categories formed as alternating optimism and pessimism which constructs the world as an essentially a good or bad place, and whether human beings can or cannot change it. The four categories are thus:

1   essence optimism and influence optimism – the world is good and humans can make it better;

2   essence optimism and influence pessimism – the world is good but it goes of itself and humans cannot alter the course of events;

3   essence pessimism and influence optimism – the world is bad but humans can make it better;

4   essence pessimism and influence pessimism – the world is bad and there is nothing humans can do about it.

The image of a society characterised by emancipatory action is, we believe, the metaphor drawing our work towards it. It is using Polak's style of analysis, an image which is firmly influence optimistic. It is characterised by hope that liberated humans can make the world better, but optimism is sobered in its estimates of human capacities by the hubristic excesses of the technological revolution. The characteristics of this underlying metaphor are likely to be embedded in all our choices of fields in which to work and of the strategies we choose to take.

However, it should not be assumed that this metaphor is beyond question or critique. Indeed, the implication for future practice of this insight is that it is necessary to make our myths and metaphors problematic if we are to ensure that our actions are consistent with our beliefs and values. Now that we are more aware of a dominant metaphor or vision driving our choice of paradigms and actions we can be alert to the effects it might have in both a positive and negative way.

Second, the field of community development practice is a rich one for those of us working in to promote educational change and social justice in schools. It is a field of work which is highly consistent with the emancipatory metaphor or vision espoused by many with a commitment to the fight against injustices in education and in society.

The two aspects of our work in the field which we have found most useful are: (a) the basic step-by-step cycle of bonding – seeing the world through the eyes of others in order to get alongside them, and banding – bringing people together in order to work to address an issue or issues which affect them; and (b) the development of a practice framework which gives a structure with which to view a situation from a range of perspectives and a language with which to talk about the views one has of the situation from that range of perspectives. The example given above of the insights developed into the dilemmas facing us in our projects earlier in 1995 by applying the thinking dimension of the 'head, heart, hand' framework serves to demonstrate the power of such a framework to analyse situations and change practices.

Clearly, community development practices will form a prominent part of our future practices. A priority for each of us will be to develop our own individual practice framework based upon the head, heart, hand one that formed the basis of our training in the second half of 1995.

Finally, we have learned much about the processes of action learning/action research. Kemmis and Wilkinson in Chapter 2, this volume, have given some criteria by which project participants can reflect on the principles and assumptions of their proejcts. Our own reflection on this project showed that there are certainly some major difference between the surface image one gets of PAR when one reads the standard guides to the practice (Kemmis and McTaggert 1988; Wilkinson 1995; Grundy 1995, etc.). However, when one reads deeper to judge what is the essence of critical practice in PAR, then our work in 1995 starts to fit the image quite well.

Action research projects are not always the neat and tidy processes that they can sometimes appear to be in textbooks. The collaborative nature of these processes in real-world settings means that they are far from being objective laboratory exercises. They are in fact very human processes. This does not detract from them in any way in terms of the learning that it is possible for participants to gain by taking part. It would be very wrong, for example, to view the events of Roger's project in the second half of 1995 as a failure just because of the course of events that one would have liked to predict for it. There was much to be learned from the events as they did occur and further, there were many new opportunities to apply the insights gained by participants to ensure that newly emerging practices worked to counter injustices.

At this point in time, we would argue that the success of our action research/action learning practice will be measured by the extent to which we have been able to work together to investigate our practices in order to change them and the extent to which we have been able to participate in improving our social situation. In seeking to measure this we can only reflect that the satisfaction our group felt as participated in the community development training course we undertook, and the anticipation we shared that we would be able to use the knowledge, skills and processes we were gaining in order to work alongside school communities in the tasks of school improvement are positive indicators that our learning together is making a difference.

NOTES

1   School Support Centres are established by the Queensland Department of Education to provide resources and expertise in support of curriculum change and development in schools in their local areas.
2   At the time of writing this chapter, the Australian Labor Party was in government. The educational policies and structures giving rise to this project have since ceased to exist.

REFERENCES

Boulding, E. (1979) 'Remembering the future: reflections on the works of Fred Polak', *Alternative Futures: The Journal of Utopian Studies*, Fall, 3–11.

Egan, K. (1989) 'Balancing equity and culture', *Curriculum Perspectives*, 9: 22–40

Grundy, S. (1987) *Curriculum: Product or Praxis*, London: Falmer Press.

—— (1995) *Action Research as Professional Development*, Perth, West Australia: Innovative Links Project Murdoch University.

Habermas, J. (1971) *Towards A Rational Society*, London: Heinemann.

—— (1972) *Knowledge and Human Interests*, 2nd edn, London: Heinemann.

—— (1974) *Theory and Practice*, London: Heinemann.

Innuytella, S. and Wildeman, P. (1995) Ways of knowing and the pedagogy of the future, paper presented at the Teaching Future Generations workshop, University of Toronto, Canada.

Kelly, T. (1995) Gift of a methodology of working step by step, handout at the Community Development workshop at the Valley School Support Centre, Brisbane, Australia, August.

Kelly, T. and Sewell, S. (1988) *With Head, Heart and Hand: Dimensions of Community Building*, 3rd. edn, Brisbane, Australia: Boolarong Books.

Kemmis, S., Cole, P. and Suggett, D. (1983) *Orientations to Curriculum and Transition: Towards the Social Critical School*, Melbourne: Victorian Institute of Secondary Education.

Kemmis, S. and McTaggert, R. (1988) *The Action Research Planner*, Geelong, Australia: Deakin University Press.

Polak, F. (1962) *The Image of the Future*, trans. E. Boulding, New York: Ocean Press.

Sarra, C. (1995) Aboriginal and Torres Strait Islander behavioural management project, paper presented at the National Aboriginal and Torres Strait Islander Education Programme state-wide conference, Brisbane: Queensland Government Department of Education, August.

Standing Conference on Community Development (1990) *A Working Statement on Community Development*, Sheffield: SCCD.

Slee, R. (1995) *Changing Theories and Practices of Discipline*, London: Falmer Press.

Taylor, M. (1992) *Signposts to Community Development*, London: Community Development Foundation.

Wilkinson, M. (1995) *Action Research: For People and Organisational Change*, Brisbane: Queensland University of Technology.

Young, I.M. (1990) *Justice and the Politics of Difference*, Princeton, NJ: Princeton University Press.

Zohar, D. and Marshall, I. (1993) *The Quantum Society: Mind, Physics and a New Social Vision*, London: Flamingo.

10

ACTION RESEARCH FOR PROFESSIONAL DEVELOPMENT ON GENDER ISSUES

Ross Brooker, Georgia Smeal, Lisa Ehrich, Leonie Daws and Jillian Brannock

In their chapters in this volume, Grundy, Kemmis and Wilkinson, and Rizvi offer three conceptual frameworks which link the various chapters in this book. Grundy, for example, in Chapter 3 in this volume suggests that there are two ways of conceiving professional research partnerships: 'researching for the profession'; and 'researching with the profession.' She points out, the first form of partnership refers to the commissioning of 'university-based researchers ... to undertake research on behalf of the profession'. This, she suggests, is often externally funded (e.g., from government) research. The second form of partnership that Grundy highlights, refers to the 'development of professional collaborative research enterprises between groups of educators' (e.g., between school-based teachers and university-based researchers, students, parents, etc.). Grundy articulates the dimensions of the second form in some detail. In our work, the authors of this chapter found both conceptions of partnership to be significant and interrelated. In our case, 'researching for the profession' provided the opportunity for 'researching with/in the profession'.

In Chapter 2 in this volume Kemmis and Wilkinson discuss a conceptual framework which centres around the notion of participatory action research (PAR) as a process to bring about change in educational contexts. They argue that PAR goes beyond concerns about the 'methodological and procedural task of using particular techniques to collect data about practice' to make explicit the collaborative efforts to theorise the practice itself. They explain that this theorising activity involves 'describing the way a particular practice is embedded in particular social media and social structures, and in the knowledge and agency of particular individuals in particular places'. Based on this viewpoint, they provide a checklist of criteria for deciding if a study can be thought of as participatory action research. While the authors of this chapter are supportive of the values articulated by Kemmis and Wilkinson, we contend that these criteria will necessarily be shaped and modified by the context(s), in which a project occurs. Hence, the suggestion that a project may not be a PAR project unless it meets each of these criteria becomes redundant.

Although the process of our project was participatory, the levels of participation by the teachers and academics involved differed. Given the differing levels of involvement, is the project then disqualified from being framed as action research? On the contrary, we believe that action research, and any other research for that matter, is inevitably shaped (constrained or liberated) by the context in which it occurs.

Rizvi's conceptual framework (in Chapter 4 in this volume) concerns the need for research to be positioned in social justice ideals that result in 'cultural and social changes to the ways schools are structured' and changes to the 'way things are named and represented, the manner in which difference is treated and the ways in which values, significations and norms which govern life in schools are negotiated and established'. In the following account of our project, we reveal how in certain school contexts our project facilitated progress towards this ideal.

Yes, it was *our* project in the sense that we were commissioned to do it. We did, however, extend the *our* to embrace the involvement of partners in schools and education offices in two different Australian states. We are not suggesting that a 'parity of esteem' (see Grundy's chapter) necessarily existed between the partners. In one sense the project was mutually exploitative of the partners. The university researchers had needs and goals which were oriented to developing a product. To achieve goal this required the contribution of school personnel and schools. Although we attempted not to privilege our needs as paramount, they were a significant factor in shaping the direction of the project. Schools recognised, and acted on, an opportunity to access funds to pursue gender agendas in their school, which in the case of one school was marginal to the direction of the project. Despite these limitations in terms of working within the action research paradigm, positive outcomes did eventuate. Changes in school structures did occur. Values were problematised and existing practices challenged. There was a 'deepening' of 'conceptual knowledge about teachers, school cultures, and the process of school change' (Lieberman 1992: 6).

Consequently we believe that our project characterised authentic action research.

Action research and professional development

According to some commentators (e.g., see Owen 1990; Ingvarson 1987) there are two alternative orientations to professional development: the innovation-focused and action-research models. The former implies learning from others, while the latter implies learning for ourselves. The innovation-focused professional development model is based on the assumption that teachers need concrete and continuous support from credible people to enable them to implement new programmes or practices. In contrast, action research is based on the assumption that teachers use their own contexts to generate solutions to problems and issues they identify as important.

A key question is, is there a role for an outside person/consultant/academic in an action research project at the school level? While the innovation-focused approach is predicated on the belief that there may be such a thing as 'expert knowledge' (Ingvarson 1987: 210), the role of an outsider in action research is not settled. Purist action researchers maintain that action research must begin with problems identified by teachers themselves and must enable teachers control over the entire process of planning, acting and reflecting. Furthermore, purist notions of action research suggest that the process is sufficient unto itself to bring about change, that the gathering of and reflecting upon data will automatically result in the development of new insights and improved practices. At the other end of the continuum, however, there are authors (e.g., see Henry and Kemmis 1985; Hopkins 1987; Ingvarson 1987) who are supportive of the idea that outsiders have a role to play in providing external support to action research projects.

For example, Hopkins (1987) argues that action research is not a practitioner-initiated mode of inquiry but is instigated by outsiders for the benefit of insiders and the wider academic community. Henry and Kemmis highlight the important role of 'outsiders' in facilitating action research. They allude to this point when they state that groups in schools interested in action research may arrange 'legitimising rituals' which means that 'consultants or other outsiders can help to show that respected others are interested in what the group is achieving for education in the school' (Henry and Kemmis 1985: 4).

Kemmis (1987) in a later paper, argued that while there is a role for outside specialists in the development of educational programmes using action research, 'self evaluation is the bedrock upon which program evolution rests' (p. 75). In other words, there are some conditions under which outsiders *can* be helpful in action research projects, but fundamentally, the impetus for action research must come from participants themselves.

It is our contention that it is very difficult for teachers to adopt a critical stance about their work and practice, particularly when what is to be viewed afresh is something that has been instilled as common sense. For example, if teachers believe that they have always interacted equally with boys and girls in their classrooms, then what fresh evidence might cause them to question this belief? If teachers perceive their existing practice is fair and equitable, then there is the likelihood that what is looked for and seen will be what is already believed to be happening. Our project therefore was premised on the recognition that in order to tackle the inequalities that arise from the social construction of gender, 'teachers, parents, students and other members of the community need to participate in school activities which critically reflect on the impact of gender on their lives and relationships' (Australian Education Council 1993: 7). As the university researchers who were commissioned to undertake the project, our role was one of providing the initial stimulus for, and focus of the project, as well as ongoing support to teachers and schools. The project provided the impetus for teachers, administrators, parents and students to reflect critically upon their beliefs and practices in relation to gender equity.

The project's philosophical backdrop was informed by the view that gender is socially constructed. This view makes a distinction between biological sex and socially constructed ideas about masculinity and femininity. It challenges the idea that men and women have biologically determined positions in the world, arguing that schooling oriented to equality of outcomes should not constrain students to rigid gender boundaries but rather should provide students with opportunities to take up a range of positions on the masculinity/femininity continuum. At the same time, the project team acknowledged that the everyday actions and recurring practices of all individuals significantly shape gender relations and in order to move towards more equal gender relations in schools, as educators we must be equipped to critique the value positions and taken-for-granted behaviours which shape our practice.

This chapter then discusses the role of action research in professional development based on our experiences in a ten-month project commissioned and funded by the Australian Federal Government's Department of Employment, Education and Training and Youth Affairs (DEETYA). The project aimed to design and produce professional development modules for school teachers and administrators that addressed classroom and school practices contributing to equality of outcomes for girls and boys in Years 7–10. Action research contributed to the project in three ways. First, it was the underpinning framework for the conduct of the project. Second, it was the research process adopted by staff in the partner schools to explore and influence the thinking and practices about gender equity in those schools. And third, it was written into the modules as a recommended approach for bringing about change in gender understandings and practices in school. The next sections of the chapter provide insights into the project from two perspectives, that of the university researchers and that of the school-based researchers. The voices of the school personnel are recorded in two ways. First, comments from evaluation data collected as part of the workshop process are included in the researchers' account. Second, a case study written by teachers from one of the schools in the project is reproduced in full.

Action research in a gender equity project

The task for the project was to develop professional development modules for school teachers and administrators that addressed classroom and school practices which contribute to equality of outcomes for girls and boys in Years 7–10. The project was framed by two conditions: (a) schools from two states had to be involved in developing the professional development material; and (b) the trialling of any materials had to incorporate a 'train the trainer' approach. In order to meet the requirements of the project, partnerships were established between university-based researchers and personnel from four school sites, two in one state and two in another. It was significant that the project provided both a structure for research partnerships to exist and a process for the professional growth and development of the partners. There were two key outcomes from the project. The first was changed practices in the partner schools (i.e., research with the profession) and the second was the publication of seven professional development modules which focused on how teachers can tackle gender inequality in schools using an action research approach to professional development (i.e., research for the profession).

The process of selection of schools from both states to participate in the project was guided by consultations with appropriate state and national education advisers. The main criterion for school selection centred on their interest or involvement in gender equity issues and a willingness to contribute to a national project. After discussion and consultation, two Queensland (one secondary and a nearby primary feeder school) and two northern New South Wales secondary schools were approached and agreed to become involved in the project. The combination of secondary and primary schools was chosen because in Queensland, Year 7 marks the final year of primary school whereas in New South Wales, Year 7 is the first year of secondary school. Gender equity officers in regions where the schools were located were also involved in the project mainly through participation in the workshops, and in follow-up visits to participating schools.

Within each of the schools, the teachers who volunteered to be part of the project did so from a variety of motives. Two teachers from a school in New South Wales became involved because of previous interest and involvement in girls' education strategies and projects, while another, from the second New South Wales school, saw it as an opportunity to raise the profile of gender equity within her school. Other reasons teachers identified for their participation in the project ranged from curriculum area needs to an interest in what was being done for the boys. Their interest in initiating change to improve some aspect of practice was an important criterion for inclusion because of the intended use of action research. Furthermore, to explore a sensitive area such as gender, which evokes resistance and defensiveness among many men and women in the community, it was crucial to enlist schools which were prepared to invest time and energy into this important issue.

From our experience in gender-based research, we anticipated that participants would encounter resistance from some staff in their schools. This reinforced our desire to engage schools and personnel with the commitment necessary to persevere in the face of such resistance. At the same time we recognised that the action research approach which builds awareness and collaboration was an appropriate vehicle for professional development and had the potential to reduce the effects of resistance and challenge the resistors.

One of the key issues for the university researchers was the desire and commitment to model action research throughout the module development process. We drafted a working set of principles drawn from personal experiences of leading successful professional development activities on gender issues in schools, together with perspectives from the literature. The principles were as follows:

- Collaborate with and value the input of the school personnel.
- Be responsive to the school personnel's intimate knowledge of school staff and contexts.
- Make available on-site support for the school personnel at every stage of the development process.
- Value individuals in the process.
- Bring together practical and theoretical perspectives on gender issues.
- Explore personal beliefs and understandings of gender issues as a starting point.
- Accept that real change is a gradual process and that because individuals are at different points of understanding and practice, resistance would be encountered and, as far as possible, addressed.

First stage of project

First workshop: planning for action

Following a number of weekly meetings among the university researchers in the early stages of the project, a full-day workshop was held bringing together school and education regional office personnel from southern Queensland and northern New South Wales and the university researchers responsible for the project. Each of the four schools was represented by two staff members. The workshop was designed for participants to meet one another and to discuss the focus of, and boundaries for, the project. It provided the opportunity to establish the partnerships which would take the project forward. The workshop agenda was as follows:

- Introduction and overview of the project.
- Project update.
- Open session for questions and comments.

- Exploring 'relationships' as a theme for the project.
- Introduction to action research as a means of exploring gender issues in the school.
- School groups action planning (undertaken by school personnel).
- Feedback on action plans (from university researchers and school personnel).
- Allocation of university researchers to work with schools in subsequent phases of the project.

The workshop was facilitated by the university researchers and designed to foster the development of collaborative practices among a group of people (many of whom did not know each other) with diverse understandings of and interests in gender issues. We also addressed a number of critical issues for the conduct of the project. Participants were exposed to gendered material from the popular media as a way of raising consciousness about the area and providing stimulation for the development of ideas for school-based research. Perspectives on action research processes were also shared. The final session at the workshop was devoted to school personnel identifying focus areas for school-based research and planning data collection to inform those areas.

While teachers' reactions to the workshop process were mainly positive and its value as a professional development opportunity was described as 'an excellent opportunity to meet and discuss issues on a professional basis with people from another state and institution', they pointed to the need to develop a framework to guide their involvement:

Although the process is up for negotiation it needs a certain amount of structure to enable us to carry on. We are so busy, we cannot think.

Other comments from teachers included:

[The] cooperative style was appreciated.

The clarity and intention of action research took some time to arrive at. Maybe some further talk around the objectives to be achieved would have avoided this.

[The workshop] sharpened my awareness of the media's role in the definition of cultural versus biological gender.

[Enhanced] self-esteem by being recognised for a worthy contribution. We have the choice to negotiate so we all feel like team members.

Data gathering

Following this workshop, school staff returned to their respective schools to begin a month-long process of exploration of their self-selected gender issues. Data collection focused primarily on teachers, administration staff and students, but in some cases involved ancillary staff and parents. On occasions, teachers called upon the university participants and regional personnel to assist with planning the data collection process and, in the case of two schools, university participants were asked to conduct interviews with teaching staff and a small number of parents. Teachers expressed the view that the involvement of outsiders in the interview process would help to reduce any potential hesitancy of staff and parents to provide open and honest perspectives.

Teachers focused data collection activities in areas that they perceived were of most concern to their schools. One school, for example, focused on three areas for data collection in the initial stage: classroom interactions; curriculum leaders' perceptions of their department's teaching strategies and practices in terms of equality of outcomes for girls and boys; and student subject choice. Data collection strategies utilised by teachers included: a questionnaire distributed to heads of departments which focused on issues associated with inclusive curriculum; a questionnaire distributed to Year 11 students which focused on student subject choice and preferred learning styles; and a similar questionnaire distributed to fifty-eight teaching staff. Classroom interactions became the focus for more intensive investigation, with results from classroom observations being fed back to the staff involved. In one school, a classroom observation instrument was developed and used by teachers working in pairs to monitor their classroom interactions with boys and girls in the areas of eye contact, control, examination of work and informal chats.

Paralleling the school-based data collection process, the university researchers gathered a range of existing professional development materials. These resources were used to supplement the school-based data to inform the writing of the modules.

Constraining factors

The competing demands on teachers' time and the short project time frame were constraining factors in the data collection process. One participating teacher reported:

> Much of the research had to be conducted in a very short time frame and had to compete with other demands on the project team's time. . . . Difficulties existed in finding a time to conduct research with the whole staff in a school the size of River High [pseudonym].

Hence, it was not only difficult for teachers to find opportunities to fit additional activities into a school day, but time was also limited in terms of engaging the whole staff in professional development opportunities. Resistance from other teachers was also identified as a major concern in the action research process. Resistance occurred to varying extents in all of the schools. One teacher commented that there was 'ongoing polarisation in her school and that there was personal resentment of me as the vehicle of the initiative'. Another concern expressed by teachers was the non-co-operation of some of their colleagues: 'I feel disappointed that I couldn't have got more people enthused in our school. People are reluctant to get involved unless there is something in it for them', and another said that some staff showed 'resistance, hostility and/or apathy towards gender equity issues and the project itself'.

While staff reported that the action research process had generated significant interest and awareness, particularly among teaching staff, it was also evident that undercurrents of resistance to raising gender issues existed, and responding to resistance would have to be addressed in the modules. At the same time, however, it was recognised that resistance is a common response to change initiatives, it can manifest itself in positive ways and is a key concept in understanding how some kinds of change actually come about. History shows, for example, that challenges to, and resistance against injustices to women has led to slow but gradual change.

The resistance phenomenon and the professional development of teachers

Resistance in the context of gender issues may be better understood if read within the current social and educational climate. The media have paid particular attention in recent years to the notion of the 'male as victim', and this attention has recently focused on schools. Woodley's article entitled 'Is it the boys' turn for special help?' (*The Sydney Morning Herald*, 19 April 1994, p. 15) talked about 'the general overpowering of boys by girls in the 1993 HSC' whilst the Melbourne-based *Age* newspaper reported: 'Ministers act on boys' problems in education' (30 April 1994).

In August 1994, a national newspaper ran an article in which Bettina Arndt asserted that: 'It's well recognised that girls are out-performing the opposite sex in the classroom. As the economy shifts further into the services sector, that trend is expected to be reflected in the jobs market too' (*The Weekend Australian*, 27–28 August 1994, p. 20). Such media publicity has tended to create a community perception that affirmative action, and in the case of schools, attention to the needs of girls, have robbed boys of their 'rights' and jeopardised males in terms of education and employment.

Given this current climate, it is doubly important to deal with the notion of resistance in professional development programmes that are focused on gender issues. For this reason, the content of the project modules included a section on resistance in the broader community, in the schools, and how one deals with resistance. The research team recognised that resistance at one level is a predictable and healthy response to rapid change. It is not to be feared, but should be faced honestly. Understanding the current context means highlighting the following issues :

- the role of the media in playing the 'male as victim' theme;
- the part played by the economic recession and competition for jobs (along with calls for married women to surrender jobs);
- the resurgence of fundamentalism and political conservatism (agendas which clearly include an assertion of 'biology as destiny');
- a perception that community fragmentation and family 'breakdown' are somehow due to feminism and the changing roles of women and men.

In a school, resistance may take different forms, and the partners in the project talked about their varied encounters with resistance. Male and female teachers often responded differently. In the secondary schools, different subject departments interpreted the issues quite differently. Teachers may respond differently from administrators, especially if they perceive change is being forced on them from above. It is important for teachers to recognise the signs of resistance, and the steps that people take as they work through an issue that challenges their assumptions about the world. Responses range through: denial there is a problem; trivialisation of the issue as not important; feeling powerlessness (along with the alibi that 'it is someone else's responsibility to change things'); coming to terms with the issue; and finally, taking action to initiate change, rather than waiting for change to occur. In the design of the project, the process of resistance was acknowledged, and regarded as a predictable part of professional change. Understanding the process, and the way different members of the school community: parents, students, administrators and classroom teachers, experience this process, were integral to the project.

Second workshop: group reflection and further planning

Five weeks after the initial workshop, a second was held with three purposes in mind: (a) to consider the data that the teachers had collected and how that might develop into ideas for the modules; (b) to discuss issues that arose through the processes of data collection; and (c) to collaboratively identify strategies that could be adopted by teachers to engage their colleagues in a consideration of the gender issues that they had identified. Specifically, the workshop pursued the following agenda:

- Project update.

- Action research reports from schools which focused on: key questions/issues addressed by the schools; problems or difficulties encountered and how they were addressed; the nature of the data collected; personal perceptions of the data collection process; and key issues arising from the action research.
- Identification of tentative topics for the modules.
- Identification of intervention/staff development strategies.
- Establishment of criteria to judge the effectiveness of the proposed strategies.
- Planning the way forward for school personnel.

While the university researchers facilitated the workshop and acted as 'critical friends' to sharpen the focus on gender, the workshop agenda was largely controlled by the teachers. The workshop provided us with an opportunity for further reflection to discover and understand the different ways in which schools had taken up the issues, to consider what we could have done better, and what this meant for subsequent professional development planning and action.

It was with interest that we noted that the project agenda and resources had in some cases been partially diverted to accommodate other agendas in the school. As partners we worked with teachers to maintain the focus of the project, while at the same time respecting the agendas of the participating schools. Negotiating the project focus with teachers became a necessary aspect the project.

School-based research had uncovered issues relating to: gender inclusive curriculum, especially in mathematics; gendered use of playground space; gendered behaviour and relationships in the classroom; gender relationships and power amongst staff; and gendered nature of school administrative hierarchies. The focuses for the modules had begun to form. Teachers commented on the processes of the second workshop:

I feel we were all more at ease with one another this time.

I appreciated the opportunity of hearing some of the similar problems encountered by other data gatherers.

Case studies and reports were very interesting and prompted thinking and discussion of ideas I hadn't thought of beforehand.

It was valuable sharing experiences with others from both similar and different areas; having the opportunity to reflect on the project intent, direction and possibilities; having time to think through where we have been.

Having identified a range of current gender concerns in schools, the workshop participants addressed the question: 'What can be achieved in schools?' and generated tentative ideas, suggestions and examples of intervention and staff development strategies appropriate to respond to those concerns. Teachers had mixed reactions to this process:

> I was a little unclear as to how to transfer action research into professional development priorities. The school's action plan was really needed.

> It was good. I am still a little unclear how the professional development modules relate to the process proposed.

> It was valuable sharing ideas for research and action; having the opportunity to focus the action plan.

Each school left the second workshop with an action plan that had an identified gender concern and some strategies for addressing that concern in their school.

The second workshop brought the first stage of the project to its conclusion. Some significant achievements had been made in this first stage, including the identification of: module topics; ways of conducting effective professional development activities on gender issues; the principles for professional development; principles and a framework for module development; and evaluation criteria to measure the success of the professional development.

Second stage of project

School-based action

After the second workshop teachers returned to their schools, in some cases to re-focus their efforts and in others to move the project forward by engaging staff in their schools in processes that directed attention to the issues relating to equality of outcomes for boys and girls. Concurrent with this activity, the university academics commenced initial work to shape the modules. By a careful sorting of all of the available information, focus areas for the modules were identified and then presented.

While the processes of data gathering created new awareness for the school staff, the actual implementation of action plans highlighted the ways in which gender shapes the daily lives of members of the school community. Some action plan strategies included the presentation of project findings to whole-staff meetings, meetings with heads of department and principals, supporting girls to lobby for more access to playground space for physical activity and raising concerns about the girls' school uniform with the parent body. When requested, university participants supported the implementation of these strategies. In one school this involved attending a planning meeting with the principal to discuss ways of responding to a gender imbalance on the school executive, in another, sitting in on a somewhat hostile science staff meeting from which one member walked out and in another, organising a staff information session conducted by a senior policy officer from the Queensland Education Department's Gender Equity Unit on gender and violence in schools.

Third workshop: reflection and sharing

At the third and final workshop, held five weeks after the second, teachers shared and discussed their recent experiences. The objectives for this workshop were as follows:

- to identify the assumptions and principles underpinning effective professional development programmes;
- to refine a set of principles and develop a framework for the modules;
- to prepare and plan for one professional development strategy to be trialled in schools, using the proposed module framework.

Achievement of these objectives required the integration of the teachers' data collection and action plans with the resources and literature collected and collated by the university researchers. In the third workshop, school personnel took the opportunity to interrogate one another about the implementation of their action plans. This often generated suggestions for alternative ways of bringing about change in beliefs and practices. Teachers also provided written feedback about their experiences in the project to date and indicated how they thought they may have changed as a consequence of their involvement in the project:

A greater sense of personal power – feeling that I can have more impact within the school decision-making system.

Greater contact with certain staff members and the principal.

[I] found it personally awareness raising – good professional development.

A better understanding of professional development and other theories of professional development.

I appreciate the power of action research as a model for changing attitudes and practices when personnel are actively involved.

Preparedness to make changes.

I have developed some of my own strategies to help ensure equality of teacher resources for boys and girls.

Increased awareness of unintentional bias.

These three workshops have been valuable in terms of professional and personal development, awareness of gender issues and in conducting action research in schools.

At the end of this workshop it was agreed that the university researchers would take the responsibility for writing first drafts of the modules and that the school personnel begin to develop a network of teachers from other schools in their locations with whom they could trial the draft modules. The third workshop involved all participants in the development process to date and brought to a conclusion the crucial second stage of the project.

Third stage of project

Module writing

Following the third workshop, drawing on the work of teachers and regional personnel, the university researchers developed the modules to first draft stage. The data collection process, implementation of action plans and collation of existing literature and resource materials revealed seven obvious areas of focus: getting started; femininity and masculinity; working with boys; working with girls; inside the classroom; outside the classroom; and staff.

Where possible, the university researchers used the data collected from the school-based personnel to form part of an activity or as an illustration in the discussion of the issues in the modules. As part of the module development process, school personnel frequently contributed by reworking and rewriting some activities to better suit their school environments.

Module trialling

The trialling was a vital stage in module development as the modules were intended to be stand-alone products which could be used by school staff without external support. Trialling was undertaken in two phases.

In phase one, four staff from each of the original participating schools took responsibility for trialling one of the modules with four staff from a partner school. They:

- selected a module and became familiar with its contents (this was typically the module that had been generated from the action research in the participating school);
- identified a partner school and negotiated the involvement of four staff from that school;
- developed an appropriate strategy for the trialling and training process-developed an evaluation process for the trial;
- arranged dates and a suitable venue.

In phase two, staff from the two schools repeated the process with staff from two other schools in the region. University researchers provided limited assistance with the trialling process but did attend the trialling sessions to provide moral support and to provide an 'outsider's' perspective on the content and professional development processes in the modules. Feedback from phases one and two of module trialling informed subsequent module redrafts.

The action research process continued to enhance our learning about gender-based professional development. We recount the following as one example of that learning. In the course of the trialling, both school and university participants became impatient with what we perceived to be a lack of progress in schools identifying, understanding and responding to seemingly obvious issues. However, out of our reflective deliberations on this matter we came to the realisation that what was obvious for some constituted 'new' discoveries for others and that the modules would have to make provision for different levels of awareness of, and commitment to, addressing, gender issues.

The draft modules were constantly redrafted and refined as feedback was received from school-based personnel and other interested parties. We issued copies of the draft modules, not only to teachers involved intimately in the project, but to other teachers to whom we had access, for example, those undertaking postgraduate study at the university. By involving a number of different people in the evaluation process, we received rich insights and relevant advice as to how to make the modules more workable and in some cases, more 'user friendly'.

Reflection on the effectiveness of the action research process

As a further stage in our monitoring of the effects of our actions during the project journey, we bring together reflections under the banners of participation and collaboration, action and reflection.

Participation and collaboration

As far as possible within the boundaries of the project, there was an enacted commitment to genuine participation and collaboration at both the level of the project and within the participating schools. Teachers commented:

> [I valued] meeting [university researchers] who I know share my passion for equality of outcomes.

> The project has enabled a strong sense of collegiality to develop between the staff in the participating schools.

> I met useful contacts and widened my experiences of other school programmes.

> Involvement in the programme provided a platform for sharing ideas and initiatives amongst participating schools.

> I have had a demonstration of the collaboration between national and local agents.

The extent to which all staff members within each of the four key schools embraced the spirit of the project and actively co-operated with the key teachers involved was in some contexts problematic. Reports from teachers illustrate that, in some schools, only small numbers of teachers became involved. In terms of outcomes for schools, the quote below sums up one school's response:

> Outcomes for schools [were] fairly limited because of small numbers involved, but awareness has been raised and a lot of gender issues have been brought forward again after being forgotten.

While the preceding and following quote suggest that only a small group of staff had been involved, the overall feeling was that teachers were pleased with the inroads they made – even if small:

> Initially I felt that our input was only token, but when I saw the results of the evaluation we did on the first draft, I felt that our input had been accepted as valuable and I am now satisfied with the process.

The university-based researchers like the school-based researchers were faced with competing demands on their time having to balance project commitments against teaching and other research responsibilities. This posed limitations on the professional partnership between academics and teachers in terms of moving the project towards the sort of 'researching community' to which Grundy refers in Chapter 3, this volume.

It was an enormous project. Fitting it into such a narrow time frame meant that collaborative work between academics and teachers at the school site was limited.

School action towards gender equity

Action research is a political process because it means that change impacts on others. Changes in the four schools were evidenced in different ways. While some of these were evident in current practices, others were planned for the future. For example, increase in playground space for girls and changes to the girls' uniform were two specific changes identified by schools. Regarding future changes and plans, schools identified the following: monthly meetings for staff to discuss issues and share ideas about gender issues; refining research instruments; setting up structures for more equitable use of the playground for girls and boys; trialling single-sex physics and chemistry classes in Year 11; introducing the 'alternatives to aggression' programme, a whole-school emphasis on gender in education and one school making a commitment to another DEETYA-funded gender and professional development project.

Other teachers stated that structures such as regular committee meetings would be established to address particular gender-related concerns in the school:

> . . . a steering committee will be formed with the aim of investigating pupil–pupil discourse. This steering committee will communicate its research findings to the school staff and form an action plan to react to the research findings.

Another school went on to set up monthly meetings to discuss issues and share news and journal items as they relate to gender issues. This same school stated its plan:

> to hold some sort of forum early in fourth term with guest speakers and/or a panel of people whose jobs or professions challenge students' ideas about career opportunities outside often-held gendered perceptions.

One school invited two female members of staff to join the School Executive meeting for a period of six weeks in order to redress gender imbalance in the participation level and contributions to decision making in the school. This proved to be a worthwhile exercise which alerted the school structure to the importance of gender balance in meetings and committees. What followed was the appointment of three female head teachers to the School Executive, lowering the gender imbalance in the School Executive and Committee membership.

Another teacher commented that:

> what we have grown together can be continued within the school's social justice and studies agendas.

Teachers' reflection

The project provided participants the opportunity for partners to clarify their own values and their teaching practice. Perhaps the most telling personal reflection on the project comes from a teacher who openly admitted that:

> at that time [time of project commencement] I had no more interest in gender equity issues than any other professional who is obliged to consider all groups within the class.

She went on to reflect:

> I feel privileged at having had the opportunity of working with the project group in spite of living through some very worrying times when the enormity of the task we'd agreed to undertake dawned on me. I had read little about the topic and often felt unsure of the ability of myself and our willing but inexperienced and very busy work group to fulfill our part of the project. At first I found some of the assumptions which the project group made about the treatment of girls very challenging.
>
> Working with the project team and later trialling the modules was a great learning experience for me. It forced me to clarify formerly unconsciously held beliefs and assumptions about the construction of gender and to consciously evaluate my classroom practices and the part they play in helping or hindering the development of my students.

Another teacher commented that:

> [the project] broadened my perceptions on boys' education which I believe is an area to change.

Other staff who took part in the data collection and trialling in the schools commented that they have an increased awareness of the effect their curriculum choices and treatment of children have on gender expectations.

In all of the schools involved in the project, participants claimed that an overall increase in awareness of gender issues and sensitivity to gender resulted within their schools:

> school staff were shown to be pro-active in gender related issues;

> [there was an] increase in sensitivity to gender differences.

Most teachers indicated that gender equity and specific gender issues would continue to be addressed and the interest of all staff members would develop in this area. The following comment sums up the feelings of one teacher regarding gender equity:

> [an] acceptance of the issue as one which is here to stay and which must be addressed.

Case study – Kadina State High School

The purpose of presenting this case study is to provide the reader with an opportunity to gain an insight into the work of the project from the perspective of the teachers. This unedited narrative from one school provides such an insight. In some measure it is providing an opportunity for the 'voice' of the teachers to be heard.

School profile

Kadina High School is located on the Far North Coast of New South Wales in a rapidly expanding suburb of Lismore. Goonellabah has a growing population with a mixture of Housing Commission develop-ments and new housing estates bringing young families into the area. The 1993 enrolment was 1,015 with 720 students in Years 7 to 10. (Ratio 389 males : 331 females.) In 1994, the school enrolment is 1,013 with 742 students in Years 7 to 10. (Ratio 375 males : 367 females.)

The staff in 1993 consisted of 9 executives/head teachers in the ratio of 8 males : 1 female, and 65 teaching staff (permanent and casual) in a ratio of 42 males : 23 females. While in 1994, the school executive/head teacher ratio changed to 9 males : 3 females, and the teaching staff increased to 68, in a ratio of 42 males : 26 females.

Kadina High School has been involved in National Schools Project initiatives, as well as local innovations such as the Lismore Secondary Schools Project. Members of the school community, including girls in the junior forms and parents, were involved in the NSW Department of School Education evaluation of educational outcomes for girls in secondary schools carried out by a Quality Assurance Team. The school principal has also encouraged our participation in regional gender equity programmes and also in the Gender and Professional Practices Project (GAPP).

The issues and how they were identified

Following an initial meeting with the GAPP Team and other participants at Queensland University of Technology (QUT), a number of key issues were identified for the participating schools. Issues such as gender relationships, power, behaviour and violence were identified. More specific issues were drawn from these broad categories:

- Playground areas;
- Use of resources – including sports equipment and facilities;
- Participation in programmes;
- Post-school pathways/vocational choices;
- Subject selection;
- Sex-based harassment in school;
- Classroom interactions.

The process

1   The background to the GAPP Project was outlined to members of the School Executive by the two participants. Head teachers were asked for their assistance in identifying and co-ordinating action research within their own faculty.
2   Teaching staff were addressed at a general staff meeting regarding the GAPP Project and their involvement in the action research.
3   Various school committees (i.e. welfare, curriculum, computer), were also approached regarding their involvement in the data collection process.

4   The Parents and Citizens Group and the Student Representative Council were advised and approached to contribute to the data collection.

5   Teaching staff were surveyed as to the various methods of data collection and asked to nominate which format they felt most appropriate for them. Strict time limits allowed little time for discussion or delay.

6   A random sample of teachers were interviewed and recorded on the issues of gender equity in education and sex-based harassment by two members of the GAPP team from QUT.

7   A great variety of data was collected by staff on various issues as outlined in the forms of surveys, questionnaires, personal anecdotes, statistical analysis, observations, comparative evaluations, gender breakdowns, project evaluations, interviews.

8   The collected data was taken to a further meeting of the GAPP Team where discussion of the findings took place. Data was divided into two main areas: (a) gender and relationships (power) and (b) gender and curriculum.

9   At two subsequent staff meetings, staff were invited to look at the summaries of the data collected and to suggest possible areas for examination and investigation, within the limited time frame for the project. The included: (a) use of the playground; (b) girls and physical education/sport (including uniform); and (c) school executive and gender imbalance.

Problems encountered

Effective communication between participants and teaching staff was hampered by the strict time limits imposed by the late start of the project and the initial resistance of the School Executive, who were already 'overloaded' with extra duties.

The 'knee jerk' reaction of staff after a full staff meeting was also a result of poor communication and fear at the size of the task being addressed. However, these fears were allayed when GAPP participants spoke to faculties separately and to individuals who had indicated their interest. Time, and the lack thereof, was the greatest stumbling block.

Some male staff and faculties expressed anger at the process where female staff were invited to attend Executive meetings without prior communication or discussion at a whole-staff meeting. Again, poor communication and time restrictions were factors in this instance. Once staff had been informed of the nature of this initiative, they accepted it.

Positive outcomes/results

- General awareness-raising of the issues such as gender equity, sex-based harassment, gender relationships, behaviour and other gender-related issues within our school.
- Invitation to two female members of staff to join the School Executive meetings to redress gender imbalance in the participation level and contributions to decision making in the school over a trial period of six weeks. (One different member of the female teaching staff was invited each week to address the meeting on various areas of concern/expertise.) Observations and responses from the participants were sought, and were found to be extremely favourable.
- Executive restructure (unsure if this is strictly related or circumstantial).
- Appointment of new head teachers in Welfare, PE/PD, English will add three extra females to the School Executive and therefore lower the gender imbalance in the School Executive and Committee membership.
- PE/Sport uniform for girls has been altered to allow shorts as an acceptable alternative to the previous short skirt which inhibited some girls from participating in sporting activities.
- Ongoing discussions with PE staff regarding the promotion of girls in team sports and lunch time sporting activities.
- Mapping of girls'/boys' usage of playground areas has identified possible projects where 'quiet' areas may be created to allow for students to sit in a protected, safe atmosphere.
- Shade and seating projects nominated by Student Representative Council, Occupational Health and Safety Committee, Grounds Committee and environmental projects underway to create appropriate protection from the sun and extreme weather conditions. i.e. 'Shade sails' erected, circular seating to be provided.

Conclusions

School-based researchers were pleased with the process and felt that the action research model was a powerful form of professional development because it grew out of their own specific contexts and therefore the data generated was relevant. It also meant that professional development was not being done to them. Rather they were in control of the process by their collective planning, action and reflection.

The project experience confirmed to us (university researchers) our belief that action research is a powerful process for fostering learning and promoting change in schools, especially in areas where uncontested beliefs and values are held by staff members. In the current context of professional development where teachers are afforded little time, if any time at all, for involvement in professional development activities inside school hours, and their access to external professional development 'experts' has been reduced, action research is an ideal framework for professional development because it is collaborative, action oriented and context specific. For an issue such as gender, which creates anxiety and sometimes outright hostility at the very thought of the concept, we believe that action research has a better chance of dealing with resistance than other models that are not based in collaborative inquiry. While resistance will never be totally minimised, action research has great potential for effecting long-term change and commitment through encouraging professionals to reflect critically on their often taken-for-granted practices.

We contend that action research, which fosters genuine partnerships between participants, is a useful way of facilitating gender-focused professional development. The outcomes of such an approach go beyond the production of materials to professional development processes that bring together theoretical and practical perspectives. From our experience in this project we further contend that it is appropriate for the impetus for action research to come from 'outsiders'. The process then, however, relies most heavily on committed groups of people who are prepared to collaborate for the purposes of improving their own and other people's practices.

REFERENCES

Australian Education Council (1993) *National Action Plan for the Education of Girls 1993–1997*, Victoria: Curriculum Corporation.

Henry, C. and Kemmis, S. (1985) 'A point-by-point to action research for teachers', *The Australian Administrator*, 6 (4): 1–4.

Hopkins, D. (1987) 'Teacher research as a basis for staff development', in Wideen, M. F. and Andrews, I. (eds) *Staff Development for School Improvement: A Focus on the Teacher*, Philadelphia: The Falmer Press.

Ingvarson, L. (1987) 'Models of in-service education and their implications for professional development policy', *Independent Education*, 17 (2): 23–32.

Kemmis, S. (1987) 'Critical reflection', in Wideen, M. F. and Andrews, I. (eds) *Staff Development for School Improvement*, Philadelphia: The Falmer Press.

Lieberman, A. (1992) 'The meaning of scholarly activity and the building of community', *Educational Researcher*, 21 (6): 5–12.

Owen, J. M. (1990) 'Perspectives from down under', in Joyce, B. (ed.) *Changing School Culture through Staff Development*, Yearbook of the Association for Supervision and Curriculum Development, Alexandria, Virginia: Association for Supervision and Curriculum Development, pp. 168–81.

11

COLLABORATIVE ACTION
RESEARCH

Learnings from a social sciences project in a
secondary school

*Ian Macpherson, Charles Arcodia, Sonya Gorman, Jill
Shepherd and Ros Trost*

The Teaching for Effective Learning in Senior Schooling (TELSS) Project was
a three-year collaborative/participatory[1] action research project to facilitate
change in teaching and learning practice. The project was a partnership of
university and school community personnel at an inner suburban state high
school. Those involved in the project sought to examine and document the
change process in terms of students, teachers, society and the state education
system. The project was not interested in a simple critique of circumstances
but actively encouraged participants to define their own problems and issues
and to pursue solutions to them. It was built around a model of collaborative
or participatory action research. This is an approach whereby a facilitator
engages with a group of participants in the context of their working environment to help define and explore certain problems and needs. Such an
approach emphasises the importance of involving participants at all levels
and stages of the process, from initial problem clarification through to solution implementation and all intervening stages. It is built around principles
of constructivist theory in that it advocates the importance of aiding and
allowing participants to build bridges in their own minds between that
which is known and that which they are coming to know. As such, emphasis
is given to participants as 'generators' of learning. In all areas, theories of
critical reflection are important, in that learners need to be encouraged to
name their 'oppression'. This is the first step in the process of active liberation. As Freire puts it:

> The insistence at which the oppressed engage in reflection on their
> concrete situation is not a call to armchair revolution. On the
> contrary, reflection – true reflection leads to action. On the other

hand, when the situation calls for action, that action will constitute an authentic praxis only if its consequences become the object of critical reflection.

(Freire 1972: 41)

The methods by which critical reflection is invoked are not uniform, but may alter according to the nature of the problem to be studied and the nature of both the facilitator and the participants involved.

The aim of the project was to develop a senior school framework which takes into account recent policy documents (Australian Education Council and Ministers for Vocational Education, Employment and Training 1992; Australian Education Council Review Committee 1991; Employment and Skills Formation Council 1992; Wiltshire 1994), initiatives such as the Key Competencies, links with industry and the need to increase student autonomy, organisational flexibility and staff professional development.

It was responding to the world-wide trend in developed industrial countries for industry and education authorities to collaborate to improve the quality of education and to develop a greater level of mutual understanding between these two sectors.

A focus on an action research approach that is collaborative/participatory opened up the possibility of engaging in a process that was emancipatory and empowering for all participants – emancipatory in the sense of creating an environment for critiquing current policy trends and reconstructing practices in the context of such critique, and empowering in the sense of participants' developing a feeling on authority to contest, politicise and advocate for actions considered appropriate within the context of critique. The project, in some ways, became an action project on the project itself. The project became an advocate for action research as an empowering agent; it valued parity of esteem for all partners or participants in the project; and it certainly addressed notions of social justice in its advocacy for changes to research and school cultures.

The principles of collaborative action research as documented in applications for funding the project sounded fine on paper, but getting started with the various sub-projects was another story. The Social Sciences Project, a sub-project of the TELSS project, was no exception and getting started was a very slow process. Teachers had lots of questions and suspicions and time was definitely needed to build a working relationship. The Social Sciences Project became an example of developing a living educational theory about educational change.

Initially meetings were held which involved social science teachers and university personnel. The overall project was outlined and possibilities for the Social Sciences Project were discussed. The detailed agenda for the project, it was stressed, had to emerge from the people who were going to work together on it.

From these initial meetings, a small group of teachers emerged as being interested and wanting to be involved. It was this group who joined with the university personnel to develop a research agenda and to begin implementing it. This group considered it had a responsibility to report both to the management committee of the overall project and to the social science teachers at the school.

This chapter tells the story of the five people most directly involved in the project over the three years.

The social sciences project

Research in 1993

The Social Sciences Project was one of four investigations within the TELSS Project. It began with the social sciences staff raising a number of issues about effective teaching and learning in the social sciences. Of particular concern were the decreasing numbers of students choosing the social sciences in the senior school in comparison to other subject areas. The main purpose of the initial meeting between the university researchers and the teachers was to discuss relevant issues and concerns more broadly and to define the nature and scope of the study in this curriculum area.

The collaborative research group, which was formed, developed a research focus and appropriate procedures over the ensuing months. The group decided that the study would focus on the place of the social sciences in the school curriculum by seeking perceptions from a range of persons in terms of the:

- significance of the social sciences in the school curriculum;
- relevance of the social sciences in the school curriculum;
- continuity in the social sciences from the primary to the lower secondary and the senior secondary school curriculum;
- implementation of the social sciences curriculum at the primary, lower secondary and senior secondary levels.

To provide some focus, questions asked as discussion starters generally fell under one of the following categories: definition; organisation; teaching and learning; and student perceptions.

The range of persons from whom perceptions were obtained included school administrators, social sciences teachers, other teachers at the school, teachers at nearby feeder primary schools, students and parents. Data were collected by the teachers and research assistants through interviews and group meetings.

Once these data were collected, the teachers began to reflect on and analyse the information in terms of what continuities, relevance and significance were perceived by teachers and students. The research team developed

214

an analytical summary which focused on the emerging issues and implications which was presented to the non-participating social sciences teachers at the school via a workshop. The purpose of the workshop was to discuss and decide which of the suggested implications would form the focus of research for the following year. The agreement that was reached was that the major focus would be on teaching and learning in the social sciences classrooms and that this focus would also inform in an ongoing way a shared definition of the social sciences in the curriculum generally and in the senior school particularly. The study would have three interconnecting components: research, professional development and advocacy.

At the workshop towards the end of 1993, the social sciences teachers were provided with the study's methodology, its limitations, a summary of the data collected and emergent implications under the following categories:

Definition

A range of definitions for the social sciences surfaced which pointed to some fragmentation in understanding the holistic nature of the social sciences. Issues to be addressed were:

- shared understanding of the social sciences by those involved;
- integration of the various social science disciplines;
- linking the social sciences with the Key Competencies associated with the national curriculum.

Organisation

A number of organisational issues (which could be grouped under the three categories of: organisation, management and restraints) emerged from the interviews with teachers and administrators. Major concerns dealt with whether the social sciences should be compulsory, channels of communication within the school, the use of resources and timetabling restraints.

Teaching and learning

There was almost unanimous agreement from teachers and students for the need for some improvement and variety in teaching strategies. Specific issues dealt with student motivation and creative teaching strategies.

The purpose of the workshop, involving all social science teachers at the school, was to discuss and decide which of the suggested implications would form the focus for research in 1994. The main outcome of the workshop was the development of an action plan to direct subsequent research on the identified focus of 'teaching and learning'.

Reflecting on the process in 1993

In early 1994, it was thought important that members of the group reflected individually on the project to date. A number of issues gleaned from experience and the literature, provided each member of the research team with a critical framework to reflect on the project. The reflections focused mainly on the process though there was some mention of the substantive side of the project. The commonalities in these reflections highlight the early frustrations and confusion in the beginning stages of the study. Over a period of time, however, a sense of community and common purpose emerged which allowed further frustrations and difficulties to be addressed more effectively. Together, the reflections helped to focus our thinking and action in terms of the project as a credible example of collaborative action research. The principles of collaboration, based on the reflections were to be:

- open communication;
- avoidance of jargon;
- clarity and sense of purpose;
- frameworks for critical reflection, professional development and advocacy;
- appreciation of teachers' time constraints;
- equity in decision making.

The reflections are presented as a series of vignettes which follow. They provided a context for the decisions we made and the actions which resulted later in 1994.

Initial reflections – Ros Trost

Initially, involvement in this collaborative research project, reflected my interest in personal growth as a teacher and my belief that the social sciences was the key to empowerment of students as learners for life rather than just in their school years. However, my enthusiasm was severely dented by a feeling of confusion, frustration and, at times, inadequacy, generated by a lack of communication of the history of focus of the project by school administrators and inadequate understanding of the roles and intentions of the university researchers in the process of collaboration with me as a teacher 'at the coal face' of learning.

In particular, I felt that a statement of intention in writing and wider discussion and distribution of relevant research material would have prevented:

- feelings of not knowing what I was there for;
- frustration that nothing positive was happening;
- suspecting that the researchers had a hidden agenda;
- my inexperience might compromise outcomes of interviews;
- the desire to walk away before it had a chance to get off the ground.

Also of concern to me at times was the language of academia with its inherent assumptions of shared understandings. This initially was a source of irritation; but given time and the building of a strong working partnership, this problem was easily resolved. Consequently, time is of the essence in this project. Not only the need to give it sufficient time to resolve the initial uncertainties and discomfort of someone new to research processes, but also the need to fund/allocate sufficient time and meetings to resolve feelings of frustration at apparent lack of continuity and progress towards outcomes. Finally, I believe that because we have over time as a group developed friendship and trust, I feel my contribution is valued and valuable and my original reasons for involvement and staying with the project have been more than adequately addressed and enriched.

Initial reflections – Sonya Gorman

FIRST MEETING – WHOLE SOCIAL SCIENCE STAFF

At this stage I was enthusiastic. I saw the project as a proactive way of addressing some of the grave concerns I had (as a new teacher to the school) about the state of social science here. I liked the promise of professional co-operation I felt was missing. I didn't understand HOW it would be done and felt confused about the idea of primary school interviews.

SUBSEQUENT MEETINGS RE INTERVIEW PHASE

I felt frustrated by what I felt to be a directionless and purposeless exercise. What would we do with this information in a *practical* sense and WHEN? I resented the expectations that we conduct interviews – I did not feel I had the necessary skills to ensure objective results and disliked the fact that we (school staff) seemed to be carrying the burden of 'research'. There was insecurity with the university staff. A sense of there being a hidden agenda – Key Competencies, etc. – existed. (Better information about the focus of the project needed at start.) Irritation at the 'bitty' nature of meetings due to lack of time meant I was becoming less committed/disinterested. There seemed little focus beyond getting interviews conducted and transcribed.

NOVEMBER '93 SOCIAL SCIENCE STAFF WORKSHOP

Here, things became clearer. Having to tell others what we'd done and why helped me understand and crystallise not only what we'd done but where we were going. Reading interview transcripts and discussing issues with staff pointed to broad but fairly clear areas of concern. I felt more comfortable with the 'collaborative' nature of the project and QUT staff personally. I could see the ways to address my initial concerns, and those of others, and get results.

DIRECTIONS FOR '94

We do have them (from the November meeting) but don't seem to be working towards them. The paper (for Post-Compulsory Conference) is helping us fine-tune. In some ways it's a distraction from our main goals of professional development and in-service. I still don't like the uncertain nature of our meetings. I've discovered I'm very task oriented and feel as though I'm wasting time without an agenda. A true and complete understanding of the concept and purpose of vignettes still eludes me to an extent. I feel positive about the pilot as a whole and more secure after the April 16 meeting.

GENERAL

Short meetings only raised questions, not addressed them. Longer blocks of time are needed for meetings. The nature of project needs early explanation.

Initial reflections – Jill Shepherd

Being involved in the collaborative research project with university researchers and the other social sciences department teachers at the school, has provided me with a marvellous opportunity for professional development in association with people of similar and supportive interests, and for improving the quality of teaching and learning in the social sciences at our school. Thus, I hope we can help increase student interest and numbers in the subjects offered by the social sciences department.

I had expected the university members of our research group would take a leading role in the project, guide us, tell us what to do, show where changes were needed and complete the programme as quickly as possible. But the process has been very different.

At initial meetings there was much discussion, making (it seemed to me) little headway. The teachers were waiting on the anticipated leadership of QUT members and were having difficulty in understanding the technical terminology being used. The problem was that the teachers did not understand the collaborative process in research until we read some research papers on the subject. We then understood our problems were common to collaborative work, especially where group members have a wide range of academic and work experience backgrounds.

With these new understandings, the next meeting was like an open confessional. From sharing our misunderstandings, difficulties and frustrations, a new relationship developed within the group that has allowed us to work together as equal members within the group. The 'them and us' barriers between university and school staff have been broken down; technical jargon is less frequently used and explained when necessary; we value the range of knowledge and skills that each member brings to the group; and members are very supportive, encouraging and non-judgemental.

Thus, it seems, the primary steps in any collaborative research project must include a very clear understanding of the collaborative process and development of collaborative group dynamics. These steps could not be forced nor hurried, as they involve time and individual effort.

The second stage involving research on teaching strategies is just under way and should prove just as professionally satisfying as each member takes and shares responsibility. And I'm sure we will achieve our overall goals far more effectively because of the collaborative approach to this project.

Initial reflections – Charles Arcodia

I brought to this project an interest in teaching the social sciences more effectively and a willingness to support practising teachers as they reflected on their teaching. I had spent many years in the class-room teaching a variety of subjects within the social sciences and I looked forward to the opportunity to allow our research to impact upon and renew my own teaching practice.

One of the difficulties I experienced was that whilst I understood the underlying premise of action research methodology, I had little practical experience of it. Other research work I had been involved in seemed more straightforward (and therefore easier) as it involved the analysis of texts and policy documents. The other difficulty was that I was involved with and trying to balance three other pilot studies as part of the overall project.

There is no doubt that whilst each of the studies is interesting and has the potential to improve the effectiveness of teaching and learning, the social sciences study is the only curriculum-based study in which I was involved in that seems committed to collaborative research as described in the literature.

One point that I have learned from the study so far is that it takes time to earn the trust of teachers, to develop and verbalise communal goals and to motivate busy teachers to give even more of their time to be involved with the study. As it became more obvious to the teachers that I had no 'hidden' agenda, I felt less of an interruption to their daily plans and I was able to defend the study and its 'slow but careful' progress with more conviction.

Another frustrating aspect was that some of the teachers I spoke with were resigned to the fact that nothing could be done, or at least very little could be done without the support of key school personnel. I was convinced and still am that whilst the involvement of others is more than welcome and accepting fully that organisational structures and inflexible personnel do impede advancement, lasting teacher change occurs from within.

Whilst action has been slow in coming, there is action and it is directed as much by the teachers as it is by university personnel. When the study is completed and the university researchers have moved on to new enterprises, the teachers should be empowered with the knowledge, experience, but most of all, the confidence to continue to 'plan, act, observe and reflect' on their teaching which is the very essence of action research.

Initial reflections – Ian Macpherson

My interest in the project emerged from my earlier involvement in the Senior Schooling Curriculum Framework; from follow-up research studies which focused on the process used to develop the framework; and from my continuing interest in collaborative research approaches using qualitative methodologies.

In the initial stages of such a large project, I wondered what my involvement in the project would be and how truly collaborative the project was going to be. I was concerned at some of the 'noise' which seemed to get in the way of communicating the thrust of the project to the school community. I worried about the perceptions (imagined or real – it didn't matter) of staff to one of the early projects. Initial meetings with social science teachers were difficult. I felt the project in a sense determined the agenda – quality teaching and learning in the senior school. However, I did not want to convey a sense of imposition. While I had ideas of the sort of things that could happen, I was determined not to impose an agenda. Understandably, teachers were confused, frustrated and probably cynical to some degree.

I had to learn tolerance and patience all the while contributing to an environment in which teachers' voices were heard, listened to and used as the major reference point in determining the agenda. I was endeavouring to make the Social Sciences Pilot Project one that took seriously a collaborative research approach.

I saw some of the implications relating to:

- equality of partnership amongst all members of the group;
- shared understandings re the purposes, principles and procedures of the project;

- development of a collaborative working relationship;
- awareness of the micro-political contexts in which the project is situated;
- the support of members in the group in terms of full participation in the project;
- the determination of realistic and achievable goals given the many factors operating within the context and affecting the members of the group in diverse ways;
- the communication to school and university personnel that collaborative approaches will lead to outcomes in the short term which focus on building relationships and developing action plans, and in the long term to more visible evidence relating to quality teaching and learning in senior schooling.

Thus far, the project has been a valuable learning experience more so in procedural rather than substantive terms. This learning experience has included the micro-politics of both the university-based research team and the school community; working with three teachers and a senior research assistant; and the evolving research environment where understandings, agendas, procedures, analysis and outcomes are being more comfortably shared.

These vignettes, along with the somewhat impersonal account of the early days of the project, formed the basis of a paper presentation at a national conference on Post-Compulsory Schooling in July, 1994 (Arcodia *et al.* 1994). This gave the five of us a goal and it became a discipline focus to document our work and our reflections on it.

Research in 1994

From the reflections and within the context of the principles identified above, we proceeded to focus our attention on classroom practices in the social sciences. Each teacher developed a set of observations and reflections based on this focus with reference to her own classroom practice. The observations and reflections had no rigid structure and were developed through observations and discussions with students and colleagues. The teachers offered a personal reflection of their teaching practice using the insights of colleagues and students together with their own perceptions. These reflections raised questions about the implementation and support of teaching strategies which purport to promote effective learning. The three sets of observations and reflections follow.

Reflecting on the process in 1994

Observations and reflections – Jill Shepherd

During 1994, I have utilised two very different types of strategies in the teaching of geography to a Year 12 (senior) class and to assessing outcomes. While it is too early to compare quantitative results as they have yet to complete their final assessment task, student response to the different types of teaching strategies has been obvious to the observer and in student responses to surveys.

In semester one, the students generally expected to be spoon-fed information and to pass tests well with content forming the major form of criteria. They had been used to this teacher-dependent approach during the previous year. So I used teacher-centred strategies and focused on content and skills.

Student responses to a survey seeking their comments on this semester's unit of work indicated that they:

- found some of the unit of value;
- found the most effective teaching strategy was the teacher writing information on the blackboard;
- saw the teacher's role as the provider of information and to assist understanding and achievement;
- found the work boring and could not get motivated;
- generally, did not put their best effort into this unit of work.

I found the class group uninspiring and difficult because the students lacked confidence in their ability to think for themselves; they expected all answers to be 'right' or 'wrong'. They depended on me for all instructions and information, and were not easy to motivate.

From the first day of the semester two unit of study, I established an informal atmosphere in the classroom to encourage students to be involved in discussions and decisions about course content, strategies, time management and assessment. Initially, students were very dependent on me, but as they realised their input was respected and group decisions were determining their course, they began to participate with increased confidence and took more control of their course, and accepted me more as a guide/facilitator/negotiator, less as the authority.

The first two topics in this unit involved teacher input and guidance to develop skills and independence so students could manage a totally student-directed third topic. For the final topic, very regular informal conferencing has ensured students stayed 'on track', provided support and guidance, has improved student–teacher relationships, provided positive feedback to students and ensured they have developed the necessary skills for their chosen tasks.

Student comments when asked to write their reflections on this second unit three-quarters through it included:

- 'useful in the future'
- 'interesting'
- 'enjoyable'
- 'working independently enables me to have more control and to go at my own pace'
- 'a list of benefits including development of communication skills, learning to take the initiative'.

Criticisms were mainly of the short amount of time available for research. However, for those who managed their time well, this has not been a problem.

I have observed growth in most of the students in a number of areas: affective, knowledge, research skills, self-confidence, maturity, awareness of community, local issues and people management.

The students and I are looking forward to completing this unit with their chosen means of presentation of the results of their research for assessment, though they feel a little anxious at this stage about peer assessment.

From observations and discussions with students and colleagues, and my own reflections, I must now ask:

- Do students benefit more from some teaching strategies than from others? If so, why and how?
- What is 'effective learning'?
- Did the attitudes and experiences of the previous year impact on the attitudes, learning and skills development this year?
- What should be the teacher's role in a classroom for the most effective learning?

Observations and reflections – Ros Trost

During interviews conducted with my 1993 Year 12 class, a significant number of students revealed that they felt previous years had not prepared them sufficiently for the study of documents at the level I had set them. In particular, they felt intimidated by the document studies I had prepared for examination purposes. They expressed concern that document studies had been a minor part of their work in class, and from their information, I came to the conclusion that little or no skills development had been experienced by them and the level of critical thinking they were exposed to was fairly limited. With this in mind, I prepared a number of lessons which concentrated on identifying levels of competency but at the same time starting with short, single-document studies designed to boost confidence rather than develop skills needed for more advanced critical analysis. Students confidently completed the task and expressed enthusiasm for this approach as they understood the categories of questions/responses and were aware of being extended into the higher levels of critical thinking through discussion in both small and large group situations.

To prepare the students for the more demanding skills of evaluating/comparing/contrasting, etc. several primary sources relating to a single topic, I have decided to integrate original sources with expository material over several lessons. My aim is to build on skills (acquired through study of single documents and understanding of the categories of questions/responses), to guide students towards competency in detecting bias through (a) examination of sources by a number of authors; (b) identification of purpose and audience; (c) study of language; (d) sequence/arrangement of information.

In this way, I hope that the problems of students who in the past have felt unprepared for Year 12 standards in classroom and examination use of documents will be overcome.

The topic chosen for an in-depth study of a period of history exposed students to a wide range of opinions/evaluations by ancient sources. It also encouraged small-group and class discussions which revealed a depth of understanding of the topic and clearly demonstrated that students reached this understanding because they felt confident and competent when applying developing skills of analysis, interpretation, evaluation, decision making and making value judgements.

I noted, however, a number of problems associated with my strategy of introducing a wider range of levels of thinking and applications skills. First, the process is by necessity, very time consuming if it is to be of any real value for students. Second, difficulties with continuity occurred because of the number of classes lost through internal timetabling factors.

Consequently, even though my perceptions of success or improvement were substantiated by the use and integration of original sources in the essay on the set topic, I was concerned by the need to 'short-circuit' processes when covering other topics. For me playing 'catch up' meant lost opportunities to consolidate skill development and reinforce confidence and competency in application of extended and more difficult levels of critical thinking to new areas of study. Furthermore, while I believe I have addressed with some success the problems of students being or perceiving to be unprepared in the use of document studies, I also believe that students will feel nervous about their impending document study because of the lack of time to adequately address the content of their study.

From these observations and reflection, I pose the following questions:

- Is lack of time for preparation a problem for teachers? If so, it needs to be addressed by the Department, for example, sharing/exchange of resources, smaller class sizes.
- Is more in-service training needed to meet the needs of both teachers and students?
- Do large classes affect the range of teaching strategies?
- If the recommendations for more effective teaching and learning in our schools are to be remotely possible, how should convincing arguments be presented to policy makers?
- How do we support teachers so that they, as well as the students will be interested enough to extend themselves and find reward in providing a challenging programme and using teaching strategies which cater for all levels of ability?

Observations and reflections – Sonya Gorman

I was pleased students found discussion such a useful part of their history lessons. This class is quite mature (especially for Year 10) and they discuss at quite a sophisticated level. I worried that the amount of discussion was too great, that there was too little formal noting taking, etc. Some students also felt this. My fears regarding the amount of discussion are reflected in my teaching by a panic reaction, which leads me to use text questions as a method of note taking. It is clear that students, at some level, recognise this because there is consider-able criticism of doing large numbers of questions at once and at specific times, especially as revision for exams. This was one of the aspects they disliked most and it stemmed from my lack of lesson variety.

In response to these criticisms I'd be inclined to substitute group work for the text questions and combine it with a jigsaw and judge-ment element so that students were using their discussion skills and refining them in small group work where there was no referee to ensure fairness. This method would also provide more formal and informal oral reporting opportunity to boost the confidence of those students who are intimidated by oral reports.

I'd use written group summaries made by students in the jigsaw activity and distributed them to the other students to replace text questions. Text questions would be used for revision at students' own pace or for homework. I'd try to maintain the atmosphere of the class as it allowed most students to feel comfortable to offer and justify their opinions. At the same time, I'd need to be more aware of those few students who need encouragement to join discussion.

The criticisms of the time taken to return tests/assignments, etc. are valid. That is personal organisation (or lack of it). I'm pleased assessment is seen as constructive for future work.

It was good to see some students reflecting critical thinking in their comments about textbooks and opinions. How do we keep this alive and encourage it to grow?

Questions for consideration (from observations, discussions with students and colleagues and my own reflections) include:

• How do we make the social sciences interactive?

- How do we keep enthusiasm so that students continue to see the social sciences as relevant in the senior school?
- How do we ensure, we, as a staff remain interested and enthusiastic so we promote the social sciences?
- How do we find ways of sharing our strengths and improving our weaknesses?
- How do we gain confidence?

The collaborative research group arranged a workshop with other social sciences teachers to share the results of its classroom research; to seek comment on its reflections; and to determine priority areas for investigation in 1995. The observations and reflections above formed the basis of sharing with other social sciences teachers as a means of encouraging additional teachers to become involved in the research, professional development and advocacy components of the study.

From the three teachers' observations and reflections a number of major issues were identified and grouped under the following categories:

- Professional development: sharing strengths; improving weaknesses; maintaining teacher interest; and teaching style;
- Teaching and learning: determinants of effective teaching; interactive teaching; student motivation; and teaching strategies to suit individual students;
- Resource allocation: preparation time; class sizes; and resources;
- Advocacy: political action.

Teachers were then given the opportunity to prioritise the issues which were most important and to suggest possible actions to deal with them.

Sharing strengths and improving weaknesses

Workshop participants determined that there was an ongoing need to share teachers' strengths and improve identified weaknesses. A variety of possible actions were raised such as subject meetings, which were called for the specific purpose of sharing ideas, debating strategies and calling for suggestions of how to teach a particular unit of work more effectively.

Teachers proposed not just observing each other's teaching but developing a number of team-teaching events. It was thought that team teaching would be more informative and remove some of the anxiety that teachers may experience when colleagues wish to observe their teaching. It was understood that this initiative would need the support of the school's administration because it has implications for class allocation and the supervision of classes.

228

Other suggestions included developing a process for sharing lesson plans and regular evaluations of teaching effectiveness by generating more formalised procedures for eliciting student feedback.

Improving resources

Teachers identified 'resources' as an ongoing issue which needed consistent attention. They were concerned about both physical and human resources within the social sciences. Teachers explained that while there were a number of reasons which force teachers to take a variety of units within the academic year and at various year levels, this militated against continuity in the development of the teacher's skills in a particular area of content. Without continuity in year level and class allocation, teachers moved from one unit to the next, never having the possibility of teaching the same area twice or in succession, which would allow teachers to refine and improve their teaching strategies. Furthermore, the group implored school timetablers to take more notice of recognised and documented teacher expertise in certain academic fields. They revealed that some ineffective teaching was to due to the fact that teachers were teaching outside of their area of training and interest.

Teachers identified physical resources as an ongoing area of concern. Suggestions included the acquisition of a wider variety of professional journals, improvement of a system for filing useful activities for future use, the development of focused 'learning centres' in the school and the allocation of teachers to the specific task of resource acquisition in a particular area of interest. A final suggestion was the development of a data bank of worksheets and ideas which could be easily customised by teachers when preparing their classroom activities. This initiative will require a staff which is computer literate or at the very least a 'data manager' who is willing to assist teachers in accessing the bank.

Interactive teaching

This third issue generated some debate about the nature of interactive teaching and the perceived problems of students' passivity. The classroom investigations showed that teachers needed to be more demanding in the junior years in terms of critical thinking, research, interpretation of data and analysis. Whilst many teachers see this as a valid observation, it may also be accurate to suggest that at times such activities are actually taught in the junior classes but not named as such. This would lead students to utter the common phrase 'we never did that last year'. It may be necessary then not only to increase the number of activities which require critical thinking skills but to label the endeavour as an exercise in 'analysis', 'synthesis' 'evaluation', etc.

Research in 1995

The agenda for 1995 continued to focus on the three components of research, professional development and advocacy. The three components were developed within the following context: the place of the social sciences within the senior schooling curriculum, which is increasingly geared towards workplace relevance and vocational education and the interplay of key competencies, principles of effective teaching and learning and senior schooling initiatives and imperatives.

Research included further critical self-reflection and action upon teaching approaches and strategies for effective learning in social sciences classrooms. We identified characteristics of effective teaching and learning, of critical thinking, independent learning and co-operative learning. From this, we hope that teachers will identify some of the competencies that effective teachers will possess, performance indicators that will demonstrate such competencies and learning outcomes which will illustrate effective student learning. This, we hope, will become the basis for professional development which integrates teachers' work, their reflections on their work and departmental and administrative support for their work. In regards to advocacy, we hope teachers will consider ways of politicising the role of the social sciences in a curriculum which is focusing more and more on workplace relevance.

Reflection on the social sciences project

Learning about collaborative/participatory action research

The Social Sciences Project was an example of collaborative/participatory action research. Much has been written about collaborative research (e.g., Allan and Miller 1990; Aspland *et al.* 1996; Carson 1990; Cornett 1990; Dicker 1990; Kemmis and McTaggart 1988) and several questions and issues may be raised. These include:

- How do you get started with action research?
- How do you encourage collaboration?
- Whose interests are being served?
- What are the roles of those who are involved?
- What sorts of critical frameworks are needed?

Information about collaborative/participatory forms of research drawn from a recent survey of literature, (e.g., Aspland *et al.* 1993; Feldman 1993; Johnston 1993; Levin 1993; McCutcheon and Jung 1990; Tripp 1990; Van Manen 1990) has indicated a number of limitations and benefits of this sort of research. Some of the limitations include the problematics of collaborative research such as ethical concerns and sensitivities, the possible conflict of values and the vexing issues of power and authority. The main advantages of collaborative research are that it promotes critical thinking and practice, the generation of professional knowledge and the collective interpretation of and action upon data. These advantages may consequently lead to improved professional performance and a sense of empowerment for the practitioners.

We believe that credible examples of collaborative action research will include the principles of collaboration outlined earlier in the paper. These are:

- open communication;
- avoidance of jargon (or at least a shared understanding of its meaning);
- clarity and sense of purpose;
- frameworks for critical reflection, professional development and advocacy;
- appreciation of teachers' time constraints;
- equity in decision making.

As the members of the group reflected on progress made during 1994 (via a revisiting of these principles), a number of 'lessons' emerged. These lessons are by no means exhaustive, but they do reflect a grappling with the problematics and a building upon the advantages as outlined above. A second paper presentation at a national conference on research in education was given in late 1994 (Macpherson *et al*. 1994). The lessons are:

Open communication

It is suggested that participants:

- Do not expect open communication from the start.
- Work towards open communication as relationships are developed among members of the group.
- Recognise that building relationships and opening communication channels takes time.
- Be objective, non-judgmental, open-minded and patient.
- Be aware of the range of interest in and opinions about teaching and learning and collaborative projects like this one.

Avoidance of jargon

It is suggested that participants:

- Do not make assumptions that everyone understands the language and the discourse about the project.

231

- Define terms, goals and approaches early in the project, even if the definitions are tentative.

Clarity and sense of purpose

It is suggested that participants:

- Do not make assumptions that everyone shares a common vision for the project at the beginning.
- Be aware that the early stages of projects like this one have the potential to be breeding grounds of suspicion and cynicism.
- Maintain honesty and openness in all discussions and meetings associated with the project.
- Strike a balance between giving background information and theoretical frameworks and allowing the group to develop its own living educational theory and professional knowledge.

Frameworks for critical reflection, professional development and advocacy

It is suggested that participants:

- Recognise the prior experience and expertise of all involved in the project.
- Emphasise the notion that the research is being conducted within a 'researching with' and not a 'researching on' mindset.
- Be aware that the project must be seen to be progressing and achieving something. (Definition of terms may be developed, other persons may come on board, others in the school community are told what is happening, progress is made in terms of the project's having an impact on further policy development, etc.).
- Retain an ongoing commitment to sharpening the focus of the project and ensuring that it is relevant, purposeful and effective.
- Retain a critical perspective which is informed by an awareness of broader trends and a willingness to contest these trends in constructively critical ways.
- Keep in focus an action orientation in terms of professional development and advocacy. (Emancipatory notions of action research are helpful in maintaining a commitment to empowerment for teachers and learners.)
- Avoid the problematics of collaborative action research by developing principles of procedures which are shared and understood by all participants and stakeholders.

Appreciation of teachers' time constraints

It is suggested that participants:

- Be prepared to share the multi-faceted nature of the roles of group members and associated pressures.
- Talk about the intensification of teachers' work and implications for involvement in projects like this one.
- Be creative in developing ways of integrating research, professional development and advocacy into teachers' work (recognising that a project like this one does not add critical reflection to the teacher's repertoire, rather it celebrates and formalises it).
- Be patient and understand that timelines may have to be extended.
- Celebrate the commitment that members of the group have to the project in both the short and long term.
- Take stock of what is happening on a regular basis, and note the advances, however small, which are being made.

Equity in decision making

It is suggested that participants:

- Value everyone's contribution and maintain an up-front view that equality and diversity of input are essential ingredients in a project like this one.
- Should encourage one another to work for the advancement of the group's agenda, and not to operate unilaterally as far as project matters are concerned.
- Do not begin a project like this with one person who is dominant and overtly in control and who appears to have a pre-determined agenda.
- Achieve a balance in agenda setting so that the project does not focus on esoteric criticism on the one hand, or on technocratic practice on the other. Both facets are crucial and they must work together for a meaningful sense of empowerment for both teachers and learners.

What we have learned about aspects of teaching for effective learning in the social sciences

The social sciences are a vehicle for facilitating effective teaching and learning (which focus on such areas as critical thinking, independent learning and co-operative learning). The argument is not so much that the social sciences, themselves, have a monopoly on these aspects of learning; rather that the social sciences can contribute to learning experiences and learning outcomes in these areas. Of course, it would be wonderful to value the social sciences for their intrinsic worth, but in a context largely shaped by economic rationalism, one must look for ways in which the social sciences can serve both general and vocational educational outcomes.

An argument along these lines strengthens the place of the social sciences in the curriculum (particularly in the senior years of schooling). It has become easy to marginalise the social sciences on the basis of a preconceived idea that they are a cultural frill which cannot serve the serious purposes of economic rationalism and the achievement of employment-related key competencies.

Besides the humanising elements which the social sciences can provide, the following ideas clearly show that they also can contribute significantly in preparing students for life-long learning. The social sciences can participate in the convergence of general and vocational education by encouraging students to develop relevant workplace competencies and by providing positive learning experiences which will ensure their preparedness to engage in self-motivated learning throughout the course of their vocational and social lives.

Fostering effective teaching and learning

Social sciences engender effective teaching and learning through/by:

- developing and extending critical thinking skills through exposure to activities which involve the students in comprehension, analysis, synthesis, application, evaluation, research, communication and knowledge;
- fieldwork including planning, problem solving, time management, identification and collection of primary data, observation, explanation, description, sketching, surveying, note taking, team work, independent work, debriefing, reviewing, report writing, written and oral communication, interaction with the general public/authorities or experts;
- source work, for example, identifying bias, comparison, evaluation;
- discussion to develop oral communication, interpersonal skills, identifying fact/opinion/points of view, non-verbal communication and cues, separate issue from the personality/individual;
- debriefing for evaluation of actions leading to future modification;
- reviewing for the purpose of monitoring learnings, progress, re-assessment of goals/direction;
- group/teamwork including long-term development from short-term structured group work to long-term self-directed team work . . . increasing independence, self-reliance, interpersonal and problem solving;
- developing subject-specific literacy/numeracy such as visual literacy – charts, diagrams, cartoons, posters, maps, media;

- subject literacy, for example, terminology, generic structures, emotive/persuasive devices, questioning; and numerical literacy including statistics, graphs, maps, tables;
- clear links with real experiences by identifying trends, practical application of theory and lifelike examples;
- methods of assessment which allow both teacher and student to monitor skills development and which aim to provide students with appropriate challenges so as to experience success, satisfaction and competence as a result of effort;
- acknowledging non-specific skills and modifying them to suit the purposes of the social sciences at a conscious level.

Fostering critical thinking

Critical thinking is facilitated within the social sciences by:

- creating an awareness of the variety of factors which influence 'truth', e.g., culture, gender, race, class, creed, politics, omissions;
- providing specific content or interpretations for analysis in light of the above;
- comprehending, analysing, synthesising and evaluating a variety of conflicting sources/texts/stimuli within a context;
- modelling, guiding and encouraging effective and clear communication of critical thinking, for example, argument;
- creating an atmosphere in which awareness and skills development combine and contribute to a confidence which empowers students to become active, not just informed citizens.

Independent learning

Independent learning is facilitated within the social sciences by:

- modelling, practising and encouraging confidence at each stage e.g., planning, setting goals/aims, accessing resources;
- providing a secure and supportive environment in which students feel comfortable to take risks;
- actively teaching independent learning at a conscious level so students can select and utilise those steps appropriate to a given situation be it real or simulated;
- encouraging students to take progressively increasing responsibility for their own learning;
- developing an awareness of decision making as a difficult and complicated skill and providing simulated or real life opportunities for students to experiment, practise and hone those skills;

- taking a supportive/facilitating role rather than a direct teaching role;
- monitoring the progress of each student.

Collaborative learning

Co-operative learning is facilitated within the social sciences by:

- encouraging a supportive, non-competitive atmosphere which allows students to participate in and share responsibility for achieving a common goal;
- allowing students to exercise personal preference as regards to using co-operative learning or assessment purposes or avoiding the use of co-operative learning in formal assessment;
- encouraging student reflection or their co-operative learning experiences;
- accepting casual, in-class co-operative learning between established and responsible pairs/groups (checking, clarifying, discussing).

Conclusions

Thus far, the project has progressed substantively in terms of a continuing focus on effective teaching and learning in social sciences classrooms; and procedurally in terms of an ongoing commitment by all team members to consolidating and strengthening our approaches and practices in relation to collaborative/participatory action research.

In a sense, then, this paper tells a story of the project, but very importantly for us, it documents the evolution of our own living educational theory (McNiff 1993, Whitehead 1989) about collaborative/participatory action research. The focus in the story rests upon the establishment and maintaining of partnerships in a context of incessant educational change.

It is hoped that the momentum begun during the three years of the project will be sustained by the social sciences teachers as they seek to create professional development opportunities and to advocate for the continuing place of the social sciences in the senior school curriculum. Our experience, however, would lead us to believe that three years is insufficient time to build, maintain and sustain change efforts on an ever-expanding scale which in turn will lead to institutional cultures which are empowering for all participants in the ongoing transformation of educational practice.

The project however, leaves questions unanswered – ongoing questions which must be asked about the lessons already learned. With this type of research, one thing at least is certain – it takes a long time to do very little if you want to do it well (meaning parity of esteem for all participants).

NOTE

1   The phrase collaborative/participatory implies that the project is both collaborative and participatory.

REFERENCES

Allan, K. and Miller, M. (1990) 'Teacher researcher collaboratives: cooperative professional development', *Theory into Practice*, 29 (3): 96–202.

Arcodia, C., Gorman, S., Macpherson, I., Shepherd, J., and Trost, R. (1994) *Investigating Social Science Curriculum Issues in the Senior School through Collaborative Inquiry: A Queensland Example*, paper presented at the Third National Conference of Post-Compulsory Education, Brisbane, June.

Aspland, T., Macpherson, I. and Proudford, C. (1993) Teachers' curriculum decision-making practices at the classroom level: Implications for curriculum policy formulations at the system level, paper presented at the Annual Conference of Australian Association for Research in Education. Fremantle, West Australia, November.

Aspland, T., Macpherson, I., Proudford, C. and Whitmore, L. (1996) 'Critical collaborative action research', *Educational Action Research*, 4 (1): 93–104.

Australian Education Council and Ministers for Vocational Education, Employment and Training (1992) *Putting General Education to Work (The Key Competencies Report)*, Canberra: Australian Government Printing Service (commonly referred to as the Mayer Report).

Australian Education Council Review Committee (1991) *Young People's Participation in Post-Compulsory Education and Training*, Canberra: Australian Government Printing Service (commonly referred to as the Finn Report).

Carson, T. (1990) 'What kind of knowing is critical action research?' *Theory into Practice*, 29 (3): 167–73.

Cornett, J. (1990) 'Utilizing action research in graduate curriculum courses', *Theory into Practice* 28 (3): 185–95.

Dicker, M. (1990) 'Using action research to navigate an unfamiliar teaching assignment', *Theory into Practice* 29 (3): 203–8.

Employment and Skills Formation Council (1992) *Australian Vocational Certificate Training System*, Canberra: Australian Government Publication Service.

Feldman, A. (1993) 'Promoting equitable collaboration between university researchers and school teachers', *Qualitative Studies in Education*, 6 (4): 341–57.

Freire, P. (1972) *Pedagogy of the Oppressed*, Harmondsworth: Penguin.

Johnston, S. (1993) 'Action research as a school-level change process', *Curriculum Perspectives*, 13 (1): 21–8.

Kemmis, S. and McTaggart, R. (1988) *The Action Research Planner*, Geelong: Deakin University Press.

Levin, B. (1993) 'Collaborative research in and with organisations', *Qualitative Studies in Education*, 6 (4): 331–40.

McCutcheon, G. and Jung, B. (1990) 'Alternative perspectives on action research', *Theory into Practice*, 29 (3): 144–51.

McNiff, J. (1993) *Teaching as Learning: An Action Research Approach*, London: Routledge.

Macpherson, I., Trost, R., Gorman, S., Shepherd, J. and Arcodia, C. (1994) *Collaborative Action Research: Lessons Learned from a Queensland Example*, paper presented at the Australian Association for Research in Education Conference, Newcastle, Australia, November.

Tripp, D. (1990) 'Socially critical action research', *Theory into Practice,* 29 (3): 158–66.

Van Manen, M. (1990) 'Beyond assumptions: shifting the limits of action research', *Theory into Practice*, 29 (3): 153–7.

Whitehead, J. (1989) 'Creating a living educational theory from questions of the kind, "How do I improve my practice?"' *Cambridge Journal of Education*, 19: 41–52.

Wiltshire, K. (Chairman) (1994) *Shaping the Future*, report of the review of the Queensland School Curriculum, Brisbane: Queensland Government Printer.

Part 5

PARTNERSHIPS WITHIN THE UNIVERSITY

12

ACTION RESEARCH AS REFLECTIVE COLLABORATION

Denise Scott and Patricia Weeks

After five years of co-ordinating the TRAC (Teaching, Reflection and Collaboration) professional development network at the Queensland University of Technology (QUT), we have learnt that in a university context with its potentially sterile 'academic standards' and stereotypical views of what constitutes 'real research', it is necessary to demystify the notion of 'research' in 'action research': to free it from neo-scientific connotations and quasi-quantitative constraints. Only in this way can it realise its boundless potential and possibilities. We have additionally concluded that action research's most documented (and yet most technicist) characteristic – the cyclical reflection/action process (Kemmis and McTaggart 1988; see also Kemmis and Wilkinson, Chapter 2, this volume) – is, at best, peripheral to, and, at worst, inhibitive of, open, emancipatory (in the sense of being freed from one's cellular, contextual and disciplinary confines) professional inquiry. We will argue in this chapter that action research which is not collaborative is both limited and limiting.

The TRAC Project

The clinical supervision model (cycle 1)

Originally, the TRAC project called for volunteers who would engage in the 'clinical supervision' (Goldhammer 1969) or 'peer review' process/cycle, as a means of evaluating and improving teaching. Self-selected pairs of academics were invited to learn about this process and to use it directly to address teaching/learning issues of personal interest and concern. Additionally, participants were encouraged to keep a reflective journal or diary (Holly 1984) to record their experiences, and to document the development and outcomes of the reflective, collaborative process.

The collaborative reflective spiral process encourages reflective experimentation in which academic teacher-researchers try to make sense of the complexities of the teaching/learning process. It requires 'reflective conversation' (Schön 1987: 78) and involves academic teachers, not only as learners, but as co-researchers in the learning cycles. Schön noted that 'groups of practitioners may support one another in reflective research . . . and . . . reflective research may become a part of continuing education for practitioners' (Schön 1983: 323).

In essence, this was the focus of the first stage of the TRAC project: colleagues working supportively in dialoguing and analysing each other's teaching as a form of personal professional development where 'teachers' constructs become enhanced rather than replaced' (Goldhammer 1969: 202).

Generally speaking, focusing on the clinical supervision cycle as it did at this stage, the TRAC project was neither especially innovative or revolutionary in its operation or intent. What it did do, however, was to set a reflective agenda for academic teaching practice at QUT and introduced an element of structure and predictability into the process of self-evaluation. Above all, this first cycle of our own reflective practice (as staff development personnel) gave us a broad and exciting vision of future directions and possibilities for collaborative staff development.

The action research model (cycle 2)

It soon became very clear that it was unrealistic and limiting to restrict participants to engagement in the peer review process which, by its very nature, can limit the exploration of teaching and learning to the 'presentational' and/or organisational aspects of specific teaching episodes. The concerns of tertiary teachers and their students are many and reach far beyond observable pedagogic practice. There were, for instance, issues of clinical experience to be addressed; of large- and small-scale innovation; of analysis of student learning. Some participants wished to explore the implications of reflective practice (Schön 1983; 1987) itself, or the role of assessment in the learning process. Some wished to develop personal models of specific disciplinary practice. The variations were many.

And so it happened that anyone who wished to undertake small-scale action research into any aspect of teaching and learning in their own context was welcomed as a TRAC participant. The action research cycle became the developmental model for TRAC's second semester of operation. A brief summation of the nature and methodology of action research as discussed by Kemmis and McTaggart (1988) clearly indicates its relevance to personal/professional staff development:

- It is a democratic mode of research conducted by those who wish to improve their practice through self-reflection and collaborative action; it is not research conducted by traditional 'expert', objective, or impartial observers.

- It aims to build communities of people committed to enlightening themselves about the relationship between circumstance, action and consequence in their own situation, and emancipating or liberating themselves from the institutional and personal constraints which limit their power to legitimise (and live by) their own educational and social values.
- It involves a systematic learning process in which people act deliberately to improve situations.
- It has dimensions of knowledge production and action, as well as constituting new ways of relating to one another to make the work of reform possible. It is a process of using critical intelligence to inform action, and developing it so that social action becomes *praxis* through which people may consistently live their social values.

More specifically, McTaggart (1991) outlines several characteristics for participatory action research which can be applied to this project:

- Identification of the individual and collective project. In our case, individuals worked on their own projects to improve their own work while also helping others improve their work so that the possibility for a more broadly informed common project is being created.
- Changing and studying discourse, practice, and social organisation. Reflective practice and collaborative discussion about teaching is directed towards the improvement of the social situation in QUT.
- Engaging in the politics of research action; participatory action research is a political process in so far as individual changes will also affect others. By critically analysing their work at QUT, project participants work politically and socially to overcome the accepted traditional teaching practices of the university.
- Use of various methodological resources. Participants are encouraged to use various research methods for their projects. They work through the self-reflective cycles of planning, observing and reflecting. Some use simple forms of data collection and others use more elaborate and demanding methods of investigation.
- Creating the theory of work. Action research calls for a critical reflection and justification of the educational work of its participants (cf. Schratz 1992). The project participants are creating their own practical theories of teaching in higher education in a classic practice-to-theory orientation.

Action research was not proposed as merely a 'method'; it was meant to be understood as a way of reflecting on tertiary teaching and thereby creating an 'inquiry culture' of teaching in higher education. Becoming an academic teacher is a process which, like any other professional role, requires time and experiential insight. Action research seemed an appropriate strategy for reflective professional development as it is a method of inquiry which 'engages practice while generating theory . . . one that facilitates action while generating research outcomes' (Wildman 1995: 23).

The collaborative/reflective model (cycle 3)

While we were, indeed, encouraged by the range and number of the projects undertaken, we felt, however, that the collaborative inquiry culture which epitomised an action research approach was being compromised by this very range and disparity. While reflective collaboration was an endemic part of the clinical supervision (or peer observation) process (cycle 1), collaboration was limited to the immediate situation and to the teacher and observer. While collaboration also played a role in individual action research projects (cycle 2), this role was essentially an *ad hoc* one, as teachers conferred with others in the unstructured, 'catch it as you can' mode of much practitioner discourse. As compensation for this shortfall, our monthly meetings of all TRAC participants provided the forum for a cross-disciplinary sharing and support that might otherwise never have occurred in a large university such as QUT. These meetings, it seemed, had the power to energise and inspire, to enlighten and support.

It was the realisation of the inspirational function of these meetings which encouraged us to highlight (and extend opportunities for) reflective collaboration; to raise it from its *ad hoc* status to become the central focus of our evolving model of staff development for academic teaching. We emphasised the importance of collaborative sharing within the total TRAC group, diverse as individual projects and disciplines might be. Meanwhile, we knew that more thought was needed to further facilitate this process, to somehow identify and co-ordinate both the individual and collective concerns. We realised, too, that this was necessary in order to completely exploit and validate the action research methodology. As McTaggart explains:

> Participatory action research is concerned simultaneously with changing both individuals and the culture of the groups, institutions, and societies to which they belong. But it is important to emphasise that these changes are not impositions: individuals and groups agree to work together to change themselves, individually and collectively. Their interests are joined by an agreed thematic concern.
>
> (McTaggart 1991: 172)

Practical considerations were about to suggest an expeditious solution to our perceived 'problem' and thus launch the next cycle of TRAC's operation.

Collaborative sub-groups (cycle 4)

As membership grew (by now there were eighty participants), we clearly needed to explore new avenues if we were to retain and extend the collegial, collaborative spirit we had come to regard as vital to TRAC's success and to the full and faithful exploitation of the action research methodology. With this number of participants, too, it became obvious that several sub-groups of 'like-projected' participants could be formed. For example, several participants were pursuing the introduction of problem-based learning components into their respective courses; others were interested in exploring the role of the academic teacher/'supervisor' in clinical or practical settings (for example, in the teacher education, nursing and social-work fields; others were particularly interested in problems with large classes and so on.

Thus, collaborative cross-disciplinary sub-groups were formed. Both our large membership 'problem', and its solution, were part of the continuing evolution of our project/model. Collaborative sub-groups have remained as the central focuses of TRAC participation. With 1998 approaching, there are 220 TRAC participants involved in thirteen different sub-groups on a wide range of teaching and learning issues. There is no doubt that such networks provide the basis of a strong 'inquiry culture in education' (McTaggart 1991) in QUT: a culture that fosters change and development at the personal, professional and, ultimately, social levels.

Discussion and reflection

Action research as professional inquiry

As indicated in the details above, our involvement with action research became less a matter of acquiring a relevant methodology and applying it to individual problems and projects, and more and more a matter of discovering professional partnerships with a collaborative agenda. This inquiry agenda is based on concerns that are in the final analysis, the mutual needs and goals of those who seek, as *educators*, the same professional assuredness enjoyed in their specific disciplinary context.

Mutual goals of this professional inquiry include the need to:

- test personal practical teaching knowledge and experience in a collegially supportive environment;
- measure personal theories of teaching and learning against the propositional repertoire of established educational theory (provided by the group's 'professional' educators if and when desired);
- legitimate personal feelings and emotions engendered by the broader university culture/climate.

The collaborative format then is our action research methodology *per se*: a critical inquiry process rich in reflective and critical analysis, rich in data with outcomes relevant to specific conditions and interactions. Action research according to Kemmis (1994) is open-minded. To value and discover the essential heart of research – the process itself – it is necessary to doff traditional, narrow and elitist views of prescribed methodology. It is our belief and our experience that action research, for our purposes, must be *process* rather than *product* driven. In the case of the TRAC network, this process is ongoing professional development where research and its application are grounded in professional discourse and personal reflective practice.

Such research ought not be judged, as is traditional research, on measurable, replicable results, but on the quality of the collaborative discourse as it empowers its participants, meets their dynamic needs and dilemmas and validates the personal/emotional and idiosyncratic aspects of the research process. If a purist were to insist on a framing of our research problem, this would be our reply: how best to engender and nurture continuing collaborative dialogue as a rich and diverse form of personal/professional development? Action research is intentionally personalised, idiosyncratic and contextual. It allows 'researchers' to get 'close to the data' (Wadsworth 1991).

Critical dialogue: the essential characteristic

When reading some, if not much, of the action research literature, the novice could be forgiven for perceiving that the action research process consisted of a neo-scientific cycle of self-conscious, self-centred inquiry. Thus characterised, the truly fruitful, potent characteristics of action research, collaborative inquiry, can be overlooked. Participatory action research is not just learning; it has dimensions of knowledge production and action; it constitutes new ways of relating to one another to make the work of reform possible (Weeks 1995).

The TRAC experience has shown that collaboration – an initial coming together in a sense of inquiry – is essential to the development of the critical friendships, the extra-contextual views and the collective sense of power and autonomy essential to truly critical analysis and outcome:

> Collaborative participant discourse generates a climate of skeptical, subjective inquiry, of professional interpretative judgment, of creative and proactive practice. In so doing, it initiates a problematic and dynamic interplay of the propositional and the procedural, of theory to practice and practice to theory.
>
> (Weeks and Scott 1993: 7)

The role of reflective dialogue, of critical, analytical conversation arising from professional collaboration has, in our view, been underemphasised in the action research literature. By this reasonably defensible criterion, the TRAC network is an action research network committed to educational inquiry in the broadest sense of the term. TRAC participants ask questions about teaching and learning (indeed, in many cases, they must first learn what questions to ask); they converse, speculate, compare, contrast, describe, explain, theorise, and/or hypothesise. It is people's actual teaching experience which provides a basis for development (Rowland and Barton 1994: 372). Their action research is an on-going professional, inquiring stance; their goal or problem is to do something about the phenomenon of being untrained educators in a teaching/learning environment. By comparison and contrast, Zuber-Skerritt (1991) argued that the technocratic approach to improving teaching and learning in higher education, (that is, for example, by workshops) is analogical to the 'reproducing' or 'surface' approach taken by students to learning and that an action research approach to teaching development would enable lecturers to take a 'deep' approach to improving teaching. TRAC participants explore truly 'professional knowledge' – that is knowledge which is intrinsically connected with practice; is not knowledge which 'informs' practice but reflective knowledge which is embedded in 'praxis' (see Grundy, Chapter 3, this volume).

As central to the critical inquiry process, and source of its developmental 'product', critical conversation is particularly fruitful in the cross-disciplinary TRAC context. We have seen its power to:

- challenge and change disciplinary–insular values and beliefs;
- analyse and deconstruct personal linguistic and abstract conceptions;
- explore multiple meanings and dimensions of linguistic conceptions;
- convert 'story', narrative and common sense into educational knowledge;
- elicit and authenticate 'tacit' knowledge;
- critically explore personal and collective conceptions.

To attempt to methodologically constrain such activity to the much-projected traditional action research cycle, would be a defensive reaction to the perceived need to be 'scientific', albeit in a limited sense. We do not apologise for a lack of definitional rigour, of cyclical process or progress, of scientifically acceptable experimental method. Despite a prevailing academic prejudice to the contrary, quality is not defined by quantitative or methodological rigour but by vision and commitment to improving one's situation.

It is our contention that the active reflective process of continuing professional inquiry and development is, of its very nature, a 'quality action research' process.

There is a long history of advocacy for educational practitioners to be able to control the production of their professional knowledge (see Grundy, Chapter 3, this volume). When action and research are brought together not only in one process but into the one person, we gain a true inquiring, reflective practitioner (Carr and Kemmis 1986; Schön 1987).

Conclusions

For action research to take its deserved place in professional inquiry, its proponents need to address the question of its academic acceptance, status and credibility – an accolade traditionally awarded according to scientific rigour.

At the 'product' level of the 'research' dilemma we need to demystify notions of mandatory external validity, replication and generalisation and emphasise the equal validity of research that is interpretively sensitive to specific contexts and conditions, to particular individuals and interactions; research that is open, tentative, speculative and informal. We need to emphasise, without apology, in fact, that 'research' is an ongoing dialogical process and both personal and academic reflections are a live and vital part of that process.

A clear definition of action research as critical, collaborative inquiry with the specific purposes of on-going professional development may substantially help this cause; as might the reminder that such inquiry is, in effect, an essential prerequisite of 'professional' status.

REFERENCES

Carr, W. and Kemmis, S. (1986) *Becoming Critical: Knowing through Action Research*, Geelong, Australia: Deakin University Press.
Goldhammer, R. (1969) *Clinical Supervision: Special Methods for the Supervision of Teachers*, New York: Holt, Rinehart & Winston.
Holly, M. L. (1984) *Keeping a Personal Professional Journal*, Geelong, Australia: Deakin University Press.
Kemmis, S. (1994) 'Action research', in Husen, T. and Postlethwaite, N. (eds) *International Encyclopedia of Education: Research and Studies*, London: Pergamon Press.
Kemmis, S. and McTaggart, R. (1988) *The Action Research Planner*, 3rd edn, Geelong, Australia: Deakin University Press.
McTaggart, R. (1991) 'Principles for participatory action research', *Journal of the Participatory Action Research Network*, 1: 29–44.
Rowland, S. and Barton, L. (1994) 'Making things difficult: developing a research approach to teaching in higher education', *Studies in Higher Education*, 19 (3): 367–74.
Schön, D. A. (1983) *The Reflective Practitioner: How Professionals Think in Action*, New York: Basic Books.
Schön, D. A. (1987) *Educating The Reflective Practitioner*, San Francisco: Jossey Bass.
Schratz, M. (1992) 'Crossing the disciplinary boundaries: professional development through action research in higher education', *European Journal of Education*, 25 (3): 131–42.

Wadsworth, Y. (1991) *Do It Yourself Social Research*, Collingwood, Victoria: Victorian Council of Social Service and the Melbourne Family Care Organisation.

Weeks, P. A. (1995) Facilitating a reflective, collaborative teaching development project in higher education: reflections on experience, unpublished PhD thesis, Brisbane, Australia, Queensland University of Technology.

Weeks, P. and Scott, D. (1993) *Exploring Tertiary Teaching: Papers from The TRAC Project, Volume 2*, Brisbane, Australia: Academic Staff Development Unit, Queensland University of Technology.

Wildman, P. (1995) 'Research by looking backwards: reflective praxis as an action research model', *Action Research Case Studies Newsletter*, 3 (1): 20–38.

Zuber-Skerritt, O. (1991) *Professional Development in Higher Education: A Theoretical Framework for Action Research*, Brisbane, Australia: Centre for Advancement of Learning and Teaching, Griffith University.

13

OCCASIONAL VISITS TO THE KINGDOM

Part-time university teaching

James J Watters, Clare Christensen, Charles Arcodia, Yoni Ryan and Patricia Weeks

> I find the academic environment analogous to the court of Louis XIV, so how do you interact with all these courtiers and who's making the decisions and who's sleeping with who? How would I ever know when I'm such an occasional visitor to the Kingdom?
>
> (Part-time Law lecturer)

The study reported here was conceptualised as a collaborative participatory action research (PAR) Project. It is the story of a journey involving five academics, three full-time and two part-time, who came together through a common desire to explore the situation surrounding the employment of part-time teachers in our university. The motivations of the participants differed, reflecting our individual experiences of the situation. Each participant's conceptions of research also reflected disparate experiences. Our story relates changes in consciousness of the problems facing part-timers as well as changes in understanding of research practice that might do more than describe and amplify the situation but might actually lead to reform for the benefit of all stakeholders (full-time and part-time staff and students).

This chapter describes the project at two levels. First, in coming together and forming a collaborative group we attempted to generate a shared understanding of the experiences and needs of part-time teachers and to facilitate a process in which part-timers would be empowered to challenge the constraints of their situations for the enhancement of their professional competence. Second, the collaboration also led to enriched understandings of the researchers' own academic roles, assumptions about practice and priorities for the project. These two levels illustrate both individuals engaged in action research and action research that attempted to produce a large-scale change in the culture and structures impacting on practice in an institution.

We will first describe the study at the researcher level. The processes will be mapped as illustrative of PAR projects in which a collaborative group was formed – each member with his or her own agenda, skills and concerns. These motivations will be explored as individual stories. Next, on the project level, we will report parts of the study and then, on the researcher level, each of us will reflect on the journey as it has impacted on our emerging understanding of the process.

Non-dangerous liaisons

The context of this project was the Queensland University of Technology (QUT). QUT was formed in 1990 by an amalgamation between the Queensland Institute of Technology (QIT) and the Brisbane College of Advanced Education (BCAE). Prior to this, QIT had specialised in technology, business and law, and earned a good reputation for providing professional courses with practical relevance to employers' needs and for undertaking research aimed at solving industrial problems. BCAE had provided education mainly in teaching, business, social science and the visual and performing arts. Currently QUT has an enrolment of 23,000 students, 12,000 full-time staff and 1,800 part-time academic staff.

The first scene of this project opens in October 1994 when a group of people interested in action research came together at QUT to form a support network called PARAPET, with Dr Stephen Kemmis as mentor. A number of action research projects already under way were tabled and briefly explained by their respective 'convenors'. Among the projects proposed was one that the Academic Staff Development Unit (ASDU) at QUT intended to undertake.

Advisers to the Court

The Academic Staff Development Unit at QUT operates from within the Division of Academic Affairs. It offers a university-wide service of support for academic staff. It has a mandate to improve teaching, research and professional leadership within the university. The mission of ASDU is to assist university teachers in improving the quality of educational experiences which QUT students encounter. It does this by offering programmes and activities, sponsoring visits by experts from other institutions, undertaking appropriate research and providing consultations with individual staff members.

ASDU records showed that very few part-time teachers in QUT availed themselves of these programmes and activities. ASDU staff were not sure why. It was this concern that ASDU's professional development programme was not reaching a large group of QUT academic staff that motivated some ASDU staff members to initiate this project. The project was concerned with how the professional development needs of part-time teachers at QUT could be met. This project resonated with the interests of the five individuals who eventually grouped to initiate the PAR project described in this chapter.

Action research involves participants who accrete about a common objective, frequently bonded by individual concerns of social justice and equity. In the beginning, as disparate personalities we each brought particular perspectives to the issue of part-time teaching and a complex set of relationships with each other. Establishing communication and rapport was the first consideration. The participants, Jim, Clare, Charles, Yoni and Patricia each grappled with feelings and constraints while attempting to understand and work with colleagues in a truly synergistic productive relationship. Our personal stories reveal some of the factors that impact on an action research project of the type described in this chapter.

Jim's story

Teaching in many foundation or core units within a defined programme of studies frequently involves contact with large class numbers. While the major teaching functions such as administration, co-ordination, setting of examinations and assessment are the responsibility of a unit or subject co-ordinator, much of the face-to-face contact with students involves part-time academic staff. Depending on the nature of the subject, these staff may be lecturers presenting whole or part of a programme, demonstrators working in laboratories, tutors working in interactive workshops or clinical/teaching or facilitators working in field locations with small groups of students. Communication with and management of a large teaching team can be problematic.

For example, effective learning and teaching should occur where there is smooth, efficient and equitable communication and collaboration between teaching staff, students and administrators. This is a particularly difficult task where several staff may be working with multiple groups of students all required to meet common criteria for assessment and credit. It was my belief that outcomes are positively affected by programmes that encourage student–lecturer involvement, collaborative learning, where students have a critical say in their course and where learning communities exist outside the formal class-room (Chickering and Gamson 1987).

252

As unit co-ordinator I am responsible for a major core unit that has special difficulties for students; my goals included establishing an effective community of learners which included the part-time teachers. Concern about the status, roles and competencies of part-time academic staff thus stimulated my interest in this study. What were the factors, experiences and concerns that part-time staff brought with them into the teaching situation? In what ways could I engage in dialogue with part-time staff in order to improve the teaching and learning within the unit of concern to me?

Clare's story

I have taught part-time at QUT for four years. While I enjoyed my classes and my relationship with the students, along with others I worked with I have felt unhappy about my experience in other respects. The main issue for me was the absence of a feeling of collegiality and equality with full-time staff, despite 15 years' teaching experience in secondary schools. Some teaching team meetings were held but while I felt free to speak, I perceived that my contributions were not regarded seriously but rather as annoying disturbances in a well-established routine. I was not prevented from being innovative in my classes, but little interest was shown in my innovations, although one was subsequently adopted by other staff. When the unit was reviewed, despite four years of enthusiastic and conscientious involvement in teaching the subject, I was not told about the review nor invited to contribute.

Through talking to other part-timers while I was teaching, I found that my experience was not unique. Knowing this I was pleased to have an opportunity to work towards changing the culture of part-time teaching at QUT. I was interested in working to improve the status, recognition and appreciation by QUT of the contribution and experience of part-time teaching staff. I saw this as an issue of social justice which seemed much more important when I found out that there were 1,800 part-time teachers at QUT. Since the project was based on an action research model, with part-timers being involved in formulating actions, I felt hopeful that things might change for the better.

I also work at QUT as a research assistant and I was invited to play this role on the project. I was pleased to accept this position since usually a lot of my tasks are very repetitive and this, I knew would be less stressful if the tasks were part of research that would be of personal interest.

Yoni's story

Both personal and professional concerns stimulated my interest in the project: friends and family members work casually at QUT, and had often complained about the short notice they were given for teaching activities, and their sense of powerlessness and marginalisation in the institution. As a staff developer, I had also listened to the rare part-timers who attended professional development training and empathised with their sense of inadequacy in learning to teach better and more specifically in dealing with new technology.

Charles' story

I was interested in joining the research team for this project because I had direct and recent experience as a part-time teacher at QUT. I was concerned about two main issues. The first was the quality of teaching and lack of support that a number of part-time teachers experience. The second was that there was very little recognition of those part-timers who did have teaching skills and relevant experience.

More importantly however, I felt that this was a good opportunity to do something positive about the art of teaching, which I believe is devalued in universities. There is a strongly held assumption that content knowledge is all that is required for successful teaching; there seems to be much less emphasis on communication skills and teaching strategies.

I also assumed I could bring further credibility to the research team because of my ongoing experience as a part-timer. I was aware, however, that my experience at QUT was different from the experience of the majority of other part-time teachers. I was employed as a full-time senior research assistant and so had much more of an opportunity to be part of the university's culture.

Patricia's story

As a member of staff in the ASDU I very rarely hear about or become involved in staff development activities organised by other parts of the university. Somehow or another, and I'm glad I did, I heard about the PARAPET project and decided to go along to the workshops. At the same time I had been mulling over 'doing something' for part-time staff in QUT. I had completed an initial search of the literature, talked to a few key people, and vaguely thought about how on earth to proceed. It was a real pleasure for me to meet others at the PARAPET meetings who were interested in part-timers and also interested in action research.

Thus, various motivations and pragmatic objectives influenced the researchers in initiating and collaborating in this study. Our different paths and experiences within the university (including experiences with and as part-time teachers) were a strength because we saw the issues of part-time teaching from a panorama of perspectives. A common narrative thread between the various perspectives was a sense of social justice.

The study

The teaching goal of the university, which is the setting of this study, is to ensure that its graduates (a) possess knowledge and professional competence; (b) have a sense of community responsibility; and (c) a capacity to continue their professional and personal development throughout their lives (QUT 1990). The university attempts to achieve this goal in several ways. Primarily, it argues that its teaching staff are committed to enhancing student learning and are involved in scholarly educational research within their discipline (Queensland University of Technology 1994). In addition, a range of objectives including the development of innovative learning practices, computer-based education and study skills are given high priority. The university prides itself on being a 'University for the Real World' by using strategies that ensure the relevance, currency and comprehensiveness of its courses by 'connecting directly with the world of practice' (Queensland University of Technology 1994). Thus, QUT in advertising for part-time staff actively seeks professionals who enhance the practical perspective of QUT's education. The use of practising professionals as lecturers is therefore widespread, accounting for the equivalent of 22 per cent of all effective full-time academic staff. However, the depth of dependence on part-time teachers is staggering. Although it is difficult to achieve accurate figures, there are in excess of 1,800 part-time teachers employed in some teaching capacity. This compares with the 1,200 full-time teaching staff at associate lecturer to professor levels. Thus, part-time academic teaching staff constitute a significant component of the university's resources needed to meet its goals, and they represent a major sector to which resources should be provided to support their teaching responsibilities. The study described here was designed to explore the roles, functions and conditions of the part-time staff.

While the philosophies and goals described above, though not unique to QUT, are laudable, external pressures (e.g., government-funding policies) are also changing the structure of employment within universities. Holley asserted that 'it has been clear for some time that the pay and conditions of academic staff employed on a casual (part-time) basis is one of the great scandals of the higher education sector' (Holley 1995: 14). A secondary concern identified by Holley was that increasing casualisation threatened the workloads of full-time staff, particularly as it involves extra administration by full-timers, increased demands on co-ordinators and a further burden on students.

However, is the real situation known? In the fourteen years since the report of the national Academic Salaries Tribunal chaired by Mr Justice Ludecke (1981) addressed employment issues, no substantial research on part-timers has been recorded in Australia. Indeed, the situation of 'adjunct staff' is so marginal throughout the Western university sector that the major US study in the area is entitled *The Invisible Faculty* (Gappa and Leslie 1993) and, with similar emphasis, a Canadian study was titled, *Hidden Academics: The part time faculty in Canada* (Rajagopal and Farr 1992). Only in the last few years have part-timers attracted the attention of staff development units, concerned that a substantial proportion of academic staff have been untouched by development programmes designed to improve teaching and learning. Curtin University, for example, has a programme for tutorial staff, the University of Technology, Sydney has a limited school-based programme and the federally funded Queensland Higher Education Staff Development Consortium has implemented a 1995 Queensland-wide programme.

Yet, we still lack basic data on the qualifications, experiences, motivations, financial situations and teaching abilities of part-time staff, and furthermore, we do not know the issues that concern them in relation to their employment circumstances or their teaching. We do not know whether they are primarily graduate students seeking entry to academic careers; professionals who 'do a little teaching on the side' for the love of it; temporaries wanting 'pin money' or a thin connection to an institution which might later offer them employment as their personal circumstances change; or victims of tighter economic times, a cheap, exploited, yet expendable labour force. Nor do we know if there are gender or equity issues hidden in this lack of information. The university as a supporter of equal opportunity needs to be aware of these issues if statements such as the following are to be meaningful:

> Commitment to a socially-just university is reflected by equity and affirmative action programs in staff recruitment and promotion as well as by staff development measures which aim ultimately to provide better representation and career advancement for groups traditionally under-represented in the university community.
>
> (Queensland University of Technology 1994: 7)

We do know that the Committee for Quality Assurance in Higher Education lauded QUT for its high proportion of industry-based part-time staff, presumably for the practical relevance they brought to their teaching. We do know that the National Tertiary Education Union has been adamant that the proportion of part-timers should be capped to protect full-time staff interests, as in the latest 2 per cent productivity agreement conducted at QUT (though it is obvious that part-time staff are difficult to unionise).

There is, therefore, an unexamined tension between the professional relevance part-timers bring to their teaching, the common perception that full-timers' jobs are at risk, the suspicion that part-timers are 'untrained' and 'undedicated' and the complete dependence of most universities on their services.

It is within this context that we investigated the problems and concerns of lecturers who are employed on a part-time basis across a range of disciplines at QUT. The study aimed to build on research undertaken by Franz (1993) who identified in one school within the university a number of factors associated with part-time teaching that were likely to impede the development of effective teaching and learning environments.

It was expected that the outcomes of the project would benefit:

- part-time teaching staff, who would have better support and recognition, greater access to professional development activities and the opportunity to work towards improving their employment conditions;
- students, as recipients of more innovative and effective teaching;

- full-time staff, who would be able to enter into more effective dialogue with part-timers;
- administrators, who may appreciate further the contribution of part-time staff and who may implement practices and programmes to alleviate the practical systemic difficulties experienced by part-timers;
- the community, through the graduation of students with relevant, effective and practical problem-solving skills which are enhanced by their contact with part-time teachers drawn from the professions.

In summary, the project identifies the factors affecting the quality of part-time teaching and seeks to assist individual lecturers to improve their own practice as well as to challenge the institutional culture and practice that inhibits change (Carr and Kemmis 1986). The research team adopted a co-ordinating and facilitative role as well as one of active advocacy to bring about systemic changes.

Our action research model

Throughout most of this century the dominant models of educational research have been the natural science model, based on positivist research paradigms used in the physical sciences and, more recently, the interpretive model. Researchers in the interpretive model aim to discover and interpret the perspectives of the participants in the process (Kember and Gow 1992). Action research, which we used for this project, presents a challenge to these models, especially when it is located in a critical perspective, as action researchers aim 'to change the world, not just to study it' (Wadsworth 1991: 44).

Action research means different things to different people. Some are very demanding and exclusive in their definition of what does and does not count as action research (McTaggart 1991; McTaggart and Garbutcheon-Singh 1986); others use the term more loosely (Zuber-Skerritt 1991). Our project was influenced considerably by the work of Stephen Kemmis. According to Carr and Kemmis (1983) there are three types of action research: technical, practical and emancipatory. The phases of our project have, in fact, moved through each of these types of action research. In the first phase, which we have termed the reconnaissance phase, when we established through the use of questionnaires, who the part-timers in QUT were, we were certainly dealing at a very technical level. As the project progressed we moved through a practical phase before the emancipatory action phase of the project. Carr and Kemmis (1983) argued that only emancipatory action is real action research. We would argue that in order to be emancipatory, we first needed to deal with the technical and practical problems.

Carr and Kemmis (1986) believe that three conditions are necessary before a project can be classified as action research. First, the subject matter must be a social practice susceptible to improvement; second, the project must proceed through a spiral of cycles of planning, action, observing and reflecting; and third, the project should involve the practitioners and widen its audience so others may benefit from their experience. Our project has satisfied each of these conditions. Part-time employment practices are certainly a social practice in need of improvement. We have proceeded through a spiral of five phases which have included a planning phase, an action phase, observing, reflecting and further planning and action.

Elliott (1991) noted that action research is being used in education faculties all over the world to promote reflective practice amongst teachers. In education, action research seems to have become synonymous with the school sector (see, for example, Kemmis and McTaggart 1981; 1988; McNiff 1988; 1993). Consideration of action research in the higher education sector has largely been concerned with the professional development of teachers in education faculties. From the literature, it appears that the concept of action research has only recently been explored in conjunction with the improvement of teaching in higher education (Chism *et al.* 1987; Elliott 1991; Gibbs 1989; Weeks 1995). To our knowledge this is the first time action research has been used to improve teaching by part-time staff in higher education.

Action research is intentionally personalised, idiosyncratic and contextual. Questions for study arise from needs which are unique to individuals in particular settings (Kyle and Hovda 1987). Dealing with part-time staff, we had no formula to follow. Everything we did was new and unique to the particular needs of part-time staff in QUT. Action research allows researchers to get 'close to the data' (Wadsworth 1991). We wanted to know more about part-time staff from as many perspectives as possible. Action research allowed us to get close to our participants. PAR has dimensions of knowledge production and action, as well as constituting new ways of relating to one another to make the work of reform possible. This project has produced knowledge about part-time teachers at QUT which was previously unknown by the institution and part-timers themselves. The action phase of the project aims to give part-time teachers the opportunity to be involved in changing aspects of the culture and practices of part-time teaching at QUT. Action research integrates evaluation, research and philosophical reflection, into a unified conception of a reflective educational practice. Action research aims to contribute both to the practical concerns of people in an immediately problematic situation and to the goals of social science by joint collaboration within a mutually acceptable ethical framework (Rappaport 1970). Through an emphasis on critical evaluation of practice, action research capitalises on the shared concern of practitioners from a variety of backgrounds who are committed to improving practice and understanding the process of practice (Whitehead 1988). The strength of action research as indicated by Whitehead lies in the creative and critical dialogue that develops between members of a community of practice. Each of us came to

259

the project with different perspectives but sharing a common concern about practice. Action research has allowed us to integrate the variety and diversity of the experiences we brought to the project. In this research paradigm we focus on a context in which a number of stakeholders may be identified.

At a broader level we acted as advocates for stakeholders, including the part-timers themselves, and for students, for the co-ordinators and administrators and for the social organisation of the university. Improvement in conditions of employment through appraising administrators of the situation of part-time teachers, increasing the level of professional development of part-time lecturers and encouraging them to negotiate better conditions will contribute to the wellbeing of the whole organisation. Consequently, we envisaged a process in which the part-timers would themselves become reflective practitioners.

The part-time teachers in many instances would see themselves as embedded within the disciplines they are responsible for teaching. Encouragement or expectations of evaluation with implications for self-improvement of their teaching practice is limited. In higher education there has been an unfortunate tendency to dichotomise teaching and research, rather than view them as complementary. For lecturers, the problem is doubly unfortunate because they tend to be categorised as either researchers or teachers. This has perpetuated a separation between teaching and research on teaching activities. The challenge, therefore, was to facilitate and encourage part-time teaching staff to engage in research on their teaching practice.

Our story about research on teaching now details the implementation of the model commencing with the reconnaissance phase.

Reconnaissance

The first component of this project was to develop an understanding of the situation of part-time teaching staff. In one sense we were reconnoitring the territory, exploring the situation or evaluating the processes and relationships. This process involved several stages including a demographic survey, focus groups, selective interviews with various stakeholders and collecting anecdotal assorted data (Figure 13.1). However, each stage informed and complemented others. Indeed, the procedure adopted was congruent with that described by Guba and Lincoln (1993) as 'responsive evaluation'. Responsive evaluation focuses on the claims, concerns and issues raised by the stakeholders in the system under evaluation. Claims are assertions that are favourable. However, concerns mostly would be critical, whilst issues tend to be controversial and not amenable to negotiable conclusions. The major task in evaluation then becomes one of seeking different views and engaging in mutual reconciliation of these viewpoints.

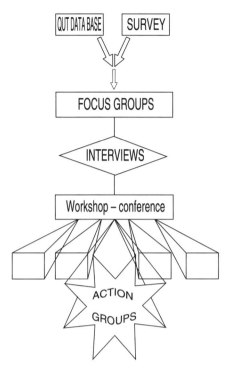

Figure 13.1 Conceptualisation of project stages

> One of the major tasks of the evaluator is to conduct the evaluation
> in such a way that each group must confront and deal with the
> constructions of all the others, a process we shall refer to as a
> hermeneutic dialectic.
>
> (Guba and Lincoln 1993: 41)

The procedures thus involve (a) identification of stakeholders; (b) recording
and sharing claims, concerns and issues for comment, refutation, agreement
or reaction to enable resolution; (c) further exploring unresolved claims,
concerns or issues among all stakeholders; and (d) negotiating among stake-
holding groups concerns or issues in order to reach consensus on each
disputed item.

Each of the stages that comprise the reconnaissance component will be
described in detail (Figure 13.1).

Stage 1 – Demographic survey

As an initial step, a database on part-time staff, was compiled through interrogation of the QUT personnel and statistics database and by contacting all

departmental secretaries. As limited information was available from these sources, a questionnaire was necessary. The questionnaire, which was mailed to home addresses of all identifiable part-time teachers, explored the composition of the part-time academic community in terms of age, sex, contact hours, qualifications, teaching experience, motivation for part-time employment, professional background, primary activity (e.g., student, research assistant, professional) and distribution across schools and faculties. Provision was also made for open-ended responses to several questions. The distribution of the questionnaire also raised consciousness among part-timers that some action was being undertaken by the university to address their concerns and hence a number of part-timers responded directly to the researchers in person or by telephone, contributing rich descriptions of events and experiences and pleas for involvement.

Stage 2 – Focus groups

Seven focus groups comprising twenty-nine part-time staff were convened to identify and explore major concerns. Potential participants were targeted by two methods. First, individual schools were requested to nominate key part-time teaching staff whose participation would be desirable. Second, a representative selection of all part-time staff, identified from the survey respondents, were invited to participate in the focus group for the purpose of brainstorming and identification of issues that impact on the provision of quality teaching.

Stage 3 – Interviews with individuals

Two deans and four heads of school, one co-ordinator of part-timers (at professorial level), the equity officer and a representative of the student guild were interviewed in an unstructured format on a range of issues. The interviews focused on claims, concerns or issues related to the selection of part-timers, quality of teaching, availability of professional development, management structures, working environment and safety conditions.

A limited number of part-time teachers (ten) were selected as representative of a range of constituencies identified in the demographic survey, focus groups and interviews with heads of school and deans. These teachers included full-time PhD students, professionals employed as specialist lecturers and who were not dependent on the university for financial support and tutors solely employed by the university. These were interviewed about experiences in the following areas: interactions with QUT's administrative and teaching systems; staff development; contributions to establishing QUT's teaching and learning environments; opportunities for career development; occupational health and safety; extrinsic factors impacting on part-time teaching (for example, child care, security, parking); and other issues arising out of the focus group sessions.

Analysis of these interviews provided a basis for planning and implementing next stage of the project.

Stage 4 – Workshop–Conference

A one-day workshop–conference was conducted to provide an orientation to the project for QUT part-time teachers and to skill them in appropriate strategies to explore and improve their own teaching skills. This workshop–conference was to be facilitated by an expert in action research and supported by other contributors. The agenda for the workshop drew upon the issues and concerns identified through stages 1–3. Invitations to all part-time teachers in QUT were to be distributed by mail.

Stage 5 – Action groups

Groups of 6 to 8 workshop–conference participants were to be selected on the basis of need, willingness to participate in action research and formed into action or Teaching, Reflection and Collaboration (TRAC) groups. These sub-groups would undertake cycles of action research with regular reference to the project co-ordination team. The team or key personnel in the team would also investigate issues of constraint imposed by the university systems and work in parallel with the teaching action researchers to advise, react and support their research. The team would adopt the role of critical friends and advocates for the part-time teachers.

The situation of part-timers

The outcomes of Stage 1, the demographic survey, are in part described below. An analysis of the focus groups, the interviews with administrators and selected part-timers will follow.

Questionnaire

The questionnaire was to incorporate issues raised in Franz's (1993) study and concerns of the research group. As a pilot exercise, a draft questionnaire with provision for extended comments was distributed to 14 teachers within one faculty. These teachers' suggestions were incorporated into the final design. The questionnaire comprised 27 questions which probed 4 issues: working conditions, aspirations, demographics and qualifications of staff in Semester 2 1994. The format included provision for multi-choice and open-ended responses. Comparative statistical data for full-time staff were extracted from personnel records.

Eight hundred and fifty one responses received by the due return date or after the reminder represented a return rate of approximately 55 per cent, which was considered satisfactory given an apparently high transient population and difficulties in identifying part-time teachers involved in sustained teaching. The questionnaire provided a demographic description of the part-time establishment at the university.

Findings and implications of the survey

Almost 75 per cent of part-time staff indicated that they were either self-employed or in salaried positions. The dependence on non-QUT income varied according to sex, faculty, primary role and age. For example, among female part-time staff, 65 per cent were either self-employed or in a salaried position in contrast to 82 per cent of males. A large variation was also noted across faculties with the lowest dependence on non-QUT income in the Education, Health and Science Faculties.

In relation to primary role, clinical facilitators (20 in the Faculty of Health) and demonstrators (25 in the Faculty of Science) were the most dependent on part-time employment. Of part-time staff over 40 years of age, 78 per cent (63.5 per cent of all females and 88.9 per cent of all males) were in receipt of a salary or self-employed. Six per cent of part-timers were dependent on a scholarship and undertaking graduate studies, a figure well below the 21 per cent reported in the US study (Gappa and Leslie 1993).

As the first stage of an action research project, this study is a reconnaissance of the situation of part-time teaching staff in QUT and provides the basis for exploring issues in depth with part-timers (Di Chiro *et al.* 1988). It is clear even at this early stage that while there are systemic issues which concern staff in all faculties, questions of sex balance, levels of qualification, teaching qualifications and financial vulnerability differ between faculties (Arcodia *et al.* 1995). The professional schools of business, engineering, architecture, education and nursing require skilled 'real world' practitioners who appear to have less dependence on the university for employment and have more industry-based experience. These staff are also less likely to be involved in higher study or possess formal teaching qualifications; equally, they are less likely to possess more than an undergraduate degree. Low levels of academic qualifications appear to be related to their primary professional background (e.g., nursing or engineering), where a first degree is standard. To what extent they can be motivated towards or are interested in professional development programmes related to their teaching remains a question to be answered.

Sex distribution across faculties aligns with traditional gender roles particularly in nursing and engineering. There appear also to be indications that staff employed in some schools may be undertaking duties beyond those commensurate with their level of remuneration.

Focus groups

Twenty-nine part-timers participated in seven focus groups. Participants represented all eight faculties and 23 of the 39 schools and they were drawn from staff employed as demonstrators, tutors, lecturers and clinical facilitators. The focus interviews were audio-taped and the audio tapes reviewed to reveal a number of recurring categories, which represented claims, concerns and issues. These are summarised in Table 13.1, Table 13.2 and Table 13.3, where the frequency of occurrence of claims and concerns indicates the number of sessions in which the topic was discussed. These claims, concerns and issues reflect the particular circumstances that each participant has experienced and through the focus groups has shared with their fellow contributors. They therefore represent assertions and interpretations that need to be confronted and refined by the hermeneutic process (Guba and Lincoln 1993).

By way of explanation, the claims listed in Table 13.1 were expressed strongly by many of the members of the focus groups. For example, although only two groups made the claim that returning something to the profession was important, the focus group facilitator was conscious of the breadth of support attached to this claim in the groups where it was discussed.

Insights into the concerns (Table 13.2) and issues (Table 13.3) of part-timers are particularly evident in the following excerpts from the focus sessions. Feelings of isolation and invisibility, of never meeting other tutors or lecturers, and of relegation to the bottom of the priority list for support by administrative staff are evident in a comment by one participant:

> I don't have much contact, I feel very much insulated. . . . I don't feel very much part of the faculty, I'm just an outsider who comes in and helps out, sort of, to fill a gap. . . . I turn up Monday afternoons at 5 o'clock, go to my little drawer, see if there's anything there, like, notices for me, and then take off for the lecture . . . so I'm very much a fly-by-nighter.
>
> (Part-time lecturer)

Table 13.1 Claims identified by part-time academic staff through focus group sessions

Claims	*Frequency* *
Communication with QUT excellent	2
Excellent administrative support	1
Motivation:	
Enjoyment of teaching	7
Returning something to the profession	2
Enhances professional status or self-esteem to teach at university	4

Note: Frequency relates to the number of times the claim was made across groups; it does not reflect the number of individuals who supported each claim.

Table 13.2 Concerns identified by part-time academic staff through focus groups

Concerns	Examples	Frequency
Physical facilities	locked rooms, no phone, poor meeting space, lack of technical support at night, need to do photocopying privately	7
Induction information insufficient	duty statement, policies re assessment	2
Pay rates and policies	variable, unrealistic for marking, co-ordination not allowed for, delays	6
Administration of pay	forms, tax deductions	2
Marking guidelines vague	liaison poor within teams	2
Course organisation	lack of adequate notice, never met course co-ordinator	4
Quality of teaching	class sizes, no consideration of teaching ability in selection, lack of commitment by colleagues, seen as a reward for undertaking postgraduate studies	6
Support for teaching	no sense of being valued, need to know content, no consultation about unit development or feedback, not advised of student results	5

The power structure inherent in the relationship between full-time and part-time staff was a frequently expressed theme. Teaching support was non-existent, especially when a problem arose concerning discipline. One part-timer sensed the feeling that administrators had little trust in him:

There's a definite culture and, I've studied here for nine years, I'm still studying here, I work here full-time as well as part-time teaching and tutoring, so I've got good insight as to the corporate culture and there is a real doctor–nurse-type culture, like you know happens in hospitals, where you've got the doctors who are on a plane much higher than the nursing staff, even though it's the nursing staff that are doing the day-to-day activities and keeping the place running. There is a real culture problem with academics being, or seeing themselves on a much higher plane than all the non-academic tutoring or part-time teaching staff. And I have a real problem in the other direction and it's just because you're an academic doesn't necessarily make you a good educationalist. In fact often the reverse applies and my greatest concern is that there is not enough feedback or interaction between academics and their tutors or teachers when there should be because we are the ones that are working with the kids at very close quarters, we know their strengths, their weaknesses, whether they're picking up the material, whether they're learning anything or not. Often the academics sail on straight over the top in this world of nebulae and have no concept that they're missing the point completely. And yet we're never consulted, we're never asked. We'll sit there and mark their exam papers, their assignments for them, but we're never asked to comment, to put in any input because of this doctor–nurse type of culture – we're the academics, we're the ones who should know.

(Part-time lecturer)

Table 13.3 Issues raised by part-time academic staff through focus groups

Issues	*Elaboration*
Powerlessness to act	feelings of not being able to protest – beliefs about autonomy, some felt free to protest others not
Role of subject co-ordinators	senior staff member should be responsible for co-ordination of part-timers – some agreed some did not
Relevance of teaching content	real world practical skill vs. theoretical knowledge frameworks of full-timers, involve part-timers in unit development – the role of theory and practice
Professional development	teacher training for part-timers – strong feelings held for and against

Feelings of pessimism and disempowerment to change, to contribute or to become involved in the culture permeated many of the focus sessions. Cases where part-timers had developed units, implemented innovative practices and reflected on their practice were identified but subsequent events were often disheartening. More often than not these part-timers were shifted to other units, full-timers took credit for practices or the cost of change was personally prohibitive. Systemic pressures were a disincentive to change as one part-timer mused:

> I sense that there are forces at work over which I have limited control so I should just accept the gruel that is offered me rather than give any other recipes to the cook! . . . I find the academic environment analogous to the court of Louis XIV, so how do you interact with all these courtiers and who's making the decisions and who's sleeping with who? How would I ever know when I'm such an occasional visitor to the Kingdom? The energy I would have to expend to improve my environment one iota would be disproportionate to what I have available.
>
> (Part-time lecturer)

Although informal feedback from many participants acknowledged the usefulness of this whole project, some scepticism was evident among a few:

> I'm just amazed that someone has asked. After running around the maze, someone's checking the cheese.
>
> (Part-time lecturer)

Part-timers, however, were equivocal about a number of the issues identified in Table 13.3. For example, professional development involving 'teacher training' was seen by some as important and by others as undesirable.

Interviews with heads of school and deans

Interviews were undertaken with senior representatives of each faculty and some teaching units. The interviews were conducted by two members of the research team in an unstructured format and concentrated on three major areas: selection and training, administration and resources. In all, two deans, five heads of school, one nominee of a head of school, the equity officer and a member of ASDU were interviewed. The extensive data gathered through this process will not be explored in depth here but some generalisations will be made to illustrate some findings. Significantly, as a step in the design of this study, the data were revealing in two broad aspects.

First, there was some general correspondence between many of the 'claims' and 'issues' identified in the interviews and focus groups with the part-timers and the views of the senior academics but there was notably little recognition of the 'concerns'. The senior academics in general were less concerned with accreditation of teaching of part-timers than they were with professional qualifications in the selection process. However, they expressed major concerns about the quality of teaching which ranged from poor interactions with students, lack of availability for consultation to attempting to impart '20 years' experience in four lectures. Some concern was expressed that many industry personnel may be lacking in skills to interact with students in an academic environment. A related concern was that part-timers, although they may have currency in the workplace, may not have a theoretical framework from which to analyse their practice. Administrative and funding problems and the consequent need for flexibility to meet changes in student numbers and course structures were raised as concerns. Several senior academics advocated fractional appointments including teaching assistantships and adjunct lectureships as an alternative to casual appointments. Differential funding was also a concern of one senior academic who was unable to attract high-quality part-time staff in a highly paid industry.

Second, there was a common concern that professional credibility be maintained in the university's courses. For example, one interviewee stated:

> even if you have a professional background, the minute you work in an institution you're seen as an academic and no longer have any credibility, well that's an exaggeration, but have less credibility than in the professional world, so in a sense we maintain that professional approach by bringing in industry people who are up to date with what's happening.
>
> (Senior academic)

Many of the senior academics were unaware of the day-to-day administration and involvement of part-timers. Some were unsure of how many were employed or who they were. Few schools provide any form of common induction programme and only two schools could provide any specific documentation aimed at new part-time staff. Where relevant, there was an explicit policy of giving employment priority to graduate students.

Indeed, one head of school considered that employing graduate students and encouraging integration of part-timers in the teaching culture of the school a part of his professional responsibility as head of school. In other areas, however, part-timers had little input into planning of units and in some areas such involvement was actually discouraged. The model of a part-timer described by one interviewee was explicit:

> A good part-time staff member is someone who doesn't turn up a minute before and leave a minute after, but is prepared to say (to a student) 'if you've a problem then come and see me'.
>
> (Senior academic)

Clearly, poor communication between academic staff and part-timers is endemic in the university at the school and faculty levels. Insights obtained through these interviews provided an overview of the interactions between part-timers and schools and was important in developing the next phase of the project – initiating action.

Action

The next phase of this project was to develop the conference, drawing on the data gained from the first stage of the project. The conference was seen as an opportunity to develop networking and action research cells of part-time teaching staff.

This phase of the project proceeded smoothly and with a substantial degree of support from senior administration in the institution. A preliminary report of the findings of the project was disseminated to senior administrators responsible for areas such as finance, library, information technology, human resource management and selected deans. In that report the results of the questionnaire, focus groups, interviews and other probes were presented and discussed. Informed by the preliminary findings, these administrators and managers, including the Deputy Vice-Chancellor, came together with approximately 140 part-time academic staff (all part-time academics were invited to attend) at the conference to listen, to explore issues and concerns and to suggest mechanisms to improve the teaching and learning environment and opportunities for professional development for part-time academic staff.

The conference was structured in two phases. In the first phase preliminary findings from the data were reported to the participants. Representatives from QUT administrative support units then responded to the issues raised by these findings. Considerable discussion between administrators and part-time academic staff followed. In the second phase the part-time staff participants brainstormed in small groups their claims, concerns and issues and proposed actions for change. Summaries of the small group findings were then presented to the whole conference. Further discussion followed. In the last phase of the conference described above, fifty part-time academic staff agreed to become actively involved in the process of change.

Outcomes of the conference

As part of the hermeneutic process described earlier, part-time academic conference participants' claims, concerns and issues were compared with the preliminary findings of the earlier stages of the project. These findings were confirmed and thus validated by the major stakeholders of the study. Other immediate outcomes of the conference were as follows:

1   The conference provided a unique opportunity for part-time academic staff (hitherto an 'invisible force' and an unheard sector the university) to voice their claims, concerns and issues in the presence of senior university administrators, thus facilitating the opening of dialogue between the two groups of stakeholders.

2   Senior management publicly acknowledged (both at the conference and in a subsequent QUT newspaper editorial) the vital role that part-time academic staff play in the achievement of the university's goals.
3   The Deputy Vice-Chancellor made a public commitment (at the conference) to support recommendations from the conference participants to improve the situation of part-time academic staff, and to maintain regular liaison with them.
4   Through the involvement of administrators in the conference process and discussion of the project's findings, the development and delivery of university support services and professional development is now informed by knowledge of the needs of part-time academic staff and increased awareness of the important role they play in achieving the university's goals.
5   Through participation in the conference, many part-time staff were encouraged to become involved in professional development, particularly in relation to their teaching. As well as becoming aware of support services and teaching workshops available to them, many participants appreciated the opportunity to meet other part-time staff and begin to form informal supportive networks with them.

Following the conference, the next phase of the project (see Figure 13.1) was the formation of action groups of part-time academic staff. The purpose of these groups was to become engaged in the process of changing the practice of part-time teaching at QUT. From the 50 conference participants who volunteered to become involved in this process, 23 of these staff attended a meeting several weeks after the conference. Project team members were also present with the intention of providing support to the newly formed group. A range of options for implementing change was discussed at this meeting, but the consensus of the meeting was that priority should be given to the formation of a professional association. It was proposed that an association could then address specific issues of concern to part-time academic staff.

In parallel with this process, a professional development workshop was organised by the Academic Staff Development Unit specifically for part-time academics, addressing some of the needs described by participants at the conference. A meeting of part-time academics, publicised to all part-time staff, was held in conjunction with this workshop. Thirty part-time academic staff attended this meeting and voted on a proposal and a series of motions to form a Professional Association for Part-time Academic staff at QUT, with the acronym PAPTA. The meeting elected an organising committee comprised of representatives from all the faculties and teaching units employing part-time teaching staff.

Representatives of this committee then met with the Deputy Vice-Chancellor who had addressed the conference and who had made a commitment to resolve some of the difficulties presently facing part-time academic staff. He accepted a detailed request from the committee for administrative support for the association and for action on certain urgent issues such as delays in payment.

Since communication was identified by part-time staff as one of their major concerns, one of the committee's first actions was to organise the setting up of an email list for discussion and the posting of information. However, only a small proportion of part-time academic staff have access to a computer in their workplace, thus this issue is being addressed concurrently.

These initiatives have begun the process of action in which part-time academic staff themselves are engaged in changing the practice of part-time teaching at their institution. The overall aim of the association is to provide support for part-time academic staff.

The committee envisages that this will be done first, by representing the professional interests of staff to QUT administrators, thus improving communication with the institution. Second, the group will provide information to part-time academic staff regarding QUT support services and processes and work for more formal processes such as induction, handbooks and professional development opportunities. Third, through forums such as the email discussion list and an annual conference the association aims to support networking amongst part-time staff.

Reflection by collaborating researchers

Jim's reflections: diary of a journey through a different paradigm

My motivation for research stems from a personal curiosity to understand my practice and the world with which I personally interact. Coupled to this curiosity is a sense of need to contribute to the solution of problems associated with education. The empirical model grounded in a realist epistemological stance – derived from a former life in the natural sciences – has framed my research. Consequently, my research philosophy is associated with scientific realism (House 1991). The scientific realist position argues that events are explained by examining the structures that cause the events, and thus events are produced by multiple interactions of causal entities. In particular, reality is not what we can necessarily see but also the underlying causal entities that are not always directly observable. Given the complexity of events in social systems one might hope only to observe or infer 'transfactual causal structures that influence events'. In other words we hope to be able to glean some understanding or recognition of events that might influence outcomes. Much debate asserts that the adoption of a positivistic approach to educational research implies a relationship between the researcher and the researched in which the researcher speaks about people as subjects of research and seeks solutions in terms of explanations and technological knowledge (Carr and Kemmis 1986). Also influential in framing my practice is the concern that research is not impacting on educational practice. Richardson (1994) articulates the dilemma in advocating the teacher researcher and the role of practical enquiry through which teachers take the responsibility of improving their own practice through any functional methodology. The dilemma facing a university academic, then, is one of how to bring about partnerships between those with academic and practice expertise.

Other issues that emerged as the project developed were the nature of assumptions held about fellow collaborators: the role of expertise, our status, responsibilities and roles within the organisation. The original group came together with what I perceived was a sense of common interest with little concern for hierarchical structures. However, given that two collaborators fulfilled three formal roles as part-time tutors, graduate students and research assistants, with competing obligations and responsibilities, tensions were possible. My own administrative position in relation to these research assistants further complicated relationships. My personal beliefs and actions were, however, never clearly articulated leaving an atmosphere of confusion and feelings of tension to which I was oblivious. Compounding this confusion was the tacit assumption of roles to be played by the respective collaborators. One collaborator was not only a research assistant, but she was also deliberately assigned to tasks associated with the project. This was done for both pragmatic and theoretical reasons. A number of tasks associated with the project were considered best undertaken by a person with her qualifications, experiences and identification with part-time teachers. The issue of concern centred on acknowledgement of the collaborator's original contributions to the analyses, writing and planning of these tasks. Similarly, I undertook certain tasks that benefited from the expertise that I could bring to them. Whereas this role was perceived to be appropriate for an academic and needed no explanation, she was clearly concerned with identification with two roles – assistant and collaborator.

Analysis of my diary revealed a singularly egocentric and technical approach to the project. Meetings were planned, agenda constructed, tasks planned and analysed, issues discussed in relation to meeting 'the project' plan. I seem to have recorded little discussion about values, feelings and motives of individuals within the team. These, on reflection, did occur, but as is usual in the research paradigm, their significance was not registered or acted upon. The team did evolve structural relationships that did eventually facilitate more meaningful exchange of ideas but in retrospect, more should have been done to encourage clarification of these issues through clear communication at an earlier stage.

Clare's reflections

I feel that our collaboration has been effective in some ways but not in others. I found our meetings friendly and respectful and in some ways enjoyable, and I was pleased to be involved in a project where I liked the other people. The research seemed to me to be something of value because it was addressing what I saw as injustice, and I felt that these academic staff were perhaps different from others I have worked with, who are fairly detached from the subjects of their research and less concerned with social issues.

At some stage, however, I became aware that I felt less than an equal partner in the project. I realise now that this is partly because of my research assistant role in this project, which I also play with other full-time academic staff on other projects. The research assistant role has the status of a technician supporting others' research. Because my principal involvement in this group was organising and conducting interviews, I felt like a research assistant on the project and thus not an equal partner. From other research contexts I saw writing about the research as the important part, which gave one a real voice and equal status with other researchers. I was not involved in any writing and although this could be explained in terms of time or convenience, it still felt to me like exclusion, with the automatic doubts this raises about one's capability. It also echoed my experiences as a part-time teacher, where I felt useful but not quite good enough.

Looking back now, it seems to me that we should have discussed our respective roles and levels of contribution explicitly at the beginning of the project. Obviously there will be differences of expertise in the group and different degrees of interest in different tasks but these should be made explicit and negotiated. I feel that collaborating on writing is perhaps the most difficult part of collaborative research and for this reason should be discussed early in the project.

Charles's reflections

I have learned a number of useful points about action research from this project so far.

Effective communication is essential if the research is to be collaborative. I believe that other research methodologies are far more efficient and perhaps 'productive' in a narrow sense of the word. PAR needs more time for collaboration, discussion and argument. Without a commitment to group reflection this methodology cannot be successful.

It is important to recognise the role the participants have within the university and any other duties they have which may impact on their perspectives or participation in the research group. My role within the university is to support research projects, but my role in this group is as one of a team funded by the university to carry out the project. It is useful to spell out the different roles which are necessary in the carrying out of successful research and then to negotiate who will be responsible for them. Without such clarity the task can lose its momentum and leave individual researchers uncertain about their responsibilities.

The strength of PAR is the diversity of perspective that each member brings to the team but herein lies its potential weakness. It is difficult for participants to leave behind the primary role they play in the university and to open themselves to the vulnerability of genuine group decision making.

Yoni's reflections

The difficulties of collaboration have been that none of the researchers have been involved with such a large project before, and that we struggled with methodological imperatives, and practical difficulties such as accessing the names and addresses of part-timers from a system which at that time was not attuned to such interrogation. Coming from two campuses and with high demand levels on our time in both the faculty and staff development, there was also the problem of energy levels each of us could muster, and the initial difficulty, for me, of working in a quantitative paradigm (stage 1) when I have always worked in qualitative modes. Yet throughout, the personal qualities of all participants and pleasant atmosphere of meetings have added to our motivation to empower and improve the situation of part-timers.

Patricia's reflections

Reflecting on this project has been interesting. When I first went along to the PARAPET meetings I had a small research project vaguely in mind, I certainly did not have a project of the size and complexity in my mind which this one has grown to be. I find it fascinating how this project 'threw up' five such different collaborators. Forming an action research team has certainly not been straightforward. It appears to me, reflecting on that time, that the five of us who became the PETPAR team, brought multiple perspectives and different agendas to the project. This has been interesting to observe and participate in as we have conceptualised improving teaching by part-timers in QUT as an action research project. Our connection with our own areas has taken most of our time and in my case I have felt unable to give as much time to the project as I would originally have wished and envisaged. We represent such varied points of view. We have had very little time to think about our working relationships, which is probably similar to the situation in many action research projects. I think we did not put enough time into finding out more about ourselves and our reason for joining the project. We did not ask ourselves what we felt we could bring to the project and what part we would like to play. We made many assumptions, originally, about who would do what. We spent what little time we had getting started immediately, with the technical requirements of the project. We are all, in fact, part-time on the project and this in some ways has given us a 'feel' for how our participants must feel. I recognise that some of our concerns mirror those of part-time teaching staff. For instance, the feeling of marginalisation some members of the team has reported have also been discussed by our participants. Some members' strengths were very soon put to use. Some jumped in and started writing, others took on the role of research assistant because it seemed 'natural'. In fact, by doing this we opened up a whole range of concerns by those who, for one reason or another, felt either unable or unqualified to offer their help in these ways.

I had not worked in a quantitative paradigm before and the large-scale reconnaissance we undertook at the beginning of this project was, for me, quite scary. I felt it was like a huge mountain we had to climb before we could start. I felt we were trudging along, hoping one day, to really get into it. On reflection, I think I wondered if we were actually doing action research – it did not feel right to me. My interests lay in the action phases of the project and I found it very hard to really 'get into' the demographic data. I also had no knowledge of the data analysis methods and with very little time available I found it difficult, at times, to sustain my interest in the project. Once I started actually working with part-time staff, talking with them, listening to them, and hearing about their concerns whilst teaching them during a series of workshops run by the ASDU, my interest levels immediately rose and I felt more able to contribute to the project.

Conclusions: breaching the castle walls

The overall project outcomes have been threefold: first, acknowledgement by QUT administrators of the contribution of part-time academic staff to the life of the institution and a commitment to ongoing dialogue with them; second, the beginnings of structural change in the institution; and third, the formation of a professional association of part-time academic staff to provide support and a voice for dialogue with the university administration.

Thus, through the process of action research begun in this project a group of practitioners has become involved in the process of changing practice. Essential to the success of this process however is an ongoing dialogue with the administrators of the institution. To sustain their efforts the association needs some administrative support from the institution. It has already been the experience of the organising committee that their survival and thus their role in changing practice depends on accessing knowledge of the structures and processes of the institution. The isolation they have experienced as individual part-time academic staff could operate against their chances of changing practice as a group if the institution is not also committed to the process of improvement and to breaking down the first barrier by providing administrative support, that is, knowledge.

Implementing this project has been a significant experience in terms of the researchers' need to acquire new skills. As individuals in a collaborative group we have had to redefine our own objectives and goals and test them against those of other members of the group. We have had to learn to value the collaboration and to become reflective about the process of collaboration. In retrospect the project was very demanding in so far as reconciling the many demands on our time with the need to be actively participating in the project. Competing responsibilities to ourselves as researchers, to the part-timers with whom we were attempting to build a process and to the university who provided funding and expected accountability had to be balanced. For example, as researchers, reporting, publication and theorising were tiring and often conflicted with advocacy roles, where energy was needed in interacting with part-timers. For some of the researchers the development of research skills involved near-quantum leaps. However commitment and interest in the project were sustained by the hope that significant cultural change for part-time academic staff at QUT would result from it.

REFERENCES

Arcodia, C., Christensen, C., Kemmis, S., Ryan, Y., Watters, J. J. and Weeks, P. (1995) 'Part-time teaching: the invisible force', *Research and Development in Higher Education*, 18: 91–6

Carr, W. and Kemmis, S. (1983) *Becoming Critical: Knowing through Action Research*, Geelong, Victoria: Deakin University Press.

—— (1986) *Becoming Critical: Education, Knowledge and Action Research*, Lewes: Falmer Press.

Chickering, A. W., and Gamson, Z. (1987) 'Seven principles for good practice in undergraduate education', *Wingspread Journal*, 9 (2): 1–4.

Chism, N., Sanders, D. and Zitlow, C. (1987) 'Observations on a faculty development program based on practice-centred inquiry', *Peabody Journal of Education*, 64 (3): 1–23.

Di Chiro, G., Robottom, I. and Tinning, R. (1988) 'An account of action research in a tertiary context' (pp. 133-43), in Kemmis, S. and McTaggart, R. (eds) *The Action Research Planner*, 3rd edn, Geelong, Vic: Deakin University.

Elliott, J. (1991) *Action Research for Educational Change*, Milton Keynes: Open University Press.

Franz, J. (1993) Factors affecting the quality of part-time teaching, unpublished report to the School of Architecture, Interior and Industrial Design, QUT.

Gappa, J. and Leslie, D. (1993) *The Invisible Faculty: Improving the Status of Part-timers in Higher Education*, San Francisco: Jossey-Bass.

Gibbs, G. (1989) *Improving Student Learning: A CNAA Funded Project*, Oxford: Oxford Polytechnic.

Guba, E. G. and Lincoln, Y. S. (1993) *Fourth Generation Evaluation*, Newbury Park, CA: Sage Publications.

Holley, C. (1995) 'Time to sort out the casual academic mess', *National Tertiary Education Union Advocate*, 2 (2): 14–15.

House, E. R. (1991) 'Realism in research', *Educational Researcher*, 20 (6): 2–9.

Kember, D. and Gow, L. (1992) 'Action research as a form of staff development in higher education', *Higher Education*, 23 (3): 297–310.

Kemmis, S. and McTaggart, R. (1981) *The Action Research Planner*, Geelong: Deakin University Press.

—— (1988) *The Action Research Reader*, 3rd edn, Geelong: Deakin University.

Kyle, D. W. and Hovda, R. A. (1987) 'Action research: comments on current trends and future possibilities', *Peabody Journal of Education*, 64 (3): 170–5.

Ludecke, J. (1981) 'The part-time academic saga', *Journal of Advanced Education*, 4 (3): 3.

McNiff, J. (1988) *Action Research: Principles and Practice*, Basingstoke, Hampshire: Macmillan Education Ltd.

—— (1993) *Teaching As Learning: An Action Research Approach*, London: Routledge.

McTaggart, R. (1991) *Action Research: A Short Modern History*, Geelong, Victoria: Deakin University Press.

McTaggart, R. and Garbutcheon-Singh, M. (1986) 'New directions in action research', *Curriculum Perspectives*, 6 (2): 42–6.

Queensland University of Technology (1990) *Mission Statement*, Brisbane: QUT.

—— (1994) *Quality and Excellence in Teaching and Learning: A Submission to The Committee for Quality Assurance in Higher Education*, Brisbane: QUT.

Rajagopal, I. and Farr, W. (1992) 'Hidden academics: the part-time faculty in Canada', *Higher Education*, 24: 317–31.

Rappaport, R. N. (1970) 'Three dilemas in action research', memo given to the Social Science Research Council Conference, York, in Elliott, J. and Adelman, C. *Classroom Action Research*, Cambridge, England: Cambridge Institute of Education.

Richardson, V. (1994) 'Conducting research on practice', *Educational Researcher*, 23 (5): 5–10.

Wadsworth, Y. (1991) *Do It Yourself Social Research*, Collingwood, Victoria: Victorian Council of Social Service and the Melbourne Family Care Organisation.

Whitehead, J. (1988) 'Foreword', in McNiff, J. *Action Research: Principles and Practice*, Basingstoke, Hampshire: Macmillan Education Ltd, p. xi.

Weeks, P. (1995) Facilitating a reflective, collaborative teaching development project in higher education: reflections on experience, unpublished PhD thesis, Queensland University of Technology, Brisbane.

Zuber-Skerritt, O. (1991) *Action Research in Higher Education: Examples and Reflections*, Brisbane: Centre for the Advancement of Learning and Teaching, Griffith University.

14

A PATHWAY FOR POSTGRADUATE TEACHING

Tania Aspland and Ross Brooker

This chapter shares, in an instructive way, a continuing attempt by two academics to challenge and reshape the constructs of higher education programmes for professional educators enrolled in curriculum studies in a new university context. Action research has become a central construct in this process, a process that in many ways still remains problematic, yet has offered to us a framework in which to transform a discourse that has remained unquestioned for too long. This chapter portrays and analyses the pathway we have taken in reconstructing and theorising our teaching through action research over a period of four university semesters (two years) with two different cohorts of students enrolled in an in-service postgraduate diploma in education course. Each cohort undertook the same two curriculum studies subjects, one in each semester of the year in which they studied.

The chapter is structured to give the reader not only a sense of the historical development of the pathway but, more importantly, to articulate the critical inputs from the various participants (students, lecturers, literature) and the deliberations that transformed those inputs into meaningful actions.

Cycle One

The problem

For some time now, it has been argued (Bullough 1992; Cornett 1990; Goodman 1986) that the teaching of curriculum studies should be a core component of teacher education and training programmes. The most central reasons are outlined here as:

- the need for teachers to develop a broader understanding of the political, cultural, social and historical relations in which their curriculum practices are set;
- the desire for teachers to generate a more informed view of curriculum in terms of a vision for socially just learning opportunities provided within a particular setting;

280

- to heighten awareness that teachers are a means through which sustained change can occur;
- to enhance teachers' professional capacities to use a range of skills and strategies that are central to curriculum decision making in local, systemic and national contexts.

Curriculum studies are means by which educators can examine, clarify and reconstruct their values and their practices in ways that are better informed and enhance the quality of teaching and learning experiences for their student clientele.

Considerations of how curriculum studies should be taught at the postgraduate level must take into account, not only principles of adult learning and emerging propositions about 'best practice' for professional development, but also the very nature of curriculum as a field of endeavour. Further, as higher education becomes more accessible to a broader clientele, it becomes the responsibility of universities to cater for a variety of professional contexts in which curriculum takes on different meaning and modes of expression. A growing literature in the field is presenting a convincing argument that curriculum as praxis is a proposition that is vital to the successful teaching of curriculum studies. Curriculum decision making is no longer considered a technical process that can be enhanced through the dissemination of theories intent on refining the curriculum tools available to educators. Therefore, the teaching of curriculum studies is no longer a recipe book outlining the application of theory to practice. Rather, it involves complex processes of theorising about one's practice; weighing up curriculum options; critiquing what has always been taken for granted – analysing the constructs of why we do things that way we do – with a view towards ongoing improvement; taking an informed stance on curriculum issues; and arguing for unique ways to address what is problematic in particular learning communities. Curriculum decision making has been recognised as a highly personal process and curriculum studies has a vital role to play in assisting educators towards personal and professional understandings and transformations in a field that is fraught with curriculum complexities, contestations and concerns.

It is argued here that the teaching of curriculum studies has, in the past, failed to respond to the challenges outlined above. For the past fifteen years academic staff, despite some exceptions, have continued to provide 'distanced learnings' from the disciplines (Aoki 1990: 111) that surrounded curriculum decision making. We argue that this type of teaching has failed to centralise educators' practice at the heart of curriculum studies, instead it continues to 'preach' predetermined and prescriptive procedures and models of curriculum as ways to addressing curriculum problems.

The project reported here began following anecdotal concerns from students, about the inappropriateness of the traditional mode of delivery (a

3-hour class each week for fourteen weeks dominated by lecture input) adopted to teach a compulsory curriculum studies component within a post-graduate course. In response, an informal needs assessment was undertaken in order to identify the specific concerns of the students. They indicated that they were being taught in ways that were more appropriate to undergrad-uate orientations and were dissatisfied with university teaching that they believed trivialised their professional (and personal) contexts and needs. They argued that the links to their everyday professional practice were tenuous and a significant proportion of the theoretical concepts in the unit were presented too late to inform assignment work based in their work contexts.

The group, consisting predominantly of women students, expressed feel-ings of disempowerment, frustration and anger as they perceived the subject to be inappropriate to their needs. Students expressed disappointment and a lack of support for learning experiences that 'were theoretical and removed from reality'. They did not respect lecturing staff who 'hadn't seen the inside of a classroom for a long time' arguing that links between professional prac-tice and curriculum theory were lacking in credibility. Students who were not given the opportunity to challenge and critique existing research and professional practice felt that curriculum studies as it was presented in this context, was 'a waste of time' and a 'meaningless experience'. It was most evident that students expected a critical approach to learning to be an inte-gral part of a postgraduate programme.

An initial response

Because we had only a few weeks between semesters to rethink the teaching and learning approach for the second curriculum studies unit with this cohort, our deliberations were somewhat intuitive and drew upon our existing knowledge bases and experience rather than from any informed reading of the literature or dialogue with other curriculum workers. This came as the semester progressed.

Consequently, the students were offered an alternative teaching and learning path of which 48 of the 60 students chose as a more appropriate mode of learning. This alternative approach was offered in modules that moved away from weekly meetings (see Appendix), but more importantly, central to this approach was a form of teaching and learning that was responsive to their professional needs and focused on the teachers completing classroom research about their practice. A critical approach to action research was offered to the students as a framework that was congruent to their professional needs. Implicit in this was a requirement for each student to engage in an action research project that began with 'some-thing that they believed was problematic' within their professional context as the focus of their learning. During formal classes, we began with the reporting of these works in progress through seminar presentations, and integrated traditional form of curriculum studies lectures and workshops in response to common curriculum issues that arose out of the works in progress. The formal lecturing component of the programme focused, not on the dissemination of curriculum theory, but rather on a critique of the existing literature, with a view to offering teachers a framework to further develop and reshape their own projects and practices. The guiding question for the group was 'why do we do things the way we do – and do we do want to continue to do so?'

In attempting to theorise this new and responsive approach to teaching and learning, we were able to articulate a complex interplay of principles of procedure that needed to be considered and shared with the group. While we did not formally engage in action research about our own teaching, we certainly engaged, as a teaching team in a process of careful reflection and informal theorising about our practice 'being inquisitive about circumstances, action and consequences and coming to understand the relationships between circumstance, actions and consequences' (Kemmis 1994) in our work.

In so doing, our discussions focused on, a range of existing social and political practices that shape the lives and work of: (i) professional people involved in the course (the students); (ii) practices of university teaching in times of transition; and (iii) the constraints of the subject: curriculum studies.

It became our responsibility (our obsession at times) to analyse the complex interplay of such practices with a view to making decisions about our teaching in order to generate transformative actions that would ensure a more effective presentation of the subject, that more appropriately met the needs of the clientele. In hindsight, we have been able to articulate at least three separate but interrelated practices and sets of assumptions that we believe were useful in reshaping our interactions with the group. Each of the separate practices and assumptions will be briefly outlined in order to highlight the distinctive nature of each, and then, the interplay amongst them and the impact this had on the learning environment will be discussed.

Practices in higher education: a context in transition

As a teaching team we were able to identify the following beliefs about higher education teaching that underpinned our practice in postgraduate contexts.

- Learners should actively construct their own knowledge.
- Learners should be encouraged to engage in different orientations to learning according to their goals.
- Learners who succeed shape their knowledge through the interplay of formal and informal theory.

- Learners need to engage in a process of learning that is active, reflective and collaborative.

Second: the changing needs of professional practitioners

As our clientele diversified across professional contexts, including education, police, health and community welfare, we had to carefully consider what was meaningful learning across the professions. We argue here that:

- The starting point for teaching and learning is the professional needs and interests of the clientele.
- Professional learning emerges through a research orientation that articulates what is problematic about practice, investigates why it is problematic within a particular context and how this can be addressed in ways to ensure transformative action.
- Professional learning is a long-term process promoting ongoing personal and group critical reflection that promotes self-renewing practices.
- Professional learning actively focuses on existing ongoing educational practices which, together with theorising from the literature, combine to form the basis of ongoing development.
- Professional learning is enhanced through critical collaborative dialogue with peers in a context that is conducive to open and informative debate.
- Professional learning attempts to monitor the congruence between ideology and practice.
- Professional learning engages the learner in studying the impact of the social, cultural and political contexts on one's practice.

The complex practice of teaching curriculum studies

As we had been presenting curriculum studies in predominantly pre-service teacher education contexts for some time, we had to reconsider our thinking in meeting the demands of the postgraduate context. We identified the following principles to guide our practice.

- One way in which educators can achieve coherence in professional practice in higher-degree work is the study of curriculum.
- The study of curriculum becomes a powerful force in developing educators images of professional practice while they practice.
- The study of curriculum is essential for current and future educators and trainers because it integrates their understanding in the context of practice.
- The study of curriculum should reveal the complexity of curriculum decision making underpinning professional practice. In so doing, profes-

sional educators need to develop the corresponding capacities to enable them to further partake in decision making in powerful ways.

- The study of curriculum is seen as a field of inquiry by which educators can develop a framework for formulating arguments for their practice and demonstrating accountability for what they do.
- The study of curriculum provides a means for educators to develop a contextual understanding of curriculum policies and their implications for curriculum practice, providing opportunities for critiquing policy, analysing its impact on practice, providing the basis for transformative responsible action (curriculum change) when necessary.
- The teaching of curriculum studies, in higher degree settings calls for an interactive or 'praxis' orientation that encourages professional practitioners to engage in critical theorising about their practice ensuring a better understanding of a continuing involvement in the complex multi-faceted and value-laden social practice of curriculum decision making.

The confluence of our thinking and our teaching

We reached a point where we were able to argue that it was the interplay of these three sets of assumptions that set the scene for more appropriate teaching and learning processes for the student cohort engaged in learning about curriculum studies and are able to document the following achievements as the basis for further discussion.

First, an extensive number of students acknowledged that they thought the knowledge base we incorporated into the programme was appropriate in the field of curriculum studies. Many indicated that a full understanding of curriculum concepts, curriculum orientations, curriculum models, processes of curriculum development and curriculum evaluation were' all necessary components of a curriculum studies programme. Whilst no extensive rationale was offered as a basis for inclusion other than the status quo of existing courses, a number of students did suggest that the inclusion of such a knowledge base needed to be linked with practice. It was overwhelmingly stated that the input of theory that was devoid of context and lacked application to practice was regarded as inappropriate in a postgraduate course. A small number of students argued that such theory in isolation could be placed in a pre-service course as a preparation for teaching but this was not supported across the sample group A very strong argument was put by a group of students that such a knowledge base was useless in a postgraduate course, unless it was directly linked to their own professional practice. These students argued that theory of this nature was 'difficult to grasp', 'failed to have an impact on practice' and 'was useless in terms of professional development'.

Second a large number of students welcomed that curriculum studies should focus more clearly on the teaching and learning processes in which they were actively involved. They perceived curriculum studies to evolve from their role as educator in a highly complex process of curriculum decision making and curriculum development. The knowledge base that they preferred was one that was elicited from current research and readings, bringing theory to their practice in a way that allowed them to better understand their practice and improve it as required. The content of such a knowledge base remained ill-defined from the perspective of students but fell within the parameter of personal ideology, professional practice, curriculum change and innovation. This group argued the basic concepts of curriculum studies should be established in a pre-service course, as a preparation for entry into the field. Postgraduate work like this may need to revise and refine these basic concepts, but the knowledge base at this level should focus on 'widening educators' knowledge of curriculum practice and on becoming familiar with current curriculum research, policy development and contextual changes.' It was argued that the knowledge base of postgraduate courses should bring practising educators in touch with issues and development of this nature with a view to 'enriching existing curriculum practices'.

Whilst many educators in the group attempted to delineate the content that should be offered in pre-service or in service courses, no shared view emerged. However two significant points became obvious. First, curriculum studies *should* be a component of both pre-service and in-service programmes, but in a way that strengthened professional practice. As students moved into the field, a greater degree of critiquing practice should be fostered through curriculum studies. Second, whatever the knowledge base, it needs to be planned in a way that is *developmental* and *responsive* to the specific needs of particular groups. It should be clearly articulated and sufficiently diverse to cater for the changing professional needs of clients who return to postgraduate study at different points in their career. The following sentiments expressed by one student were reflected across the group.

> Before this new approach was designed curriculum studies at this institution was very narrow and repetitive . . . students were discouraged at the prospect of regurgitating the same content developed from a similar rationale and objectives . . . What is new? This approach has given us new scope and challenge as educators. We don't have to put up with more of the same? If this approach does not continue, is the Masters course and PhD work going to prove to be as narrow.
>
> (Postgraduate student)

The processes of teaching and learning that were deemed most appropriate by the group were those that fostered the making of links between teachers' knowledge, beliefs and the implementation of curriculum (Bullough 1992). A high level of support and commendation was provided to us, as lecturing staff who offered to students an opportunity to explore their curriculum decision-making practices in a systematic, sustained and critical manner. The students overwhelmingly supported this as the most appropriate teaching mode at the postgraduate level: one that called on previously acquired curriculum knowledge in a manner that further refined understanding of such concepts in a way that was enriching. One student declared that 'this was achieved by encouraging students to stand back from practice and critically analyse what was happening'.

Students argued that this approach introduced them to a form of research-based learning that brought new insights to their curriculum work that had previously been unquestioned. They also valued appropriate readings that provided the basis for ongoing dialogue and field-based research. They condoned 'good lecturing that integrated, context, curriculum theory and professional practice'.

The process of critical reflection and its contribution to the positive professional development of teaching as curriculum decision-makers was recognised by all participants. It brought to many students, for the first time, an opportunity to 'get outside' professional practice and develop a richer understanding of teaching behaviour that for many years they had taken for granted. Students valued the opportunity to expose the ideology that underpinned their practice. They also acknowledged that by becoming aware of the contextual variables that were continually reshaping their work, they were better able to understand the complexities of their curriculum practice.

Students valued the opportunity to thoroughly research the impact of policy on their daily practice and argued that this gave them new insights into the present educational context. This allowed them to make more informed curriculum decisions at the level of school policy as well as in classroom practice.

> I knew nothing about the National Curriculum ... now I am considered a leader in the field at school and I can better prepare my work for future changes. . . . I don't know how I could have been so blind to national change.
>
> (Postgraduate student)

Many students commented that this postgraduate work in curriculum studies empowered them to participate more fully in school–community forums dealing with curriculum decision making. They indicated that their increased knowledge in the field allowed them not only to contribute to the forums but also to challenge administrators and departmental personnel in a way that enhanced their professional image and enriched the decision-making process. 'I am no longer just a classroom teacher isolated and removed from policy debates!'.

Students claimed that they have developed a new understanding about the generation of curriculum documents and how the underlying values of such documents may 'contradict the basis of daily practice'. A number of students indicated that they had never questioned the impact of such documents on their practice and always 'accepted curriculum documents as the Bible'. They feel now that they will no longer 'blindly accept curriculum constraints' such as these, by being proactive in critiquing future policy and curriculum documents in light of their 'teaching ideologies, the nature of knowledge and preferred teaching and learning processes'. As one student stated 'curriculum studies in this subject has addressed who has power over curriculum decisions, who should have power and how teachers fit into the big picture. This has been an invaluable experience.'

It is very evident from this analysis that this pathway offered to educators as professionals an orientation to learning that was empowering, engaging, and most importantly made meaningful connections with professional practice. As a result of our teaching transformations, we were able to conclude the following:

- Personal/professional concerns and practices need to be linked closely with higher education programmes.
- Such a process had led to change in personal professional practice for 60 per cent of participants.
- The content and process of the subject was considered significant for all participants (71 per cent) fair significance (29 per cent major significance).
- The intensive two-day workshops were well received professionally but proved to be 'heavy' in terms of intellectual and physical demands. A small group of students remained committed to traditional modes of learning.
- Students expressed ownership and commitment of the unit and were proactive in reshaping it where necessary.
- Many have developed a new confidence in themselves as teacher–researchers.
- Many have developed a new world view about their professional responsibilities and roles as they actively engage in challenging much of what they have taken for granted for many years.

A way forward

While feedback suggested that the process was generally well received by the participants, as the teaching team we wanted to explore more fully the implications for higher education teaching and learning processes. What was it about our teaching that was so welcoming from the student perspective and could we theorise what we did in ways that could be instructive to our colleagues as well as ourselves? Further, in theorising our practice, how could we better confront the existing inadequacies of our teaching that were still problematic for a number of participants, and troubled us as teachers.

What remained problematic for us can best be described using the framework of Fay (1987). Fay has argued that the work of projects such as these should generate social practices that move through four phases, the first of which centres on a theory of false consciousness whereby the participants engaging in action research come to realise the incoherence or contradictory nature of their self-understandings and how these have manifested themselves through their practices, the essence of which are often maintained by the institutional hegemonies that subtly dictate the shapes of such practices in ways that are in complete opposition to the practitioners' world view. It is contended here that this project was successful in raising the consciousness of the participants through action research on their practice eliciting complex issues for discussion that were new and insightful. Such critique, as is evidenced above, effectively confronts the essence of false consciousness implicit in their/our professional world. This moved the debate about their curriculum work to a point that Fay identifies as the theorising of crises whereby the participants clearly identified a number of crises that they were experiencing in their professional work. As a result of the ongoing dialogue within our teaching forums they were able to examine the sociopolitical, sociocultural and sociohistorical constructs of such crises.

These *revelations* formed the basis of insightful dialogue, follow-up reading, responsive lecturing and an ongoing process of critique. In many cases this led to continuing developments of individual action research projects, developments that each student took back to his or her own community for further elaboration. Despite the euphoria that permeated the group as each participant came to 'see the light' and they continued better to understand the complexities of their taken-for-granted practice, so, too, did they experience feelings of anxiety, anger and frustration as they came to realise the differing levels of negative impact and manipulation that they had been experiencing and accepting for such a long period of their professional life. What remained problematic within this development, however, is that most individuals in the group failed to move forward, in Fay's terms, to address such crises in ways that had the potential to change and reshape their practices. Simply stated, the teachers, through the notions of action research fostered in cycle one, came to understand why they do things the way they do, yet they were not willing to take the necessary steps to transform aspects of their work that remained problematic.

Cycle Two

The challenge

It became our challenge as 'lecturers' to confront what it was about *our* teaching that failed to engage the learning community in relations that provided teachers with the opportunity to address the professional crises that they were facing, crises that were ultimately having a negative impact on the effectiveness of their curriculum work, yet that they felt disempowered to address.

In preparation for the following year's work, teaching the same two curriculum studies units but with a new cohort of students, we read more widely to involve a broader network of 'participants' into our deliberations. Two significant 'participants' were Simon and Dippo (1986) and Smith (1987; 1990) and their contributions are discussed in the following two sections.

Calling on critical ethnography

Whilst the theorising of our work during 1995 has been inspired by Dorothy E. Smith, the formation of the teaching practices described here were shaped by the principles of critical ethnography. Simon and Dippo (1986) characterise critical ethnography, as a research methodology, in the following way, the principles of which we extended to what we called research based teaching within our learning community.

Our teaching must be organised around a phenomenon that is problematic and thus determines the nature of the posing of research/learning questions and consequently, the processes of data collection and analysis. By identifying the nature of the phenomena under study as problematic, it is places the questions in the broader discourse of history, power, gender, class and race relations that inform the social relations that lie at the heart of the work. As such, the participants of the research learning community are invited to view their taken-for-granted world in new ways, ways that are designed to emancipate themselves through a better understanding of the relations that have emerged within existing as well as transformed practices.

The learning process in which we are engaging must be situated in a public domain with a view to exposing the critique that forms the integral focus of learning about how things got to be the way they are and what is essential to enact the necessary transformations to alleviate conditions that are problematic.

The research implicit in our learning must be aware of its own limitations due to the very nature of the historical relations of power and material conditions that shape its constructs as social practice (adapted from Simon and Dippo 1986: 197).

Most importantly, critical ethnography offered a framework that placed our teaching and learning as a learning community in a new discourse – a critical research-based teaching discourse that was intent on democratic, collaborative and empowering purposes; that not only captured the lived curriculum experiences of a group of people who have traditionally been marginalised through teaching orientations that effectively disconnect them from their practice, but also offered a dialogue, a conceptual framework and a way of thinking to release them from their existing oppressive practices.

As a learning community, critical ethnography, enhanced by the work of Smith (1987; 1990), discussed below, offered us an opportunity to engage in action research that was not only about emancipation from traditional curriculum restraints but more importantly allowed each of us the opportunity for self-articulation and self-determination. We reshaped our teaching to pursue our aspirations, the students transformed their practices to address what was problematic in their context. This action process generated possibilities for each of us in our curriculum work to reposition our subjectivities away from assymmetrical relations that permeated our professional world. Further, it invited us to engage in an active form of agency in dealing with our curriculum work that for too long has been manifested in disempowering ways due to the cultural, historical and political constructs in which it is immersed. It is difficult to describe just exactly how we went about pursuing our teaching aspirations for, as in any relations that are responsive, things predominantly just happened. It is possible, however, to articulate a number of guiding principles:

- As a group we established a learning community (lecturers and students) that was intent on engaging in curriculum studies by considering a common starting point – what is problematic about our curriculum work?
- In order to pursue this question, we needed to articulate a shared (but not the same) language of curriculum. We attempted to clarify through a consensus-seeking mode (as opposed to a lecturing mode) issues relating to the nature of knowledge, orientations of teaching and learning, procedures of assessment and evaluation, conceptions of schooling/education, as we searched for an understanding as to why we do things the way we do.
- We agreed upon three basic processes to stimulate our dialogue: that of the spoken narrative, informed by appropriate readings and action research.

The narrative invited all participants to share within the learning community recounts from their practice through stories that bring to the fore 'the images, rituals, habits, cycles, routines and rhythms that constitute their daily experiences' (Connelly and Clandinin 1985: 184) and highlight the problematic nature of their curriculum work. It was put to the group that such a process gave each participant an opportunity to access their own thinking about their curriculum experiences in a particular setting at any point in time. As participants listened to the recounts, it was their responsibility to elicit from the tales more complex issues that so often remain unspoken, and pose questions as an integral part of the learning dialogue, that centred on challenging each teacher as to why they do things the way they do. In an atmosphere that emerged as predominantly non-threatening, individual participants tried to theorise their practice, ably assisted by colleagues confronting similar situations.

The questioning procedures together with the emerging processes of clarification were followed up with appropriate reading materials that formed the basis of ongoing discussions in future meetings. These readings contributed to a literature review that was useful in assisting each teacher articulate what was problematic about her work in an informed and critical manner. Action research became the mode of inquiry that was useful in sustaining an investigation into the curriculum problem identified by each person. The notion of action research that was agreed upon, and adopted for this project was that of an emancipatory nature (Carr and Kemmis 1986) with the specific shared purpose of initiating changes in teachers' curriculum rather than simply identifying the need to change. As such, the shape of each participant's action research project, including our own, took on many differing forms but was continually being critiqued in terms of a number of requirements outlined more fully elsewhere, that we referred to as authentic action research (Kemmis and McTaggart 1988).

The classroom research implicit in teachers' action research projects formed the basis of reporting ongoing works in progress – the heart of our curriculum conversations at each of our learning community meetings (small-group, individual and whole-group sessions). During these sessions, as people reported on their evolving practices, curriculum issues continually arose and became the 'content' of the learning experiences. A range of narratives emerged as the projects changed shape and as a consequence, critical reading was pursued to further inform people about their curriculum work. And so the learning cycle continued as the semester and, in fact, the year (co-requisite subjects) unfolded.

Women in curriculum studies

One of the important factors that informed our thinking was the (very obvious) realisation that almost all of our students were women. In fact, of the sixty students taught in the first year, only three were male and in the incoming cohort of forty, there were only three males. It was at this point we turned to the work of Smith (1987; 1990) for inspiration – as a framework in which to theorise our struggles, and hopefully reshape our own teaching practice.

Smith's work primarily addresses the problem inherent in the discipline of traditional sociology which, she argues, has been written from the standpoint of men located in the relations of ruling in western society. Her lifetime of work has been dedicated to withdrawing women's assent to a knowledge, culture and ideology that has been created and recreated by men and endorsed by women despite their exclusion at the level of conceptualisation. She proposes an alternative sociology that confronts the patriarchal constructs of the existing body of knowledge through the articulation of a feminist sociology that signifies the value of the problematic nature of the everyday world of women.

This has important implications for research in general and this study in particular for it suggests a 'feminist mode of inquiry might . . . begin with women's experience from women's standpoint and explore how it is shaped in the extended relations of larger social and political relations' (Smith 1987: 10)

It is argued here that the teaching of curriculum studies has similarly been shaped by *extra local* world views that are implicit in a patriarchal, capitalist and unjust educational community. As such, they have traditionally portrayed women as metempirical beings, theorising curriculum relations as 'extra local, impersonal, universalised forms of action, . . . the exclusive terrain of men, while women became correspondingly confined to a reduced local sphere of action organised by particularistic relationships' (*ibid*: 5), thus diminishing the significance of the latter (the local) to the point where it is totally overwhelmed, regulated and distorted by the former (the extra local). This seemed to us to capture what was problematic in our work from the previous semester.

What was required was a reconstruction of the discipline of curriculum studies placing the concept of woman, (here – woman as teacher) as the primary organiser of an emerging political discourse, at the centre of the debate. This proposition was considered insightful, and offered a way to reshape our teaching of curriculum studies to become more responsive to people, predominantly women, who were struggling with their curriculum work in local contexts.

A number of issues implicit in Smith's work has implications for the theorising and redesign of our teaching and included the following: First, traditional approaches to teaching curriculum studies are misrepresentative in a number of ways because they were shaped by 'relations of ruling' of the curriculum elite. The students in the first cycle of this project suggested that our approaches to teaching were different in this sense, yet as has been noted, not sufficiently different to address the real curriculum crises implicit in their curriculum work.

It was significant that we tried to confront the domain of a powerful curriculum elite who continue to dominant the literature yet are clearly removed from the everyday realities that permeate teachers' lives. This group of curriculum theorists have been portrayed as 'specialists occupying influential positions in the ideological apparatus (the educational system, communications, etc.) . . . ' (Smith 1987: 19) who have manufactured our (curriculum) culture in deliberate ways that overlook the spontaneity of lived experiences. As such they have created a mode of ruling that loses sight of and devalues the local actualities that are very much a part of teacher's daily lives and the very essence of curriculum research.

This implies that curriculum studies projects for too long have portrayed their findings from the standpoint of those men in dominant positions, who control and regulate widely accepted curriculum perspectives, curriculum perspectives that endorse the silences of teachers and other minority groups. Smith argued that this is not simply a problem of gender. Rather, Smith postulated a more complex thesis that challenges the essentialist world view, underpinning the dominant curriculum discourse as 'partial, limited, located in a particular position and permeated by special interests and concerns' (Smith 1987: 20), a curriculum world view that has been constructed through the silencing of teachers and as such is misrepresentative of the standpoint of the most valuable participant in curriculum theorising. Teachers as speakers have no authority, lack any proper title to membership (*ibid.*: 31) in the circle constructing ideology, although they are often complicit in the social practices of their silence (*ibid.*: 34). Women as teachers have learned to be partners in trivialising their curriculum experiences – the most essential elements of curriculum studies.

Second, Smith argues that the everyday world of women is organised by social relations not fully apparent in it nor contained in it. In fact, it is impacted upon by social relations external to it. Curriculum research so often fails to recognise this interplay. The starting point for cycle two of this project was to be at the 'line of fault' where, it is contended, individual women as teachers experience a sense of incongruence between the reported social forms of curriculum consciousness and the reality of their own curriculum world. It was considered essential that this initial catalyst be captured by a teaching process that enables the learning community (lecturers and students) to examine the incongruencies (the 'line of fault') of their own curriculum work, as experiences located in the social relations that organise, regulate and determine the points of contestation inherent in curriculum studies. To capture the essence of such disjuncture is essential to teaching of this type (cycle one), but to go one step further in this cycle, and ask how is this organised, how is it determined and what are the social relations that generate it. Smith (1987: 50) invites the community to rupture, through research-based teaching, those forms of social relations that for too long have alienated women as teachers from their experience and sustained the domination of the curriculum ruling elite. For the group of women as teachers that formed the basis of the incoming student cohort, it was necessary to address this void through a process of consciousness raising, and further, initiate a process of transformative action that previously had failed to emerge in their professional contexts. We believed we would be able to pursue this in the 'safety' of the university class.

It was essential that our research-based teaching in cycle two presented women as teachers, as well as ourselves, with the opportunity to begin the formulation of a new discourse that articulates ways of speaking about our curriculum subjectivities, speaking it politically as well as personally in support of the limited work emerging in curriculum studies at the present time (Gore 1993; McWilliam 1994; Yates 1993).

Third, the students' experiences are made more complex by a 'bifurcation of consciousness' that occurs as each one confronts curriculum studies and moves from the local and particular as a way of knowing to the conceptual level of knowing (Smith 1987). Traditionally the teaching of curriculum studies had restrained, and at times, forbidden this movement. It was our vision to address this through action-oriented teaching that was initiated from the local and particular rather than imposed from a standpoint that alienates people from their own practice. We wanted to confront traditional teaching practices that for too long, have confirmed the invisible nature of what is really the most significant part of women as teachers' consciousness, that which is local, particular and subjective. This creates a sense of alienation for students who become misrepresented in the literature and whose roles are further manipulated through the design of ongoing curriculum research. So often the researcher's knowledge of the substantive curriculum field is already situated in a conceptual framework prior to the design of the project (as perhaps we did in cycle one!). The world as we know it is largely organised by the articulation of the discourse to the ruling apparatus of which it is a part (Smith 1987: 63).

What was required in this teaching cycle was to make overt many of the assumptions that we have taken for granted about curriculum studies that are built into the discourse – thus interrupting the flow in the discourse in the interests of those, to date, who have been silenced by it.

In this way, the curriculum studies content became relocated in the actual working practices of those at the heart of curriculum rather than within the conceptual apparatus that has traditionally removed curriculum phenomena from the social relations which form its very constitution. Such an apparatus has eventuated in a viewpoint of curriculum and social relations that Smith describes as 'extra local'. This became clearly evident in the lead-up to this project when we witnessed an 'institutionalised form of knowledge and practices of social control . . . that [were] externalised, objectified' (Smith 1987: 77) and not locatable in a curriculum space. In the past this has allowed curriculum staff in higher education contexts to transform the essence of local material and social relations into conceptual phenomena that are positioned within the hierarchical framework of institutional ruling, detached from the local and particular world of students in which learning experiences are positioned. The curriculum discourse has failed to touch base with the reality of teachers' curriculum experiences.

Fouthly, the very nature of the students' experiences have rarely been conceptualised as problematic through the teaching of curriculum studies. This teaching exercise provided a rich opportunity to do so. It has too long been the case that these issues have been reported from the perspective of traditional frameworks, the knowledge base and ideological platforms continuously being repossessed by those situated in the domains of the ruling apparatus (Smith 1987: 88). What was required was an alternative conception of curriculum teaching and research that relocated the research subject at the heart of the inquiry. Further, it was essential to generate an alternative that did not focus only on capturing the essence of everyday experience as we did in cycle one, but to devise a means of 'explicating for members [of the learning community] the social organisation of their experienced world, including in that experience the ways in which it passes beyond what is immediately and directly known, including, therefore, the structure of a bifurcated consciousness' (Smith 1987: 89). A call was made for the learning community to make the everyday world of curriculum decision making problematic (Smith 1987).

The focus of teaching and research in cycle two celebrated the world as it is known by the participants, a world in which the participants are historically, socially and materially located. Implicit in the focus is the everyday world of curriculum decision making as it evolves within social relations that are not directly observable from the inside. It was *not* the purpose of our work in cycle two to highlight an everyday world that is filtered through a predetermined theoretical framework by a teaching team aspiring greater control over evolving social relations and educational ideology as we may have been prone to doing in cycle one (and for many years prior to this!). What was required of this learning community was the pursuit of what was problematic in everyday curriculum work for each woman, to 'begin from a different assumption when as premises we begin with the activities of actual individuals whose activity produces the social relations that they live' (Smith 1987: 90).

In cycle two a clear delineation was made on the one hand between pursuing and engaging in the everyday world as problematic, and on the other, researching the everyday world as a phenomenon that is overtly recognisable as an object of study. The latter determines a teaching process that emerged in cycle one, whereby the theories, methods and practices of curriculum research become divorced from and separate to the complexities of the everyday world. Implicit in this approach such complexities are sifted through a predetermined theoretical framework and are classified and sorted in ways that suggest coherence, order and system. Normative teaching of this nature result in 'generalisable' findings that portray curriculum behaviours as predominantly conforming behaviours. This has typically been the case with teaching in this field in this university since 1980. Those who have not conformed have been labelled deviants or trouble makers. What is omitted in these accounts, and what was missing prior to the introduction of this project, is what is central to the everyday world of curriculum studies: 'what is missing is an account of the constitutive work that . . . arises . . . as a locally realised organisation . . . [and] how this course of action is articulated to social relations' (Smith 1987: 155).

Contrary to this way of thinking about curriculum studies, the problematic nature of teaching generated through this project was deeply immersed in the lived experiences and 'constitutive actions' of the learning community (experiences that are oft times incoherent, nonsystematic, disorganised and 'fuzzy') with a view to 'direct attention to a possible set of questions that may not be posed or a set of puzzles that do not yet exist in the form of puzzles but are "latent" in the actualities of the experienced world' (*ibid.*: 91). By so doing, the refining of our teaching emerged in naturalistic ways from within, from the lived experiences of members of the group as the generators of knowledge, rather than as course content imposed on the students through an ideological framework that distorts the nature of curriculum studies in furthering the interests of the 'ruling apparatus', and promoting normative modes of teaching. This did not deny the learning community the opportunity of advancing conceptual arguments about their curriculum practice, rather, the theorising was devised through more representative ways as the transformations to existing practice evolved.

As it was envisaged by Smith, the pursuit of the problematic as the focus of our teaching began with a social actuality, an episode, found within the everyday world of teachers' curriculum work, from which we were able to generate a conceptual teaching framework that was truly representative of the participants' curriculum thinking through the disclosure and explication of its properties. In proposing such a conceptual framework, the learning community was cognisant of the everyday world of curriculum decision making as complex and determined by social, cultural and political relations that are external to and removed from the visibility and control of the participants:

> The everyday world is not fully understandable within its own scope . . . there are important differences in the fundamental form of social organisation. The problematic character of the everyday world is an essential property of this social form.
>
> (Smith 1987: 92–3)

By pursuing an approach to teaching and learning that centred on locating the subject in her everyday world of curriculum work, focusing on how everyday experiences are shaped and how they articulate with the larger constructs that determine the everyday world of curriculum work, the learning community was better placed to enter a phase of transformative action and the reshaping of their practice. Our teaching was extended beyond capturing the essence of those experiences, or simply examining the processes from both the micro and macro levels of analysis by stepping outside the everyday world. The focus of teaching and learning was on each woman as teacher, positioned in differing and evolving curriculum relations that determined her experiences as problematic. This, in turn, invited the learning community to gain valuable insights into curriculum relations that have traditionally been portrayed in ways that misrepresent curriculum decision making; ways that have located the subjects outside the reported curriculum experience; ways that have conceptualised curriculum as an 'object' of study; ways which, as a result, have alienated teachers from the origins of their knowledge base.

The centrality of lived curriculum experiences as a teaching problematic fostered a more honest and true interplay between the located subject – the student, and the generation of a systematic body of knowledge articulating the social, cultural and political relations of the everyday world of curriculum work through which 'the latter may become a means to disclose to the former the social relations determining her everyday world' (*ibid*: 98).

Positive student outcomes

At the end of cycle two data were collected from individual interviews with the students and some of the conclusions from the formal evaluation of the second cycle are reported below.

- These teachers indicate that the content of the units has enhanced their professional understandings of how to deal with change and of how to be more reflective. They indicate that their understandings and awareness of curriculum related issues have been broadened. Many now have a new, more enlightened, view of curriculum policy and curriculum documents. For some, the units have sharpened their thinking about their curriculum needs. Some of those interviewed have referred to a heightened awareness and understanding of their subject area. Many have indicated that they now feel more empowered and self-confident in their teaching role.
- Teachers are also positive about the impact of these units on their professional practice. They see themselves as more reflective, as more focused on student learning, and as more 'problem' oriented. Reflecting on the personal learnings they gained from the practical, action research activity they undertook as part of these units, the teachers discuss their greater understanding of their 'content area'. They refer to their

increased self-confidence, particularly with regard to their acceptance of responsibility and accountability within curriculum-related areas. Some perceive that their sensitivity to the points of views of others has been heightened.

- There is overwhelming support for action research as a valuable method-ology in educational contexts. There is also clear evidence that these teachers have a thorough understanding of action research as a process and that they feel confident and competent in applying it in their own educational settings. Many indicate that they will use it as a process beyond the requirements of the course.

Consequently in our collective work in this project as a cohort of educators, we have achieved a number of outcomes. Through research-based teaching, we have been able to resituate ourselves in history, identify elements of crises that permeate our work, reclaim the possibility of curriculum transforma-tion and relocate our practices in a world that we better understand and hence, over which we assume greater control.

From the lecturers' perspective, this approach has moved our teaching forwards towards an orientation of postgraduate teaching that calls for new social visions of curriculum studies and a set of pedagogical processes that are pursued by academics and students as a learning community through research based teaching juxtaposed with classroom action research.

Conclusions

At the heart of our teaching was a professional learning community investi-gating the diverse complexities that permeate curriculum work, processes fraught with struggles occurring within inchoate conditions, continually confronting the participants with dilemmas at both the personal and collec-tive levels. In addressing these types of contestations as an integral part of the teaching process, the learning community generated a research process that captured a 'living scan' or an 'X ray vision' of the transformative possi-bilities of curriculum studies in order to gain insights into the complex everyday processes of their work. They did so through a sustained and systematic process of looking inward and outward, searching for phenomena oft times distorted by the reality of the experience and creating false illu-sions of curriculum experiences. The articulation of the contestations, tensions and dilemmas that permeated their work (the problematics of their work) became the focus of an ongoing learning process for teachers in the field, and the essence of the ongoing teaching and learning dialogue in the university classroom. Teachers not only came to understand what was prob-lematic about their curriculum work, but began actively to reshape their work and deal with continually emerging curriculum dilemmas. This continued and is continuing in the short term within university classes, as well as in the long term through a newly constructed orientation to curriculum work.

It is argued here that the problematic nature of teaching curriculum studies can be articulated in innovative ways that are successful in addressing the curriculum questions that evolve. Of particular significance to us was the key question: 'how does it happen to me/us as it does?' As a result, this teaching project generated curriculum theories, methodologies and practices that incorporated, but moved beyond the essentialist nature of current teaching approaches to identify the features of the socially, culturally and politically constituted relations that underpin curriculum work.

Appendix

The subject structure

- An initial 3 hour meeting in Week 1.
- A full weekend in the first two weeks of the semester in which the theoretical foundations were presented in ways that catered for the diversity of the group. These sessions moved from formal inputs to dialogical workshop to individual consultations/independent work.
- A series of individual/group consultations to identify clarify and refine the focus of research projects.
- A further two weekend days at which students engaged in critical dialogue concerning works in progress. This was conducted as a mini conference whereby professional colleagues identified areas of interest. The roles of presenters and participants was clearly delineated and agreed upon prior to commencement.
- A final 3 hour symposium in the last week of lectures.
- Submission and publication of final papers.

REFERENCES

Aoki, T. (1990) 'Themes of teaching curriculum', in Sears, J. and Marshall, J.D. (eds) *Teaching and Thinking about Curriculum: Critical Inquiries*, New York: Teachers College Press, pp. 111–14.

Bullough, R. (1992) 'Beginning teacher curriculum decision making: personal teaching metaphors and teacher education', *Teaching and Teacher Education*, 8 (3): 239–52.

Carr, W. and Kemmis, S. (1986) *Becoming Critical: Knowledge, Education and Action Research*, London: Falmer.

Connelly, F. M. and Clandinin, D. J. (1985) 'Personal practical knowledge and the modes of knowing: relevance for teaching and learning', in Eisner, E. (ed.) *Learning and Teaching the Ways of Knowing: Eighty-fourth Yearbook of the National Society of Education (Part 3)*, Chicago: University of Chicago Press, pp. 174–98.

Cornett, J. (1990) 'Utilizing action research in graduate curriculum courses', *Theory into Practice*, 29: 185–95.

Fay, B. (1987) *Critical Social Science: Liberation and its Limits*, Cambridge: Polity Press.

Goodman, J. (1986) 'Teaching pre-service teachers a critical approach to curriculum design: a descriptive account', *Curriculum Inquiry*, 16 (2): 181–201.

Gore, J. (1993) *The Struggle for Pedagogies: Critical and Feminist Discourses as Regimes of Truth*, New York: Routledge & Kegan Paul.

Kemmis, S. (1994) 'Action research', in Husen, T. and Postlethwaite, N. (eds) *International Encyclopedia of Education: Research and Studies*, London: Pergamon Press.

Kemmis, S. and McTaggart, R. (eds) (1988) *The Action Research Reader*, 3rd edn, Geelong, Victoria: Deakin University Press.

McWilliam, E. (1994) *In Broken Images: Feminist Tales for A Different Teacher Education*, New York: Teachers College Press.

Simon, R. and Dippo, D. (1986) 'On critical ethnographic work', *Anthropology and Education Quarterly*, 17: 195–202.

Smith, D. E. (1987) *The Everyday World As Problematic: A Feminist Sociology*, Boston: Northeastern University Press.

——(1990) *The Conceptual Practices of Power: A Feminist Sociology of Knowledge*, Boston: Northeastern University Press.

Yates, L. (ed.) (1993) *Feminism and Education*, Melbourne Studies in Education, Melbourne, Australia: La Trobe University Press.

15

ACADEMIC GROWTH THROUGH ACTION RESEARCH

A doctoral student's narrative

Mary Hanrahan

When I began my PhD, I still had a lot to learn about research, but I thought that there were some things I could take for granted: what research was, how best to do it, and who should do it. About every six months after that, however, there seemed to be a revolution in my thinking, so that I was repeatedly discarding old 'certainties', and the research plans that depended on them, in favour of a new research project which would be the ultimate one. Now, my PhD is in its third year, and I can take a broader view of this process. What may appear to some people as a messy series of false starts and changes of direction, now appears to me to be a rational progression in my ideas about the most appropriate goals and methodology for research in education.

However, the progression was not apparent at the time, and I experienced the changes as failures to produce the required product (an extended proposal for the research was normally due within 12 months of beginning and mine was only forthcoming after 30 months). Consequently, I suffered guilt and shame and sometimes despair at the ineptitude that this failure implied, especially since I interpreted my principal supervisor as having little faith in my decisions.[1] Instead of questioning the conventional method of doing a PhD, or of seeing myself as an ideal candidate for action research, we all seemed to conclude, at least from my point of view, that there was something wrong with me and my methods. And even when I did come up with what seemed like the perfect solution to my problems, that solution – action research – seemed to have its own internal contradictions and dilemmas for me.

Dealing with these, however, has been a very rewarding experience for me, and one which has not only taught me how to learn from research, but has also led to much personal growth for me and a new zest for life. In this chapter, I wish to discuss a research approach which is simultaneously theoretical, practical, rigorous and personal, and I hope to show how it has helped me become a better researcher, and a more proactive member of the education community.

This chapter will take the form of a narrative. This should not be taken as a sign, however, that it will deal with the problematic nature of action research in a superficial manner, but rather as a sign that it will provide a rich context in which to examine many important issues related to action research.

Contexts of the research

To help you understand my experience, I will begin by describing two of the contexts which provide the background to my research. One is the traditional context for a PhD study, a review of the literature in the area from which the research question arises. In my case, this is the science education research literature specifically, and the literature on effective learning generally and I will turn to that shortly in as far as it is relevant to the story of my own learning. The other is the personal history of the researcher which influences how he or she interprets what is taking place and theorises it. I include this personal context because I believe that, in social science research, where people are relating to each other on several levels as they do research together, it is inevitable that personal factors will play an important part in the meaning making that takes place.

The psychology of learning: the problem of superficial learning

A major portion of the research in science education over the past decade or two has focused on the persistence of misconceptions (or alternative frameworks) in students' thinking despite teaching methods specifically structured to dispel them. Such research indicated that school learning appeared to be superficial in comparison to the learning which took place outside the classroom. The latter informal learning, developed in a meaningful physical and social context, seemed to have the characteristics of strong beliefs embedded firmly in robust frameworks for interpreting experience (White and Gunstone 1989).

Research on approaches to teaching which had been shown to have the most impact on such alternative frameworks, generally stressed one or more of several common factors. Such 'conceptual change' teaching, as science researchers called it, emphasised the importance of relating new learning to prior learning (Posner *et al.* 1982), of nurturing positive motivational beliefs (Pintrich *et al.* 1993) and of nurturing self-regulation of learning (Baird 1986). Another factor considered important was a learning environment which affirmed students' personal thoughts and feelings (Hanrahan 1994b; Watts and Bentley 1987). Finally, I was impressed by the apparent importance of developing a community ethos for what could be thought of as a cognitive apprenticeship (Collins *et al*. 1989).

At the early stages of my research I had read only the part of the research which recommended an individualistic approach to solving problems in learning science, but as time went on I became more influenced by writing that emphasised the importance of the classroom as a mini-culture, which either reinforced or helped modify students' alternative frameworks and the beliefs they had about themselves as learners in science. While reading and thinking about this research literature, I could not help but see the implications of it both for my own learning as a PhD student, and for teacher change.

If meaningful learning was a deeply personal process influenced by social and psychological factors, how could I believe that my own learning was a coldly rational process uninfluenced by my own personal assumptions, beliefs and history. It would be inconsistent of me to ignore the possibility of such influences on me, and on my actions and interpretations as a researcher. As part of my research method, therefore, I adopted the practice of writing a personal journal, where I reflected not only on my reading and other formal research activities, but also on the likely effect on me of my motivational beliefs, assumptions and personality, which in turn meant that I had to reflect on my personal, family and cultural history.

Similarly, it seemed likely that such principles of conceptual change would apply to teachers as well. There was much discussion in the science education literature about the difficulty of teacher change, since teachers did not tend to adopt or, if they did adopt, were not likely to persist in using strategies that the research literature advocated as being the most likely to be successful (Taylor 1992). I came to believe that their lack of change was likely to be related to their lack of personal involvement in the reforms being foisted upon them.

The personal research context

The personal factors which I think probably had the most influence on the way I went about my research, and the problems I had with action research, were the negative effects on me of an authoritarian family and church background (at least from my point of view), and the results of the comparatively permissive approach which I had taken in bringing up my own children. As I perceived it, in my family of origin my father's word was law and it served no purpose to have ideas of my own, especially since speaking them was likely to lead to punishment or at least feelings of guilt. The Catholic Church community to which I belonged seemed to reinforce his authority and also the apparent wrongness of having independent ideas. I gradually learnt that my roles in life meant that I should not allow myself to trust my own thinking but rather be obedient to rules that others provided for me.

Nevertheless, at some deeper level, I grew increasingly uncomfortable and resisted, albeit silently, such thought control. By the time I had finished secondary school, I had given up any allegiance, not only to my father, who seemed to me to be lacking in understanding about human nature and individual differences, but also to a God who was, from what I could gather, judgemental and inflexible. I then fled to a safely distant city (by electing to go to university when there was no university locally) and hoped that there I could be free of such constraints on my thinking. I failed to see that the problem was not simply a matter of the personal relationship between myself and those in my environment, or to see that my father's behaviour and that of influential members of the Church were as culturally bound as my own conditioning was. Where I differed from those in positions of authority was in believing that the disadvantages of this cultural system outweighed its advantages.

During my first stint at university, consequently, I was shocked to discover that I myself could be labelled as having a highly authoritarian personality. Even now, in spite of what seem to me enormous changes in my attitudes over the intervening years, I still sometimes find that I react to the world as though there may be disastrous consequences of my not following the dictates of those who claim to hold the highest moral ground. In relation to action research, this was to lead to much anxiety when my attempt to implement a particular action research methodology clashed with my own judgement of how I should proceed in a particular situation.

In conflict with this tendency, one of the results of having felt powerless and voiceless as a child, was that, in my research, I wanted to give others the chance to think their own thoughts and act on them whenever possible, without undue influence from me. My having done this to excess with my own children, however, may have been influential in their resistance to schooling, and in their leaving school early, and (in my estimation at the time) with no positive plans for their futures. On the other hand, my experiences in adult literacy teaching suggested that affirming students' own thinking could have a positive and powerful effect on their engagement in learning.

The following story of my 'getting of wisdom'[2] will certainly show the signs of my personal philosophy as well as the influences of my reading in the research literature. The more I read, and the more classroom research I did, the more my ideas changed, not only about what exactly the heart of the problem was in science education, but also about the appropriate methodology to use when researching the problem. In the following section, I recount the story of my quest for research methods which would result in positive change in science classrooms, and hence, more scientifically literate students. Then I inspect my research through the lenses of action research principles and finally, I begin to evaluate the outcomes of my research.

Finding the appropriate research methodology

A positivist approach to change

In stage 1 of my PhD, I blithely put forward a proposal to do an intervention in a classroom, to solve the problem involved in teaching for conceptual change, using instruction in self-regulatory strategies in a peer learning setting which would deal explicitly with emotional aspects of learning. As I was not teaching at that time, I proposed to recruit a willing teacher to trial my planned intervention, and perhaps provide the 'control' class as well. My role would be to observe, interview, do pre- and post-tests and, of course, write up the research report.

An interpretivist approach to research

Stage 2 began when I started to be influenced by the constructivist (e.g., Tobin 1993; Guba and Lincoln 1989) and interpretivist (Erickson 1986) research literature. The certainty I had of being able to find answers that would be practically independent of context rapidly faded.

As well, there seemed to be an inherent contradiction in *directing* or *training* students to use *self-regulatory* strategies. After reading some of the literature on the expert–novice difference (e.g., Jones and Idol 1990), it seemed to me that a crucial fact about expert learners was that they were self-starters to a large extent. Experts, it seemed, tended to use self-regulatory strategies in a goal-directed way, with great persistence and energy.

I doubted that the same outcomes would result from taking unsuccessful students, who would probably have low self-esteem and low motivation, and getting them to go through the motions used by expert problem solvers. This approach seemed to me to be less likely to produce large changes than an approach which directly helped students to have goals, and helped motivate them to work towards achieving them. This dilemma also had implications for my plan of sub-contracting out the actual intervention part of my research to teachers, since getting them to follow *my* strategies to produce *my* goals seemed likely to be doomed to a fate of being exercised in a half-hearted manner, if the teachers concerned did not share my goals, or my beliefs in those particular strategies.

In any case, other events conspired to help me see more clearly the limitations of positivistic thinking. First, there was the visit to our research centre by Ken Tobin, a science education professor, who was an advocate for qualitative research and who subsequently strongly influenced my reading at that time. I was shocked by Guba and Lincoln's (1989) strong condemnation of quantitative research, and inspired by both Erickson's (1986) seminal chapter on qualitative methods for research on teaching, and Bruner's (1990) book on narrative modes of meaning making. Consequently, I decided that, rather than do an intervention, I would do ethnographic classroom research to try to understand more about learning environments for science. I was offered an opportunity to study one Year 11 Biology class in depth and I seized the chance.

After four years of psychology courses in statistics, however, I was still steeped in a behaviourist tradition of doing research, and had great difficulty adapting to this new way of doing research. I worried a lot about not noticing the 'right' behaviours, and not finding whatever it was that I 'should' be finding – what any objective researcher would have found in my place. The things that seemed immediately significant to me seemed to fall rather flat when I reported them to my principal supervisor, and yet I could not find whatever it was that *would* be a significant finding for him. I went through a dark period, and in the end decided that I would have to resign myself to the discovery that, whereas I might have been considered a successful quantitative researcher in an earlier degree, I was only a second- or third-rate researcher when it came to the difficult business of interpreting what was going on in the complex social situation of a classroom. I was still hoping, however, that when I had analysed all my data in some detail, significant findings would emerge.

My principal supervisor, however, convinced me that I was getting nowhere with this case study, and I accepted his advice to give it up and 'get back to work' on preparing my proposal. I gave in because I had to admit that I had not come up with any clear insights about the classroom culture after six weeks of observing and interviewing, and I still felt rather insecure about what to do with the nebulous data I was accumulating. Nevertheless, this action on his part confused me because I thought that what I had been doing was the 'real thing' – what qualitative researchers did. I didn't understand what I had to produce to please him, but I supposed some kind of intervention study was called for – something PhD examiners would see as more 'solid'.

I was disappointed to have apparently failed at 'interpretive' research but I was also glad to get back to what I was more comfortable with, and I had to admit that I didn't really understand or believe some of the rules that texts like Guba and Lincoln (1989) seemed to me to be setting down for researchers, such as giving up the use of words like 'cause' and 'effect' in social science, and renouncing practically all further use of inferential statistics or generalisations. These concepts were still meaningful to me. I found my loyalties see-sawing between experimental and qualitative notions of research.

On the one hand, I began to understand how I could be successful as an ethnographer. At the same time as my principal supervisor seemed to be disaffirming me as a researcher, I was communicating with another academic who seemed to be listening with interest and respect to my ideas, which encouraged me to continue to develop them and eventually find the strength of my own convictions. (I will say more about the importance of responsive listening to the process of emancipation in a later section.)

As I started to listen to my own interpretations more, and to use interviews to explore my developing theories, I started to realise that my interpretations of the Year 11 class situation were largely based on frameworks derived first from my psychology background, particularly in clinical and counselling psychology, and, second from the professional development adult literacy teaching course which I had been doing the previous year. I suspected that my supervisor shared neither of these perspectives, and decided that his failure to acknowledge the significance of my observations was related to the difference in our cognitive frameworks rather than to my ineptitude.

This was a very liberating experience for me, especially as it was linked with my growing realisation that there was no one true way that contexts *should* be perceived or that research *should* be done, and that the best that I could do was to act on my own convictions based on as much direct and indirect experience as I could access, and that to expect more of myself than that was unreasonable. The accumulated shame and guilt dropped away, leaving me free henceforth to make my own decisions about research. I felt that I was becoming a researcher in my own right, prepared to reflect about and take responsibility for my own actions and conclusions, rather than being more like a research assistant who allowed others to make all the major decisions about the research project.

This interpretivist perspective also meant, however, that I found it hard to believe that ethnographers could go into a situation with an open mind (as Guba and Lincoln (1989) seemed to me to be suggesting they should) and find out about the culture from the *participants'* point of view. I for one could not honestly claim to be able to interpret a situation from the other participants' points of view. Even though all participants might agree about the data collected at some factual level, it seemed to me that while researchers were interpreting it in terms of *their* theories and the language available to them, frameworks largely in place before they went into the situation, the other participants might be putting a very different complexion on it, but might keep this to themselves because of differences in power relationships within the research.

My final fling at 'number crunching'

On the other hand, a desire to create theory and test it still kept gnawing away at me and I wanted to argue that this could be done in an interpretive rather than a positivistic frame of mind. Although I was starting to grasp what an ethnographic approach to research might mean, part of me still wanted to talk in terms of generalisations.

Why could one not theorise about causes and effects in education? What was the goal of education research if not to find theories and methods that could generally help those in schools and in pre-service education to improve their teaching? I still thought that quantitative measures could test theory in a rough way, as long as one did not try to overgeneralise one's findings but rather treated them as relating to a particular context, that is, treated them as one would any case study.

Consequently, now working independently and motivated by a new level of faith in my own ideas and also by my success in such exercises in the past, I wrote a questionnaire, based on factors which had emerged for me as of special interest in the Year 11 case study (Hanrahan 1995). These factors included how students perceived teacher affirmation of their worth, teacher support for autonomy in their thinking, teaching approaches and their own learning approaches.

Based on a secondary knowledge source about the characteristics of the particular classes to whom I wished to administer the questionnaire, I created items specifically designed to be meaningful to them. The results were statistically significant (in many instances evenly highly so) in the direction I wished, but I soon realised that there were quite a few competing hypotheses which could explain them, for example, any number of interactions between class and teacher factors such as gender, personality, prior knowledge and class expectations. Still, when I presented a paper on this study at a conference it was received with interest, and it was also accepted without hesitation for publication (Hanrahan 1994b), all of which helped restore my confidence in myself as a researcher, even while my enthusiasm for quantitative research methods was failing.

I was relinquishing the idea of quantitative data being very useful as a basis for theorising and planning about changes to make in teaching and learning situations. There were so many factors interacting in a social situation, not only at any one moment, but changing in a complex way over time, that making any strong generalisations seemed unwarranted. Still, my principal theory had not been disconfirmed and I continued to search for a way of allowing teachers and students to be responsive to personal factors involved in student learning. From that point on, however, I wanted to do intensive qualitative research in a single classroom, where I could become familiar with some of the psycho-social factors operating, factors such as the teacher–student interpersonal relationship, the ethos of the classroom and teacher and student expectations for the class.

A more direct approach to change

Although I have been characterising my research in stages, in actual fact the changes were happening sometimes gradually, sometimes in sudden bursts of insight, and while I was making progress in one area, I might be standing still in another. Consequently there was a lot of overlap between the stages.

The questionnaire study, for example, happened concurrently with my gradual move towards working more collaboratively with a teacher. It was a kind of aside, not intended to be part of my PhD thesis, but rather a private investigation aimed at exploring my lingering doubts about the apparent dogma being advanced by some qualitative research advocates.

A feature of ethnographic research which had troubled me, in addition to the ones I have already mentioned above, was the lack of an explicit intention to bring about change. I believed strongly that change was needed in science education if more students were to gain either academically or personally from learning science, and so I wanted research to do more than *explain* what was going on in a learning environment. I was impatient to be involved in change and, after all my reading, prior experience and recent research, I believed I had possible answers to some of the problems in science education, and could play a part in such change.

At the same time I had begun to read the teacher change literature, and realised that isolated academic research, whether experimental or qualitative, no matter how well it was received in the research community, would probably have little effect on what was going on in schools. I wanted to do 'real' research for my PhD, which meant for me research which would be useful in the education community. I could not see the point of research which satisfied academic requirements but was unlikely to affect teachers and teaching, so I decided that I would need to involve teachers actively in my research.

In any case, as I began to apply my theories about learning to teacher change (see Taylor 1992), it no longer made sense to me to expect teachers to change without involving them personally in the process. And just as I thought autonomy and positive feelings about oneself and about learning played an important role in student learning (at any level, including post-graduate degrees), I believed teachers should have autonomy and dignity as they learnt more about teaching and learning in the context of working towards their own goals (see Grundy 1987). Such thinking prepared the ground for my later being receptive to ideas about action research but my thinking at this stage was based on pragmatic rather than ethical grounds.

A major event in the PhD calendar for students at my institution was confirmation of candidature through successful presentation of a research proposal, and although I had been moving ahead in my thinking, I had still not produced my research proposal. However, I was becoming more convinced of what I should do and how I should go about it.

My research proposal at this stage involved working with a teacher in a non-threatening learning environment (Watts and Bentley 1987), on ways to encourage students to take a more active role in their own learning, using journal writing and/or small group discussion. I felt so sure that I was ready to start that at the end of the school year, I had visited what seemed to me to be a suitable school (in terms of developing autonomy in its students) and had found at least one (similarly suitable) volunteer teacher who seemed willing to collaborate with me in my research.

My principal supervisor again disaffirmed my progress – at least this is how I saw it – by telling me that my proposal was still unsatisfactory and would take at least another six months to become acceptable enough for me to even begin to approach a school. I also interpreted him as expressing a lack of faith in personal journal writing, both for me as a stage in the writing of my PhD proposal, and for science students as a way of promoting conceptual change. I felt at odds with him over many issues and I started to suspect there was a widening gap in our beliefs about how to promote deep learning, and perhaps also in our ways of seeing the research endeavour generally.

I was left with the options of continuing in a conflictual situation which I saw as unresolvable as long as I was true to my own convictions, or of changing my supervisory team. (My associate supervisor had been absent much of the time referred to above, and although he was usually very understanding, he generally seemed to me to go along with the decisions of my principal supervisor.) I chose the latter course, and fortunately was able to find two new supervisors who had confidence in what I wanted to do, realised the importance for me of doing research that was consistent with my personal convictions and were prepared to give me the necessary support to carry the research through.

During all this confusion over whether or not I should commit myself to qualitative research methods and whether or not I had ideas worth supporting, I had begun to work with the teacher who had volunteered to trial the use of student journal writing with me. I had to postpone the actual intervention until after I had formally presented my proposal, and unfortunately the teacher went on leave before that happened, and was vulnerable to re-posting as soon as she returned, so our (it would probably be more honest to say 'my') planned intervention ended before it began.

This was still an important period in my research, however. By the end of the six-month period I spent visiting the school, I had started to have some new insights into the nature of the language problems students from lower socio-economic status backgrounds were having with learning science. (I should mention that, before I did a science degree, I had, many years earlier, done an arts degree and had been an English and foreign language teacher for many years.) While working with this science teacher, I had also developed a new style of recording my observations, giving up what Erickson (1986) so aptly described as 'writing like crazy' and writing instead detailed post-class reflections in which I pondered over anything that stood out for me in what I had experienced.

As well, I had begun to experience some of the dilemmas of trying to establish trust and a good working relationship with a classroom teacher at the same time as continuing to behave like a detached scientist. Because I feared 'contaminating the data' by being honest about my reactions to what I was experiencing, I kept quiet and this placed a strain on the relationship. Even though I helped in the classroom where I could, the teacher was the one taking all the risks of action and self-disclosure, while I was obviously the one who would benefit most from the arrangement. Towards the end I tried to be more self-disclosing myself, but I still played the executive role in the research, and could see that the nature of our roles put the teacher at a distinct disadvantage in the relationship.

Action research as the answer?

While I was in the middle of the research stage just described, Stephen Kemmis arrived at our university to run a series of workshops on action research, which then prompted me to begin reading the texts he had been involved in writing. Eureka! At last, *here* was the method of doing research that I had been looking for, and it had landed right on my door step! Action research was concerned with change, and it was also concerned with issues of empowerment and emancipation. The ideological reasons Stephen gave for doing action research may not have been the pragmatic ones I have given above, but the idea of doing collaborative research seemed consistent with my aims.

Six months later I had reconceptualised and rewritten my PhD proposal as action research – both on my own practice and with a teacher. This allowed me to include all the previous stages as important steps in my learning. The changes that were formerly interpreted as signs of failure – and hence excluded from my proposal or at best smuggled in under the guise of pilot studies – were now seen as positive aspects of my progress towards greater knowledge of my research area.

My conviction of having reached the end of my quest for the right research methodology was short-lived, however. A few short weeks later, after reading in more detail about action research, I had several misgivings so serious that I rewrote the proposal methodology as narrative inquiry (Connelly and Clandinin 1990), and even hesitated over calling my collaborative research with a teacher 'action research'. All the while, however, I continued to read and learn more about action research, because there was something about it that appealed to me strongly. The second part of the chapter deals with the dilemmas I faced as I came to read and understand more about critical theory and what was involved in what Stephen Kemmis and his colleagues (Carr and Kemmis 1986; Grundy and Kemmis 1988; Kemmis and McTaggart 1988a, 1988b) called 'action research'.

Can a PhD study really be action research?

In the previous section I have outlined the early struggles I had in my PhD, as I tried to determine an appropriate topic for research, the most appropriate research methods to use, and the most appropriate role for the researcher to play, at the same time as adjusting to the notion of sharing my experience of the research situation with the other participants. These struggles are still present in this section. However, another prominent theme in this section is the problem of satisfying the requirements for justifying my research methodology when PhD research in science education has traditionally had, on the whole, stable rather than evolutionary goals and methods, and an individualised rather than a group focus.

Difficulties and dilemmas in relation to participatory action research

I shall begin by briefly outlining my current research project and the research methodology I came to use. The project consisted of working with a volunteer teacher towards a goal of improving the scientific literacy of the students in his Year 8 Science class. We planned to use personal writing in a dialogue journal, to get students expressing in their own words their personal experiences in learning science. This began with my modelling the kinds of activities I thought might get students more cognitively involved in learning, and with the two of us collaborating to evaluate their effectiveness and plan modifications in an ongoing fashion. The students were invited to participate in the research evaluation and gave their comments both in focus group interviews and periodically in their journals. To assist my own thinking, I used an interpretive research model (Erickson 1986), collecting data by interviewing the teacher and other relevant staff, and observing as I participated regularly in the classroom. All the while I wrote detailed analytic memoranda which included both my interpretation of what I had experienced and critical reflections about it.

Although I was satisfied that the research I was doing with a teacher and his class was useful to both of us, and at least meeting some of the needs of the class, I was unsure of how I was going to justify it as 'real' research in my PhD, as it did not seem to fulfil all, or even most, of the requirements of the action research model I had intended to follow. In some instances these requirements seemed to be in conflict with PhD requirements, and in some cases they seemed to be in conflict with the precepts I seemed to have developed for myself about appropriate ways for me to interact with other people.

Theoretically, I had been impressed by what I had learnt about the Habermasian school of critical social educational research, but how to put these principles into practice remained problematic for me. Initially this learning was through reviews of Habermas's influence on educational theory by writers such as Ewert (1991) and Young (1990), who frequently used long quotes from Carr and Kemmis's (1986) *Becoming Critical* to explain the implications of Habermas's ideas for education. The notion of the competing knowledge–constitutive interests was particularly meaningful for me, as it explained the stages of my research journey, from technical/ experimental to practical/interpretive to emancipatory/action research. However, the logical conclusion of accepting such a critical social science view of educational science, according to Stephen Kemmis and his colleagues (Carr and Kemmis 1986; Kemmis and McTaggart 1988a, b) was to accept their version of action research, and their advice about how to put it into practice.

Kemmis and McTaggart defined action research in such a way that it was possible that the research I was planning to do was not, in fact, action research. They described it as:

> a form of *collective* self-reflective inquiry undertaken by participants in social situations in order to improve the rationality and justice of their own social or educational practices, as well as their understanding of these practices and the situations in which these practices are carried out.
>
> (Kemmis and McTaggart 1988a: 5)

At this present moment, when I re-read the seventeen 'Key points about action research' and the 'Four things action research is not', in the *Action Research Planner* (Kemmis and McTaggart 1988a), I can say to myself that I am working along the lines indicated, at least in principle. However, when I read them twelve months ago, when I was about to justify my research as action research in my research proposal, that did not seem good enough since I was contravening several important aspects of the stated rules and methods of this model of action research.

There were two main levels of practice involved in my research and on neither of them, it would seem, was I doing exemplary action research, according to this model. First, there was my collaborative research with a teacher and his students, and, second, there was my own practice as a post-graduate research student.

Problems of participatory research within a school

Until very recently in my school research, it seemed to me that it was impossible to satisfy at the same time both the emancipatory concerns of critical action research and the procedural prescriptions I thought I must follow about how it should be carried out. There seemed to be problems in several areas. To begin with, my host teacher and I did not really have the same 'thematic concern' (Kemmis and McTaggart 1988a). He did not seem to want to contribute equally to the decision making at all stages. He was not sure he would have time to do regular reflective writing, and neither of us could be said to have a clear peer reference group in relation to the research. The students were even less involved in the proposed action research.

Looking back at my reflections of several months ago, I see now that what I saw as major problems then, are no longer such problems for me. This has come about partly through further reading about dialogical research in writing by Kemmis (1995) and Guy (1994), where solutions to such problems were explored, and partly because I am learning more about participatory research by doing it.

As I have already mentioned, my concern about not having identical 'thematic concerns' with my collaborators in the research turned out in the end to be unwarranted. It was enough that we shared a hope that the situation could be improved, because it meant that we were prepared to work together to realise that hope. On the other hand, in my research on my own practice as a research student (see following section), I did find that dialogue was most useful when it was undertaken with those who shared my goals for education.

Another concern was one that I had lost the thread of my thesis, that the substantial focus of my research had changed beyond recognition. At first I thought that moving from being concerned about scientific conceptual change to being concerned about scientific literacy, would be a serious flaw in my thesis, but it is no longer of concern to me. It was only a concern as long as I clung to positivistic notions that goals for research about educational problems should not change from the beginning to the end of research. As one of my supervisors pointed out to me, the changes in my research were, in fact, signs that good action research was taking place.

As Kemmis insists (see Chapter 2 by Kemmis and Wilkinson, this volume), action research is itself about change. With action research, whether collaborative action research or reflective practitioner research (e.g., Schön 1983) an important aspect is that the research is responsive to the problems as they are perceived in the particular situation by the participants, rather than remaining faithful to some predetermined aim which may turn out to be inappropriate. Such research is not weakened but rather strengthened by being responsive to practitioners' needs as they emerge in the practical situation.

Other kinds of research work are based on models which separate the research from the change deemed necessary, and discriminate between those who do the research (and so gain 'expert' status) and those who will carry out the follow-up changes prescribed by the experts. This is true for both experimental research that has compared different factors (teaching strategies, etc.) using inferential statistics, and for ethnography, which uses in-depth exploration of a particular case to increase understanding of an educational situation. Action researchers make a point of doing research in ongoing practice so that it can be adapted and refined by those who will be most affected by the changes, in ways which are meaningful to them, the practitioners, who will then be implementing them in ways consistent with their own beliefs and values (Carr and Kemmis 1986; Grundy 1987).

The problem that I used to refer to as the 'insider–outsider problem' or the concern about being a research facilitator from outside the school system has also been a false problem. I have expanded my research role to become part of the school system, and the classroom teacher has expanded his teaching role to become part of the research system. As Guy (1994) points out, the insider–outsider problem is only a problem in a positivistic system. In a world where difference is allowed and dialogue replaces domination or consensus, inclusion or exclusion become less relevant terms. As Grundy has argued in Chapter 3, this volume, it is better to see schools and universities as partners where research can be part of the teaching role in schools and researchers can have active roles in school systems, including an advocacy role in helping teachers gain time away from teaching duties to pursue their own research.

Related to this theme was the initial worry I had about being a single author of a thesis even though action research has many participants. This also is less of a concern now that I know that there are ways of representing the many voices in a single thesis, and, in any case, participating collaboratively in research means that single voices lose some of their individual perspective and become part of a shared perspective.

On reading the above account the reader may have thought it was debatable whether what *I* was doing as my part of the school research was action research. I was doing research on classroom teaching and learning, but in the sense of 'practitioner' research, it was the teacher who was doing action research on his practice as a teacher, and, to a lesser extent, the students who were doing research on their practice as science students. My role was to initiate this period of practitioner research and to facilitate it by acting as a 'critical friend', but my main practice throughout this period was the practice of being a researcher, or more precisely, that of being a research student. Thus, although the above research may have been action research to different degrees for the *other* participants, my overall practice needs to be looked at before one can decide whether I, too, was observing the principles of practitioner research in my own practice as a research student.

Critical action research on my own practice as a research student

The second level on which it made sense to me to say that I was involved in action research was my PhD study. However, although the PhD process seemed to have several clear aspects of action research, it seemed to be less clearly action research in other aspects.

As part of a PhD thesis, this research was certainly part of a collective, critical endeavour as my supervisors and the wider research community to which I belonged helped me to make decisions about my research and how it was to be (re)presented. For example, they discussed my proposals with me and gave me feedback in seminars on my research. However, whereas my intention had expanded to include being self-critical about the morality of what I was doing in terms of appropriate goals for education and research, it seemed that many of the members of this community seemed more concerned with my conforming to traditional practices than with critically examining the goals and practices of research.

As far as reflectivity went, I had also kept a reflective journal right from the start of my PhD. Most of my insights took place in the process of writing, and, without it I doubt that I would have been reflective enough to 'become critical' about my own research and the PhD process itself. At times the narrative imperative might take over, but at other times I treated it as a confessional, where I should examine my motives critically and look more carefully into situations where I may have ignored or glossed over discrepant facts in an attempt to hold on to my beloved theories.

My journal writing had begun as solitary reflection on my readings and thinking, but as time went by, it became much more a site for dialogue, as I used it for rehearsals for real dialogues with critical friends with whom I wanted to talk out my ideas and get some feedback. Such dialogues included discussions with academics who supported or opposed my ideas about research, letters to researchers and email posts to the PARAPET-L and other electronic discussion groups. I saw my reflections as an individual activity but also as very much part of the practice within a particular cultural community, albeit a loose community.

My journal writing and letter writing thus could be seen as combining the ongoing reflection and dialogue with others that Kemmis and McTaggart (1988a, b) saw as being crucial to action research, but it could be said that I had not been creating the formal structures and following the formal procedures that Kemmis and McTaggart (1988a, b) described as 'action research'. Consequently, some might see the above description of my practice as stretching too far the notion of a collaborative, self-reflective group.

For me, however, it has provided the advantages of a face-to-face group without the disadvantages. The latter include having to think quickly in order to participate, and being unduly influenced by non-verbal communication from the higher-status members of the group which might otherwise subtly influence my actions, for example, by causing me to refrain from unwanted dissent. In fact, after my own experience, I do not believe that the members of a group of critical friends need to be present to each other physically to promote critical thinking. The fact that they are likely to report back to each other from time to time, even in writing, may be enough to encourage a self-critical attitude at other times. This approach is supported by research by Guy (1994) in which a self-reflective collaborative community was developed through writing among distance education students in Papua New Guinea, one of whom commented that the distance arrangement allowed them to be more reflective than they could have been in a face-to-face interview or conversation where they would feel pressured to answer quickly.

Thus, although I had had critical friends from the start, rather than being part of an explicit ongoing community of self-critical researchers with shared goals, these critical friends had waxed and waned over time and did not interact with each other, except as part of a loose community of education researchers, and did not always have a reciprocal relationship with me. This meant that, although I found that they fostered reflexivity in me, the Habermasian 'ideal speech' situation was limited in my interactions with them. Often I found that I had to act largely as my own critic, taking both my moral support and challenges from the writings of researchers who had similar values to mine. These writers provided a virtual dialogue with me that was none the less valuable for being spread over both time and space. However, it was only when I joined the PARAPET group, that I could say that I had a reference group of practising researchers who were helping me to improve the rationality and justice of my practice.

Except in the very last stages, therefore, the method I was using could be seen as individualistic rather than collaborative, and better described as responsive reflection-in-action (Schön 1983). For Schön (1983), a reflective practitioner was one who was doing ongoing research into his [sic] practice in an attempt to make his actions more responsive to each new situation, in terms of a client's needs, his own beliefs about the goals of his practice, his judgements about moral questions involved, and the constraints and opportunities of the immediate situation. Such an approach to practice would allow appropriate answers to problem situations to be found which might deviate from traditional methods of dealing in the profession, in contrast to a positivistic approach to practice in which practitioners saw their role as carrying out practices designed by scientific experts to achieve established ends, without testing their appropriateness to the situation in question.

In *The Action Research Planner* (Kemmis and McTaggart 1988a), individual and group action research are treated as irreconcilable opposites, but, in the spirit of Stephen Kemmis's more recent writing (e.g., Kemmis 1995), which advises moving from thinking in dichotomies to thinking in dialectical terms, seeing individual reflection as inevitably part of a wider dialogue would seem preferable (cf. Bruner 1990: xii, citing Bakhtin's writings, 'All single voices are abstracted from dialogues').

Using this reasoning, it makes less sense to see a gulf between what Kemmis (1994) describes as the two main views of action research: the 'critical social science' view and 'the practical reasoning' view. Schön, who could be seen as belonging to the latter group, in fact sees reflection-in-action as involving reflecting on one's frames of action and theories of action as one responds to the problems of a particular case, and as likely to involve or lead to participation in a 'larger societal conversation' (Schön 1983: 346).

However, reflective practice such as he recommends, may not be possible in many contexts. Not all practitioners feel empowered to make decisions about their practice, based on both their professional and personal judgment, or to participate in potentially critical groups via such vehicles as professional journals. I myself as a fledgling researcher have only recently begun to see myself as empowered in such a role, and only then because of the processes of support, mentoring and reflectivity that I have referred to or implied above. In professions such as teaching, the need to create a formal group, such as an action research group may be much greater, to improve participation in decision making by practitioners.

The transformative nature of action research on my own practice

When I began my PhD, the seeds for being critical were already there, but I was prepared to do it in a conventional manner, without questioning my own basic assumptions about learning and research. The practice, however, of doing regular intensive, reflective writing, and the dialogue it grew into with other questioning researchers, led me to a new understanding of my roles as a PhD student and as a researcher. I began to see the deeper and original purposes of postgraduate education and research and to see how these practices had lost much of their value by serving as little more than empty vehicles for achieving credentials or promotion goals, having the appearances of being beneficial to the education community, but in actual fact, often disempowering it from being an active learning community capable of fostering a more effective education system.

This reflectivity and dialogue which I originally saw as being *outside* my research methodology – a somewhat personal self-indulgence – in fact became the main features of my methodology, once I realised their power to help me learn more deeply and critically, by allowing me to see the cultural boundedness I shared with others in my context. They helped my practice change in the cyclical manner of action research, and empowered me to become more active on behalf of myself and other research students.

In fact, the more I write of this chapter, the more I can see that in several areas of my PhD, I had been moving inexorably towards the principles of action research long before I learnt to call it that. In the first instance, the literature which stood out when I was exploring the problem of alternative conceptions in science was the literature that asserted that students learnt better when social aspects of learning were recognised, values and emotional responses were explicitly taken into account, learning was seen as continuous rather than discrete and when autonomy in learning was encouraged.

With regard to my own learning processes, similar factors became important. I decided that my learning became more meaningful when, in regular journal writing, I reflected critically on its moral and emotional aspects as well as on other aspects of its rationality, and when I entered into dialogue with 'critical friends' to develop in myself a more intellectually honest approach to my study. This led inevitably to my recognition of the necessity of cyclical updating of my research question and methodology, to my becoming aware of their broader social and historical implications, and to my joining a collective of educational practitioners concerned with improving the rationality and social justice of institutions for education.

Similarly, when I began research in science classrooms, I noticed the negative effects of not allowing students sufficient active involvement in decisions about what should be studied or how they should go about studying it. I also noticed similar negative effects of not involving teachers enough in the various stages of research on their own practice, from deciding which research questions should be addressed, to judging which findings were most significant and what should – and, in practice, could – be done in response to these findings. I also concluded that teachers, if they were to continue to be effective in responding to societal changes affecting their students, needed more time for reflection and discussion with other educational practitioners about theoretical and practical educational issues, and more autonomy in making decisions about their own practice.

In all these areas, I also noticed an upsurge in energy and a new interest in learning when individuals were allowed greater participation in decision making which affected their daily lives, and when learning became personally meaningful, that is, based on their personal interests or goals and their relevant cultural values. Conversely, I noticed corresponding drops in energy and motivation when autonomy was removed and agendas which were not personally meaningful were imposed on individuals. This suggests, at least in our cultural context, that people of a range of ages and occupations are happier and more vital, not to mention more productive, when they are allowed to participate in a personally meaningful way in cultural activities.

Conclusions

This has been the story of my emancipation as a researcher while doing a Doctor of Philosophy degree in the area of education. At the beginning of my research degree, although I had an inkling that learning had a personal component, I had a concept of knowledge as something impersonal and 'academic' which came mainly from books. Now, well into my PhD, I have come to believe that if learning for social situations such as education, is to be of any use beyond accreditation, it cannot or should not be detached from any of its social, personal and moral implications.

Before I could see this however, I had to become liberated from relying and acting on other people's knowledge and had to find out how to learn for myself. Knowledge in books could be useful, but it was only part of the knowledge people needed to act in complex and evolving social and political situations such as research and teaching. This has been the story of how I came to change my understanding of knowledge and to learn that the practical and theoretical parts of my research could not be separated. Just as importantly, I found out that relating to people was an essential part of the whole process, that research in social situations was most effective and useful when it involved people working together to help each other learn and improve situations.

I learnt that methodology was not simply a matter of the practicality of matching the method to the research question, but also involved ethical and political dilemmas about such issues as whose questions counted, and whose answers, and about what part the goals of teachers and students should play in the education process. I learnt that pleasing supervisors and examiners in the academic world of the PhD was not necessarily synonymous with doing worthwhile research as defined by others who were concerned with improving the rationality and justice of education in schools.

Seeing research change from being an individualistic pursuit to a collaborative one, even within a PhD, has probably been the biggest change I have had to accommodate in becoming a participatory action researcher. I have learnt that my own insights can be greatly enriched by feedback from 'critical friends' on my reports about the research. For example, writing this chapter, knowing that such 'critical friends' would be reading it, has given me a different perspective on how I behave as a researcher from the one I had before I began writing it.

I have realised that the problem of not wanting to make demands on the teacher and students for fear of reducing their autonomy is similar to my not wanting to make demands on my own children, and that in both cases, it would probably have been much better if I begun much earlier to be more forthcoming about my own agendas. Then, instead of trying to get my own way by being manipulative, we could have begun our productive dialogue earlier. In fact, it was only when I did decide to make my hidden emancipatory agenda explicit to my host teacher that dialogue about the purpose of science education began between us.

Part of the reason that I wanted to tell this story is that I think that emancipation is as much a personal matter as it is a political matter. As long as I had not granted myself the right to participate in decisions affecting my life, it was of little consequence that others had actually given me such speaking or voting rights long before. For me, this learning to respect myself was essential to my being able to participate powerfully with others in research, so I would like to dwell on this briefly before I go on. I think there were three factors involved.

The first factor was finding the language to name experiences or states that had previously been inchoate and therefore not given consideration in my dealings with others. In other words, I needed to hear myself or others articulate what I intuitively felt to be true, before I could begin to take my own experience seriously. The second was learning that there was no one 'right' way to be and think, a principle I had already accepted in other spheres of my life, but had to re-learn in the academic sphere.

The third factor – and this is closely related to what Shirley Grundy refers to as the issue of 'parity of esteem' (see Chapter 3, this volume) – was having significant others take seriously what I was already saying but thought must have been unimportant in the grand scheme of things as it had previously been disregarded by those who held the reins of power. I would want to emphasise, however, the distinction between 'being listened to' and 'being heard', since those whose actions I have suggested were disempowering to me, could rightly claim that they always allowed me a voice and time to speak to them – they simply did not seem to me to treat what I had to say as significant enough to dignify with a serious response. Responsive listening to different points of view must be an important feature in any attempt to foster useful dialogue between those with different points of view. If we are to temper a 'distribution' notion of social justice with a notion of justice which recognises difference, as Fazal Rizvi has argued in Chapter 4, this volume, then different voices must be heard and respected.

There have also been several unexpected side effects of doing this action research PhD. One is the personal development I have undergone. From being a retiring and polite person with a dread of public speaking, of teaching or even of having to ask anyone to do research with me, I have become an active student representative on two research committees, I have done some teaching, I have given four seminar papers on my research, and have become bold enough to volunteer my services to help facilitate a possible teacher action research group in a school. This looks like a very different person from the one who half-flippantly wrote to the PARAPET-L email list a year earlier,

> Working with other people is almost an entirely unknown quantity for a comparative hermit like me but I'm willing to give it a go. Who knows, I may even end up becoming fully human, a 'mature individual', or even 'communitarian' (I wonder what that means?)!
>
> (Hanrahan 1994a)

One sign that I had changed from the isolated individual over the period of my PhD was the difference in my physical appearance over time. At the beginning I felt as though I was doing disembodied research, as though I was an invisible observer and critic, looking through a peephole at the world of the classroom, and I dressed and acted accordingly – drably. By the end, I had started to see myself and to act like someone who had an active social role to play in my world, and I had started to wear more appealing clothes and to take more pride in my appearance. Part of this change I think has resulted from moving from seeing research as just a matter of collecting and analysing scientific information (about 'subjects') to seeing research as relationships between people (see Chapter 3, by Grundy, this volume).

I will finish with a recent quotation of mine to another electronic action research forum, since I believe it shows the extent of change in my ideas after having participated in action research for over a year:

> In the end I decided that if the problem you were addressing was merely a technical one, then non-critical action research could address it, but that most problems, once you looked into them deeply enough, were found to be intricately woven into the social and cultural fabric, and not amenable to change without changing the whole culture to some extent.
>
> And changing the whole culture, I believe, is fairest – and works best – when participation is as complete as possible and voluntary. Having one-sided manipulation of the culture presumes that some have the right to impose their view of what is right on others. Once I believed that was the case, but I find now that I can't maintain that belief any more.

(Hanrahan 1996)

NOTES

1 To be fair, I should note here that my former supervisor's interpretation of the situation differs from mine both here and later in the story.
2 Cf. *The Getting of Wisdom*, a novel by Henry Handel Richardson.

REFERENCES

Baird, J. R. (1986) 'Improving learning through enhanced metacognition: a classroom study', *European Journal of Science Education*, 8: 263–82.

Bruner, J. (1990) *Acts of Meaning*, London: Harvard University Press.

Carr, W. and Kemmis, S. (1986) *Becoming Critical: Education,Knowledge and Action Research*, revised edn, Victoria, Australia: Deakin University.

Collins, A., Brown, J. and Newman, S. (1989) 'Cognitive apprenticeship: teaching the crafts of reading, writing and mathematics', in Resnick, L. (ed.) *Knowing, Learning and Instruction: Essays in Honour of Robert Glaser*, Hillsdale, NJ: Erlbaum, pp. 453–93.

Connelly, F. M. and Clandinin, D. J. (1990) 'Stories of experience and narrative inquiry', *Educational Researcher*, 19: 2–14.

Erickson, F. (1986) 'Qualitative methods in research on teaching', in Wittrock, M.C. (ed.) *Handbook of Research on Teaching*, 3rd edn, New York: Macmillan, pp. 119–161

Ewert, G. D. (1991) 'Habermas and education: a comprehensive overview of the influence of Habermas in educational literature', *Review of Educational Research*, 61: 345–78.

Grundy, S. (1987) *Deakin Studies in Education Series: 1. Curriculum: Product or Praxis?* London: Falmer.

Grundy, S. and Kemmis, S. (1988) 'Educational action research in Australia: the state of the art (an overview)', in Kemmis, S and McTaggart, R. (eds) *The Action Research Reader*, 3rd edn, Geelong, Australia: Deakin University, pp. 321–35.

Guba, E. G. and Lincoln, Y. S. (1989) *Fourth Generation Evaluation*, London: Sage.

Guy, R. (1994) Distance, dialogue and difference: a postpositive approach, unpublished PhD dissertation, Deakin University, Geelong.

Hanrahan, M. (1994a) 'What do we have in common?' Post to PARAPET-L@qut.edu.au, 23 November.

—— (1994b) 'Student beliefs and learning environments: developing a survey of factors related to conceptual change', *Research In Science Education*, 24: 156–65.

—— (1995) *The Effect of Learning Environment Factors on Students' Motivation and Learning*, paper presented at the 26th Annual Conference of the Australian Science Education Research Association, Bendigo, Australia, July.

—— (1996) 'Re: ARLIST: Technology Education and AR', Post to ARLIST-L@scu.edu.au, 21 May.

Jones, B. F. and Idol, L. (eds) (1990) *Dimensions of Thinking and Cognitive Instruction*, Hillsdale, NJ: Erlbaum.

Kemmis, S. (1994) 'Action research', in Husen, T. and Postlethwaite, N. (eds) *International Encyclopedia of Education: Research and Studies*, London: Pergamon.

—— (1995) 'Action research and communicative action: changing teaching practices and the organisation of educational work', adapted from an address to the National Forum of the Innovative Links Between Universities and Schools for Teacher Professional Development Project, Melbourne, August.

Kemmis, S. and McTaggart, R. (1988a) *The Action Research Planner*, 3rd edn, Wauru Ponds, Australia: Deakin University Press.

——(eds) (1988b) *The Action Research Reader*, 3rd edn, Geelong, Australia: Deakin University.

Pintrich, P. R., Marx, R. W. and Boyle, R. A. (1993) 'Beyond cold conceptual change: the role of motivational beliefs and classroom contextual factors in the process of conceptual change', *Review of Educational Research*, 63: 167–99.

Posner, G. J., Strike, K. A., Hewson, P. W. and Gertzog, W. A. (1982) 'Accommodation of a scientific conception: oward a theory of conceptual change', *Science Education*, 66: 211–27.

Schön, D. A. (1983) *The Reflective Practitioner: How Professionals Think in Action*, New York: Basic Books, Inc.

Taylor, P. C. S. (1992) 'An interpretive study of the role of teacher beliefs in the implementation of constructivist theory in a secondary school mathematics classroom', (unpublished PhD dissertation), Curtin University of Technology, November.

Tobin, K. (ed.) (1993) *The Practice of Constructivism in Science Education*, Washington, DC: AAAS Press.

Watts, M. and Bentley, D. (1987) 'Constructivism in the classroom: enabling conceptual change by words and deeds', *British Educational Research Journal*, 13: 121–35.

White, R. T. and Gunstone, R. F. (1989) 'Metalearning and conceptual change', *International Journal of Science Education*, 11: 577–86.

Young, R. E. (1990) *A Critical Theory of Education: Habermas and Our Children's Future*, New York: Teacher's College, Columbia University.

POSTSCRIPT

16

COLLABORATIVE WRITING IN PARTICIPATORY ACTION RESEARCH

Clare Christensen and Bill Atweh

Many action research advocates have identified writing and publishing as an integral and important process in action research projects. McKernan (1991) argued that 'action researchers must become writers too. They must communicate the life of the projects and those who live and breathe them'. Further, Cloake and Noad described the process of writing itself as action research since it involves planning, acting, observing, reflection and re-planning; moreover, the processes of writing and of project work are intrinsically related:

> Action research and the writing process are interdependent and iterative, and can be compared to cogs in a machine, in the way they interact to drive the machine along. If we view the action research process as a spiral of planning, acting, observing, reflecting and reviewing, the process of analysis and writing can be seen as cogs driving the action research up the spiral to its conclusion.
>
> (Cloake and Noad 1991: 1)

Although some action research texts discuss various forms of writing that may be appropriate for action research and/or provide guidelines and advice for novice writers, the specific problems stemming from collaboration in writing are very rarely explored. Most participatory action research (PAR) projects involve collaborative writing, yet the process is seldom problematised and is seldom itself the subject of reflective writing.

Reflecting on writing about action research is an important part of reflecting on our own practice as action researchers. The experience of compiling this book, as discussed in the Preface, and the wide range of processes adopted by the various teams of authors, presented us with a unique opportunity to reflect on collaborative writing. Further, the emphasis of PARAPET on the unifying themes identified in the introduction made us even more aware that collaborative writing involves issues of social justice and partnerships.

Our interest in collaborative writing arose from our observations and discussions during the PARAPET working conferences for writing this book. To facilitate the articulation of the themes and issues raised, interviews were conducted at the end of chapter writing with ten authors from seven chapters in this book. The sample included university academics, research assistants, staff from the school support centres and teachers. The authors interviewed had varying degrees of experience in writing and varying aims in participating in the writing process.

Benefits from collaborative writing in PAR projects

There are several reasons why writing and publishing action research projects are important. First, as Kemmis and Wilkinson argue in Chapter 4 in this volume, participatory action research is a social activity. The PARAPET group's decision to write this book for sharing its learning from the projects with a wider audience is a part of that social commitment. Second, there is a more practical reason. Many authors in this book are associated with a university system that has strong expectations that research will be published. Undoubtedly, for some authors their engagement in the writing was, at least partly, motivated by a desire to satisfy this demand of their employment.

Further, many of the chapter authors in this book have identified some special benefits from writing collaboratively. First, writing collaboratively can assist in the professional development of less experienced members of the team by providing them with an opportunity to develop their skills and confidence in writing. This was possible particularly during the two working conferences where each author critically reflected on one or two other chapters, and writers received feedback from three 'discussants'. According to one author, the writing process was considered useful for building the skill of critical reflection.

> This provided an interesting process of peer review and support. As a novice writer it has been most beneficial to have the inputs of the other writers, some with well-established research credentials and others like me, with little or no previous writing experience . . . my novice attempts at critique were well received and valued. All in all, these experiences have proved to me that I *do* have a capacity for writing and critique.
>
> (An author)

Second, most interviewed authors found the collaborative writing process, and especially discussions concerned with the writing, to be invaluable in helping them clarify and sharpen their individual thinking and under-standing of action research and of their own projects. Often the process of writing allowed action researchers to reflect on the primary focus of their projects, their undeclared assumptions, the major hurdles encountered and the resulting learning. Inevitably, a significant amount of soul searching and self-questioning occurred in this process.

Third, collaborative writing can assist in the development of a shared vision between the collaborators. In the experience of the PETPAR project team (see Chapter 13, this volume), which consisted of university researchers, research assistants and staff involved in professional develop-ment, the writing process revealed significant differences in assumptions, perspectives and expectations among the project participants. Discussion of the roles and expectations of the participants led to the development of a shared vision of the project. This would suggest that writing early in the life of a project could help in building closer partnerships among the project team throughout the project.

Ways of writing collaboratively

The degree to which participants integrated the process of writing into the life of the project varied from one project to another. Some action research projects maintained notes or minutes of meetings. In cases where these notes contain sufficient detail, not only of group decisions but also of the issues raised, these notes may form the basis of the report writing. According to one of the authors interviewed, the project participants developed writing as an integral component of action research very early in the life of the project. Writing was used in the spiral of action and reflection in order to 'see where have we come from, what's been happening, where we are going . . . in thinking about the various helping forces, stopping forces, to try and clarify what was really going on'. Some participants took brief notes of meetings, others wanted:

> to file away everything that happened to them along the way . . . at other times we'd go to the boardroom and we'd do a whiteboard and we'd prioritise. Another time we'd meet at a parent's house and have pasta and wine and do mind-mapping and try to solve a partic-ular problem such as sport, that was confronting parents and schools and teachers and students and the principal.

In most other projects, however, writing did not commence until later in the project and had the function of reporting on the project.

Collaborative writing is a process where two or more authors are involved in the development of a single piece of work. No two PARAPET groups followed the same approach to this task. However, based on the interviews with the authors, at least three broad approaches could be identified. The first approach could be called 'progressive writing'. In some projects, a first draft was written by one person then passed around the group for further contributions and editing. Often, in addition to this, there were meetings for group discussion. One writer described this process as follows:

> The process was sort of like throwing a ball around. Someone would say, 'Here you have a go at it, see what you can do', and then they'd bring it back and then throw it at someone else and say, 'Here you have a go at it'. Every now and then we'd get together and look at how it was shaping, the way in which we wanted it to go and the direction of the writing itself.
>
> (An author)

The second approach adopted by some of the groups could be called 'shared writing'. One group reported that they always wrote together, setting aside considerable blocks of time, 'a lot of late nights and weekends', for this. A variation of this model reported in another group consisted of different authors writing separate accounts prior to a group meeting. The reading of each other's accounts was the first step towards understanding the perspectives of other team members. Negotiation at meetings often led to the development of a shared vision. According to one author interviewed: 'We looked at what it is, the common things that we have, what it is that we share, what are the things that connect us.' This approach may be particularly appropriate when different members of the group are responsible for different components of the action research project.

The third approach adopted by some projects could be called 'directed writing'. In some groups one person took the main responsibility for writing the first draft and the subsequent editing based on individual and group feedback. This person took the individual stories and synthesised them into a whole with which the other writers were satisfied. It was not unusual for this person to be an academic with considerable expertise in writing. According to this approach, this leading person was not speaking for the group; rather they were acting in a direct leading role in the process. The group was involved in the critical reading and editing of the manuscript.

In identifying these three approaches we do not intend to say that they are mutually exclusive. Nor is one approach necessarily preferable for collaborative writing. The particular context of the project, including the number of participants, their access to each other, their experience and interests determined to a large extent the actual procedures followed in the writing process. Whatever approach is followed, careful and open negotiation between the participants, preferably early in the life of the project, increases the likelihood of true collaboration and a smooth writing process.

Not all members of the action research teams chose to participate in the formal writing of the chapter. Some non-writing participants associated the writing of the chapter with academic writing, which did not correspond with their professional values and interests. Their role as non-writing participants was negotiated with the rest of the team. The question arose of whether their names should/could be on the chapter as authors. In the case of one chapter, the non-writing participants did not desire to be identified as authors. In another case they agreed to being named as co-authors and were happy to limit their participation to commenting on the chapter's drafts. In the latter case, their involvement in the authorship of the chapter was considered appropriate since through their involvement in the project, they were the source of many of the ideas reported in the chapter. In most chapters in this book, however, all members of the research group have directly participated in the writing and editing process.

Issues in collaborative writing

As described above, collaborative writing in action research can be valuable in developing both individual expertise and group cohesion. However, as discussed by many of the authors, the process of writing collaboratively is not easy nor without, at times, significant conflict. Some of the issues faced by the writers may present considerable limitations to the act of full and equal collaboration. Some of these issues relate to parity of esteem, some to voice, and others relate to the development of appropriate group dynamics for the task at hand.

Parity of esteem

In her chapter (Chapter 3 in this volume), Grundy argues that collaborative projects should be based on parity of esteem between the different participants. The author says that mere elimination of hierarchy within a project does not eliminate the problems of parity of esteem. The experience of some authors in this volume has raised examples of possible sources of perceived inequality in status or extent of contribution between the collaborators in the writing process.

The first cause of this perceived inequality was the confusion between the work-related positions of the collaborators and expectations of co-authorship. In more than one chapter, the writing teams consisted of people who are in either subordinate or supervisory roles in their normal work situations. Often relationships between people at different levels of work are not based on equal say and power. Conflict may arise for those who assume that co-authorship automatically implies equality in status. Some authors in subordinate work situations were well aware of their difference in status, as expressed by one participant:

There's the difference in hierarchy as well. And even though people don't believe in hierarchies or creating differences between people at different levels of operation, it was still something for me to come to terms with . . . I felt it within myself, I had very traditional notions of the way in which leadership was formed and, there's still that social protocol that's entrenched from when you're very young, right through, about what a leader does and how you [act] within [their] presence.

(An author)

The difficulty in clarifying multiple roles is best illustrated in the PETPAR chapter (Chapter 13). The aim of the PETPAR project was to explore the experiences and needs of part-time academic staff at the university. Two research assistants were invited to join the team because they were part-time tutors. Their awareness of the issues faced by part-timers was considered a valuable attribute. In addition, the project proposal provided for the employment of them as research assistants to carry out the research and the many administrative tasks of the project. This dual role in the project was never discussed and there was uncertainty in the research assistants' minds about their primary role on the project team. The collaborative writing process brought out this underlying confusion.

The research assistants performed tasks that are usually expected of the research assistant role; at the same time they were considered to be co-authors by the rest of the group and were involved in editing a conference paper and drafts of the chapter. However, they were not specifically asked by the group to do any writing themselves. This raised for them some concern about their status with the rest of the team. Importantly, they did not feel confident even to share their concern with the rest of the group. Eventually, at a meeting of the group where an outsider was present, one of the research assistants did speak about the issue. As a result of the discussion which followed, one of the two research assistants became much more involved in the writing of the chapter. This situation may have been avoided had there been explicit discussion and negotiation of roles early in the project.

The second source of perceived inequality in collaborative writing is related to the varying levels of experience and confidence in academic writing possessed by the different authors. Irrespective of the variety of writing styles adopted in the different chapters, the perception of the task at hand as 'academic' caused some reduction in the involvement of some participants. Many of these participants were closely involved in the planning, implementation, reflection on, and day-to-day documentation of the project. However, when it came to writing the chapter they felt less confident in contributing equally with other members. In many situations an academic researcher took a leadership role in the writing, with other participants contributing either to the story part of the chapter or simply to editing and commenting on drafts. In the words of one participant:

> My biggest disadvantage was that I hadn't done enough reading, in terms of theoretical background of what we were writing . . . I wasn't very skilled in writing articles. I let other people do that for me. I had got into the project for a different reason. . . . [However] I don't feel uncomfortable because I've always been offered equal rights and a share in [all decisions].
>
> (An author)

Voice

The PARAPET writers were very conscious of the problem of the voice represented in the telling of the stories of their projects. Questions of voice include: Who has developed the learning and who is reporting it? Who is representing whose voice? How can different voices be represented in the one chapter?

The first aspect of this problem is representing the voice of the non-authoring participants in the project. Early in the process of writing and critical discussions, the authors were aware that in some cases they represented only a small part of the projects' participants. Stephen Kemmis summarised the guidelines adopted by the group in one of the meetings as follows:

> Of course every story is told from the point of view of its author(s). We may want to disrupt the smooth expectation that our chapter authorship is the authorship of our projects. Our projects contain many stories – so we may want to ensure that the perspectives and voices of other project participants are present in the chapters. We may not be able to tell other people's stories for them, but we can ensure that other voices are present in our texts (so they become 'multivocal').

The second aspect of the question of which voice(s) are represented in the chapters is related to the group of authors involved. The task of combining different voices in one chapter gave rise to serious difficulties for many authors. In some groups these differences became obvious only at the stage of project documentation. In the words of one author:

> The difficult part of the collaborative writing was that there were five people involved with different agendas, coming from different perspectives, motivations, philosophies and understandings of the project.
>
> (An author)

How the different groups of authors dealt with the problem of multiple voices differed from one group to another. Most teams of authors adopted a traditional style, with a group of authors telling a unified story in their chapter. The final version of these chapters was the result of collaborative writing and negotiations, where the end product represented the shared view of all participants. At times this process was a result of compromise. According to one author:

> There were places [in our chapter] where we were three voices in one, and other places where it sounded like three in one but [in reality] there was just one of us speaking. There's a lot of implicit diversity in the voices which maybe the readers are never going to pick up but the people who [wrote] it know. And we could live with that.
>
> (An author)

Other teams opted for having sections of their chapters authored and attributed to individual writers. This approach was appropriate in different chapters for different reasons. For example, in the Valley School Support Centre group (see Chapter 9), each of the co-authors was co-ordinating a separate project. At the writing stage the group decided to write their individual stories connected with a unified theoretical discussion on which they all agreed. On the other hand, the authors of the PETPAR (Chapter 13) and Social Science projects (Chapter 11) also wanted to stress the individual experiences and learnings of each participant; they did this by having sections of their chapters attributed to individual authors.

Developing appropriate group dynamics

In the previous sections we have identified several instances where negotiation about the roles and procedures of writing would have been beneficial to the group. None of the interviewed authors indicated that such negotiations were done prior to starting writing. Often problems and conflict arose after the writing commenced. It is clearly important for understandings of collaboration to be discussed early in the life of a project and for roles and responsibilities to be clarified and negotiated openly. Such negotiations can be seen as part of what one participant described as a 'birthing process' of the group. This process also involves the development of a shared vision of the project, or, in the words of one author, developing 'a shared understanding of what it is we were to do and where it is we were to go'. Another author considered that the birthing process was never experienced in his group and that, as a consequence, 'we didn't learn very much about writing or working collaboratively'.

Individual working-style preferences within the group may vary and need to be taken into account. Working or writing collaboratively does not necessarily 'come easily' to everyone. Some people prefer to work independently. These people may feel that considerable compromise is being asked of them to work closely with others. It may be necessary to allow space for independent work within a collaboration. This was the case in the Valley School Support Centre group. One member of the team indicated that: '[We] only worked together when we really had to and that maybe stemmed from the fact that we're quite independent in the way in which we work.'

Another source of difficulty may arise when participants come together with different expectations of collaboration. For one author in the PETPAR project (Chapter 13) collaboration meant equal participation in the writing by all team members. Another member of the same team, however, felt that:

> Collaboration only works well if somebody takes the initiative and sits down and starts doing something and relies on other people to give support and backup and interpretation . . . someone has to be in charge.
>
> (An author)

A practical issue which may hinder collaborative writing is the question of efficiency. Collaboration as a way of writing is time consuming. At least one author was concerned about the apparent inefficiency of writing in a group, since sharing inputs and decision making takes much more time and energy than working independently, especially in the larger groups. The process of writing is often carried out under tight time limitations due to busy schedules and deadlines. Often these constraints cause the group to adopt more efficient ways of getting the job done. While efficiency is a positive aim to achieve, this concern could compromise the group's commitment to deep individual and group learning.

Last, collaborative groups who were able to develop rapport between the participants faced less conflict. Often this rapport was based on the group's previous experience of shared writing. In other groups this rapport required some effort to achieve.

Learnings and issues in publishing action research stories

The previous sections have considered the benefits of collaborative writing for individuals and the group, ways of writing collaboratively, and some issues which arose in the experience of PARAPET participants. Publishing action research writing is another important aspect of writing. Publishing is the means of sharing the contextual learning developed in the project with others who may be in similar situations.

The means available for publishing action research writings are varied. When the PARAPET group was considering sharing its learnings, it was decided that compiling an edited book containing the different stories would allow us to illustrate the common issues and themes and the different ways the projects have dealt with them. Also we expected that the compilation of the book would be an enriching experience for all the people involved. (See the Preface for the story of the book.)

A significant amount of learning occurred in the process of editing the individual chapters and collating the stories into a book. The main issues we faced related to style of writing and ownership of publication. Learning came through facing these issues in a context of interaction with critical friends.

Writing style

One of the early issues faced by the group was writing style. It became obvious from the early stages of our planning that each author had a preference and expertise in certain styles of writing. Concerns were expressed that one style would be imposed on every chapter and that these demands might be used to censor some stories. It became clear to the group that the question of style was closely related to the question of intended audience and that the different stories reported in this book may be of interest or benefit to a diverse group of audiences. Some stories may be of direct interest to school teachers; others may be more appropriate to administrators or school support staff; some directly aim to address parents' concerns; and others may be of interest to researchers and lecturers at educational institutions. How could one style of writing suit everybody? The group had to reach an understanding of these issues before commencing the writing task. Stephen Kemmis recorded the following reflections on one of the authors' meetings:

> There was agreement that the project chapters should *tell the story* of their projects. This seemed to imply adopting a more <u>personal</u> style than had been preferred in some draft chapters. The idea is that we try to convey that our projects are grounded in the lives and experience of particular participants (not the universal subject, the impersonal 'academic' style – some chapters may aspire to being more personal than in the current draft, some to being less). At the same time, we want to show that we are critical reflective practitioners, able to stand back from our own work and think about it as a basis for reorienting ourselves and our action (not people whose perspective is immutably fixed by our location, as if we could never see beyond the boundaries of our own prejudices or points of view).
>
> Different authors will want to tell the story of their projects in different ways. We do not expect a strict uniformity about what our stories should be like.

Our projects have 'lives'. Perhaps they have particular beginnings and endings as <u>projects</u>, but they also have pre-histories and postscripts. . . . We need to acknowledge that they are lived in <u>relationships</u> <u>and</u> <u>communities</u> beyond their 'project-ness'. If our stories focus too much on the 'project-ness' of our projects, we may give the impression that they are just 'jobs' to be done (getting a project up and running and done and delivered); if we can focus less on the 'project-ness' of projects, we may be able to <u>show</u> how they are constructed in real, living relationships between people who are aiming not only to 'produce results' but also <u>to</u> <u>investigate</u> <u>reality</u> <u>in</u> <u>order</u> <u>to</u> <u>transform</u> <u>it,</u> <u>and</u> <u>transform</u> <u>reality</u> <u>in</u> <u>order</u> <u>to</u> <u>investigate</u> <u>it</u>.

(Stephen Kemmis [underlined in the original])

Editing individual chapters

While PARAPET participants engaged in the process of group editing, as in the working conferences (see Preface), understanding of the role of critical friends developed. Members of the PARAPET group had widely varying levels of experience in editing and publishing; some had no such experience. The collaborative process of writing the chapters and editing the book brought new learning to all participants. For example, prior to the conference some less-experienced participants expressed concern about critiquing the writing of academics. Through the conference they developed significant confidence, especially when they realised that their point of view as practitioners was valued by all. On the other hand writers with more experience also valued the opportunity to receive critical feedback from other authors with a variety of backgrounds and different perspectives.

When the conference started, many of the authors did not know each other and many of them started attending PARAPET meetings only when work on the book commenced. Hence, it was not possible to develop rapport and trust between participants prior to their becoming critical friends at the working conference. Care was taken by all to provide a balanced critique of each other's work and to avoid personal 'put-downs'. The process of collation of the stories created a sense of common target and task. Friendships developed out of being critical and not the other way around.

Book editorship

The process of developing this book was marked with some controversy. Issues concerning the rationale and processes of the book and its editorship were discussed at meetings and decisions were reached. Although time consuming, these discussions were intended to ensure that all authors had similar expectations of the book and had similar opportunities to learn from the process.

The issue of editorship of the whole book was considered in a number of meetings. The question arose of the possibility of continuing with the process of shared decision making right to the end of publication. However, some members' previous experience with the demands of dealing with external publishers and the tedious mechanical process of final editing led to the consideration of alternative arrangements. After discussion in several meetings the group decided that a smaller group would be designated as editors to carry the book forward after the second conference. This decision did not mean that the editors would assume ownership and control of the book. PARAPET was still committed to the spirit of collaboration and co-operation. However, in dealing with publishers the small group, consisting of people who all had had previous experience in publishing, was to handle the day-to-day process of final editorial changes to meet publishing requirements.

A related problem was the difficult task of deciding whose names would appear on the cover as editors. The largest part of chapter editing was undertaken by the whole PARAPET group. Should we list all the names (about 20 of them!) as editors? Should we list one or two with the addition of the phrase 'In conjunction with the PARAPET Group'? Would we simply say 'Edited by the PARAPET project'. In making the decision, once again practical considerations prevailed. The meeting of authors felt that these alternatives, although reflecting the spirit of collaboration under which the book had developed, would cause some practical problems. The first concern was that they might not be acceptable to the publishers. Second, the conventions for referencing books according to the standard style manuals make it easier to have a small number of people identified as editors. We also noted that in similar cases in the past, even though a book was developed by a team, only the first author was often cited as an editor. In this case the group decided to follow the traditional conventions by using the names of the selected group of editors on the cover.

Conclusions

Collaborative writing is often taken for granted by researchers and advocates of action research methodology. This chapter has discussed the process of collaborative writing in action research. In the experience of the authors of this book, collaborative writing about action research has brought benefits to individuals and to the group. It has led to deeper understanding of the assumptions, actions and outcomes of projects and assisted in the development of shared understanding of action research. The experience of PARAPET authors has shown that there is a variety of approaches to collaborative writing and to the issue of style. The experience of developing and collating the different stories in this book has shown that there are several issues that may need to be addressed early in the life of the project for writing to achieve its purpose and maximise its benefits. Negotiation of roles is important and, in the spirit of action research, it is an ongoing process, not something that is done once and for all. Finally, reflection on the process of writing should follow the pattern of action research: cycles of critical reflection alternating with action.

REFERENCES

Cloake, P. and Noad, P.N. (1991) 'Action research and the writing process', in Colins, C. and Chippendale, P. (eds) *Proceedings of The First World Congress on Action Research and Process Management*, Brisbane, Australia: Acorn Publications, pp. 1–5.

McKernan, J. (1991) *Curriculum Action Research: A Handbook of Methods and Resources for The Reflective Practitioner*, London: Kegan Page.

NAME INDEX

342

SUBJECT INDEX

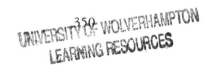